A·N·N·U·A·L E·D·I·T·I·O·N·S

Business Ethics *06/07*

Eighteenth Edition

EDITOR

John E. Richardson

Pepperdine University

Dr. John E. Richardson is a professor of marketing in the George L. Graziadio School of Business and Management at Pepperdine University. He is president of his own consulting firm and has consulted with organizations such as Bell and Howell, Dayton-Hudson, Epson, and the U.S. Navy, as well as with various service, nonprofit, and franchise organizations. Dr. Richardson is a member of the American Management Association, the American Marketing Association, the Society for Business Ethics, and Beta Gamma Sigma honorary business fraternity.

Contemporary Learning Series

2460 Kerper Blvd., Dubuque, IA 52001

Visit us on the Internet
http://www.mhcls.com

D1279447

Credits

1. **Ethics, Values, and Social Responsibility in Business**
   Unit photo—© Getty Images/Alistair Berg
2. **Ethical Issues and Dilemmas in the Workplace**
   Unit photo—© Digital Vision
3. **Business and Society: Contemporary Ethical, Social, and Environmental Issues**
   Unit photo—© Digital Vision
4. **Ethics and Social Responsibility in the Marketplace**
   Unit photo—© Getty Images/Lawrence Lawry
5. **Developing the Future Ethos and Social Responsibility of Business**
   Unit photo—© Punchstock Images/Stockbyte

Copyright

Cataloging in Publication Data
Main entry under title: Annual Editions: Business Ethics. 2006/2007.
1. Business Ethics—Periodicals. I. Richardson, John, *comp.* II. Title: Business Ethics.
ISBN-13: 978–0–07–352837–3   ISBN-10: 0–07–352837–4   658'.05   ISSN 1055–5455

© 2007 by McGraw-Hill Contemporary Learning Series, Dubuque, IA 52001, A Division of The McGraw-Hill Companies.

Copyright law prohibits the reproduction, storage, or transmission in any form by any means of any portion of this publication without the express written permission of McGraw-Hill Contemporary Learning Series, and of the copyright holder (if different) of the part of the publication to be reproduced. The Guidelines for Classroom Copying endorsed by Congress explicitly state that unauthorized copying may not be used to create, to replace, or to substitute for anthologies, compilations, or collective works. Inquiries concerning publishing rights to the articles herein can be directed to the Permission Department at Contemporary Learning Series. 800.243.6532

Annual Editions® is a Registered Trademark of McGraw-Hill Contemporary Learning Series, A Division of The McGraw-Hill Companies.

Eighteenth Edition

Cover image © 2006 Keith Brofsky/Getty Images and Maggie Lytle
Printed in the United States of America   1234567890QPDQPD9876   Printed on Recycled Paper

Editors/Advisory Board

Members of the Advisory Board are instrumental in the final selection of articles for each edition of ANNUAL EDITIONS. Their review of articles for content, level, currentness, and appropriateness provides critical direction to the editor and staff. We think that you will find their careful consideration well reflected in this volume.

EDITOR

John E. Richardson
Pepperdine University

ADVISORY BOARD

Archie B. Carroll
University of Georgia

Gerald R. Ferrera
Bentley College

William J. Kehoe
University of Virginia

Tom Mahaffey
St. Francis Xavier University

Tim Mazur
University of Maryland

Thomas Mulligan
Brock University

Patrick E. Murphy
University of Notre Dame

Lisa H. Newton
Fairfield University

Andrew Sikula
Marshall University Graduate College

Roberta Snow
West Chester University

Marc D. Street
University of South Florida

Michael van Breda
Southern Methodist University

Jon West
University of Miami

Staff

EDITORIAL STAFF

Larry Loeppke, Managing Editor
Susan Brusch, Senior Developmental Editor
Jay Oberbroeckling, Developmental Editor
Bonnie Coakley, Editorial Assistant

PERMISSIONS STAFF

Lenny J. Behnke, Permissions Coordinator
Lori Church, Permissions Coordinator
Shirley Lanners, Permissions Coordinator

TECHNOLOGY STAFF

Luke David, eContent Coordinator

MARKETING STAFF

Julie Keck, Senior Marketing Manager
Mary Klein, Marketing Communications Specialist
Alice Link, Marketing Coordinator
Tracie Kammerude, Senior Marketing Assistant

PRODUCTION STAFF

Beth Kundert, Production Manager
Trish Mish, Production Assistant
Jade Benedict, Production Assistant
Kari Voss, Lead Typesetter
Jean Smith, Typesetter
Karen Spring, Typesetter
Sandy Wille, Typesetter
Tara McDermott, Designer
Maggie Lytle, Cover Graphics

Preface

In publishing ANNUAL EDITIONS we recognize the enormous role played by the magazines, newspapers, and journals of the public press in providing current, first-rate educational information in a broad spectrum of interest areas. Many of these articles are appropriate for students, researchers, and professionals seeking accurate, current material to help bridge the gap between principles and theories and the real world. These articles, however, become more useful for study when those of lasting value are carefully collected, organized, indexed, and reproduced in a low-cost format, which provides easy and permanent access when the material is needed. That is the role played by ANNUAL EDITIONS.

Recent events have brought ethics to the forefront as a topic of discussion throughout our nation. And, undoubtedly, the area of society that is getting the closest scrutiny regarding its ethical practices is the business sector. Both the print and broadcast media have offered a constant stream of facts and opinions concerning recent unethical goings-on in the business world. Insider trading scandals on Wall Street, the marketing of unsafe products, money laundering, and questionable contracting practices are just a few examples of events that have recently tarnished the image of business.

As corporate America struggles to find its ethical identity in a business environment that grows increasingly complex, managers are confronted with some poignant questions that have definite ethical ramifications. Does a company have any obligation to help solve social problems such a poverty, pollution, and urban decay? What ethical responsibilities should a multinational corporation assume in foreign countries? What obligation does a manufacturer have to the consumer with respect to product defects and safety?

These are just a few of the issues that make the study of business ethics important and challenging. A significant goal of *Annual Editions: Business Ethics 06/07* is to present some different perspectives on understanding basic concepts and concerns of business ethics and to provide ideas on how to incorporate these concepts into the policies and decision-making processes of businesses. The articles reprinted in this publication have been carefully chosen from a variety of public press sources to furnish current information on business ethics.

This volume contains a number of features designed to make it useful for students, researchers, and professionals. These include the *table of contents* with summaries of each article and key concepts in italics, a *topic guide* for locating articles on specific subjects related to business ethics, and a comprehensive *index*.

Also, included in this edition are selected *World Wide Web* sites that can be used to further explore article topics.

The articles are organized into five units. Selections that focus on similar issues are concentrated into subsections within the broader units. Each unit is preceded by an overview which provides background for informed reading of the articles, emphasizes critical issues, and presents key points to consider that focus on major themes running through the selections.

Your comments, opinions, and recommendations about *Annual Editions: Business Ethics 06/07* will be greatly appreciated and will help shape future editions. Please take a moment to complete and return the postage-paid *article rating form* on the last page of this book. Any book can be improved, and with your help this one will continue to be.

John E. Richardson

John E. Richardson
Editor

Contents

UNIT 1
Ethics, Values, and Social Responsibility in Business

UNIT 2
Ethical Issues and Dilemmas in the Workplace

The concepts in bold italics are developed in the article. For further expansion, please refer to the Topic Guide and the Index.

The concepts in bold italics are developed in the article. For further expansion, please refer to the Topic Guide and the Index.

UNIT 3
Business and Society: Contemporary Ethical, Social, and Environmental Issues

The concepts in bold italics are developed in the article. For further expansion, please refer to the Topic Guide and the Index.

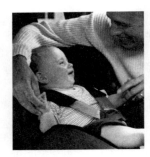

UNIT 4
Ethics and Social Responsibility in the Marketplace

The concepts in bold italics are developed in the article. For further expansion, please refer to the Topic Guide and the Index.

UNIT 5
Developing the Future Ethos and Social Responsibility of Business

The concepts in bold italics are developed in the article. For further expansion, please refer to the Topic Guide and the Index.

Topic Guide

This topic guide suggests how the selections in this book relate to the subjects covered in your course. You may want to use the topics listed on these pages to search the Web more easily.

On the following pages a number of Web sites have been gathered specifically for this book. They are arranged to reflect the units of this *Annual Edition*. You can link to these sites by going to the student online support site at *http://www.mhcls.com/online/*.

ALL THE ARTICLES THAT RELATE TO EACH TOPIC ARE LISTED BELOW THE BOLD-FACED TERM.

Auditing
8. Corruption: Causes and Cures
18. Birth of the Ethics Industry

Brands
22. Does It Pay to Be Good?
23. Trust in the Marketplace
28. Debate Flares Anew Over Violence in Video Games
31. Fakes!
34. Truth in Advertising: Rx Drug Ads Come of Age

Business and government
18. Birth of the Ethics Industry
27. Eminent Domain: Is It Only Hope for Inner Cities?

Business and law
11. The Under-Reported Impact of Age Discrimination and Its Threat to Business Vitality
13. How Corporate America is Betraying Women
18. Birth of the Ethics Industry
27. Eminent Domain: Is It Only Hope for Inner Cities?
28. Debate Flares Anew Over Violence in Video Games
35. Rejuvenating Wal-Mart's Reputation

Business environment
3. Advice from Aristotle on Business Ethics
4. Truth or Consequences: The Organizational Importance of Honesty
9. Where the Dangers Are
13. How Corporate America is Betraying Women
17. On Witnessing a Fraud
24. How Women Are Changing Corporate America
30. Managing Ethically with Global Stakeholders: A Present and Future Challenge
35. Rejuvenating Wal-Mart's Reputation
39. Patagonia's Founder Seeks to Spread Environmental Gospel

Business ethics
2. Business Ethics: Back to Basics
5. Why Good Leaders Do Bad Things
18. Birth of the Ethics Industry
41. Hiring Character

Code of ethics
2. Business Ethics: Back to Basics
6. Best Resources for Corporate Social Responsibility
18. Birth of the Ethics Industry
29. Values in Tension: Ethics Away From Home
36. Managing for Organizational Integrity
37. An Ethical Delimma: How to Build Integrity into Your Sales Environment
39. Patagonia's Founder Seeks to Spread Environmental Gospel
42. Why Corporations Can't Control Chicanery

Conflicts of interest
7. Flip-Flop Over Faculty Fingerprints
8. Corruption: Causes and Cures
15. Into Thin Air

16. Hall Monitors in the Workplace: Encouraging Employee Whistleblowers
17. On Witnessing a Fraud
19. Academic Values and the Lure of Profit
20. Like the Smoke of a Blazing Room
21. The Parable of the Sadhu
22. Does It Pay to Be Good?
23. Trust in the Marketplace
27. Eminent Domain: Is It Only Hope for Inner Cities?
34. Truth in Advertising: Rx Drug Ads Come of Age
37. An Ethical Delimma: How to Build Integrity into Your Sales Environment
40. Ethics for a Post-Enron America

Consumer protection
9. Where the Dangers Are
16. Hall Monitors in the Workplace: Encouraging Employee Whistleblowers
20. Like the Smoke of a Blazing Room
26. The Truth About Drug Companies
28. Debate Flares Anew Over Violence in Video Games
31. Fakes!
32. The Perils of Doing the Right Thing
33. Is Marketing Ethics an Oxymoron?
34. Truth in Advertising: Rx Drug Ads Come of Age
38. The Right Balance

Crime
7. Flip-Flop Over Faculty Fingerprints
9. Where the Dangers Are
18. Birth of the Ethics Industry
20. Like the Smoke of a Blazing Room
28. Debate Flares Anew Over Violence in Video Games
31. Fakes!
37. An Ethical Delimma: How to Build Integrity into Your Sales Environment
38. The Right Balance

Discrimination
10. Sexual Harassment and Retaliation: A Double-Edged Sword
11. The Under-Reported Impact of Age Discrimination and Its Threat to Business Vitality
12. Where Are the Women?
13. How Corporate America is Betraying Women
14. 50 and Fired
23. Trust in the Marketplace
25. Old. Smart. Productive.
35. Rejuvenating Wal-Mart's Reputation
42. Why Corporations Can't Control Chicanery

Diversity
2. Business Ethics: Back to Basics
4. Truth or Consequences: The Organizational Importance of Honesty
24. How Women Are Changing Corporate America
35. Rejuvenating Wal-Mart's Reputation

Downsizing
14. 50 and Fired
15. Into Thin Air

Internet References

The following internet sites have been carefully researched and selected to support the articles found in this reader. The easiest way to access these selected sites is to go to our student online support site at *http://www.mhcls.com/online/*.

AE: Business Ethics 06/07

The following sites were available at the time of publication. Visit our Web site—we update our student online support site regularly to reflect any changes.

General Sources

CBSR (Canadian Business for Social Responsibility)
http://www.cbsr.bc.ca

CBSR says this is a "one-stop shop" for information on corporate social responsibility in Canada. You'll find news articles, member news, best practices, and resources.

Center for the Study of Ethics in the Professions
http://ethics.iit.edu

Sponsored by the Illinois Institute of Technology, this site links to a number of world business ethics centers.

GreenMoney Journal
http://www.greenmoneyjournal.com

The editorial vision of this publication proposes that consumer spending and investment dollars can bring about positive social and environmental change. On this Web site, they'll tell you how.

Markkula Center
http://www.scu.edu/SCU/Centers/Ethics/

Santa Clara University's Markkula Center strives to heighten ethical awareness and to improve ethical decision making on campus and within the community. A list of published resources, links to ethical issues sites, and other data are provided.

U.S. Department of Labor
http://www.dol.gov

Browsing through this site will lead to a vast array of labor-related data and discussions of issues affecting employees and managers, such as the minimum wage.

U.S. Equal Employment Opportunity Commission (EEOC)
http://www.eeoc.gov

The EEOC's mission "is to ensure equality of opportunity by vigorously enforcing federal legislation prohibiting discrimination in employment." Consult this site for facts about employment discrimination, enforcement, and litigation.

Wharton Ethics Program
http://ethics.wharton.upenn.edu/

The Wharton School of the University of Pennsylvania provides an independently managed site that offers links to research, cases, and other business ethics centers.

UNIT 1: Ethics, Values, and Social Responsibility in Business

Association for Moral Education (AME)
http://www.amenetwork.org/

AME is dedicated to fostering communication, cooperation, training, and research that links moral theory with educational practices. From here it is possible to connect to several sites of relevance in the study of business ethics.

Business for Social Responsibility (BSR)
http://www.bsr.org/

Core topic areas covered by BSR are listed on this page. They include Corporate Social Responsibility; Business Ethics; Community Investment; the Environment; Governance and Accountability; Human Rights; Marketplace; Mission, Vision, Values; and finally Workplace. New information is added on a regular basis. For each topic or subtopic there is an introduction, examples of large and small company leadership practices, sample company policies, links to helping resources, and other information.

Enron Online
http://www.enron.com/corp/

Explore the Enron Web site to find information about Enron's history, products, and services. Go to the "Press Room" section for Enron's spin on the current investigation.

Ethics Updates/Lawrence Hinman
http://ethics.sandiego.edu/index.html

This site provides both simple concept definitions and complex analysis of ethics, original treatises, and sophisticated search engine capability. Subject matter covers the gamut, from ethical theory to applied ethical venues.

Institute for Business and Professional Ethics
http://commerce.depaul.edu/ethics/

This site is interested in research in the field of business and professional ethics. It is still under construction, so check in from time to time.

National Center for Policy Analysis
http://www.ncpa.org

This organization's archive links lead you to interesting materials on a variety of topics that affect managers, from immigration issues, to affirmative action, to regulatory policy.

Open Directory Project
http://dmoz.org/Business/Management/Ethics

As part of the Open Directory Project, this page provides a database of Web sites that address numerous topics on ethics in business.

Working Definitions
http://www.workingdefinitions.co.uk/index.html

This is a British, magazine-style site devoted to discussion and comment on organizations in the wider social context and to supporting and developing people's management skills.

UNIT 2: Ethical Issues and Dilemmas in the Workplace

American Psychological Association
http://www.apa.org/homepage.html

Search this site to find references and discussion of important ethics issues for the workplace of the 1990s, including the impact of restructuring and revitalization of businesses.

www.mhcls.com/online/

International Labour Organization (ILO)
http://www.ilo.org

ILO's home page leads you to links that describe the goals of the organization and summarizes international labor standards and human rights. Its official UN Web site locator can point you to many other useful resources.

UNIT 3: Business and Society: Contemporary Ethical, Social, and Environmental Issues

National Immigrant Forum
http://www.immigrationforum.org

The pro-immigrant organization offers this page to examine the effects of immigration on the U.S. economy and society. Click on the links to underground and immigrant economies.

Sympatico: Workplace
http://sympatico.workopolis.com

This Canadian site provides an electronic network with a GripeVine for complaining about work and finding solutions to everyday work problems.

United Nations Environment Programme (UNEP)
http://www.unep.ch

Consult this UNEP site for links to topics such as the impact of trade on the environment. It will direct you to useful databases and global resource information.

United States Trade Representative (USTR)
http://www.ustr.gov

This home page of the U.S. Trade Representative provides links to many U.S. government resources for those interested in ethics in international business.

UNIT 4: Ethics and Social Responsibility in the Marketplace

Business for Social Responsibility (BSR)
http://www.bsr.org/

BSR is a global organization that seeks to help companies "achieve success in ways that respect ethical values, people, communities, and the environment." Links to Services, Resources, and Forum are available.

Total Quality Management Sites
http://www.nku.edu/~lindsay/qualhttp.html

This site points to a variety of interesting Internet sources to aid in the study and application of Total Quality Management principles.

U.S. Navy
http://www.navy.mil

Start at this U.S. Navy page for access to a plethora of interesting stories and analyses related to Total Quality Leadership. It addresses such concerns as how TQL can improve customer service and affect utilization of information technology.

UNIT 5: Developing the Future Ethos and Social Responsibility of Business

International Business Ethics Institute (IBEI)
http://www.business-ethics.org/index.asp

The goal of this educational organization is to promote business ethics and corporate responsibility in response to the growing need for transnationalism in the field of business ethics.

UNU/IAS Project on Global Ethos
http://www.ias.unu.edu/research/globalethos.cfm

The United Nations University Institute of Advanced Studies (UNU/IAS) has issued this project abstract, which concerns governance and multilateralism. The main aim of the project is to initiate a process by which to generate jointly, with the involvement of factors from both state- and nonstate institutions in developed and developing countries, a global ethos that could provide or support a set of guiding principles for the emerging global community.

We highly recommend that you review our Web site for expanded information and our other product lines. We are continually updating and adding links to our Web site in order to offer you the most usable and useful information that will support and expand the value of your Annual Editions. You can reach us at: *http://www.mhcls.com/annualeditions/*.

UNIT 1
Ethics, Values, and Social Responsibility in Business

Unit Selections

1. **Thinking Ethically: A Framework for Moral Decision Making**, Manuel Velasquez et al.
2. **Business Ethics: Back to Basics**, William I. Sauser, Jr.
3. **Advice from Aristotle on Business Ethics**, James O'Toole
4. **Truth or Consequences: The Organizational Importance of Honesty**, Erline Belton
5. **Why Good Leaders Do Bad Things**, Charles D. Kerns
6. **Best Resources for Corporate Social Responsibility**, Karen McNichol

Key Points to Consider

- Do you believe that corporations are more socially responsible today than they were 10 years ago? Why or why not?

- In what specific ways do you see companies practicing social responsibility? Do you think most companies are overt or covert in their social responsibility activities? Explain your answer.

- What are the economic and social implications of "management accountability" as part of the decision-making process? Does a company have any obligation to help remedy social problems, such as poverty, urban decay, and pollution? Defend your response.

- Using the recent examples of stock, financial, and accounting debacles, discuss the flaws in America's financial system that allow companies to disregard ethics, values, and social responsibility in business.

Student Website
www.mhcls.com/online

Internet References
Further information regarding these websites may be found in this book's preface or online.

Association for Moral Education (AME)
http://www.amenetwork.org/

Business for Social Responsibility (BSR)
http://www.bsr.org/

Enron Online
http://www.enron.com/corp/

Ethics Updates/Lawrence Hinman
http://ethics.sandiego.edu/index.html

Institute for Business and Professional Ethics
http://commerce.depaul.edu/ethics/

National Center for Policy Analysis
http://www.ncpa.org

Open Directory Project
http://dmoz.org/Business/Management/Ethics

Working Definitions
http://www.workingdefinitions.co.uk/index.html

Ethical decision making in an organization does not occur in a vacuum. As individuals and as managers, we formulate our ethics (that is, the standards of "right" and "wrong" behavior that we set for ourselves) based upon family, peer, and religious influences, our past experiences, and our own unique value systems. When we make ethical decisions within the organizational context, many times there are situational factors and potential conflicts of interest that further complicate the process.

Decisions do not only have personal ramifications—they also have social consequences. Social responsibility is really ethics at the organizational level, since it refers to the obligation that an organization has to make choices and to take actions that will contribute to the good of society as well as the good of the orga-

nization. Authentic social responsibility is not initiated because of forced compliance to specific laws and regulations. In contrast to legal responsibility, social responsibility involves a voluntary response from an organization that is above and beyond what is specified by the law.

The five selections in this unit provide an overview of the interrelationships of ethics, values, and social responsibility in business. The essays in this unit offer practical and insightful principles and suggestions to managers, enabling them to approach the subject of business ethics with more confidence. They also point out the complexity and the significance of making ethical decisions.

thinking ethically

A FRAMEWORK FOR MORAL DECISION MAKING

DEVELOPED BY MANUEL VELASQUEZ, CLAIRE ANDRE, THOMAS SHANKS, S.J., AND MICHAEL J. MEYER

Moral issues greet us each morning in the newspaper, confront us in the memos on our desks, nag us from our children's soccer fields, and bid us good night on the evening news. We are bombarded daily with questions about the justice of our foreign policy, the morality of medical technologies that can prolong our lives, the rights of the homeless, the fairness of our children's teachers to the diverse students in their classrooms.

Dealing with these moral issues is often perplexing. How, exactly, should we think through an ethical issue? What questions should we ask? What factors should we consider?

The first step in analyzing moral issues is obvious but not always easy: Get the facts.

The first step in analyzing moral issues is obvious but not always easy: Get the facts. Some moral issues create controversies simply because we do not bother to check the facts. This first step, although obvious, is also among the most important and the most frequently overlooked.

But having the facts is not enough. Facts by themselves only tell us what *is*; they do not tell us what *ought* to be. In addition to getting the facts, resolving an ethical issue also requires an appeal to values. Philosophers have developed five different approaches to values to deal with moral issues.

The Utilitarian Approach

Utilitarianism was conceived in the 19th century by Jeremy Bentham and John Stuart Mill to help legislators determine which laws were morally best. Both Bentham and Mill suggested that ethical actions are those that provide the greatest balance of good over evil.

To analyze an issue using the utilitarian approach, we first identify the various courses of action available to us. Second, we ask who will be affected by each action and what benefits or harms will be derived from each. And third, we choose the action that will produce the greatest benefits and the least harm. The ethical action is the one that provides the greatest good for the greatest number.

The Rights Approach

The second important approach to ethics has its roots in the philosophy of the 18th-century thinker Immanuel Kant and others like him, who focused on the individual's right to choose for herself or himself. According to these philosophers, what makes human beings different from mere things is that people have dignity based on their ability to choose freely what they will do with their lives, and they have a fundamental moral right to have these choices respected. People are not objects to be manipulated; it is a violation of human dignity to use people in ways they do not freely choose.

Of course, many different, but related, rights exist besides this basic one. These other rights (an incomplete list below) can be thought of as different aspects of the basic right to be treated as we choose.

- *The right to the truth*: We have a right to be told the truth and to be informed about matters that significantly affect our choices.
- *The right of privacy*: We have the right to do, believe, and say whatever we choose in our personal lives so long as we do not violate the rights of others.

the case of
maria elena

Maria Elena has cleaned your house each week for more than a year. You agree with your friend who recommended her that she does an excellent job and is well worth the $30 cash you pay her for three hours' work. You've also come to like her, and you think she likes you, especially as her English has become better and you've been able to have some pleasant conversations.

Over the past three weeks, however, you've noticed Maria Elena becoming more and more distracted. One day, you ask her if something is wrong, and she tells you she really needs to make additional money. She hastens to say she is not asking you for a raise, becomes upset, and begins to cry. When she calms down a little, she tells you her story:

She came to the United States six years ago from Mexico with her child, Miguel, who is now 7 years old. They entered the country on a visitor's visa that has expired, and Maria Elena now uses a Social Security number she made up.

Her common-law husband, Luis, came to the United States first. He entered the country illegally, after paying smugglers $500 to hide him under piles of grass cuttings for a six-hour truck ride across the border. When he had made enough money from low-paying day jobs, he sent for Maria Elena. Using a false green card, Luis now works as a busboy for a restaurant, which withholds part of his salary for taxes. When Maria Elena comes to work at your house, she takes the bus and Luis baby-sits.

In Mexico, Maria Elena and Luis lived in a small village where it was impossible to earn more than $3 a day. Both had sixth-grade educations, common in their village. Life was difficult, but they did not decide to leave until they realized the future would be bleak for their child and for the other children they wanted to have. Luis had a cousin in San Jose who visited and told Luis and Maria Elena how well his life was going.

After his visit, Luis and Maria Elena decided to come to the United States.

Luis quickly discovered, as did Maria Elena, that life in San Jose was not the way they had heard. The cousin did not tell them they would be able to afford to live only in a run-down three-room apartment with two other couples and their children. He did not tell them they would always live in fear of INS raids.

After they entered the United States, Maria Elena and Luis had a second child, Jose, who is 5 years old. The birth was difficult because she didn't use the health-care system or welfare for fear of being discovered as undocumented. But, she tells you, she is willing to put up with anything so that her children can have a better life. "All the money we make is for Miguel and Jose," she tells you. "We work hard for their education and their future."

Now, however, her mother in Mexico is dying, and Maria Elena must return home, leaving Luis and the children. She does not want to leave them because she might not be able to get back into the United States, but she is pretty sure she can find a way to return if she has enough money. That is her problem: She doesn't have enough money to make certain she can get back.

After she tells you her story, she becomes too distraught to continue talking. You now know she is an undocumented immigrant, working in your home. What is the ethical thing for you to do?

This case was developed by Tom Shanks, S.J., director of the Markkula Center for Applied Ethics. Maria Elena is a composite drawn from several real people, and her story represents some of the ethical dilemmas behind the immigration issue.

This case can be accessed through the Ethics Center home page on the World Wide Web: http://www.scu.edu/Ethics/. You can also contact us by e-mail, ethics@scu.edu, or regular mail: Markkula Center for Applied Ethics, Santa Clara University, Santa Clara, CA 95053. Our voice mail number is (408) 554-7898. We have also posted on our homepage a new case involving managed health care.

- *The right not to be injured*: We have the right not to be harmed or injured unless we freely and knowingly do something to deserve punishment or we freely and knowingly choose to risk such injuries.

- *The right to what is agreed:* We have a right to what has been promised by those with whom we have freely entered into a contract or agreement.

In deciding whether an action is moral or immoral using this second approach, then, we must ask, Does the action respect the moral rights of everyone? Actions are wrong to the extent that they violate the rights of individuals; the more serious the violation, the more wrongful the action.

The Fairness or Justice Approach

The fairness or justice approach to ethics has its roots in the teachings of the ancient Greek philosopher Aristotle, who said that "equals should be treated equally and unequals unequally." The basic moral question in this approach is: How fair is an action? Does it treat everyone in the same way, or does it show favoritism and discrimination?

Favoritism gives benefits to some people without a justifiable reason for singling them out; discrimination imposes burdens on people who are no different from those on whom burdens are not imposed. Both favoritism and discrimination are unjust and wrong.

The Common-Good Approach

This approach to ethics presents a vision of society as a community whose members are joined in the shared pursuit of values and goals they hold in common. This community comprises individuals whose own good is inextricably bound to the good of the whole.

The common good is a notion that originated more than 2,000 years ago in the writings of Plato, Aristotle, and Cicero. More recently, contemporary ethicist John Rawls defined the common good as "certain general conditions that are... equally to everyone's advantage."

In this approach, we focus on ensuring that the social policies, social systems, institutions, and environments on which we depend are beneficial to all. Examples of goods common to all include affordable health care, effective public safety, peace among nations, a just legal system, and an unpolluted environment.

Appeals to the common good urge us to view ourselves as members of the same community, reflecting on broad questions concerning the kind of society we want to become and how we are to achieve that society. While respecting and valuing the freedom of individuals to pursue their own goals, the common-good approach challenges us also to recognize and further those goals we share in common.

The Virtue Approach

The virtue approach to ethics assumes that there are certain ideals toward which we should strive, which provide for the full development of our humanity. These ideals are discovered through thoughtful reflection on what kind of people we have the potential to become.

Virtues are attitudes or character traits that enable us to be and to act in ways that develop our highest potential. They enable us to pursue the ideals we have adopted.

Honesty, courage, compassion, generosity, fidelity, integrity, fairness, self-control, and prudence are all examples of virtues.

Virtues are like habits; that is, once acquired, they become characteristic of a person. Moreover, a person who has developed virtues will be naturally disposed to act in ways consistent with moral principles. The virtuous person is the ethical person.

In dealing with an ethical problem using the virtue approach, we might ask, What kind of person should I be? What will promote the development of character within myself and my community?

Ethical Problem Solving

These five approaches suggest that once we have ascertained the facts, we should ask ourselves five questions when trying to resolve a moral issue:

- What benefits and what harms will each course of action produce, and which alternative will lead to the best overall consequences?
- What moral rights do the affected parties have, and which course of action best respects those rights?
- Which course of action treats everyone the same, except where there is a morally justifiable reason not to, and does not show favoritism or discrimination?
- Which course of action advances the common good?
- Which course of action develops moral virtues?

This method, of course, does not provide an automatic solution to moral problems. It is not meant to. The method is merely meant to help identify most of the important ethical considerations. In the end, we must deliberate on moral issues for ourselves, keeping a careful eye on both the facts and on the ethical considerations involved.

FOR FURTHER READING

Frankena, William. *Ethics*, 2nd ed. (Englewood Cliffs, N.J.: Prentice Hall, 1973).

Halberstam, Joshua. *Everyday Ethics: Inspired Solutions to Real Life Dilemmas* (New York: Penguin Books, 1993).

Martin, Michael. *Everyday Morality* (Belmont, Calif: Wadsworth, 1995).

Rachels, James. *The Elements of Moral Philosophy*, 2nd ed. (New York: McGraw-Hill, 1993).

Velasquez, Manuel. *Business Ethics: Concepts and Cases*, 3rd ed. (Englewood Cliffs, N.J.: Prentice Hall, 1992) 2–110.

This article updates several previous pieces from Issues in Ethics *by Manuel Velasquez—Dirksen Professor of Business Ethics at SCU and former Center director—and Claire Andre, associate Center director. "Thinking Ethically" is based on a framework developed by the authors in collaboration with Center Director Thomas Shanks, S.J., Presidential Professor of Ethics and the Common Good Michael J. Meyer, and others. The framework is used as the basis for many Center programs and presentations.*

From *Issues in Ethics*, Winter 1996, pp. 2–5. © 1996 by the Markkula Center for Applied Ethics/The President and Board of Trustees of Santa Clara College. Reprinted by permission.

Business Ethics: Back to Basics

Abstract

With business news dominated in recent years by some spectacular examples of ethical malfeasance, confidence in the business world has been shaken. Never mind that the Enrons of the world are actually few and far between. No business or organization can afford even a suspicion of unethical behavior and must take proactive steps to ensure that no suspicions arise. Ethical behavior begins at the top with actions and statements that are beyond reproach and ambiguity. Managements may want to follow an eight-point action list presented here for establishing a strong ethical culture and also a decision checklist when ethical dilemmas loom. Sterling reputations are valuable business assets: they are earned over time but can be lost almost overnight.

William I. Sauser, Jr., Auburn University

Introduction

Enron, Arthur Andersen, Tyco, ImClone, Martha Stewart, WorldCom, Global Crossing, Merrill Lynch, Rite-Aid, Qwest, Adelphia, Kmart, HealthSouth—the list of formerly respected businesses (and business leaders) being charged with breaches of ethical conduct seems to be growing by the day. This is having adverse effects on our economic well-being, on investor confidence, and on the perceived desirability of pursuing business as a respectable calling.

Commenting on the ethical crisis in business leadership, Eileen Kelly (2002) observed, "Recently a new business scandal seems to surface each day. The current volatility of the market reflects the apprehension, the sense of betrayal, and the lack of confidence that investors have in many large corporations and their managements" (p. 4). Marcy Gordon (2002), reporting on a speech by United States Securities and Exchange Commissioner Paul Atkins, noted, "The string of accounting failures at big companies in the last year has cost U.S. households nearly $60,000 on average as some $5 trillion in market value was lost" (p. C4).

Accounting failures are not the only ethical concerns facing modern business organizations. The Southern Institute for Business and Professional Ethics (2002) lists on its Web site an array of issues that put pressures on business enterprises. These include the globalization of business, work force diversification, employment practices and policies, civil litigation and government regulation, and concerns about environmental stewardship. The institute (on the same Web site) concluded, "Despite such powerful trends, few managers have been adequately equipped by traditional education to recognize, evaluate, and act upon the ethical dimension of their work."

Columnist Malcolm Cutchins (2002), an emeritus professor of engineering at Auburn University, summed up the problem concisely: "We have seen the effect of not teaching good ethics in business schools. If we continue to neglect the teaching of good principles on a broad scale, we all reap the bad consequences" (p. A4).

Business Ethics

Ethics has to do with behavior—specifically, an individual's moral behavior with respect to society. The extent to which behavior measures up to societal standards is typically used as a gauge of ethicality. Since there are a variety of standards for societal behavior, ethical behavior is often characterized with respect to certain contexts. The Ethics Resource Center says, "*Business Ethics* refers to clear standards and norms that help employees to distinguish right from wrong behavior at work" (Joseph, 2003, p. 2). In the business context, ethics has to do with the extent to which a person's behavior measures up to such standards as the law, organizational policies, professional and trade association codes, popular expectations regarding fairness and rightness, plus an individual's internalized moral standards.

Business ethics, then, is not distinct from ethics in general, but rather a subfield (Desjardins, 2003, p. 8). The subfield refers to the examination and application of moral standards within the context of finance; commerce; production, distribution, and sale of goods and services; and other business activities.

It can be argued that an ethical person behaves appropriately in all societal contexts. This may be so, in which case one might prefer the term "ethics in business" to "business ethics." The distinction is subtle, but serves as a reminder that morality may be generalized from context to context. Adam Smith, for example, saw no need for ethical relativism when it comes to business. "It is impossible to determine just how business became separated from ethics in history. If we go back to Adam Smith, we find no such separation. In addition to his famous book on business and capitalism, *The Wealth of Nations*, Adam Smith also wrote *The Theory of Moral Sentiments*, a book about our ethical obligations to one another. It is clear that Smith believed that business and commerce worked well only if people took seriously their obligations and, in particular, their sense of justice" (Bruner, Eaker, Freeman, Spekman, and Teisberg, 1998, p. 46).

May (1995) echoed this important point: "The marketplace breaks down unless it can presuppose the virtue of industry, without which goods will not be produced; and the virtues of "honesty and integrity, without which their free and fair exchange cannot take place" (p. 693).

Standards of Behavior

The law (including statutory, administrative, and case law) is an important and legitimate source of ethical guidance. Federal, state, and local laws establish the parameters (Fieser, 1996), and violation of the law is almost always considered unethical (with the possible exception of civil disobedience as a mechanism for putting the law itself on trial). Pursuing business outside the law is regarded as an obstructionist approach to business ethics (Schermerhorn, 2005, p. 75). Such an individual would almost certainly be labeled unethical.

A second important source of authority is organizational policies, which are standards for behavior established by the employing organization. Typically they are aligned with the law (which takes precedence over them) and spell out in detail how things are done. All employees are expected to adhere to organizational policies. It is very important that managers at the highest level set the example for others by always working within the law and the policies of the organization.

Another important source of ethical guidance is the code of behavior adopted by professional and trade associations. These codes are often aspirational in nature and frequently establish higher standards for behavior than the law requires. Members of a profession or trade association typically aspire to meet these higher standards in order to establish and uphold the reputation of a profession or trade.

A fourth type of standard—often unwritten and commonly the community's concept of morality. These social mores, based on commonly held beliefs about what is right and wrong and fair and unfair, can be powerful determinants of a person's reputation. Behavior that—in the strictest sense—meets legal requirements, organizational policies, and even professional standards may still be viewed by the general public as unfair and wrong (Krech, Crutchfield, and Ballachey, 1962).

A fifth set of standards reflects the individual conscience. Coleman, Butcher and Carson (1980, p. Glossary IV) define "the conscience" as "the functioning of an individual's moral values in the approval or disapproval of his or her own thoughts

and actions," and equate it roughly with the Freudian concept of the superego. Highly ethical business leaders typically have moral standards that exceed all four of the lesser standards just listed. These values, learned early in life and reinforced by life's experiences, are internalized standards often based on personal, religious or philosophical understandings of morality (Baelz, 1977, pp. 41–55)

Ethical Dilemmas

An ethical dilemma is a situation where a potential course of action offers potential benefit or gain but is unethical, in that it violates one or more of the standards just described. Behaviors violating laws are, by definition, illegal as well as unethical. The key question for the business leader when presented with an ethical dilemma is: "What to do?" Behavior determines a person's ethical reputation, after all. Ethical leadership is exhibited when ethical dilemmas are resolved in an appropriate manner.

Here is a sampling of some ethical dilemmas that frequently rise in the business setting. Many of these behaviors are illegal as well as unethical.

➤ Providing a product or service you know is harmful or unsafe
➤ Misleading someone through false statements or omissions
➤ Using insider information for personal gain
➤ Playing favorites
➤ Manipulating and using people
➤ Benefiting personally from a position of trust
➤ Violating confidentiality
➤ Misusing company property or equipment
➤ Falsifying documents
➤ Padding expenses
➤ Taking bribes or kickbacks
➤ Participating in a cover-up
➤ Theft or sabotage
➤ Committing an act of violence
➤ Substance abuse
➤ Negligence or inappropriate behavior in the workplace.

Poor Ethical Choices

Why do people sometimes make poor choices when faced with ethical dilemmas? One set of reasons has to do with flaws of *character*. Such character defects include malice (intentional evil); sociopathy (lack of conscience); personal greed; envy, jealousy, resentment; the will to win or achieve at any cost; and fear of failure. There are also flaws in *corporate culture* that lead even good people to make poor ethical judgments. Weaknesses in corporate culture include indifference, a lack of knowledge or understanding of standards on the part of employees; poor or inappropriate incentive systems; and poor leadership, including the use of mixed signals such as:

➤ I don't care how you do it, just get it done.

- ➤ Don't ever bring me bad news.
- ➤ Don' t bother me with the details, you know what to do.
- ➤ Remember, we always meet our financial goals somehow.
- ➤ No one gets injured on this worksite…period. Understand?
- ➤ Ask me no questions, I'll tell you no lies.

Such statements by managers to their subordinates too often imply that unethical behaviors that obtain the intended results are acceptable to the organization. While it may be difficult—other than through termination or other sanctions—to rid the organization of employees with character flaws, correcting a poor organizational culture is clearly a matter of leadership.

Establishing a Strong Ethical Culture

Business leaders who wish to take proactive measures to establish and maintain a corporate culture that emphasizes strong moral leadership are advised to take the following steps:

1. **Adopt a code of ethics.** The code need not be long and elaborate with flowery words and phrases. In fact, the best ethical codes use language anyone can understand. A good way to produce such a code is to ask all employees of the firm (or a representative group) to participate in its creation (Kuchar, 2003). Identify the commonly-held moral beliefs and values of the members of the firm and codify them into a written document all can understand and support. Post the code of ethics in prominent places around the worksite. Make certain that all employees subscribe to it by asking them to sign it.

2. **Provide ethics training.** From time to time a leader should conduct ethics training sessions. These may be led by experts in business ethics, or they may be informal in nature and led by the manager or employees themselves. A highly effective way to conduct an ethics training session is to provide "what if cases for discussion and resolution. The leader would present a "real world" scenario in which an ethical dilemma is encountered. Using the organization's code of ethics as a guide, participants would explore options and seek a consensus ethical solution. This kind of training sharpens the written ethical code and brings it to life.

3. **Hire and promote ethical people.** This, in concert with step four, is probably the best defense against putting the business at risk through ethical lapses by employees. When making human resources decisions it is critical to reward ethical behavior and punish unethical behavior. Investigate the character of the people you hire, and do your best to hire people who have exhibited high moral standards in the past. Remember that past behavior is the best predictor of future behavior, so check references carefully. Formal background investigations may be warranted for positions of fiduciary responsibility or significant risk exposure. Base promotional decisions on matters of character in addition to technical competence. Demonstrate to your employees that high ethical standards are a requirement for advancement.

4. **Correct unethical behavior.** This complements step three. When the organization's ethical code is breached, those responsible must be punished. Many businesses use progressive discipline, with an oral warning (intended to advise the employee of what is and is not acceptable behavior) as the first step, followed by a written reprimand, suspension without pay, and termination if unethical behavior persists. Of course, some ethical lapses are so egregious that they require suspension—or even termination—following the first offense. Through consistent and firm application of sanctions to correct unethical behavior, the manager will signal to all employees that substandard moral behavior will not be tolerated.

5. **Be proactive.** Businesses wishing to establish a reputation for ethicality and good corporate citizenship in the community will often organize and support programs intended to give something back to the community. Programs that promote continuing education, wholesome recreation, good health and hygiene, environmental quality, adequate housing, and other community benefits may demonstrate the extent to which the business promotes concern for human welfare. Seeking and adopting best practices from other businesses in the community is also a proactive strategy.

6. **Conduct a social audit.** Most businesses are familiar with financial audits. This concept can be employed in the context of ethics and corporate responsibility as well. From time to time the leader of the business might invite responsible parties to examine the organization's product design, purchasing, production, marketing, distribution, customer relations, and human resources functions with an eye toward identifying and correcting any areas of policy or practice that raise ethical concerns. Similarly, programs of corporate responsibility (such as those mentioned in step five) should be reviewed for effectiveness and improved as needed.

7. **Protect whistle blowers.** A whistle blower is a person within the firm who points out ethically questionable actions taken by other employees—or even by managers—within the organization. Too often corporate whistle blowers are ignored—or even punished—by those who receive the unfortunate news of wrongdoing within the business. All this does is discourage revelation of ethical problems. Instead the whistle blower should be protected and even honored. When unethical actions are uncovered within a firm by one of the employees, managers should step forward and take corrective action (as described in step four). Employees learn from one another. If the owners and managers of a business turn a blind eye toward wrongdoing, a signal is sent to everyone within the firm that ethicality is not characteristic of that organization's culture. A downward spiral of moral behavior is likely to follow.

8. **Empower the guardians of integrity.** The business leader's chief task is to lead by example and to empower every member of the organization to demonstrate the firm's commitment to ethics in its relationships with suppliers, customers, employees, and shareholders. Turn each employee of the firm, no matter what that individual's position, into a guardian of the firm's integrity. When maliciousness and indifference are replaced with a culture of integrity, honesty, and ethicality, the business will reap long-term benefits from all quarters.

A Checklist for Making Good Ethical Decisions

A business leader who takes seriously the challenge of creating a strong ethical culture for the firm must, of course, make good decisions when faced personally with ethical dilemmas. Here is a checklist a manager might wish to follow:

1. Recognize the ethical dilemma.

2. Get the facts.

3. Identify your options.

4. Test each option: Is it legal, right, beneficial? Note: Get some counsel.

5. Decide which option to follow.

6. Double-check your decision.

7. Take action.

8. Follow up and monitor decision implementation.

Number six is key: Double-check your decision. When in doubt consider how each of the following might guide you. Take the action that would allow you to maintain your reputation with those on this list you believe adhere to the highest ethical standards: Your attorney, accountant, boss, co-workers, stakeholders, family, newspaper, television news, religious leader, and Deity.

How would you feel if you had to explain your decision—and your actions—to each of these? If you would not feel good about this, then it is quite likely that you are about to make a poor decision. Double check your decision in this manner before you take any action you may later regret.

Conclusion

A firm's reputation may take years—even decades—to establish, but can be destroyed in an instant through unethical behavior. That is why it is so important for business leaders to be very careful about the things they say and do. Taking the time and effort to establish and maintain a corporate culture of morality, integrity, honesty, and ethicality will pay important dividends throughout the life of the firm. While taking ethical shortcuts may appear to lead to gains in the short term, this type of corporate strategy almost always proves tragic in the longer term.

Every business leader will be faced at one time or another with an ethical dilemma. Many face even daily temptations. How the leader manifests moral integrity when faced with ethical dilemmas sets the tone for everyone else in the organization. This is why it is so important to "walk the talk" by making good ethical decisions every day. Understanding and applying the concepts presented in this article will enable you, as a business leader, to create and maintain an ethical corporate culture in your business. As Carl Skoogland, the former vice president and ethics director for Texas Instruments, recently advised, if you want to create an ethical business, you must *know what's right, value what's right, and do what's right* (Skoogland, 2003).

REFERENCES

Baelz, P. (1977). *Ethics and belief.* New York: The Seabury Press.

Bruner, R. F., Eaker, M. R., Freeman, E., Spekman, R.E., and Teisberg, E. O. (1998). *The portable MBA, 3rd ed.* New York: Wiley.

Coleman, J. C., Butcher, J. N., and Carson, R. (1980). *Abnormal psychology and modern life, 6th ed,* Glenview, IL: Scott Foresman.

Cutchins, M. (2002, November 20). Business ethics must be taught or we all pay. *Opelika-Auburn News,* p. A4.

Desjardins, J. (2003). *An introduction to business ethics.* Boston: McGraw-Hill.

Fieser, J. (1996). Do businesses have moral obligations beyond what the law requires? *Journal of Business Ethics, 15,* 457–468.

Gordon, M. (2002, November 18). Accounting failures cost $60,000 on average, SEC commissioner says. *Opelika-Auburn News,* p. C4.

Kelly, E. P. (2002). Business ethics—An oxymoron? *Phi Kappa Phi Forum, 82*(4), 4–5.

Krech, D., Crutchfield, R. S., and Ballachey, E. L. (1962). Culture. Chapter 10 in *Individual in society* (pp. 339–380). New York: McGraw-Hill.

Kuchar, C. (2003). Tips on developing ethics codes for private companies. *GoodBusiness,* 2(3), pages unnumbered.

Joseph, J. (2003). *National business ethics survey 2003: How employees view ethics in their organizations.* Washington, DC: Ethics Resource Center.

May, W. F. (1995). The virtues of the business leader. In M. L. Stackhouse, D. P. McCann, S. J, Roels, and P. N. Williams (Eds.), *On moral business* (pp. 692–700). Grand Rapids, MI: Eerdmans.

Schermerhorn, J. R., Jr. (2005). *Management, 8th ed.* New York: Wiley.

Skoogland, C. (2003, October 16). *Establishing an ethical organization.* Plenary address at the Conference on Ethics and Social Responsibility in Engineering and Technology, New Orleans, LA.

The Southern Institute for Business and Professional Ethics. (2002). *The certificate in managerial ethics.* Retrieved August, 14, 2002, from http://www.southerninstitute.org.

About the Author

Dr. Sauser is Associate Dean for Business and Engineering Outreach and Professor of Management at Auburn University. His interests include organization development, strategic planning, human relations in the workplace, business ethics, and continuing professional education. He is a Fellow of the American Council on Education and the Society for Advancement of Management (SAM). In 2003, he was awarded the Frederick W. Taylor Key by SAM for his career achievements.

From *Society for Advancement of Management,* 2005, No. 2, pp. 1-4. Copyright © 2005 by Society for Advancement of Management. Reprinted by permission.

Advice from Aristotle on Business Ethics

James O'Toole

Aristotle was the most practical and business-oriented of all philosophers who asked ethical questions. You may stop at the idea that a person who's been dead for nearly 2,400 years has anything practical to say about modern organizations. But Aristotle remains relevant because he is particularly interested in defining principles in terms of the ethics of leadership.

In his *Nicomachean Ethics*, Aristotle concludes that the role of the leader is to create the environment in which all members of an organization have the opportunity to realize their own potential. He says that the ethical role of the leader is not to enhance his or her own power but to create the conditions under which followers can achieve their potential.

Of course Aristotle never heard of a large business or corporation. Nonetheless, he did raise a set of ethical questions that are directly relevant to corporate leaders who wish to behave in ethical ways.

Here are some of them. (I'm only slightly paraphrasing them in turning them from a political context into an organizational context.)

- Am I behaving in a virtuous way?

- How would I want to be treated if I were a member of this organization?

- What form of social contract would allow all our members to develop their full potential in order that they may each make their greatest contribution to the good of the whole?

- To what extent are there real opportunities for all employees to develop their talents and their potential?

- To what extent do employees participate in decisions that effect their work?

- To what extent do all employees participate in the financial gain resulting from their own ideas and efforts?

If you translate Aristotle into modern terms, you will see a whole set of questions about the extent to which the organization provides an environment that is conducive to human growth and fulfillment.

He also raises a lot of useful questions about the distribution of rewards in organizations based on the ethical principle of rewarding people proportionate to their contributions.

"All Aristotle says is that virtue and wisdom will definitely elude leaders who fail to engage in ethical analysis of their actions."

For example, Disney's Board of Directors compensated Michael Eisner with something like $285 million between 1994 and 2004. Now, I don't pretend to have all the data about how much Michael Eisner deserves, but thanks to Aristotle, we do have some questions that a virtuous member of the Disney Board Compensation Committee might ask in making decisions about his compensation, including: Is the CEO's proportionate contribution to the organization 10, 100, 1,000 times greater than that of an animator at our Burbank studio or the operator of the Space Mountain ride at Disneyland?

Aristotle doesn't provide a single, clear principle for the just distribution of enterprise-created wealth, nor do I believe it would be possible for anyone to formulate a monolithic rule. Nonetheless, here are some Aristotelian questions that virtuous leaders might ask:

- Am I taking more than my share of rewards—more than my contribution is worth?

- Does the distribution of goods preserve the happiness of the community?

- Does it have a negative effect on morale? Would everyone enter into the employment contract under the current terms if they truly had different choices?

• Would we come to a different principle of allocation if all the parties concerned were represented at the table?

Again, the only hard and fast principle of distributive justice is that fairness is likely to arise out of a process of rational and moral deliberation among the participating parties. All Aristotle says is that virtue and wisdom will definitely elude leaders who fail to engage in ethical analysis of their actions. He tells us that the bottom line of ethics depends on asking tough questions.

James O'Toole is research professor at the Center for Effective Organizations, University of Southern California, and Mortimer J. Adler Professor at the Aspen Institute. This article is excerpted from a talk delivered at a meeting of the Center's Business and Organizational Ethics Partnership.

From *At the Center: Markkula Center for Applied Ethics,* Winter 2005, pp. 1, 3. Copyright © 2005 by James O'Toole. Reprinted by permission.

Truth or Consequences:
The Organizational Importance of Honesty

Erline Belton

"We do not err because truth is difficult to see. It is visible at a glance. We err because this is more comfortable."

—Alexander Solzhenitsyn, Nobel Prize Winner, Soviet Writer and U.S. Citizen

We have all experienced the public lie that goes unchallenged. It may be baldly untrue but somehow accepted as the basis for action with life and death consequences. Some of our experience of public lies may be based on differences in values or perceptions, but sometimes what is said just simply violates the facts—this is disheartening and drives people out of public participation.

The same may be said of organizations. A nonprofit may, on the surface, be making every effort to promote teamwork and "the higher good," but if its people continue to perceive a culture that supports a different and less reliable set of operating norms and assumptions than what is written or espoused, they will not bring themselves wholly to our efforts.

Here are some typical reasons for telling lies:

- to avoid pain or unpleasant consequences;
- to promote self-interest and a particular point of view;
- to protect the leaders or the organization;
- to perpetuate myths that hold the organization or a point of view together;

Regardless of why they are told, untruths and lies can cause people to disengage—and they can also diminish the spirit people bring into the workplace. This leads to a sometimes massive loss of applied human intellectual and physical capital assets. A disinvestment of human spirit results in what I refer to as a Gross National People Divestiture (GNPD). The GNPD index in any organization or society can be directly related to the prevalence and magnitude of untruths told and allowed to stand. GNPD occurs when your organization's tolerance of untruth creates a climate of cynical disbelief engendering a lack of trust in information and relationships. This automatically creates management problems that are sometimes difficult to put your finger on but are often very powerfully present nonetheless.

Our challenge is to buck the culture and engage people in building a climate of truth telling that will lead to a newly revived work ethic and heightened individual and collective energy. In order to do this effectively, we must understand the conditions that support the emergence of truth, and understand and eliminate those that routinely undermine its presence in our organizations.

Staying Safe: Are You Avoiding Pain, but Inviting Extinction?

According to psychologist Abraham Maslow, our strongest mutual instinct is to be safe from harm and to protect our sense of well-being. It is this instinct that guides us to avoid risk (or what we perceive to be risk), and to respond cautiously to changes in our environment, relying heavily on familiar patterns of behavior in an effort to promote and sustain a sense of equilibrium. As co-workers or managers, this instinct often propels us to play it safe and go along with the program. Ironically, in a quickly changing environment this is obviously counterproductive.

Thus, too often, we opt for the illusion of stability in order to promote a sense of psychological well-being. This sense is acquired in exchange for at least a fragment of the whole truth; and since we all know "the truth" is relative anyway, we hardly notice the cost. It is true that we all seek solid ground when in doubt. But does that solid ground need to be sameness? Solid ground might be, for instance, a place to stand for something we can believe in and whose integrity we can rely on when all else appears undependable and unpredictable.

Over time illusions dissolve and evaporate. When they do, those who have used them for grounding are left less safe, less secure than ever. And those who have allowed even the smallest of illusions to inform our management decisions, have placed entire organizations, teams and ourselves at risk.

Because of the diversity of perspectives and information available in any group, a collective organizational "truth" has the potential to be stronger and more accurate than any one individual's truth. But it is only when we have the combination of individual as well as collective seeking of truth, that organizational potential is realized. This requires an open atmosphere where people can depend upon one another to engage honestly, respectfully, and with spirit intact. It requires the testing of personal assumptions among people and that requires a level of trust.

More often than not, organizational potential is not realized. Why? Team meetings, team coordination, and team feedback all involve a diversity of people and personalities that have at least one thing in common: they don't want to get hurt; they don't want unpleasant things to happen; they want to feel safe; and they want to contribute. We, as fallible individuals create the environment, and environmental conditions can support either truth or lies.

Conditions That Support Untruths

Groupthink: The tendency to just go along with the crowd, avoid drawing criticism to ourselves, and assume that everyone agrees, is so subtle and unconscious that we are generally unaware of it. As a result, we often all wind up somewhere nobody really wanted to be. For instance, imagine the scenario of an organization trying to decide on whether to apply for a major contract. Most staff members are in favor of going forward while a few are privately concerned that the organization does not have the capacity to handle the work or the money. The push toward acquiring the contract is so strong that the isolated few remain silent for fear of being characterized as pessimists or naysayers. The organization lands the contract and finds itself in terrible straits trying to handle the management challenge. One variation on this is situations in which everyone knows something but there is an undercurrent of pressure not to state it aloud. Colluding in lies can be crippling. In one organization I know, the staff

was asked about the biggest lie inhabiting the organization. After much hemming and hawing, one man finally blurted out, "The lie is that we provide good services that the community wants. We don't and we treat any client who complains like a troublemaker." He went on to provide examples. Everyone else around the table nodded agreement immediately. Consider the enormous cost of having kept this silent for years! This was a key organization, serving an isolated immigrant community. Unfortunately the dialogue group did not include the executive director or board members who later did not allow the conversation to progress further. This was seven years ago, and to this day, funders see the organization as "chronically in trouble."

Imaginary conflicts: People often choose their words and edit their facts to protect themselves from anticipated reactions. One person's imaginary conflicts can warp the way information is exchanged. In a team, the distortion is amplified by the processes of repetition and groupthink. Eventually, the distorted facts may culminate in a "self-fulfilling prophecy" where our worst fears materialize precisely because we acted in fear. Think about the executive director that everyone soft pedals around for fear of hitting one of her sacred organizational cows. Rather than gently prodding for potential change or aiming for a more open debate about organizational myths, staff members assume that some topics are "off limits" and live in silence with the uncomfortable consequences. Of course, this only fulfills the idea of the executive director as a leader entrenched in her ways, and prevents her from getting accurate feedback—and so it goes.

Hidden agendas: When individuals have their own interests at heart, or believe that something is true but fail to disclose this fact, seemingly straightforward discussions have a way of going wrong. Unexpected disunity and conflict can undermine team spirit and group confidence,

preventing the group from working efficiently and effectively. Self-interest isn't so bad in itself, but when kept underground it acts like a dark matter pulling everything in its direction—down. The most distressing of these situations occur when individuals see themselves as self-righteous warriors using any means necessary in their "struggle for justice."

The Spectrum of Everyday Lies

Exaggerating or underplaying the truth: This is often done for one's own benefit, for that of the team, or for a teammate. These lies usually reflect (or exceed) desired expected outcomes.

Shading the truth: This is usually done to make a point or to protect yourself, your team, or your teammate. Again, such a lie is used to make the impression that things are more like you want or expect them to be than they actually are. These lies are often used in a noble effort to protect others from the truth.

Beating around the bush or throwing up a smoke screen: This is a delay tactic used to enlarge the insulation or cushion of safety between you and somebody who makes you uncomfortable. This category includes situations in which you withhold an opinion or fail to tell a person where he or she really stands with you for fear of creating complications or undesired reactions. It also includes instances when you fail to say no directly, when no is what you mean.

Pretending certainty or expertise: There is a lot of pressure in the workplace to provide answers now, to know the facts, the status, the scoop. These lies are often passed off as bravado, but they create unfounded expectations and dependencies in others, thus setting them up for unpleasant surprises.

Not letting others know your true position: Especially in times of ambiguity or controversy, there is a temptation to cover yourself by either making your stand unclear, or stating it in such a way that it sounds as if you are in agreement with others when, in fact, you are not. This is a common feature of groupthink and often leads to outcomes nobody really wanted, but everybody assumed they did!

Consciously withholding relevant information: This is often used as a kind of power play to leverage the value and impact of information that you have. By not fully disclosing your knowledge, you are in fact manipulating people for your own purposes (whatever they may be).

Perceptions of powerlessness: Especially in teams with strong leaders, people may feel they have no legitimate voice and are vulnerable (by proximity) to the "powers that be." Opting to assume that others know best, some people often let others make choices and decisions for them, and withhold information that might influence the discussion. Once this happens, these people have made themselves powerless to do anything but accept the consequences.

Perceptions of invulnerability: Belonging to a successful team can be exhilarating—so exhilarating that maxims such as "success sows the seeds of its own failure" seem irrelevant and only applicable to somebody else. There is a strong sense of being "in the know" and having a unique advantage over others who are outside the circle of your team. This can lead to carelessness, letting perceptions, communications, and facts slide by without diligent examination and discussion.

Misplaced loyalty or dysfunctional rescuing: Relationships that have longevity often interfere with the ability to be objective about performance, and ultimately one's competence to do the job. Loyalty to these relationships can cause individuals to look the other way and avoid listening to obvious data that suggests that either the person is in the wrong position, or that it is time to move on. Silence on the issues of lack of performance is a major untruth. If unacknowledged it creates disharmony and reduces leadership's credibility. Once acknowledged, and once actions have been taken, an environmental unfreezing occurs that revitalizes human spirit and performance.

Failing to give due credit: A common way of self-promotion in a group setting, this denies or diminishes the value of others' input and contributions. It disempowers people and leads to the inappropriate use of human resources.

Deluding yourself—self-deception: This is perhaps the most common source of everyday lies. You have both conscious and unconscious internal mechanisms that operate to protect you from cold hard facts in the misguided belief that what you don't know won't hurt you. These self-deceptions set you up for hard falls, and introduce faulty information into whatever team dynamic you are part of.

Conditions That Support Truth Telling

Individual examination/accountability: Individual organizations and teams can "build better truths." Since untruths can be intentional, the truth must be intentional. Collective truth for a team is the result of individual encouragement through consent that is informed, uncompelled, and mutual. The leader has a critical and essential role as role model and must understand that his or her behavior is under more scrutiny and will be given more weight than that of the others. If the leader fails at this, the organizational setting will also fail.

Visible commitment to truth telling: Relentlessly stating that truth telling has value is only the first step. Explaining thoughts, acknowledging the power of our words, and being accountable to one another for our actions will demonstrate that concept. In spite of our fear about telling the truth, relationships can be consistently strengthened with truth as the foundation.

Collective truths and collective responsibility: All team members need to collaborate in a dialogue that sets the foundation for an agreed-upon definition and description of "reality." This vision of reality is not complete until each member gives explicit consent and can accept the idea that the view of reality presented, even with qualifications, is one that they can sign on to. Once there is ownership and a feeling of collective responsibility, a future can be created. This kind of dialogue requires personal risk, courage, and time.

The Whole Truth: Access to reliable, solid, and truthful information is the one commodity every person, regardless of role or position, needs in order to succeed. As people who live or work together, we require information that is communicated openly and freely. Information based on the "whole truth" informs decisions, actions, behavior, and dialogue to support an outcome. Organizations that support truth telling understand that there are are four critical components to the whole truth, and to laying the foundation for achieving outcomes that have meaningful results and credibility: information must be complete, timely, accurate, and true.

Information Flow: Information creates its leaders' legacies and the values they stand for. Consider an organization's values and beliefs in the context of its history and current reality. All available facts and information (including personal stories, feelings, and visible and invisible reactions) are on the table in an accurate and accessible way; all information is understood and shared.

Free choice, sustained environmental spirit, safety: In organizations that value truth telling, each individual is free to evaluate and decide based solely on the merit of available truthful facts; there isn't even a hint of social, political, or economic coercion. The environment must show evidence that it is "safe" to tell the truth. There must be visible examples of situations where the truth was told, acknowledged, and acted on—and the consequences were *not* punitive. This does not mean that the truth may not bring a fallout; that could very well happen. People will leave organizations in which they don't fit, and that is a positive thing for the organization and the individuals involved.

Laying a Solid Foundation

Running an organization based on truth requires—and demands—the taking of personal risks and time. The perception that time is limited, or the fear that the truth will hurt us, or hurt someone or something we care about, are perhaps the greatest obstacles to organizational truth telling.

Busy men and women are always looking for shortcuts and abbreviations to help speed things along. But truth lies at the very foundation of a successful organization, and you can't lay a solid foundation when you cut corners; doing so places the whole structure in danger of even-

tual collapse. But if your culture now includes a tolerance for and comfort with lying (as it is described in the above "spectrum"), you have to be explicit about changing your culture and about what the "whole truth" must include. And then you must patiently and persistently inch your way toward it, in practice. Organizational healing and reconciliation are the natural first steps toward restoring a culture where truth telling is a value. It is through the process of making the change as an organization-wide effort that we reclaim the vital human spirit necessary for renewing our organizations, communities and country. Truth telling leads to freedom. Freedom requires that we challenge the way things are in organizations if we truly want them to accomplish what is in our collective hearts.

Erline Belton is the CEO of the Lyceum Group in Boston. She has been identified by clients as an organization healer, and feels honored to be of service as she practices organization development from her heart and head.

Editors' Note: Recent NPQ articles on organizational conflict ("Brave Leadership in Organizational Conflict," by Kenneth Bailey, Winter 2004) and defensive behavior ("Defending Defensiveness," by Sandra Janoff, Spring 2004) have brought a terrific response from readers throughout the country. It is clear that interpersonal skills and behavior, and the organizational systems that either support or undermine a healthy exchange, continue to be of central concern to people in nonprofits. The following piece by Erline Belton serves as a companion to these other articles, presenting a complementary vision of the group and personal skills that are needed to propel our organizations forward.

From *The Nonprofit Quarterly,* Summer 2004, pp. 57-60. Copyright © 2004 by The Nonprofit Quarterly. Reprinted by permission.

Why Good Leaders Do Bad Things

Mental gymnastics behind unethical behavior

In making ethical decisions, let virtuous values guide your judgments
and beware of the mental games that can undermine ethical decision making.

Charles D. Kerns, Ph.D.

As the General Manager for an industrial distributor, you have recently learned that your consistently top performing purchasing manager has violated company policy by accepting an expensive gift from a supplier. Since you believe that this was likely a one-time lapse in judgment, what would you say or do? Your response could range from "looking the other way" to firing the manager.

In this situation, as in all ethical choices or dilemmas, the leader's thought pattern (cognitive process) will significantly influence what action he or she takes. People's patterns of thinking will be influenced by their values, what they say to themselves (self-talk), and what they imagine will happen in response to their actions. At its most basic level, ethical managerial leadership involves discerning right from wrong and acting in alignment with such judgment.

Leaders with strong virtuous values are more likely to act ethically than are leaders who are operating with a weak or non-existent value system. One set of values that seems to be universally accepted includes wisdom, self-control, justice, transcendence, kindness, and courage.[1] When faced with challenging decisions, leaders who have not internalized a value system that includes these values will probably respond with more variability than will one who has such a system. It is primarily in the situation in which the leader does not have an internalized value system that mental gymnastics or mind games may cause an otherwise good person to make unethical decisions.

In this article we will review mind games that leaders may play when they face difficult decisions and lack both a strong value system and a professional and ethical approach to management. These leaders tend to react to circumstances on a situational basis. Some suggestions on how managerial leaders can deal with challenging decisions are offered throughout the following discussion.

Mind Games

Decision making can often result in managerial missteps, even those decisions that involve ethical considerations. Many common themes emerge as we look at these problematic decisions. Most significantly, various cognitive processes that leaders often unwittingly employ and which may be called "mental gymnastics" or mind games may serve to support and sustain unethical behavior.

Mind Game #1: Quickly Simplify—"Satisficing"

When we are confronted with a complicated problem, most of us react by reducing the problem to understandable terms. We simplify. Notwithstanding the considerable power of our human intellect, we are often unable to cognitively process all of the information needed to reach an optimal decision. Instead, we tend to make quick decisions based on understandable and readily available elements related to the decision. We search for a solution that is both satisfactory and sufficient. Full rationality gives way to bounded rationality, which finds leaders considering the essential elements of a problem without taking into account all of its complexities. Unfortunately, this process, called "satisficing," can lead to solutions that are less than optimal or even ethically deficient.[2]

"Satisficing" leads the managerial leader to alternatives that tend to be easy to formulate, familiar, and close to the status quo. When one grapples with complex ethical considerations, this approach to decision making may not produce the best solutions. Ethical dilemmas can often benefit from creative thinking that explores ideas beyond the usual responses. If a decision maker uses satisficing when crafting a solution to an ethical problem, the best alternative may be overlooked. David Messick and Max Bazerman, researchers in decision making, tell us that when executives "satisfice," they often simplify, thereby overlooking low probability events, neglecting to consider some stakeholders, and failing to identify possible long-term consequences.[3]

One of the best ways to guard against oversimplifying and reaching less than optimal solutions to ethical challenges is to discuss the situation with other trusted colleagues. Have them play devil's advocate. Ask them to challenge your decision. The resulting dialogue can improve the quality of your ethical decision making.

Scholar and ethics consultant Laura Nash suggests twelve questions that can help leaders avoid the mind game of over simplifying.[4] The following questions may raise ethical issues not otherwise considered, or help generate a variety of "out of the box" alternatives. Before settling on a solution, ask yourself the following questions:

- Have I specified the problem accurately?
- How would I describe the problem if I were on the opposite side of the fence?
- How did this situation begin?
- To whom and to what do I give my loyalties as a person or group and as a member of the organization?
- What is my intention in making this decision?
- How does this intention compare with the likely results?
- Whom could my decision or action harm?
- Can I engage those involved in a discussion of the problem prior to making a decision?
- Am I confident that my position will be valid over the long term?
- Could I disclose without reservation my decision or action to my boss, our CEO, the Board of Directors, my family, or society as a whole?
- What is the symbolic impact of my action if it is understood?
- Under what conditions would I allow exceptions to my position?

These questions initiate a thought process that underscores the importance of problem identification and information gathering. Such a process can help leaders guard against over simplifying an otherwise complicated ethical decision.

Mind Game #2: The Need to Be Liked

Most people want to be liked. However, when this desire to be liked overpowers business objectivity, ethical lapses can occur. For instance, when managers witness ethical transgressions, the need to be liked may cause them to overlook these transgressions. Such a situation is particularly acute for those recently promoted into management from within the same organization. Because they want to be liked by their former peers, they may have a difficult time saying, "No." Dr. Albert Ellis, author of *A New Guide to Rational Living*,[5] notes that one of eleven irrational beliefs that some people hold is the belief that one can or should always be liked. He states that people who are affected by this need carry around in their heads statements such as, "I believe I must be approved by virtually everyone with whom I come in contact."

Such an overriding desire to be liked can ultimately adversely affect the ethics of people in an organization and thus can decrease the firm's bottom line. For instance, a retail store manager who wants her employees to like her may readily give them additional hours when they request them to enable employees to earn more money. However, in so doing, the manager contributes to the accumulation of too many hours of labor relative to sales volume. Over time, excessive labor costs can then begin to eat into profit margins.

After recognizing that she is playing this mind game, one way that the manager might stem this problem is to distance herself from her subordinates (e.g., reduce unnecessary socializing) until she can establish some objective boundaries. Another successful approach would be to respond warmly and assertively toward employees while still going forward with appropriate but possibly less popular decisions. (If necessary, the manager could even take assertiveness training.) Finally, in such situations, the newly appointed manager might want to read Alberti and Emmons' book, *Your Perfect Right*.[6] This book provides excellent advice on how to say "no" while preserving a quality relationship.

Mind Game #3: Dilute and Disguise

In trying to strike a diplomatic chord, leaders can disguise the offensiveness of unethical acts by using euphemisms or softened characterizations. Words or phrases such as "helped him make a career choice" are used to describe firing someone, or "inappropriate allocation of resources" is used to describe what everyone knows is stealing. Regardless of whether people want to be seen as kinder and gentler, or just politically correct, this process merely helps wrongdoers and those associated with them to get away with unethical behavior.

Such softened characterizations serve to reduce the anxiety of the leader, but these euphemisms are dishonest. They serve to dilute and disguise unethical behavior. This form of mental gymnastics defuses discomfort that may otherwise develop among those involved in unethical "mischief," but such an approach dilutes the necessary intensity of ethical constraints that should be brought to bear in the situation. The antidote is for leaders to talk straight and to avoid euphemistic labeling or re-characterizing unethical behavior.

Mind Game #4: "Making Positive"

The mental gymnastic of comparing one's own unethical behavior to more heinous behavior committed by others serves only to avoid self-degradation. For example, the salesperson who occasionally cheats when reporting his expenses may say to himself, "I do this only a few times a year, while Tom, Dick, and Harry do it all the time." Or, "If you think I disregard my colleagues' feelings, you ought to see Andy in action. He is a bona fide bully!" Unethical behavior appears more ethical by comparing it to worse behavior.

Such justifications for unethical behavior are not valid. The tendency to diminish misdeeds by making dishonest comparisons also contributes to sustaining unethical conduct. To avoid this mind game, ask three questions about the comparison:

- Am I comparing apples to oranges?
- How self-serving is this comparison?

- What would three objective observers say about me and my objectivity regarding this comparison?

While behavior may often legitimately be compared to that of others, when ethical transgressions are involved, relativity does not excuse ethical lapses.

Mind Game #5: Overconfidence

Overconfident managers tend to perceive their abilities to be greater than they actually are. Self-perception often does not match objective reality. By indulging in the mental gymnastics of overconfidence, such leaders can discount others' perceptions and thus easily overlook the insights and talents of other people. Without benefit of input from those around them, overconfident managerial leaders may be blind to the most appropriate ethical choices in given circumstances and may consider only their own ideas regarding the best course of action. Overconfident managers act as though they are "above it all," relegating their people, useful information, and learning opportunities to the sidelines while pursuing their own courses of action.

Overconfident decision makers deny themselves fresh perspectives and thus perhaps better solutions to ethical problems. The overconfident manager is typically perceived as arrogant. Research tells us that the manager labeled thusly is headed for career derailment.[7] Arrogant managerial leaders who have performance problems, which may include ignoring, overlooking, or causing ethical concern, are likely to receive less understanding and support from others in their time of trouble. Their air of overconfidence not only interferes with the practice of quality ethical decision making, but it can also virtually wreck their careers.

One tool to counterbalance this unproductive and potentially deadly tendency is for the overconfident managerial leader to catch himself or herself when preparing to make declarative, "This is the way it is" statements, and replace them with more open ended, "What do you think?" types of inquiries. If practiced conscientiously, this simple communication tool can help the overly confident manager begin to consider others' perspectives. Accepting input from other people will improve the manager's decision making ability generally, including those issues that involve ethical consideration. Applied broadly, this practice will positively impact the ethical problem solving climate within the entire organization.

These five mind games can influence an otherwise good leader to act unethically. Each of the mental maneuvers provides an easy way around difficult decisions, with the likely outcome that some of those decisions will result in unethical behavior. However, the intrinsic benefit of pursuing an ethical course will be a source of motivation for leaders to get on track ethically and stay there. By staying the course and behaving in a way that is consistent with his or her virtuous values and attitudes, the ethical managerial leader will have less need to play these types of mind games.

A Call to Action

Examine your thoughts when confronted with ethical choice points. In making ethical decisions, let virtuous values guide your judgments, and avoid playing mental games that undermine ethical behavior. If unchecked, indulging in these games can lead you to do bad things while feeling justified by your wrongdoing, at least temporarily. You are encouraged to heed the following suggestions that can help defend against participating in these mind games.

As you approach an ethical decision, to what extent do you do the following?

- Deliberate the obvious and not so obvious circumstances surrounding the issue.

- Decide objectively without regard to being liked.

- Talk about transgressions and ethical breaches using straightforward words.

- Make valid comparisons when discussing specific ethical behavior.

- Act with an appropriate level of confidence.

If you responded favorably to these questions, then perhaps these five mind games are not stumbling blocks for you. Less favorable or more uncertain responses may impel you to consider how your patterns of thinking may be adversely affecting your approach to ethical decision making.

Notes

1. Martin Seligman, *Authentic Happiness* (New York: Free Press, 2002). For definitions of these "virtuous values," and a discussion about their role in the business environment see Charles D. Kerns, "Creating and Sustaining an Ethical Workplace Culture," Graziadio Business Report, 6, Issue 3.

2. Stephen P. Robbins, *Essentials of Organizational Behavior,* 7th ed., New Jersey: Prentice-Hall (2003).

3. David M. Messick and M. H. Bazerman, "Ethical Leadership and the Psychology of Decision Making," *Sloan Management Review* 37 (Winter, 1996), p. 9.

4. Laura L. Nash, "Ethics Without the Sermon," in K. R. Andrews (ed.) *Ethics in Practice: Managing the Moral Corporation,* Boston: Harvard Business School Press, (1989), p. 243-257.

5. Albert Ellis and R. A. Harper, *A New Guide To Rational Living*, 3rd ed., 1997, (North Hollywood, CA: Wilshire).

6. Robert Alberti and M. L. Emmons, *Your Perfect Right: A Guide to Assertive Living,* 7th ed. (San Luis Obispo, CA: Impact, 1995).

7. Morgan W. McCall, *High Flyers: Developing the Next Generation of Leaders,* (Boston: Harvard Business School Press, 1998).

From *Graziadio Business Report,* Fall 2003. Copyright © 2003 by Graziadio School of Business & Management, Pepperdine University. Reprinted by permission.

Best Resources for Corporate Social Responsibility

RESEARCH BY KAREN McNICHOL

What most of us lack these days isn't data but time. The World Wide Web is a marvelous research tool, but the sheer amount of information available can be overwhelming. How do you weed through it to find the very best sites, where someone has already synthesized masses of material for you? Well, consider the offerings below a garden without the weeds: a selection of the best of the best sites in corporate social responsibility (CSR).

1. Best Practices and Company Profiles

www.bsr.org—This may well be the best CSR site of all. Run by the business membership organization Business for Social Responsibility, its focus is on giving business hands-on guidance in setting up social programs, but data is useful to researchers as well, particularly because of "best practice" examples. Topics include social auditing, community involvement, business ethics, governance, the environment, employee relations, and corporate citizenship. New topics are being researched all the time. One recent report, for example, looked at companies linking executive pay to social performance, while others have looked at how to implement flexible scheduling, or become an "employer of choice." Visitors can create their own printer-friendly custom report on each topic, selecting from sections like Business Importance, Recent Developments, Implementation Steps, Best Practices, and Links to Helping Resources. To receive notices about updates, plus other CSR news, subscribe to BSR Resource Center Newsletter by sending a message to centerupdates@bsr.org with "subscribe" in the subject line.

www.ebnsc.org—You might call this the BSR site from Europe. It is sponsored by Corporate Social Responsibility Europe, whose mission is to help put CSR into the mainstream of business. This site includes a databank of best practices from all over Europe on topics like human rights, cause-related marketing, ethical principles, and community involvement. To give just one example of the site's capability, a search on the topic "reporting on CSR" came up with a dozen news articles available in full, plus a case study, and a list of 20 books and reports on the topic. One unique feature is the "CSR Matrix," which allows visitors to call up a complete social report on companies like IBM, Levi Strauss, or Procter & Gamble. The "matrix" is a grid, where the visitor clicks on one box to view the company's code of conduct, another box to see how the company interacts with public stakeholders, a third box to access the company's sustainability report, and so forth.

www.worldcsr.com is a World CSR portal offering one-stop access to the leading business-led organizations on corporate social responsibility in Europe and the U.S., including the two sites mentioned above. Another site on the portal—www.businessimpact.org—offers a useful databank of links to related organizations, such as the Global Reporting Initiative, Institute for Global Ethics, and World Business Council for Sustainable Development. Readers can also subscribe to the Business Impact News e-mail newsletter.

www.responsibleshopper.org For individuals wishing to shop with or research responsible companies, Responsible Shopper from Co-op America offers in-depth social profiles on countless companies. A report on IBM, for example, looks at everything from Superfund sites, toxic emissions, and worker benefits to laudatory activities. Different brand names for each company are listed, and social performance is summarized in letter ratings—as with IBM, which got an "A" in Disclosure, and a "B" in the Environment.

www.worldcsr.com offers one-stop access to the leading business-led organizations on corporate social responsibility in Europe and the U.S.

2. Social Investing

www.socialfunds.com—Run by SRI World Group, Social Funds is the best social investing site on the web. A staff of reporters researchers breaking news and posts it without charge. For socially responsible mutual funds, the site offers performance statistics plus fund descriptions. There's an investing center where you can build your own basket of social companies, plus a community banking center with information on savings accounts and money market funds with responsible banking organizations. A shareholder activism section offers a status report on social resolutions and is searchable by topic (equality, tobacco, militarism, etc.). Also available is a free weekly e-mail newsletter, SRI News Alert—which goes beyond social investing. One recent issue, for example, looked at new labeling programs for clean-air office construction, an Arctic Wildlife Refuge resolution against BP Amoco, and why greener multinationals have higher market value. A new service from SRI World Group, offered jointly with Innovest Strategic Advisors, offers subscribers ($100 annually) ratings of companies in various industries, based on environmental and financial performance.

www.socialinvest.org—This is the site of the nonprofit professional membership association, the Social Investment Forum, and is a useful pair to the above site. One unique feature is the collection of Moskowitz Prize-winning papers on research in social investing. The 2000 winner, for example, was "Pure Profit: The Financial Implications of Environmental Performance." Also available is a directory to help visitors find a financial adviser anywhere in the country; a mutual funds chart; a guide to community investing (showing resources by state and by type); and materials on SIF's campaign to end predatory lending. You can also access the Shareholder Action Network-which shows how to submit shareholder resolutions, and offers information on both current campaigns and past successes.

www.goodmoney.com.—Offering some unique investing features of its own is the Good Money site, which showcases the Good Money Industrial Average: a screened index which outperformed the Dow in 2000. Also available are social profiles and performance data for a variety of public companies—including the 400 companies in the Domini Social Index, companies with the best diversity record, the Council on Economic Priorities "honor roll" list, and signers of the CERES Principles (a voluntary environmental code of conduct). Another section on Eco Travel has dozens of links and articles.

3. Corporate Watchdogs

www.corpwatch.org—For activists, this may be the best site of all. Calling itself "The Watchdog on the Web," CorpWatch offers news you may not find elsewhere on human rights abuses abroad, public policy; and environmental news—plus on-site reporting of protests. Its director Josh Karliner was nominated by Alternet.org (an alternative news service) as a Media Hero 2000, for using the web to fight the excesses of corporate globalization. CorpWatch puts out the bimonthly Greenwash Awards, and runs a Climate Justice Initiative, as well as the Alliance for a Corporate-Free UN. An Issue Library covers topics like the WTO and sweatshops, while the Hands-on Guide to On-line Corporate Research is useful for research ideas. A free twice-monthly e-mail newsletter updates readers on recent CorpWatch headlines. One recent issue of "What's New on CorpWatch" looked at topics like the World Bank's record, the

SEARCH CORPWATCH
[GO]

CAMPAIGNS
Corporate-Free UN
Climate Justice
Greenwash
Order Publications

Press Room

RESEARCH TOOLS
Introduction
Research Guide
Hot Links

ISSUE LIBRARY
Biotechnology
Globalization 101
Grassroots
Globalization
Internet Politics
Money & Politics
Oil, Gas and Coal
Sweatshops
Tobacco
Trade Agreements
World Bank/IMF
WTO

>> More Issues

ABOUT CORPWATCH
History & Mission
Using this Site
Staff & Board
Job Opportunities
Feedback

UTILITY DEREGULATION
Nigeria's Gas Crisis: Suffering in the Midst of Plenty
By Sam Olukoya
Posted: 5/14/2001

Planned fuel deregulation in Nigeria has caused paralyzing shortages, price hikes and demonstrations against the IMF-backed policies.

Nigeria's President reviews U.S. troops while his country is paralysed by a fuel shortage.

CLIMATE JUSTICE
Human Rights vs. Oil: A CorpWatch Interview with Sarah James
Posted: 4/27/2001

A Native Alaskan activist speaks out about the devastating impact oil drilling in the Arctic Refuge would have on her community.

TOBACCO
Big Tobacco: Domestic Battles, Global Implications
By Robert Weissman
Posted: 4/26/2001

The Bush administration faces a series of domestic policy battles that have serious implications for global tobacco. They are more relevant than ever as international tobacco negotiations are held in Geneva

DONATE NOW!
Get a Free T-Shirt!

JOIN OUR EMAIL LIST
enter email [GO]

TAKE ACTION
Posted: 5/14/2001

Stop FTAA Fast Track!

IN THE NEWS
Updated: 5/18/2001

USA: Bush Calls for More Coal, Oil and Nukes

El Salvador: Government Report Details Labor Abuses

Italy: Poor Countries Are North's Radioactive Dump

International: U.S. Under Fire Over Tobacco Treaty

Nigeria: Shell Oil Spill Increases Tensions in Ogoniland

USA: World Health Threatened by Toxic Pesticide Stocks

India: Plastic Waste Plagues Tourist Destination

>> More News

BULLETIN BOARD

For activists, www.corpwatch.org may be the best site of all.

protests at the World Economic Forum, California's deregulation troubles, plus the regular "Take Action" feature urging readers to send e-mails or faxes on a specific issue. To subscribe to the e-letter, send blank message to corp-watchers-subscribe @igc.topica.com.

www.corporatepredators.org—Featuring Russell Mokhiber, editor of the weekly newsletter *Corporate Crime Reporter*, this site offers a compilation of weekly e-mail columns called "Focus on the Corporation," written by Mokhiber and Robert Weissman. They offer a valuable, quirky voice in corporate responsibility. Taking on topics not covered elsewhere, the columns have looked at how the chemical industry responded to Bill Moyers TV program on industry coverup, how little academic research focuses on corporate crime, and why it's inappropriate to legally view corporations as "persons." At this site (which also features the book *Corporate Predators* by Mokhiber and Weissman), readers can access weekly columns back through 1998. Subscribe free to the column by sending an e-mail message to corp-focus-request@lists.essential.org with the text "subscribe."

4. Labor and Human Rights

http://oracle02.ilo.org/vpi/welcome—Sponsored by the International Labor Organization, this web site offers a new Business and Social Initiatives Database, compiling Internet sources on employment and labor issues. It covers topics like child labor, living wage, dismissal, investment screens, monitoring, international labor standards, glass ceilings, safe work, and so forth. It features information on corporate policies and reports, codes of conduct, certification criteria, labeling and other programs. A search feature allows visitors to retrieve information on specific companies, regions, and business sectors. This is one of the most comprehensive labor sites out there.

www.summersault.com/~agj/clr/—Sponsored by the Campaign for Labor Rights, this site keeps activists up to date on anti-sweatshop struggles and other pro-labor activities around the world. Particularly useful is the free e-mail newsletter Labor Alerts, which updates readers on recent news about trade treaties, plant shutdowns, labor organizing, job postings, upcoming protests, recent books, and so forth. One recent issue contained a "webliography" of sites about the pending creation of the Free

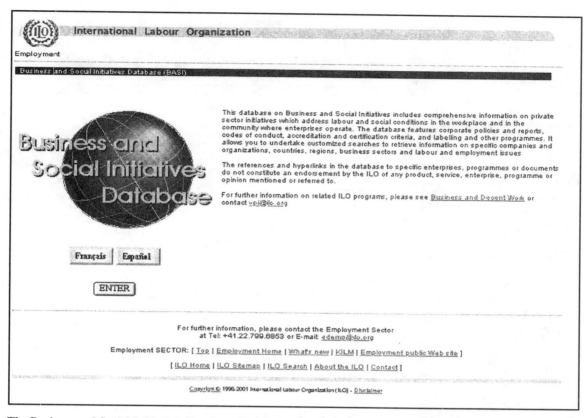

The Business and Social Initiatives Database (http://oracle02.ilo.org/vpi/welcome) is one of the most comprehensive labor compilations out there.

Trade Area of the Americas (FTAA). To subscribe contact clr-main@afgj.org.

5. Progressive Economics

www.epn.org—For the best thinking in progressive economic policy, this site managed by *The American Prospect* magazine is a one-stop source. It's the Electronic Policy Network, an on-line consortium of over 100 progressive policy centers nationwide, like the Center for Public Integrity, the Brookings Institution, the Financial Markets Center, and many more. (The focus of member groups is heavily though not exclusively economic.) A feature called Idea Central offers on-line bibliographies on topics like globalization, poverty, and livable cities. Certain topics get "Issues in Depth" treatment: One, for example, looks at campaign finance reform—including history, alternatives, and legal background, with numerous links to sites like a database of soft-money contribution, research from the Center for Responsive Politics, ACLU factsheets, and more. Another feature, "What's New," looks at recent reports and research papers by member policy centers—like a recent report from the Economic Policy Institute on privatization, or a report on state initiatives for children from the National Center for Children in Poverty. Readers can receive summaries of new research reports by subscribing to the e-mail EPN News; send an e-mail to majordomo@epn.org with "subscribe epnnews" in the message body.

www.neweconomics.org—This valuable site is run by The New Economics Foundation (NEF), a UK nonprofit think tank created in 1986 to focus on "constructing a new economy centered on people and the environment." Different areas on the site focus on powerful tools for economic change, like alternative currencies, social investment, indicators for sustainability, and social accounting. A monthly web-based newsletter reports on topics like Jubilee 2000 (the movement to cancel the debt of developing nations), May Day plans, an "indicator of the month," and more. A new bimonthly e-briefing is called "merger-watch," which looks at the hidden costs behind mergers, and who pays the price. Its first issue in April 2001 reported, for example, that a 1999 KPMG study showed 53 percent of mergers destroy shareholder value, and a further 30 percent bring no measurable benefit.

6. Employee Ownership

http://cog.kent.edu—For researchers in employee ownership, the Capital Ownership Group site is indispensable. COG is a virtual think tank of individuals—including academics, employee ownership specialists, and business leaders worldwide—who aim to promote broadened ownership of productive capital. The site's library allows visitors to browse ongoing discussions, on topics like promoting employee ownership globally, getting economists more involved in issues of capital ownership, the role of labor in employee ownership, and more. The library of-

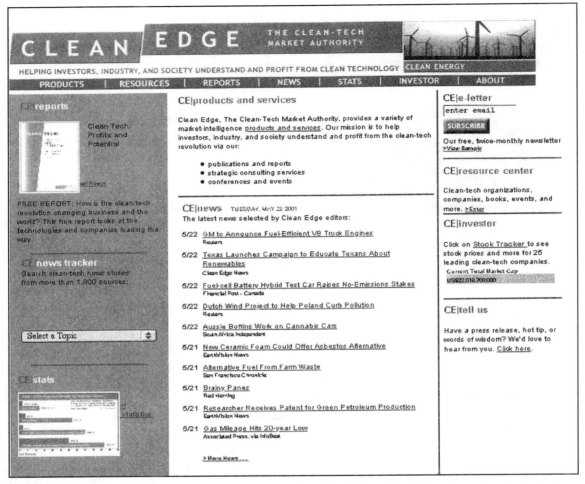

www.cleanedge.com offers news from 1,800 sources, stock trading information on 25 companies, plus lists of conferences, trade associations and research centers.

fers hundreds of papers and research reports, on topics like labor-sponsored venture capital, employee governance, case studies, and much more.

www.nceo.org—This is the site of the National Center for Employee Ownership, a nonprofit research and membership organization that is one of the best sources for employee ownership information. Its web library features a valuable introduction to the history of Employee Stock Ownership Plans (ESOPs), plus information on open book management, stock options, and alternatives to ESOPs. An "Interactive Introduction to ESOPs" lets visitors "chat" with an expert in the same way as if they spent fifteen minutes on the phone with a lawyer. Also available are a wealth of links to related sites, plus news and statistics on employee ownership.

www.fed.org—The sponsor of this site is the Foundation for Enterprise Development—a nonprofit started by Robert Beyster, founder of employee-owned SAIC—which is an organization that aims to promote employee ownership. Its focus is not ESOPs but stock options and other forms of equity ownership. A monthly online magazine features profiles of employee ownership at specific companies, articles on developing an owner-ship culture, plus news. An e-mail service updates readers on headlines.

www.the-esop-emplowner.org—From the ESOP Association—a membership and lobbying organization—this site offers a resource library, news of events, reports on legislative victories, and information on legislative initiatives. The site also offers information on the ESOP Association's political action committee, which since 1988 has helped candidates for federal office who support ESOPs and ESOP law.

7. Sustainability

www.GreenBiz.com—Run by Joel Makower, editor of *The Green Business Letter*, Green Biz is the best site on progressive environmental business activities. It enables visitors to discover what companies are doing, and to access citations of countless web resources and reports, on topics like sustainable management, green auditing, EPA programs, pending legislation, clean technologies, recycling, and all things green. A new service features free job listing for environmental professionals. Get regular updates from a free e-mail newsletter, GreenBiz, published every other week.

www.rprogress.org—Run by the nonprofit Redefining Progress—which produces the Genuine Progress Indicator (as a counterpoint to GDP)—this site offers news on topics like climate change, forest-land protection, tax reform, and congressional influence peddling. Recent stories featured a proposal to promote market-based policies for reducing sprawl, a better way to return the government surplus, plus a look at Living Planet 2000—calculating the ecological footprints of the world's largest 150 countries. Numerous studies on environmental justice, tax fairness, and community indicators are available, plus links to other climate change sites.

www.sustainablebusienss.com—The monthly on-line magazine Sustainable Business offers news on the "green economy," covering recycling, product take-back, legislative developments, and so forth. Other features are a database of "Green Dream Job" openings; plus a section to help green businesses find venture capital. A library features web sites, reports, and books.

www.cleanedge.com—The new organization Clean Edge focuses on helping investors, industry, and society understand and profit from clean technology, like wind, solar, energy efficiency, and alternative fuels. The site offers news from 1,800 sources, stock trading information on 25 companies, plus lists of conferences, trade associations and research centers. The group's premier publication, "Clean Tech: Profits and Potential," reports that clean energy technologies will grow from less than $7 billion today to $82 billion by 2010.

8. Ethics

www.depaul.edu/ethics—Sponsored by the Institute for Business and Professional Ethics at DePaul University, this site offers a large compilation of ethics resources on the web, categorized by topic; educational resources for teachers and trainers, including syllabi; faculty position announcements; calls for papers; a calendar of events; a list of other ethics institutes, and much more.

www.ethics.ubc.ca—From the Center for Applied Ethics at the University of British Columbia in Canada, this site offers a particularly valuable compilation about ethics codes—featuring sample codes, guidance on writing a code, plus books and articles on the topic. Other features are links to ethics institutes, consultants, course materials, publications, and collections of articles.

www.ethics.org/businessethics.html—Sponsored by the **Ethics Resource Center**, this site features valuable data from several business ethics surveys 1994–2000, information on character education for youth, a compendium of codes (coming soon), plus links to many ethics centers and organizations. A research bibliography covers topics like measuring success in an ethics program, or ethics in a global economy. And a provocative "Ethics Quick Test" can be taken on-line, with results available by e-mail.

Reprinted with permission from *Business Ethics*, Summer 2001, pp. 16-18. © 2001 by Business Ethics, PO Box 8439, Minneapolis, MN 55408 (612) 879-0695.

UNIT 2
Ethical Issues and Dilemmas in the Workplace

Unit Selections

Key Points to Consider

- What ethical dilemmas do managers face most frequently? What ethical dilemmas do employees face most often?

- What forms of gender and minority discrimination are most prevalent in today's workplace? In what particular job situations or occupations is discrimination more widespread and conspicuous? Why?

- Whistle-blowing occurs when an employee discloses illegal, immoral, or illegitimate organizational practices or activities. Under what circumstances do you believe whistle-blowing is appropriate? Why?

- Given the complexities of an organization, where an ethical dilemma often cannot be optimally resolved by one person alone, how can an individual secure the support of the group and help it to reach a consensus as to the appropriate resolution of the dilemma?

Student Website
www.mhcls.com/online

Internet References
Further information regarding these websites may be found in this book's preface or online.

American Psychological Association
http://www.apa.org/homepage.html
International Labour Organization (ILO)
http://www.ilo.org

LaRue Tone Hosmer, in *The Ethics of Management*, lucidly states that ethical problems in business are truly managerial dilemmas because they represent a conflict, or at least the possibility of a conflict, between the *economic performance* of an organization and its *social performance*. Whereas the economic performance is measured by revenues, costs, and profits, the social performance is judged by the fulfillment of obligations to persons both within and outside the organization.

Units 2 to 4 discuss some of the critical ethical dilemmas that management faces in making decisions in the workplace, in the marketplace, and within the global society. This unit focuses on the relationships and obligations of employers and employees to each other as well as to those they serve.

Organizational decision makers are ethical when they act with equity, fairness, and impartiality, treating with respect the rights of their employees. An organization's hiring and firing practices, treatment of women and minorities, tolerance of employees' privacy, and wages and working conditions are areas in which it has ethical responsibilities.

The employee also has ethical obligations in his or her relationship to the employer. A conflict of interest can occur when an employee allows a gratuity or favor to sway him or her in selecting a contract or purchasing a piece of equipment, making a choice that may not be in the best interests of the organization. Other possible ethical dilemmas for employees include espionage and the betrayal of secrets (especially to competitors), the theft of equipment, and the abuse of expense accounts.

The articles in this unit are broken down into seven sections representing various types of ethical dilemmas in the workplace. The initial article in this first section describes why monitoring employees is a commonplace practice in the work arena. The next article discloses the difficulty of putting in place a screening policy for new faculty hires.

In the subsection entitled **Organizational Misconduct and Crime,** articles explore the costs of organizational dishonesty, ways auditors can help deter bribery and kickbacks, and threats that information security can have on business and consumers.

The selection under **Sexual Treatment of Employees** takes a close look at how women are treated in the workplace and the expansion of sex-discrimination lawsuits.

The readings in the **Discriminatory and Prejudicial Practices** section scrutinize how the Age Discrimination in Employment Act (ADEA) is dealing with blatant forms of age discrimination, why there are still so few women in top organizational positions, and how angry women are suing their employers for sex discrimination.

In the next subsection entitled **Downsizing of the Work Force**, articles consider the trauma of getting fired at 50 and examine why many high-tech workers have lost jobs to low-wage countries because of outsourcing.

The selections included under the heading **Whistle blowing in the Organization** discloses why whistle blowing is sometimes pursued more because of monetary benefits than for moral reasons, how whistle blowing can help a company resolve problems before they become national news headlines, and analyzes the ethical dilemma and possible ramifications of whistle blowing.

The article "Birth of the Ethics Industry," which opens the last subsection of **Handling Ethical Dilemmas at Work**, reveals the recent mushrooming attention to consultants in business ethics. The next article scrutinizes how far individual sponsors have gone in seeking to use higher education and institutions for their own commercial ends. "Like the Smoke of a Blazing Room" is a case about an ethical dilemma that occurs on a company's new hotline. "The Parable of the Sadhu" presents a real-world ethical dilemma for the reader to ponder.

Flip-Flop Over Faculty Fingerprints

Rowan U. discovers how difficult it can be to put in place a screening policy for new hires

SHARON WALSH

A fingerprint is simply "an impression of the lines and whorls on the inner surface of the end joint of the finger," as defined by Mr. Webster.

That is, it's simple until it is used by university officials checking to see whether an employee has a criminal record. Then, things get complicated.

Just ask Donald J. Farish, president of Rowan University. On September 3, Mr. Farish met with his cabinet and approved a policy that would require background and fingerprint checks for all new employees—including new faculty members.

What Mr. Farish proposed was considered revolutionary. Rowan, a 10,000-student public university in Glassboro, N.J., would become what is believed to be the first college to require such an investigation for all new employees. He had the backing of the Board of Trustees, his cabinet, and union leaders on campus—or so he thought.

"I'm not willing to have a dual system, where you say one group is more likely to commit crimes than another," says Mr. Farish. "That's tantamount to profiling."

Perhaps he had not counted on the strong reaction from some faculty members. Elsewhere there had already been cries of protest from professors at some institutions where criminal background checks for all employees had begun. And the nation's largest faculty group had said that they are an unwarranted invasion of privacy (*The Chronicle*, July 30).

The policy at Rowan was introduced at the Faculty Senate meeting in September, and no one asked a question. It was posted on the university's Web site, and no one raised a concern.

But as a reporter began to make telephone calls and professors began talking to one another, it became clear that many professors still did not know about the policy. A small storm quickly brewed on campus. The Faculty Senate wanted to bring it up at another meeting. Union leaders, under pressure from their members, began to backtrack.

> **"How they can make this a criterion for every job on campus is beyond me. Number one, for the faculty, this generally raises the specter of witch hunts."**

Nicholas DiObilda, a professor of reading and head of the chapter of the American Federation of Teachers at Rowan, said last month that the AFT and other unions on the campus had supported the policy. "We thought we couldn't include one class of employees" but not others, he said of the background checks.

But now, following a meeting with union members, he has changed course. "Apparently I was wrong," he says. "Our position is that people who have unlimited access to offices, dorms, and master keys should be checked more closely."

> **"I'm not willing to have a dual system, where you say one group is more likely to commit crimes than another. That's tantamount to profiling."**

And should the policy include professors? "No, not faculty members."

Mr. Farish now says he will have an open forum to discuss the policy and let people air their views. "If, at this point, people are repudiating their former positions, I'm not going to force it," he says. "I'm willing to put the policy in abeyance until we can discuss it because it's the best way for shared governance to work.

... But I will not go forward with a separate policy for one group."

'Elitist Attitude'

The move toward fingerprinting began three years ago when unions representing maintenance workers and clerical-staff members appealed to the president and the trustees, noting that outside companies hired to do janitorial and food-service work on campus were not doing background checks on employees. That was a violation of the unions' contract with the university.

At the same time, too many things, the union leaders say, had gone missing: laptop computers, purses, equipment. None of the leaders wanted their union's members to be accused. Everyone wanted a safe campus for students and employees.

As new contracts were negotiated before the beginning of the fall semester, background checks with fingerprints were instituted for employees who worked on the campus for outside firms. Rowan's employment application asks whether a job candidate has ever been convicted of a crime. Even so, seven people were found to have lied when fingerprint checks were completed. All were fired or were not allowed to start work, including one employee who had a record as a sexual offender.

Timothy D. Michener, the director of public safety at Rowan, says that previous background checks were inadequate because they looked only into the county of residence and the Social Security number of the worker.

"We wanted a better assurance about people working on campus," he says. If a fingerprint is available, it can be sent to the State Bureau of Identification and checked against criminal records in about a month. Without the print, someone must physically go to each county in the state to look for names in the records.

Still, the fingerprint allows the examination of state records only. Mr. Michener says Rowan has asked the

state Legislature to allow them to do the check through the FBI, which requires state authorization. The state already allows fingerprint checks of public-school teachers, lawyers, and pharmacists.

Between 300 and 400 food-service, janitorial, and grounds workers have been fingerprinted under the new policy so far, using fingerprints that Mr. Michener takes manually and sends to the State Bureau of Identification. It takes from three to six weeks to get the results. The university is currently negotiating to use Live Scan technology, which takes a digital imprint of the finger and reports back within hours for about $71 a person.

Asked whether he believes faculty members will have problems with such a policy, Mr. Michener replies: "I sure hope not. That's kind of an elitist attitude. Crime transcends all socioeconomic groups. I'm uncomfortable with the notion that faculty are above being checked. They are the leaders on the campus, and they should take a leadership role."

Because faculty members had already been hired for the fall, Mr. Farish decided that the background and fingerprint checks for new professors would not begin until January. That would give everyone a chance to get used to the idea, he thought.

But not all faculty members would come around. David R. Applebaum, a history professor at Rowan, was one of the first to bring up his concerns with the president. "How they can make this a criterion for every job on campus is beyond me," he says. "Number one, for the faculty, this generally raises the specter of witch hunts for social and political dissent." In addition, it serves to unfairly exclude people from certain jobs who have paid their debt to society, he said.

Finally, Mr. Applebaum says, the notion of submitting a subset of employees—those who are new—to fingerprinting is "meaningless. Why would new employees be more likely to be criminals than those already here? It's mindless."

Although the policy was introduced by Mr. Michener to the Faculty Senate in September, Bruce E. Caswell, president of the group and a former officer of the AFT, now says the senate wants to deliberate on the matter. "There are civil-liberties issues here," he says. "There's a concern that it may have a chilling effect," he added, referring to the impact it might have on attracting and retaining faculty members.

Other union leaders who originally backed the idea of fingerprinting everyone now say faculty members should get a pass. Raymond S. Cibo Jr., head of the local chapter of the International Federation of Professional and Technical Engineers, which includes such groups as groundskeepers and electricians, says he agreed that members of his union should undergo fingerprinting because they have access to buildings and dormitories. "I'm not concerned about faculty and staff," he says.

Despite the hullabaloo raised by their colleagues over the plan to fingerprint them, some faculty members think fingerprinting makes sense. Joanne Scott, an associate professor of biological sciences, says, "I don't have a problem with being fingerprinted. We all have a responsibility to the students," many of whom work late in campus buildings and laboratories. "We have a lot of people who drive over from Pennsylvania, and we need to be sure it's a thorough background check. Otherwise, we could have a sexual predator on campus and not know it."

Who Decides?

Two significant questions arise when faculty members at Rowan talk about the new policy: Who will have access to the information that is collected? And what offenses make a person unemployable?

Mr. Farish has answers for both. Under the Rowan policy, he said, only the public-safety director, Mr. Michener, would have access to the information. In cases where offenses were discovered, Mr. Michener, the human-relations director, and the deputy attorney general assigned to Rowan would form a committee to consider the offense and make a recommendation. Then, the provost, or the appropriate vice president depending on where the person worked, would make the final decision about how the information should be used. During the process, the only one who would know the person's name would be Mr. Michener.

Those reassurances do not soothe Mr. Applebaum. "The problem with promises about how to use a policy like this is there's no safeguard for other people who might come in and occupy those jobs," he says.

Some offenses, such as being a sex offender, selling drugs, or having been denied state employment for other reasons, would cause an auto- matic rejection, Mr. Michener says. There are standards, such as the civil-service rules, that are a guide to which problems should exclude an employee.

Many cases still boil down to an issue of morals and judgment, says Mr. Michener: "That's why it's difficult to have a hard-and-fast rule."

Some faculty members wondered whether an old shoplifting conviction or an arrest for participating in a protest in the '70s might be cause for denying someone a job. "Absolutely not," says Mr. Farish. A simple charge that did not result in a conviction would be handled with care, added Mr. Michener, as would the question of whether a person had been rehabilitated.

David W. Clowney, chairman of the philosophy and religion department, contends that these checks and balances may soon be moot. "It's a matter of the consent of the governed," he says, noting that the administration did not solicit the opinions of groups on the campus before instituting the policy.

So for the time being the president has agreed to reopen the subject. Union and Faculty Senate leaders will talk to their constituents and weigh in. The president will respond to questions. And it seems very likely that, in the end, fingerprinting will be required only for some at Rowan.

"My very strong suspicion is that when all the dust settles, we will have a policy that only checks certain groups," says Mr. Clowney. "I think that would be a very appropriate policy."

From *Chronicle of Higher Education,* November 19, 2004, pp. A10, A12. Copyright © 2004, The Chronicle of Higher Education. Reproduced with permission. This article may not be published, reposted, or redistributed without the express permission of The Chronicle of Higher Education.

Corruption: Causes and Cures

Auditors can help detect and deter bribery and kickbacks.

By Joseph T. Wells

"**Y**ou'll never catch Burgin," television investigative reporter Marsha Halford said to me during an off-camera interview regarding rumors of bribery in the Mississippi senate. "He is the smartest and most corrupt politician in the state."

The Federal Bureau of Investigation had Senator William G. Burgin Jr., chairman of the Mississippi State Senate Appropriations Committee, under scrutiny. As the agent in charge of the case, I wasn't allowed to answer her. But I knew something that Halford and even Burgin didn't know: We'd just about nailed him, and he wasn't very smart after all.

Within a month of that interview, Burgin was indicted for pocketing at least $83,000 in bribes. He later was convicted and served three years in federal prison. The Burgin investigation illustrates a checklist of classic lessons that CPAs can apply when confronted with allegations or suspicions of bribery.

RUMORS OFTEN ARE TRUE

Those who accept illegal payments usually have a motive for doing so. For most people, it is debt; but once they pay their debts, they end up spending the rest of the loot. Co-workers often notice extravagances and report them; CPAs should be alert to rumors or complaints about employees who seem to live beyond their means.

Burgin's lifestyle. For years Burgin—a part-time legislator—had one of the most successful solo law practices in Mississippi and lived the life of a wealthy plantation owner. Because of his visibility as a politician, people noticed his ostentatious wealth, and it was one of them who tipped the FBI off to his illegal scheme. Evidence later showed that one of the principal reasons for his "success" was that his firm served as a conduit for the lucre of corruption.

LOOK TO THE TOP

At some point, regardless of internal controls or safeguards, a person at the top of an organization has the ultimate authority to decide how it spends its money;

lower-level employees must contend with restrictions. This means that within an entity the chief purchasing agent or similar officer would be the most likely suspect for corruption. CPAs therefore should satisfy themselves that controls over purchasing managers are adequate and are not being overridden.

Burgin's opportunity. As chairman of the Mississippi Senate Appropriations Committee, Burgin was the state's chief purchasing agent of sorts. The state neatly divided its finances according to revenue and appropriations. While the Senate Revenue Committee raised money to fund state programs, Burgin's committee was in charge of spending it. Every check the state wrote was within his powerful domain. There were controls, of course—but none the enterprising politician couldn't bypass.

THE "SNIFF TEST"

In theory, any employee authorized to spend an organization's money is a possible candidate for corruption. Those paying the bribes tend to be commissioned salespeople or intermediaries for outside vendors. The following players usually are present in a corruption scheme.

The gift bearer. Illegal inducements often begin when a businessperson routinely offers inappropriate gifts or provides lavish entertainment to an employee with purchasing authority or otherwise tries to ingratiate himself or herself for the purpose of influencing those in charge.

The odd couple. When a purchasing agent becomes the "friend" of an outside vendor, beware. A key technique bribe-givers use is to befriend their targets. They go to lunch together, take trips and engage in other social outings. But often the pair has nothing in common except for an illegal scheme.

The too-successful bidder. A supplier who consistently wins business without any apparent competitive advantage might be providing under-the-table incentives to obtain the work. Be alert to sole-source contracts and to bidders who nearly always win, who win by thin margins and who bid last. These are indicators someone at the company is supplying the winning bidder inside information.

The one-person operator. Some suppliers, rather than directly engage in payoffs, hire someone—called a bagman—to do the dirty work. Be alert to independent sales representatives, consultants or other middlemen, as they are favored conduits for funneling and concealing illegal payments.

Once an employee crosses the line and accepts kickbacks, he or she hardly is in a position to complain to the vendor about goods or services. The vendor knows this and often reacts by supplying items of poor quality and raising prices for purchases.

When a corrupt employee takes bribes, the underlying business arrangement usually is flawed. For instance, the products or services the dishonest worker contracted for, besides being substandard, are often unneeded, purchased from remote or vague sources, bought at odd times or from odd places or make little economic sense. To help uncover fraudulent transactions, CPAs should employ skepticism when examining the rationale for material purchases by the company.

Burgin's scheme. My investigation of Bill Burgin had commenced a year earlier when a confidential banking source alerted me to a contract between the state of Mississippi and Learning Development Corp. (LDC). Because the document was public record, I went down to the secretary of state's office to take a look.

I discovered there were two contracts under which the state would pay LDC a total of $860,000, purportedly to provide "educational services for disadvantaged youths in the state of Mississippi." In examining the details of the agreements, three items jumped out at me. First, they were sole-source contracts—ones with no competitive bids. The second oddity: LDC was headquartered in Nashville. With the pressure on politicians to create jobs in their own states, I wondered why the contracts didn't go to a Mississippi service provider. And there was one other thing—it was hard to decipher what the contract said and what LDC actually had to do for its money.

UNDER-THE-TABLE PAYMENTS

Being the conduit or bagman for bribe money is a profession of sorts; learning to pass bribes and get away with it takes experience and know-how. This particular profession tends to attract a small cadre of sleazy people. They typically are one-person operations and pass bribes for a variety of "clients." For example, during the Pentagon procurement scandals of the 1980s, just one bagman represented some of America's largest defense contractors. And when I investigated corruption in the private sector, I found the same trend. CPAs therefore should be alert to shadowy "consultants" on the payroll.

Burgin's "consultant." Burgin's bagman was D. Flavous Lambert, a lobbyist and former politician with a questionable reputation. On the surface the two men seemed to have little in common. I theorized that if Burgin's job was to see that the state approved the LDC contract, Lambert's task was to work with LDC to ensure the twosome got their take.

Since the contracts didn't pass the sniff test, I decided to take the investigation to the next level by examining LDC's books. The odor got worse. In tracing the corporation's receipts and disbursements, a pattern emerged. LDC received its state payments in monthly installments of $65,000 Each time LDC deposited a state check, it would immediately disburse $32,500—exactly half of the deposit amount—to Developmental Associates, a Georgia concern. The disbursement code identified it as a "finder's fee." Development Associates turned out to be nothing more than a bank account in Atlanta with only one name on the signature card: D. Flavous Lambert. The following business day, Lambert would send a share of the money to the bank account of Burgin's law firm. Believe it: Burgin was accepting bribes by check. The only reason I could figure for his flagrancy was that he had been corrupt for so long that he felt immune to discovery.

THE BRIBE-TAKER GETS INVOLVED

Anyone who takes a bribe makes a pact with the devil. Since the employee is committing a crime, he or she will go to extreme lengths to avoid discovery; that means keeping the bribe-giver happy. Corrupt employees must frequently intercede to resolve problems for the vendor, such as demanding that payments be expedited or requesting that substandard work be accepted. CPAs should look for these anomalies.

Burgin's downfall. No physical evidence linked Burgin to the crime until he interceded directly for LDC. In fact, Burgin didn't even sign the contract between the state of Mississippi and LDC. Instead, welfare commissioner Fred St. Clair signed it. Later, before a federal grand jury, St. Clair admitted he had been pressured by Burgin to approve the deal. St. Clair also told the grand jury that problems with LDC led to the checks from the state being delayed. But shortly before the holidays, Burgin showed up at the welfare commissioner's office demanding he be given LDC's overdue $65,000 check at once. Otherwise, the senator lamented, "Employees of LDC are not going to have a Christmas." It was obvious to St. Clair that LDC or Lambert had pressured the senator to intercede. Burgin, on the other hand, denied the incident ever occurred. Evidence to incriminate Burgin would be so important that, wearing surgical gloves in order not to contaminate any fingerprints on the check, I spent two days in the bowels of the dusty state archives examining canceled checks. Once I located the "Christmas check" the FBI lab found Burgin's thumbprint right in the middle of it. Sure enough, the check had been deposited to the LDC bank account.

BOOK 'EM, DAN-O

As corruption schemes progress, conspirators usually get careless.

Auteiting Vendors

Auditing Vendors

If an employee in your company is taking bribes, the illegal payment will not be reflected in your client's books, but rather it will be in those of the bribe-giver. The payments often are disguised in the vendor's records as consulting or finder's fees, commissions or similar expenses.

To help keep your vendors honest, you should insist that major suppliers agree to let you audit their books if necessary. Here is a sample of the way such an agreement could be worded.

"Vendor grants to purchaser the right to audit vendor's books and records, and to make copies and extracts, to the extent the books or records relate to the performance of this contract."

Frauds—including bribes and kickbacks—normally are not onetime events, but continuous crimes that occur over extended time periods. The Association of Certified Fraud Examiners' 2002 *Report to the Nation: Occupational Fraud and Abuse* concluded the average fraud lasted about 17 months and corruption schemes typically took about two years to be discovered.

The perpetrator's modus operandi tends to change over time. Initially, the crooked employee carefully covers his or her tracks. But as the crime progresses without being uncovered, perpetrators look for ways to accomplish the same illegal goals with less hassle. In the beginning the suspect may make sure all of the documents appear in order. Later, he or she may not even bother with any phony paperwork.

CPAs should consider major deficiencies in contract documentation to be a significant red flag. Moreover, many fraudsters don't continue to conceal their ill-gotten

gains very well. In short, they get sloppy. In fact, most of the time, the bribe-taker will deposit the illicit funds in his or her own bank account.

Burgin's last stand. Burgin's trial, held in Gulfport, Mississippi, lasted about two weeks. The government presented its case against the senator. In his defense Burgin took the stand and claimed he had no idea the money in his firm's bank account came from LDC. His story— and he stuck to it—was that he had represented Lambert in a legal matter 20 years ago and that Lambert finally was paying the bill.

During the dramatic closing of the trial, Burgin looked directly at the jury and said, "There is no way I would ever deprive the citizens of this great state of their hard-earned tax money." He then pulled a large red bandana from his breast pocket, dabbed his eyes and honked loudly into the handkerchief.

For the FBI agent in charge of the investigation, the scene was too much; without thinking, I burst out laughing. Then the jurors started guffawing. Burgin's defense lawyer was immediately on his feet shouting, "Mistrial!" The prosecutor glared at me. The trial recessed for about 15 minutes so the judge could chew me out. Then he sent the case to the jury.

In less than half a day, the jury convicted Burgin and Lambert. A reporter later asked one of the jurors about the strength of the government's evidence. In his soft Mississippi drawl, the juror said: "Well, when we saw the paper trail, we were convinced. The only way the case could have been stronger was if the checks to Burgin would've had the word *bribe* written on the description line."

JOSEPH T. WELLS, CPA, CFE, is founder and chairman of the Association of Certified Fraud Examiners and a professor of fraud examination at the University of Texas at Austin. Mr. Wells is a member of the AICPA Business and Industry Hall of Fame. He won the Lawler Award for the best *JofA* article in 2000. Mr. Wells' e-mail address is joe@cfenet.com.

From the *Journal of Accountancy,* April 2003, pp. 49-52. Copyright © 2003 by the American Institute of Certified Public Accountants, Inc. Opinions of the authors are their own and do not necessarily reflect policies of the AICPA. Reprinted with permission.

Where the Dangers Are

The threats to information security that keep the experts up at night—and what businesses and consumers can do to protect themselves

DAVID BANK and RIVA RICHMOND

In the world of cybercrime, the bad guys are getting smarter—and more ambitious.

In recent months, hackers have carried out a flurry of increasingly sophisticated attacks, highlighting the vulnerability of key computer networks around the world.

Criminals penetrated the database of CardSystems Solutions Inc., nabbing up to 200,000 Visa, MasterCard, American Express and Discover card numbers and potentially exposing tens of millions more. Leading high-tech companies in Israel allegedly planted surveillance software on the computers of their business rivals. British security officials warned of a computer attack aimed at stealing sensitive information from banks, insurers and other parts of that country's "critical infrastructure."

Security experts fear things will only get worse. As technology gets more complex, more vulnerabilities are springing up in computer networks—and more criminals, terrorists and mischief makers are rushing to exploit them.

"What people can do on computer networks and what they can find on them has increased tenfold from a few years ago," says Bill Hancock, chief security officer of Savvis Inc., a major Internet-service provider. Infiltrating those machines and using them for evil intent is easier than ever, he says.

Some of the threats are well known; home-computer users for years have battled viruses and spam and more recently have been barraged with spyware, adware and fraudsters "phishing" for sensitive information. Less visible is the constant probing of corporate networks by would-be intruders seeking trade secrets or competitive intelligence, and the data breaches caused by disgruntled or dishonest insiders.

Meanwhile, government authorities report that hackers are stepping up attempts to attack critical systems such as water, electricity, finance, transportation and communications. Last year, the Department of Homeland Security prepared a worst-case cyberdisaster scenario where criminals broke into financial-services facilities. Twenty million credit cards were canceled, automated teller machines failed nationwide, payroll checks couldn't be delivered, and computer malfunctions caused a weeklong shutdown of pension and mutual-fund companies. "Citizens no longer trust any part of the U.S. financial system," the scenario concluded.

Here's a look at the threats the security experts worry about the most—and what businesses and consumers can do to protect themselves.

TARGETED ATTACKS

The mass mailings of worms and viruses that clogged email in-boxes and corporate networks in recent years have given way to less visible but more dangerous attacks aimed at specific business and government targets.

In many cases, these invasions involve a Trojan—malicious software that hides inside another, innocuous program. Once planted on a victim's computer system, the Trojan can, among other things, steal information at will and send it back to a criminal. Trojans that are customized for a specific target are particularly dangerous, since conventional antivirus programs are designed to spot and block previously identified threats.

"Because these things are one-off, the virus scanners do not recognize them at all," says Bryan Sartin, director of technology for Ubizen, a unit of Cybertrust Inc. of Herndon, Va.

Criminals use a variety of methods to get Trojans onto their targets' systems. Often, they trick employees at a targeted company into installing the software. In the Israeli case, law-enforcement officials discovered that the alleged perpetrators gave victims floppy disks containing seemingly legitimate business proposals. The disks contained Trojans that used "key logger" software to record what users typed, and then transmitted that data, along with documents and emails, to a computer in London.

Hackers also take advantage of security flaws in Web browsers. Last year, hackers invaded the computer system of a large bank using a known, but unpatched, vulnerability in

Microsoft Corp.'s Internet Explorer, says Alfred Huger, senior director of engineering for computer-security firm **Symantec** Corp., Cupertino, Calif., who investigated the break-in. For 90 days, the criminals collected network and database passwords and intercepted secure communications, among other things. Mr. Huger says he doesn't know how much money was lost.

Security experts are increasingly concerned about break-ins that come via a company's partners and vendors. These smaller companies often have privileged access to their larger partner's computer systems, but may not be as well protected. Last year, John Pironti, a security consultant with Unisys Corp., of Blue-bell, Pa., says he helped discover a powerful Trojan that had been planted in the computer network of a major financial institution. A hacker penetrated one of the bank's custom-software suppliers and discovered the "open pipe" to the financial-services provider's network.

The most effective method for protecting against such attacks is also the simplest—disconnect databases containing sensitive information, such as credit-card data, from the Internet. "Systems like that should not have Internet access, period," says Ubizen's Mr. Sartin.

If that's not possible, all such systems should have "firewall" technology that monitors Internet connections and raises a red flag if it detects suspicious activity, such as high volumes of data sent at unusual times. Other tools can take a snapshot of legitimate system configurations and sound alarms when changes occur.

And, of course, all computers need to be kept up to date with security patches and antivirus software, and users need to be educated about opening unknown attachments or visiting suspicious Web sites.

BOTNETS

A single computer infected with a Trojan is bad enough. An army of infected computers is a weapon of mass digital destruction.

"Botnets," short for robot networks, are made up of home and business PCs that have been taken over by hackers and joined together to create remote-controlled networks. The hackers (sometimes called "bot herders") use the combined power of these machines to mount a variety of Internet attacks, right under the noses of the PCs' rightful owners. The size, and power, of such botnets is growing rapidly, as bot herders learn how to manage networks of tens of thousands of compromised "zombie" or "drone" PCs.

Here's how it works: Hackers or criminals slip Trojans carrying the bot software onto the PCs of unwitting targets. The infected computers are then programmed to listen for instructions, generally sent via instant-messaging channels.

Once assembled, the botnet can be used to send spam, launch phishing attacks or disrupt a Web site by flooding it with visits, a so-called denial-of-service attack. One popular tactic of organized cybercriminals: denial-of-service attacks against Internet gambling sites. The criminals then extort the sites for payment to halt the attack.

Home computers, which generally lack sophisticated network-monitoring tools, are most vulnerable to becoming unwitting conscripts. Early last year, Time Warner Cable began sending Matt McKay "spam ticket" citations and threatened to turn off his Internet service. The 32-year-old Charlotte, N.C., attorney wasn't moonlighting as a spammer. A hacker had hijacked his computer. "I was spamming people, and I didn't know it," he says.

The Federal Trade Commission in May urged Internet-service providers to more actively combat botnets, which the FTC estimated send as much as 80% of spam. The FTC suggested ISPs monitor their customers for suspicious emailing patterns, block Internet connections favored by bot herders and help consumers clean up infected machines.

BLACKOUTS

In last season's television thriller "24," terrorists used the Internet to penetrate control systems at dozens of U.S. nuclear power plants—and cause one to melt down. Hollywood fantasy? Security experts warn that such an attack is not as far-fetched as it might seem.

The systems used to control the nation's water, power, transportation and communication systems are increasingly being connected to corporate networks that are in turn connected to the Internet. That makes it easier to control and maintain the systems remotely, but also makes the systems vulnerable to viruses, worms and other Net-based threats.

Cyberattacks that successfully penetrate such "supervisory control and data acquisition," or Scada, systems appear to be increasing. The British Columbia Institute of Technology and the PA Consulting Group in London, which documented a handful of such incidents through 2000, have reports of at least 80 successful attacks world-wide since 2001. "Some just snoop around, some do damage," says Eric Byres, who manages the research project.

In May, the General Accounting Office reported similar findings. Security consultants cited in the report said hackers are continuously probing the power grid for vulnerabilities; in some cases, intruders gained access to utilities' control systems and affected operations, though not causing serious damage.

The vulnerability of vital networks was highlighted by the Northeast blackout of 2003. Though not caused by a cyberattack, the incident was exacerbated by one: The "Blaster" worm, which had been released days earlier, clogged communications links and hurt operators' ability to stem the cascading blackout.

Security experts say such power-control systems are unlikely to be the primary target of terrorists, who arguably are more interested in spectacular physical attacks that generate casualties. But experts are increasingly concerned that attacks on critical systems could be used in conjunction with more-violent tactics to compound the damage—for instance, by disabling emergency-response systems.

Some of the vulnerabilities of these control systems can be offset by rigorous compliance with standard cybersecurity practices. Congress is considering adding such requirements to the federal energy bill now pending. But many security experts say existing Scada systems are obsolete and need to be replaced by new sensors with multiple layers of security, including in the hardware, the network and the application.

Perhaps more important, says S. Shankar Sastry, a professor of electrical engineering at the University of California, Berkeley, are strategies for "graceful degradation," for example by installing several layers of defenses, to ensure that vital networks remain at least partly operational during and after a major attack. "We should expect in the future for attacks to succeed," Mr. Sastry says. "The question is: How do you keep the infrastructure from completely falling apart?"

CRASHING THE NET

Hackers can take down a corporate computer network. But could they crash the whole Internet? The same qualities of trust and openness that have made the Internet successful also make it vulnerable to major outages.

The experts' top worry: an arcane mechanism known as the "border gateway protocol." The protocol is used by the hundreds of networks that make up the Internet to advertise their routes so they can carry each other's traffic. By falsifying such announcements, hackers could intercept Internet traffic, modify it or simply make it vanish by directing it to bogus or nonexistent routes. And by directing a flood of traffic onto a route too small to handle it, a hacker could overload and crash at least parts of the global Internet.

"You can take out some portion of the Net for some amount of time," says Steven Bellovin, a longtime security expert at AT&T Labs and now professor of computer science at Columbia University. If a sophisticated adversary sent out fraudulent routing announcements from a dozen different points, "you could have a very serious situation," he says.

In the past decade, security specialists say, inadvertent glitches in the protocol have caused a half-dozen large network outages and many smaller ones. In December 1999, such a mistake took down AT&T's Worldnet Internet service for most of a day, leaving 1.8 million customers without Web access. An even larger outage occurred two years earlier, when a small Internet-service provider mistakenly advertised incorrect routes, causing a two-hour disruption for large parts of the Internet.

Now, security experts are seeing apparently intentional attacks exploiting the weaknesses in the protocol. In one case, the Web site of a large Internet-networking company vanished, meaning no traffic could reach it for several hours. In another, some Internet traffic went into a "black hole" along an advertised route that didn't really exist; email, Web requests and so on simply disappeared. Neither incident was considered serious, but they showed "the threat is real," says Craig Labovitz, director of engineering at Arbor Networks Inc., a network-security firm in Lexington, Mass.

Spammers are also starting to take advantage of the technique. By advertising fake Internet addresses for just long enough to launch their spam, then withdrawing the addresses, it's possible to erase any trail that law enforcement might follow. "Nobody can find it," Mr. Bellovin says. "It's not in the database. You can't map your way to it. It's just gone."

Because the Internet is used by nearly everybody but owned by no one, systemic vulnerabilities have proved difficult to correct. For starters, a change would require upgrades to thousands of routers. And there's no consensus on how to fix the border-gateway protocol.

Still, the Net has proved remarkably resilient against large-scale attacks. "We've been hearing these end-of-the-Internet stories for the last 10 years," Mr. Labovitz says. "But we haven't seen many of these mega-attacks." The most likely reason: Hackers, thieves and terrorists have come to depend on the Internet just like everybody else, and don't want it wrecked.

PHRAUD

Internet-related fraud accounted for 53% of all consumer-fraud complaints made to the Federal Trade Commission last year. Among the biggest threats are those involving scammers who use elaborate ruses to pretend to be someone else.

In "phishing" scams, fraudsters send emails that appear to come from a trusted source, like Citibank or eBay. Click on a link in the email, and you're directed to a fake Web site, where you're asked to reveal account numbers, passwords and other private information. In some cases, phishing sites plant hidden programs, such as key loggers, on victims' computers. So even if a visitor doesn't enter any data into the phony site, the phisher can try to filch it later.

Then there's "pharming," where hackers attack the server computers where legitimate Web sites are housed. Type in the address of the legitimate site, and you are redirected to a look-alike. In a similar ruse, hackers use Trojans to manipulate the browser cache on a victim's computer, where copies of Web pages are stored so that they don't have to be reloaded from scratch with each visit. When you visit a site stored in your cache, you are directed to a fake site instead.

In "Evil Twin" attacks, hackers set up Wi-Fi hot spots that trick your computer into thinking it's accessing your home wireless network or a safe public network. While you use the network, attackers can monitor your moves and steal the information you enter into a Web site, if the site doesn't have the right safety measures.

To combat phishing, assume that any email asking for personal information is a fake, says Robert C. Chesnut, senior vice president of rules, trust and safety at **eBay** Inc. Consumers can also get help from new phishing-site blockers from service providers **Time Warner** Inc.'s America Online unit and **EarthLink** Inc.

As for pharming, some banks are beginning to look at ways to help consumers distinguish real sites from fake ones, such as letting consumers choose personalized images that appear on the site whenever they visit. To combat the variation on pharming that involves meddling with PCs, consumers should be sure to regularly sweep for Trojans with antivirus and anti-spyware programs available from companies such as Symantec, **McAfee** Inc. and **Webroot Software** Inc.

For Evil Twin attacks, wireless users should enter private information only into sites that protect data with encryption technology, which is signified by a little lock on the bottom of the page.

Rogues' Gallery

Threats to the security of computer systems come in many forms. Here are profiles of some of the people behind them and their motivation:

• BOT NETWORK OPERATORS
Hackers who take over multiple systems in order to distribute phishing schemes (the use of fradulent email and Web sites to deceive people into disclosing personal information), spam and malware (viruses and other software designed with malicious intent).

• ORGANIZED CRIME GROUPS
Criminal groups use spam, phishing and malware to commit identity theft and online fraud.

• CRIMINAL SPIES
Conduct industrial espionage by breaking into competitors' systems.

• FOREIGN INTELLIGENCE SERVICES
Gather information by penetrating computer systems. In addition, several countries are working to develop the capability to disrupt the supply chain, communications and economic infrastructure that support the military power of an enemy.

• HACKERS
Break into networks for the thrill of the challenge or for bragging rights in the hacker community.

• INSIDERS
The disgruntled insider is a principal source of computer crime, and often is able to gain unrestricted acess to cause damage to the system or steal data.

• PHISHERS
Individuals or small groups who use fradulent email and Web sites to extract personal information from their victims that can then be used for monetary gain.

• SPYWARE/MALWARE AUTHORS
Individuals or organizations with malicious intent carry out attacks against users by producing and distributing malware, like viruses or worms, and spyware, which is software secretly put on victims' computers gather information about them.

• TERRORISTS
May seek to destroy, incapacitate or exploit critical infrastructure in order to threaten national security, cause mass casualities, weaken the economy or damage public morale. Also may use phishing or other schemes to generate funds or gather sensitive information.

Source: GAO analysis based on data from the Federal Bureau of Investigation, the Central Intelligence Agency and the Software Engineering Institute's CERT Coordiantion Center.

HIJACKING

Many hackers who covertly take control of your computer are looking to draft it into a botnet. But there are a host of other ways to get hijacked. Aggressive marketers are using "adware" to hijack Web searches, display pop-up ads and drag surfers to unwanted Web sites. Adware's more insidious cousin, spyware, can capture users' keystrokes and follow their browsing activities. These programs often arrive bundled with free software or sneak onto users' computers when they visit dodgy Web sites.

Viruses, meanwhile, have become a tool for delivering malicious payloads and not just a form of causing mischief. Hackers are using them to install bots and Trojans that give them control of PCs, allowing them to send spam and steal private personal information silently.

After Mr. McKay, the Charlotte attorney, cleared up his botnet problem, the home page of his Web browser was hijacked by an adware program, forcing him to view a "flashy, gaudy" page featuring links to mortgage lenders and pornography. Only when his girlfriend refused to touch the computer did he cave. "I said, 'All right, this is embarrassing,' " he recalls. " 'I'm going to fix it.' "

Mr. McKay had to undergo a crash course in Internet security to get rid of the programs that hijacked his computer. He ran a battery of different security programs, killing anything that looked suspicious. But after a slew of software failed to clean out his machine, he turned to extracting the pests manually.

Security experts advise consumers to make sure they install and use firewall and up-to-date antivirus programs, combined with regular sweeps with a spyware-removal program. Increasingly, Internet-service providers are offering their embattled customers security tools. Many people are also switching to Apple Computer Inc.'s Macintosh machines and the Firefox Web browser, which have rarely been the target of malicious code.

AIRBORNE ASSAULT

In the future, security attacks will come out of thin air. Smartphones and some personal digital assistants boast always-on wireless connections and run more-sophisticated software than standard cellphones, making them susceptible to viruses, worms and data theft just like PCs.

The hackers' current pathway of choice: Bluetooth. This radio technology allows short-range wireless communication for sending messages, exchanging electronic business cards and using wireless headsets. But hackers can exploit flaws in Bluetooth to steal information from digital gadgets or spread viruses.

For now, mobile viruses have done little more than drain their victims' phone batteries and send off text messages using their account. But bigger threats may be coming. The invasions so far were merely "science projects" for hackers wanting to see if they could attack mobile devices, says Victor Kouznetsov, senior vice president of mobile solutions for McAfee. "They discovered it's not that hard."

Mr. Pironti of Unisys says people should use built-in Bluetooth security features that let only authorized headsets and PCs talk to their phones. They should also change default passwords for wireless headsets. Meanwhile, security-software companies are rushing to offer antivirus protection for mobile devices. Japanese carrier **NTT DoCoMo** Inc. sells phones with built-in antivirus software from McAfee. A number of large carriers offer similar protection from **F-Secure** Corp. of Finland.

But the best defense will come from wireless carriers blocking attacks within their networks, before they can reach people's phones, says Gartner Inc. analyst John Pescatore. Cell-phone users should start asking their providers what protection they offer or intend to provide, he says. F-Secure, for one, says its network-level technology has been deployed by nine wireless operators that altogether serve 32 million subscribers.

YOUR KIDS

What's the quickest way to get your computer infested with spyware, bots and Trojans? Let your kids use it.

Kids often use music and video file-sharing programs like Kazaa, LimeWire and BitTorrent, where they can unwittingly download adware and spyware. They also pick up nasty programs at "code and cheat" sites, which help them get higher rankings in online games. And curiosity will take them to plenty of other risky places, including porn sites.

Some security experts advise parents to have a separate computer for the kids. John Esposito of Ridgewood, N.J., keeps financial records on his own laptop, so they won't be endangered if nine-year-old Zoe or 13-year-old Zach inadvertently lets in a hacker program.

In addition to protecting their PC with the usual array of security software, parents can use parental-control tools to restrict access to inappropriate sites. Parry Aftab, executive director of WiredSafety Group, a New York-based advocate for online safety, recommends kid-safe search engines, such as Yahoo Inc.'s Yahooligans and Ask Jeeves Inc.'s Ask Jeeves Kids. These sites won't steer kids to sites meant for adults, including porn sites that try to lure visitors with misspellings of popular keywords.

Parents should also talk to their children about online dangers and set ground rules for computer use. Parents may even want to use some spyware tools of their own to monitor what kids do online. Ms. Aftab recommends monitoring software from SpectorSoft Corp. because it's able to capture instant messaging in multiple formats.

---

*—**Mr. Bank** is a staff reporter in the Wall Street Journal's San Francisco bureau, and **Ms. Richmond** is a reporter for Dow Jones Newswires in Jersey City, N.J.*

Write to David Bank at david.bank@wsj.com and Riva Richmond at riva.richmond@dowjones.com.

From *The Wall Street Journal*, July 18, 2005. Copyright © 2005 as conveyed via the Copyright Clearance Center. Reprinted by permission.

Sexual Harassment and Retaliation: A Double-Edged Sword

Ann C. Wendt
Raj Soin College of Business, Wright State University

William M. Slonaker
Raj Soin College of Business, Wright State University

Introduction

"She was just so thrilled they believed her," said the plaintiff's attorney following a $2 million jury verdict for a woman who experienced retaliation after complaining about sexual harassment (Cruz, 2001, p. 1D). The plaintiff had been fired and escorted off the employer's premises within two hours after reporting sexual harassment to her boss. If harassment *displays* power over another, then retaliation *flaunts* power. Its origin is Title VII, which provides for separate relief if an adverse action ("retaliation") is taken against a complainant "because he has opposed any practice made an unlawful employment practice… " (Title VII, 1964). Retaliation is an attorney's "gotcha." That is, even if a woman would have lost her original sexual harassment claim for lack of proof, she will win if she can prove that she experienced retaliation for having complained about sexual harassment (*Morris v. Oldham County Fiscal Court*, 2000).

Aggrieved employees claiming retaliation under Title VII must prove that they engaged in a protected activity, that the employer took an adverse action against them, and that there was a causal connection between the protected activity and the adverse action (*Burger v. Central Apartment Management Inc.*, 1999). Implicit in these requirements is that the employer knew of the employee's participation in a protected activity, and that the adverse action follows sufficiently close in time to justify an inference of retaliatory motivation (*Wille v. Hunkar Laboratories, Inc.*, 1998).

Retaliation for complaining about sexual harassment can be expensive. Over the last five years, employers have lost a higher percentage of retaliation lawsuits than suits for age, disability, race, or sex discrimination (Oppel, 1999, p. C8). Consider recent examples:

- A jury award of $152,500 was upheld by a U.S. Court of Appeals for a woman who was fired after complaining to police that her supervisor had grabbed her breast (*Worth v. Tyler, et. al.*, 2001).

- A New Jersey jury awarded $1.5 million to a female police officer who was demoted after she took legal action for being sexually harassed (*Mancini v. Teaneck*, 2000).

- A U.S. Court of Appeals upheld a $410,156 judgment in favor of a female employee who lost her office and her secretary, and who was demoted from her six-figure job following harassment that included sexual harassment (*Durham Life Insurance Co. v. Evans*, 1999).

Retaliation is becoming *the* form of employment discrimination of the new decade. Retaliation for all forms of employment discrimination (not just sexual harassment) is increasing. In 1992, the Equal Employment Opportunity Commission (EEOC) reported that 14.5% of claims filed included a claim of Title VII retaliation. By 1998, the percentage had increased to 21.7% (U.S. EEOC, 2001), and by 2000, it was 25% (The Bureau of National Affairs, 2001, p. 1324).

Claimants may identify more than one basis (race, age, *etc.*) when filing a claim. EEOC's data include all bases that each claimant used, without distinguishing a primary basis. Thus, EEOC's data on the bases on which claims are filed totals more than 100%. For example, for 1998 claims, the data total 144.4%. However, the authors' database prioritizes each claimant's bases, enabling analyses based on 100% of the bases on which the claimants filed. Using this approach, in 1992, 10.1% of the claims were for retaliation. By 1998, the percentage was 21.9%, having more than doubled. Regardless of the counting method, retaliation claims are rising.

Brief Review of Sexual Harassment

"Sex" under Title VII includes two types of harassment. The first, *quid pro quo*, occurs when an employee is pressed to exchange "this for that," e.g., a promotion for sexual favors. The second type is where discriminatory actions have created a hostile or abusive working environment (*Meritor Sav. Bank, FSB v. Vinson*, 1986). "For [hostile environment] sexual harassment to be actionable, it must be sufficiently severe or persuasive to alter the conditions of employment and create an abusive working environment" (*Meritor*, p. 2405). Whether a working environment rises to this level is determined on a case-by-case basis, by looking at all the circumstances. "These may include the frequency of the discriminatory conduct; its severity; whether it is physically threatening or humiliating, or a mere offensive utterance; and whether it unreasonably interferes with an employee's performance" (*Harris v. Forklift Sys., Inc.*, pp. 20–1).

There are two possible sources of the sexual harassment: nonsupervisors, e.g., co-workers, customers, others; or, supervisors, immediate or higher level. Courts have held that employers will not be liable for harassment by nonsupervisory personnel if employers implement effective policies and promptly take action to rectify any harassment. The question has been more difficult, however, when the source of the harassment is a supervisor. Supervisors are agents for employers. Thus, when a supervisor is the source, it is as though the employer itself was the harasser ("vicarious liability"), even though harassment is not a typical job duty.

The U.S. Supreme Court recently (*Burlington Industries, Inc. v. Ellerth*, 1998; and, *Faragher v. City of Boca Raton*, 1998) reconciled the two types of sexual harassment, clarified when employers would be vicariously liable for their supervisors' behavior, and recognized an affirmative defense for employers in certain situations. First, the Court clarified that *quid pro quo* includes situations where a supervisor's threat is carried out, while "hostile environment" includes both situations where there is an unfulfilled threat or offensive conduct with no threat. Second, the Court rejected the notion that employers are vicariously liable for supervisors' behavior only in *quid pro quo* situations. Employers also will be liable for hostile environments created by supervisors with immediate- or higher-level authority over the victim. Finally, in cases where an employee suffered no adverse tangible employment action (such as discharge, demotion, etc.), the employer may have an affirmative defense to their supervisor's harassing behavior if two conditions are met. First, the employer must have "exercised reasonable care to prevent and correct promptly any sexually harassing behavior" (including having a policy); and second, that the employee must have "unreasonably failed to take advantage of any preventive or corrective opportunities provided by the employer or to avoid harm otherwise" (including failing to follow policy procedures) (*Burlington*, p. 2264).

The Claim Process

The EEOC is the primary federal agency charged with enforcing the federal anti-discrimination laws. However, it has delegated much of its responsibilities to state agencies, called "706 agencies," or "deferral agencies." It is within the state agencies that most formal claims are filed,

investigated, and resolved. As a practical matter, this is as far as most formal claims are pursued. An employee needs only go to an office and complete a form, under oath and with agency assistance, describing the essential facts.

The agency will conduct investigations as it deems appropriate. Some are limited to requests for documents concerning the allegations. Others include documents, on-site investigations, and interviews with the parties and witnesses. Usually, the agency will then attempt to help the parties resolve the claim. If conciliation fails, then the agency will refer the claim to EEOC, which may further attempt to resolve the dispute. Ultimately, if the dispute is not resolved, and regardless of whether the state agency found that there was "probable cause" that discrimination occurred, the claimant is entitled to a "right to sue" letter. The letter is necessary if the claimant wishes to file a lawsuit in the courts.

In 1998, 23,735 employment discrimination cases were filed in federal courts. Thirty-nine percent were settled, 14% were dismissed voluntarily, 5% went to trial, and the remainders were pending at the end of 1998. Most (78%) of the cases that went to trial were heard by juries. Of the cases that went to trial, plaintiffs won 36%, with $137,000 being the median award. However, the verdicts in 11% of the cases were $10 million or more (The Bureau of National Affairs, 2000, p. 62). These statistics reflect only employment discrimination cases filed in federal courts. Increasingly, plaintiffs are filing in state courts.

Sample and Methodology

To better understand the current level and characteristics of employment discrimination, the authors have been conducting a longitudinal study, *The Ohio Employment Discrimination Studies*. To date, they have examined 7,072 claims of employment discrimination closed by the Ohio Civil Rights Commission (OCRC) from 1985 through 1999. The claims were randomly drawn as a stratified random sample (8.7%) from the 81,355 cases closed during that time. The authors used a content analysis research method to analyze the variables (discussed in this article) within each claim. The claims were filed under federal (85%) and state (15%) laws, against all types of employers, whose sizes ranged from micro-businesses to Fortune 500 firms.

Based on a comparison of sample claimants to the workforces of both Ohio and the U.S., the findings of this research are generalizable to those workforce populations. Women compose 46% of the Ohio and the U.S. workforces. Ohio is seventh in the country for gross state product (Ohio Bureau of Employment Services, 1998, p. 1–2) (U.S. Department of Labor, 2000, Table A-1). Ohio's goods producing industries are slightly higher (at 25%), and service producing industries slightly lower (at 75%) than those of the U.S. (20% goods and 80% service). For Ohio, local and state government employment is about 12.5%, while nationally it averages about 13.5% of total employment (Ohio Bureau of Employment Services, 1998, Table 2; U.S. Department of Labor, 2000, Table B-1).

Of the 7,072 claims in the authors' database, women filed 3,760 (53%). Of these, 515 (14%) were based on retaliation for having previously complained of employment discrimination. Of the 515 claims, 35 did not identify the basis of their original complaint, leaving 480 claims where the original basis was identified. Cumulatively for the 15 years of the authors' study, retaliation-based claims ranked third in frequency of all bases for women's claims, following only race (30%) and sex-based (29%) claims. Of the women's retaliation claims, 129 (25% of the 515 claims) identified sexual harassment as the original basis, and these are analyzed in this paper. The authors' analyses included only claims of sexual harassment of a woman by a man.

Outcomes

For the 129 retaliation claims made by the sexually harassed women, the outcomes were as follows:

- "no probable cause" was found in 50% of the claims;

- employers settled 27% of the claims;

- women withdrew their claims in 17% of the cases (mostly to proceed directly to court);

- "probable cause" was found in just 4% of the claims; and,

- no jurisdiction occurred in 2% of the claims.

"No probable cause" (50%) means that there was not sufficient evidence to prove the claim, while "probable cause" (4%) means there was sufficient evidence. These outcomes are typical. In Ohio, for all employment discrimination claims, "no probable cause" was found in 58% of the claims, while "probable cause" was found in only 6% (OCRC, 1992–1999). An immediate question might be why employers and managers should worry about any form of employment discrimination, including retaliation against women for complaining about sexual harassment. When asked this question, LeAnn Dickerson, Western Region Director of Human Resources for Delta Air Lines said that "such an employer or manager would send two harmful messages: first, to employees not to bother reporting discrimination, with the result that management does not learn about serious problems; and second, a message to perpetrators of discrimination that it is 'OK,' only encouraging them to continue. At Delta, we take every employee's concerns very seriously."

The authors also believe that to conclude that employers and managers need not worry about discrimination is erroneous. First, the authors' primary explanation for the low percentage of "probable cause" findings is that employment discrimination claims are very difficult to prove. Specifically, retaliation complainants must demonstrate, by a preponderance of the evidence, that reporting sexual harassment motivated the employer's adverse

action, i.e., the retaliation (*McNairn v. Sullivan*, 1991). In 57% of the women's retaliation claims, their employers gave reasons for their allegedly retaliatory actions. The most common reason was that the complainant engaged in an improper work behavior, such as absenteeism, insubordination, or interpersonal conflicts. The next most common reason was simply inadequate performance. Thus, in at least 57% of the retaliation claims, the agency is faced with evaluating the alleged retaliation versus the employers' alleged legitimate reasons for their actions. Further, proof almost always is complicated by a lack of "smoking guns." Based on analyses of more than 7,000 employment discrimination claims spanning 15 years, the authors believe that in recent years, employers, managers, and supervisors who discriminate, or who will not take action against those who do, have become much more subtle. Additionally, state agencies (such as the OCRC) and the EEOC have limited budgets for investigations. By necessity, many are phone or paper investigations, without the benefit of personal visits to the workplaces. Also, with rare exception, employees who file complaints with these agencies do not have legal counsel. They have stated their claims as best they can and rely on the agencies to investigate.

A second reason why employers and managers should be concerned about every discrimination claim is that 90% of employees who perceive that they are experiencing discrimination will not complain to anyone in authority within the organization (Samborn, 1990, p. 1; Dubois, Faley, Kustis and Knapp, 1999, p. 202). Thus, on average, for every reported instance of discriminatory retaliation, there are nine possible complaints lurking in the wings.

Finally, a third reason that employers and managers to be concerned is the inherent cost. Employees who believe they are the victims of discrimination will not be as productive or loyal to their organizations. Their decreased morale can infect co-workers. A national study by the Families and Work Institute found that, "The *perception* of discrimination, or unequal opportunity in one's work place seems to exact a toll on workers' attitudes and behavior—*whether or not their perceptions would be found to have an objective basis* [emphasis added]" (Galinsky, Bond, and Friedman, 1993, p. 31). Because no employer would rationally allow its employees to be surveyed regarding sexual harassment experiences, it is virtually impossible to impute actual monetary costs to discrimination. However, a former EEOC investigator, Susan Crawford, estimates that sexual harassment costs the 500 largest companies $3.4 billion (average $6.7 million each) annually due to absenteeism, low productivity, and turnover (Feminist Majority Foundation, 2001).

Thus, the focus should not be on what percentage wins or loses formal discrimination complaints. Rather, employers and managers should consider unreported claims and the inherent costs of discrimination. They should take steps, such as training, to prevent both perceptions and actual discrimination.

Table 1 *General Characteristics of the Sexual Harassment Retaliation Claimants (n=129)*

To Whom The Women First Complained	Percentage	Quickness to File	Percentage
Immediate Supervisor	21	Same Day	2
Higher Manager	13	1st Week	13
Human Resources	13	2nd Week	11
Other Company Rep.	35	3rd & 4th Week	20
State 706 Agency	13	2nd Month	13
Other*	5	3rd Month	28
		4th + Month	13
Total	100	Total	100

* For example a union representative

Table 2 *General Characteristics Continued (n=129)*

Terms of Employment	Percentage	Jobs Held by Claimants	Percentage
1 Year	43	Managerial/Executive	12
2 to 5 Years	33	Professional Specialties	5
6 to 10 Years	10	Technicians	5
11 to 15 Years	4	Sales	9
16 to 20 Years	2	Clerical	20
21 to 30 Years	2	Service	20
Not Identified	6	Production	13
		Transportation/Labor	12
		Miscellaneous	4
Total	100	Total	100

Regarding the other outcomes, for the 27% of claims that settled, terms varied from as little as an apology to $21,800. The average financial settlement was $4,498. Overwhelmingly, these retaliation complainants did not have legal counsel, but the authors believe settlement costs would have been higher if lawyers had been involved. Additional settlement terms varied, including: firing or disciplining the harasser, rehiring the complainant, neutral letters of reference, and instituting new anti-discrimination policies and training programs. For the 17% of women who withdrew their claims, most did so to proceed directly to court. These complainants had legal counsel.

General Characteristics of Sexual Harassment Retaliation Complaints

Table 1 shows that most women (82%) complained to someone within the employer's organization: their boss (21%); a higher-level manager (13%); human resources (13%); or another company representative (35%). Only 13% went outside of the organization and filed a formal complaint with Ohio's 706 agencies. The other 87% of the claimants gave their employers an opportunity to manage the alleged sexual harassment complaint in-house.

Ultimately, these employers lost this opportunity when the female complainants perceived that they were experiencing retaliation for complaining and then filed with the state 706 agency.

Table 1 shows the women's quickness to file. While only 2% file the same day, and another 13% file within the first week, a total of 39% will file within the first four weeks following the retaliation. Thus, if employers needed an additional reason to promptly respond to initial complaints of sexual harassment, they have it. Some suggestions for managing sexual harassment to avoid complaints include: having a written anti-harassment policy; communicating the policy to all employees; training supervisors and employees; investigating all allegations promptly; and, remediating the problem when allegations are found to be true (Bland and Stalcup, 2001).

A rapid response to a complaint of sexual harassment must include a message to all involved that there must be no retaliation. Suggestions for avoiding retaliation claims include: have a separate anti-retaliation policy; encouraging complainants to come forward without fear of retaliation; and, not treating complainants differently than they otherwise would have been treated (Kandel, 1999).

Table 3   *Women's Retaliation Claims By Original Bases Compared to Nonretaliation Claims Filed During 1985 through 1999*

Basis	Retaliation Claims	Nonretaliation Claims	Percentage
Race	158	1,114	14
Sex-Gender	77	543	14
Sex-Pregnancy	4	255	2
Sex-Harassment	129	275	47
Disability	56	453	12
Age	43	345	12
National Origin	7	48	15
Religion	6	37	16
Not Identified*	35	0	N/A
No Basis**	0	175	N/A
Total	515	3,245	N/A

*Original basis not identified
**Claimants failed to state a prima facie case.

Nearly half (43%) of the female complainants had been employed for one year or less (with the employer against whom they filed their retaliation claim) when they first experienced the sexual harassment and the retaliation (see Table 2). Another 33% were employed for two to five years. Thus, it appears that if sexual harassment and retaliation are going to occur, it does so relatively soon after they are hired.

Most women (40%) who complained of retaliation for reporting sexual harassment worked in either clerical (administrative support) or service jobs (Table 2). Both types of jobs have traditionally been filled by women and often serve as entry-level jobs. However, sexual harassment can occur at the highest levels of the organization. For example, in one complaint within the authors' database, the male chairman of the board literally chased the female president around her desk attempting to initiate sexual contact. Finally, claimants identified the persons who were the harassers (not shown on any Table). Thirty-seven percent identified immediate supervisors, while 20% identified higher managers. Overall, 57% were supervisors or managers, that is, agents of the employer. Under the most recent U.S. Supreme Court decisions discussed earlier, employers with supervisors and managers who engage in sexual harassment are risking financial liability.

Nearly One-half of Women Who Complain Can Expect Retaliation

As Table 2 reports, women who experience sexual harassment initially complain to a variety of authorities, and only a small percentage (13%) file a formal complaint with a state 706 agency. Even for those who do initially file with a state agency, it is not feasible within the authors' database to track individual sexual harassment complainants to see if they subsequently report experiencing retaliation. However, to gain a better perspective on the significance of the women's 129 claims of retaliation where sexual harassment was identified as the original basis, the authors made some comparisons. They compared all retaliation claims filed by women (not just those related to sexual harassment) to all women's employment discrimination claims (claims not involving retaliation) filed during the same 15-year period. Table 3 reports the results.

Table 4   *Retaliatory Actions Identified by Claimants (n=129)*

	Percentage
Termination	61
Economic Loss	15
Aggression	13
Sexual Harassment	2
Miscellaneous Actions	9
Total	100

Retaliation claims based on sexual harassment compared with original sexual harassment claims occur substantially more frequently than any of the other retaliation claims compared with their respective original basis. From this comparison, the authors conclude that nearly half (47%) of all women who complain of sexual harassment can expect to experience retaliation.

What accounts for the high rate of retaliation? The authors believe that sexual harassment is fundamentally unlike any of the other forms of employment discrimination. The underlying purpose of a male sexually harassing a female is a display of power through sexual acceptance. When the victim complains or reports the perpetrator, she is rejecting his power and his implicit sexual advances. By comparison, the perpetrator in a race, pregnancy, gender, disability, age, or national origin situation is not seeking acceptance from the victim; to the contrary, he (or she) is expressing rejection of the victim. Conversely, when the victim of sexual harassment complains or reports the harasser's actions, she is rejecting the harasser. As a final display of power, and potentially to save face, the harasser "evens the score" by retaliating against (rejecting) the victim.

Forms of Retaliatory Actions

What were the retaliatory actions alleged by the complainants? The good news is that only 2% of the 129 retaliation claimants said that the sexual harassment continued. The bad news is what they allege as the retaliatory actions in the other 98% of the claims. Table 4 identifies the harmful retaliatory actions. Unfortunately, termination was the most frequently reported (61%) retaliatory action. In the workplace, discharge is the ultimate rejection. Not surprisingly, 27% of the terminations were "constructive discharges." This is when a woman resigns because the working conditions are "so difficult or unpleasant that a reasonable person in [the] employee's shoes would have felt compelled to resign" (*Chertkova v. Connecticut General Life Ins. Co.*, 1996).

The second most frequently identified retaliatory action, economic loss, included such actions as demotions, reduced wages or hours, and denial of training. These harmful actions were likely intended to force the complainants out of the organizations. While complainants can likely prove from employer records that they were terminated or experienced one or more of the economic actions, the following identified actions may be more difficult to prove as most complainants alleged that they were committed one-on-one by the perpetrators.

Most unexpected were retaliatory actions the authors categorized as "aggression." Such actions included: stalking, destruction of personal property, public humiliation, screaming, threats of physical violence, assaults, and others. These are dangerous conditions. "Physical aggression is almost always preceded by verbal aggression. Physical abuse does not just arise out of nowhere—it follows hostile, competitive verbal acts" (Wilmot and Hocker, 2001, p. 153).

Recommendations

Effective Supervisors and Managers

Three of the top five reasons that employees consider "very important" in deciding to accept a job with their current employer are open communications, management quality, and their supervisor (Galinsky, et al., p. 17). A woman needs these the most when she perceives that she is the victim of sexual harassment. As reported in Table 1, 21% of the claimants originally reported the sexual harassment to their immediate supervisor, and another 13% reported it to a higher manager. How might job satisfaction and motivation suffer when these very supervisors and managers fail to protect her from retaliation? Job satisfaction and performance are even more negatively affected when her supervisor (37%) or a higher manager (20%) is the source of the harassment, as reported by the claimants in the authors' study.

The authors recommend that organizations invest training dollars in frontline supervisors and managers. Traditionally, supervisors are selected because they have demonstrated task proficiency, and therefore, can supervise others performing the same tasks (Taylor, 1903, p. 1394). Organizations should also consider a candidate's people skills. For example, has the candidate demonstrated a willingness to stand up to discrimination in the workplace? Or, has the candidate participated in discriminatory remarks, jokes, harassment, assignments, hiring, or other discriminatory decisions? Will the candidate model the behaviors that will help to prevent sexual harassment, retaliation, and other forms of discrimination?

Policies and Procedures

"The court makes it clear that if employers have adopted clear policies regarding harassment and discrimination—if employers have clearly informed and trained employees and managers and has published clear policies—and if the employer can show it is taking clear and decisive action to address issues, then the employer is likely to be able to establish in many cases a sufficient affirmative defense to win on liability or to minimize or avoid punitive damages" (Pagano, 2000, p. 1230). Policies should tell potential complainants the procedure for reporting discrimination. There should be more than one person or office to whom a claimant can turn, in case the immediate supervisor is the cause. Next, all complaints of discrimination should be taken seriously and should be investigated by those with special training or experience. Colleen McHugh, a management attorney, suggests that an employer should investigate a complaint "with the assumption that a judge and a jury will be evaluating everything you have done" (Pagano, 2000, p. 1230).

Talk with Female Employees Who Report Sexual Harassment

Reassure a complainant there will be no retaliation for reporting sexual harassment and instruct her to report any perceptions of retaliation. Periodically engage her in conversation to confirm that she is not experiencing anything out of the ordinary in her job. For example, following a report of sexual harassment, a waitress' table assignments were changed, she was required to work longer hours, and to regularly stay until closing (*Reed v. Cracker Barrel Old Country Stores, Inc.*, 2000). Talking with the waitress following her initial report might have alerted managers or human resources that adverse actions were occurring, giving them a chance to avoid the subsequent retaliation charge.

Prior Review of Discipline and Termination Decisions
Smart employers will have a procedure for rapid review of any disciplinary decisions concerning a sexual harassment claimant—before they are implemented. Additionally, the authors recommend that employers use an internal review procedure before any termination decision is made. So often top managers watch the "front door" to make sure that women are being recruited and hired but fail to monitor what occurs after they are hired, including terminations.

Plan for the Iceberg—Not Just the Tip
Sexual harassment is much more prevalent than reported incidents would indicate. A *New York Times* poll found 40% of women reported experiencing sexual harassment. The *National Law Journal* reported that 60% of female attorneys said they experienced sexual harassment. *Parade Magazine's* survey found that 70% of women who served in the military, and 50% of women who worked in congressional offices on Capitol Hill had been sexually harassed. Yet, only about 5% of sexual harassment in the workplace is ever reported (Bennett-Alexander and Hartman, 2001, p. 254). Fears of being sexually harassed (or being accused of sexual harassment) are among Americans' top fears (*USA Weekend*, 1997, p. 5). This perspective should motivate greater efforts to prevent both acts and perceptions of harassment and retaliation. (See Greenlaw and Kohl, 1996.)

Insurance
Recently, some insurers have offered Employment Practices Liability Insurance (EPLI). Typical coverage includes discrimination, wrongful discharge, harassment, negligent retention and supervision, and hiring. Some include retaliation and tort claims. There is no standard for EPLI policies, so employers must shop carefully. Further, some insurers have very specific requirements, such as the employer having anti-harassment policies and human resource professionals (Newhouse, 1999, pp. 14–16).

Conclusion
Nearly half (47%) of women who complain of sexual harassment report that they subsequently experience retaliation. We believe that sexual harassment claimants essentially want two things. First, they want to be

"heard," meaning they want to be understood and valued (Edelman and Crain, 1993, p. 3). Second, if there is sexual harassment, they want it to stop. "Unfortunately, in the legal arena, there is no such thing as taking 'no action.' Doing nothing can have deep legal consequences." (McAfee, Deadrick, Kezman, 1999, p. 79) Victims are not looking for special treatment or money. As shown in Table 1, they do not want to file a formal complaint, and they do not want to go to court. Primarily, they want to do their job free of harassment.

The authors' 15-year study examined retaliation claims filed by 129 women who previously reported sexual harassment. Good news was that in 98% of the claims, sexual harassment ceased after the women reported it. The bad news was that in 98% of the claims, the women reported experiencing other forms of retaliatory adverse actions. A number of variables were examined and discussed, including the source of harassment, harmful retaliatory actions, and the quickness of women to file retaliation claims. While not all claims are meritorious, all are important symptoms of organizational ailments. They are real to the individual and have negative effects on that employee, co-workers, supervisors, and the employer—regardless of who ultimately prevails (Galinsky, et al., 1993, p. 31). These negative effects reduce job satisfaction, promote turnover, and ultimately increase costs. Only top executives, managers, and supervisors can create an environment free of sexual harassment and retaliation.

Acknowledgements
The authors gratefully acknowledge the cooperation and encouragement that they have received from the Ohio Civil Rights Commission, Pastor Aaron Wheeler, Sr., Chairman, G. Michael Payton, Executive Director, and Alan J. Clark, Director of IT and Workforce Design, and the assistance of Jennifer Davis, Graduate Research Assistant. This article is part of *The Ohio Employment Discrimination Studies* that have been supported by grants from Wright State University and the Raj Soin College of Business and created in partnership with the Ohio Civil Rights Commission. The authors are solely responsible for the contents.

REFERENCES
Bennett-Alexander, D. D., & Hartman, L. P. (2001). *Employment law for business* (3rd ed.). New York: Irwin McGraw-Hill.

Bland, T., & Stalcup, S. (2001, Spring). Managing harassment. *Human Resource Management, 40* (1), 51–61.

Bureau of National Affairs, Inc. (2000, January 24). *Human Resources Report* (Washington, D.C.) *18* (3), 62.

Bureau of National Affairs, Inc. (2001, December 10). *Human Resources Report* (Washington, D.C.) *19* (48), 1324.

Burger v. Central Apartment Management Inc., 168 F.3d 875 (5th Cir. 1999).

Burlington Industries, Inc. v. Ellerth, 524 U.S. 742 (1998).

Chertkova v. Connecticut General Life Ins. Co., 92 F.3d 81, 89 (2d Cir. 1996).

Cruz, S. (2001, February 11). Jury awards ex-Seagate employee $2 million. *Star Tribune* (Minneapolis), p. 1D.

Dickerson, L. (2002, January 27). Western Region Director of Human Resources, Delta Air Lines, Inc. Personal communication.

Dubois, C., Faley, R., Kustis, G., & Knapp, D. (1999, Summer). Perceptions of organizational responses to formal sexual harassment complaints. *Journal of Managerial Issues, 11* (2), 202.

Durham Life Insurance Co. v. Evans. 166 F.3d 139 (3d Cir. 1999).

Edelman, J., & Crain, M. B. (1993). *The Tao of negotiation.* New York: Harper Collins Publishers.

Faragher v. City of Boca Raton, 118 S. Ct. 2275 (1998).

Feminist Majority Foundation. 911 for women: Sexual harassment resources. Retrieved May 3, 2001, from http://www.feminist.org/911/harasswhatdo.html.

Galinsky, E., Bond, J., & Friedman, D. (1993). *The national study of the changing workforce.* New York: Families and Work Institute.

Greenlaw, P., & Kohl, J. (1996, Winter). Creative thinking and sexual harassment. *Advanced Management Journal, 61* (1), 1–10.

Harris v. Forklift Sys., Inc., 510 U.S. 17, 20–1 (1993).

Kandel, W. L. (1999, Summer). Retaliation: Growing riskier than 'discrimination.' *Employee Relations Law Journal, 25* (1), 5–27.

McAfee, R. B., Deadrick, D. L., & Kezman, S. W. (1999, March–April). Workplace harassment: Employees v customers. *Business Horizons,* 79–84.

Mancini v. Teaneck, No. BER-L-5491-96 (N.J. Super. Ct. 2000).

McNairn v. Sullivan, 929 F.2d 974 (4th Cir. 1991).

Meritor Savings Bank, FSB v. Vinson, 477 US 57 (1986).

Morris v. Oldham County Fiscal Court, 201 F.3d 784 (6th Cir. 2000).

Newhouse, D. (1999, May/June). Are you covered? *Ohio Lawyer,* 14–16.

Ohio Bureau of Employment Services. (1998, November). Ohio job outlook to 2006, Labor Market Information Division (Columbus, Ohio).

Ohio Civil Rights Commission. Historical Data 1992–99 (Columbus, Ohio).

Oppel, Jr., R. (1999, September 29). Retaliation lawsuits: A treacherous slope. *The New York Times,* p. C8.

Pagano, S. (2000, November 13). Preventive policies, prompt investigations important to minimizing employers' liability. *Human Resources Report, 8* (44), 1230.

Reed v. Cracker Barrel Old Country Stores, Inc., No. 2-99-002 (M.D. Tenn. 2000).

Samborn, R. (1990, July). Many Americans find bias at work. *The National Law Journal,* 16.

Taylor, F. (1903). Shop management. *Transactions of the American Society of Mechanical Engineers, XXIV.* New York: Published by the Society.

Title VII of the Civil Rights Act of 1964, 42 U.S.C.A. Sec. 2000e *et seq.* (West 2000).

U.S. Department of Labor. (2000, December 8). News. Washington, D.C.: Bureau of Labor Statistics.

U.S. Equal Employment Opportunity Commission. (Charge statistics from the U.S. EEOC FY 1992 through 2000. Retrieved May 3, 2001 from http://www.eeoc.gov/stats/charges.html.

USA Weekend. (1997, August 22). Exclusive poll: What Americans fear, p. 5.

Wille v. Hunkar Laboratories, Inc., 132 Ohio App. 3d 92 (1998).

Wilmot, W., & Hocker, J. (2001). *Interpersonal conflict* (6th ed.). New York: McGraw-Hill.

Worth v. Tyler, et. al., No. 00-2414 (7th Cir. 2001)

Dr. Wendt, who teaches human resource courses, previously worked in the human resources area in the private sector. Dr. Slonaker, who teaches business law and human resource courses, formerly practiced law. The authors are co-developers of The Ohio Employment Discrimination Studies, *the most complete database of employment discrimination in the U.S.; both served as labor arbitrators for the Federal Mediation and Conciliation Service.*

From *SAM Advanced Management Journal,* Autumn 2002, pp. 49-57. Copyright © 2002 by Society for Advancement of Management. Reprinted by permission.

The under-reported impact of age discrimination and its threat to business vitality

Abstract The Age Discrimination in Employment Act (ADEA, 29 USCA, 621) is credited with helping eliminate many blatant forms of age discrimination in employment. For example, before the ADEA was enacted 37 years ago, it was common for employment ads to list age limitations, indicating people over 40 need not apply. Across the board, mandatory retirement policies went unchallenged. Despite advancements in these areas since the founding of the Age Discrimination in Employment Act, it remains to be seen whether the ADEA has completed the job it set out to do. Has it proven to be an effective tool for eliminating the unreasonable prejudices that make it difficult for older workers to achieve their full potential? Has it provided adequate compensation for victims of discrimination? The following article takes a snapshot of the current work environment to gain a perspective. Based on extensive interviews with academics, employment lawyers, advocates for older workers, and older workers themselves, it reveals the need for reforms. It finds that, in a legal environment slanted toward employers, older workers continue to face bias and stereotyping, that most victims of discrimination are not made whole, and that society's lack of concern for this type of discrimination may prove more costly in the future as employers look more to older workers to fill projected workforce gaps.

Robert J. Grossman
School of Management, Marist College, Poughkeepsie, NY 12601, United States

1. The ADEA: an introduction

Thirty-seven years ago, Congress passed the Age Discrimination in Employment Act (ADEA) which makes it illegal for an employer or union to discharge, refuse to hire, or otherwise discriminate on the basis of age. Looking back, it is easy to forget the overt discrimination faced by older workers at the time. It was common for employment ads prior to 1967 to list age limitations, indicating people over 40 need not apply. Mandatory retirement policies, applicable to almost everyone but Supreme Court Justices, went unchallenged. Although some states had antidiscrimination laws on the books, they were not enforced, giving employers a free hand to discriminate. But now, almost four decades later, it bears asking whether the ADEA has done more than address age discrimination in its most blatant manifestations. Is it really effective in preventing age bias? Has it been successful in "alleviating serious economic and psychological suffering of persons between the ages of 40 and 65 caused by unreasonable prejudice?" (Polstorff v. Fletcher (1978, ND Ala) 452 F Supp 17). What role has it played in transforming the U.S. culture to be more accepting and appreciative of older workers?

2. Stereotypes survive

Despite protestations to the contrary, there seems to be little indication that attitudes have changed significantly since the enactment of the ADEA. The notion that older people have had their day and should make room for the next generation continues to be deeply ingrained. "We think maybe it's okay because it's an economic issue, not a civil rights issue," says Laurie McCann, Senior Attorney for AARP in Washington, D.C. "Until we view it as just as wrong and serious, we may not be making the inroads we need to address the intractable, subtle discrimination that is so pervasive. I don't think employers want to discriminate; they don't hate older workers. It's the stereotypes. They may not even know they harbor these biases, but they do" (McCann, 2003).

Such attitudes are evident in the case of Ann Klingert, a 64-year-old resident of the Bronx, who recalled with astonishment the public response to an article in a local New York City newspaper regarding an EEOC lawsuit she had filed. Klingert filed with the EEOC after she was fired by Woolworths and then prohibited from applying for newly created part-time jobs which were filled mostly by student applicants. "When the lawsuit was reported in a local New York City newspaper, *Our Town*, people were outraged," she said. "They wrote letters to the editor saying things like 'why don't you just retire and just take your social security and go away'" (Klingert, 2003).

Although most employers are sensitive to the issues of sexism and racism, "the idea that you cannot teach an old dog new tricks does not seem to carry the same taboo status in society and the workplace," says Todd Maurer, Associate Professor of Industrial-Organization Psychology at the Georgia Institute of Technology. Maurer says that generalizing is dangerous in the range of older workers; perhaps even more so than in other categories. "One size does not fit all," he says. "There can be older individuals who are both interested and able when it comes to learning. Research has found large differences within older groups in things like training performance and in abilities like memory and reaction time" (Maurer, 2003). However, too often, as in the case of Maryland resident Mort Beres, employers are influenced more by stereotypes than skills or experience. When Beres, then in his late 50s, lost his job, the prior owner of small businesses and successful salesman in the auto parts manufacturing industry knew he had skills that should have been in demand, yet he was turned away repeatedly. Any offers he did receive were salaried at much less than he had earned previously, and the positions were often demeaning in nature. Beres held on as long as he could, but admitted that, out of desperation, he took some sketchy jobs. "You take every jerky job you can get just to have some income; some of them make you nauseous" (Beres, 2003).

Eventually, Beres found his niche, working as a trainer and sales rep for Irvine, California-based BDS Marketing. Assigned to the Canon account at a Best Buy in Maryland, his job was to help store personnel sell Canon printers, for which he was paid a salary plus commission. After 5 years on the job, working with a series of regional supervisors, at age 67, Beres achieved a noteworthy record by helping his store become one of the top five in the territory. However, when a new supervisor took over, Beres's star began to fall. "He'd call me and make stupid comments about my age, like 'you're too old, I think it's time for a change." Finally, Beres got the axe. When he asked why he had been fired, the manager told him, "I'm not telling you and I don't have to." Beres recalls hanging up and thinking about what had happened. "I got angry; really angry. It was a little, unimportant job, but they had no right to treat me that way." *(BDS Marketing's Vice President for Human Resources, Jeffrey Sopko, refused to comment specifically but denied Beres's version of what happened and claimed that there were other reasons for Beres's dismissal).*

Beres's plight is not uncommon, yet society appears to be less outraged at age bias than other types of discrimination. "It seems more politically correct to discriminate against older people," says Mindy Farber, Managing Partner at Farber Taylor, LL.C. in Rockville, Maryland. Farber recalls hiring a new associate for the firm who was in her mid-fifties. "It was shocking. I was surprised how open people were about talking about the wisdom of my decision in light of her age. If I had hired an African American, they would have been silent. Here they told me straight out that I had made a mistake" (Farber, 2003).

3. Perspective: how older workers see it

From their perspectives, older workers see little evidence that they are competing on a level playing field. Sixty-seven percent of employed workers aged 45 to 74 surveyed by AARP in 2003's *Staying Ahead of the Curve* said that age discrimination is a fact of life in the workplace (AARP, 2003) (Table 1). This percentage is even higher among African Americans and Hispanics, both at 72%. Age is viewed as so critical to employees that respondents listed it, along with education, as more important in how workers are treated than are gender, race, sexual orientation or religion. Sixty percent said they believe that older workers are the first to go when employers make cuts.

A 2002 Conference Board survey of 1,600 workers aged 50 and older found that 31 percent of workers intending to retire within five years said they would stay on if given more responsibilities. Twenty-five percent said they were leaving because they were being held back or marginalized because of their age (The Conference Board, 2002). Linda Barrington, Labor Economist at The Conference Board, says the high percentage of dissatisfied workers is cause for concern. "It's twice as big as I might have expected," she says. Perceptions, of course, are not necessarily reality, but Barrington says that does not matter. "Perceptions affect the way you work; if you're feeling undervalued, that discouragement will affect your work. Is it perception or reality? Either way, it has to be dealt with" (Barrington, 2003).

It also bears noting that far fewer of the respondents said they have suffered personally from ageism. About 9% say

Table 1. Workers over age 45 reporting presence of age discrimination ($n=1500$)

Do not Know	2%
No	31%
Yes	67%

Source: AARP Work and Careers Study Summary (2002).

they believe they have been passed up for a promotion because of their age, 6% said they were fired or laid off because of age, 5% said they were passed up for a raise because of age, and 15% attributed their not being hired for a job to their age. However, the survey only queried current workers and did not include individuals in the same age category who were no longer in the workforce.

4. Advantage: employers

Compared to its sister statutes aimed at race, religion, gender, and disability, the ADEA offers less protection. Court interpretations have proven to be less rigorous and more employer-friendly, ceding to employers the right to make bonafide business decisions even when age is linked. In practice, instead of preventing discrimination, the law serves as a roadmap for employers, enabling all but the obtuse to avoid liability and shield all but the most egregious ageist actions from public scrutiny.

Under the ADEA, if there is a valid reason for an action, it is considered acceptable if age happens to be an accompanying factor. "If you can show you would have done it anyway, you're off the hook," says Harlan Miller, an employment attorney with Miller, Billips, and Ates (Miller et al., 2003) in Atlanta, Georgia. As a result, it is almost impossible to catch a crafty employer discriminating. "I can always get around it if I'm smart. Only idiots get nailed," agrees David Neumark, a nationally recognized expert on the ADEA and Senior Fellow at the Public Policy Institute of California in San Francisco (Neumark, 2003).

Employers are not infallible, however, and they still mess up on occasion. Often when they do, it is because of retaliation: reacting badly to an employee whose initial complaint does not rise above the threshold set by the ADEA. "We tell them to go back and complain about their treatment," says James Rubin, an employment attorney with Farber Taylor. "Then the employer does something really bad. It's not the original claim; it's the reprisal. You can bring an action based on the reprisal even if the original claim is weak" (Rubin, 2003).

Employers also get caught when the rationale for their business decision falls apart. "Typically, the employer comes in with some kind of bogus selection process that says they're trying to keep the most competent," Miller says. "Gulfstream Aerospace's decision to cut from 200 to 230 of its nearly 2000 management-level employees during the period from August through December, 2000, is a case in point. Gulfstream had a rating device based on flexibility and adaptability; code words for old or young…and not subject to any kind of objective analysis. Our analysis showed a complete correlation between age and those factors" (Miller et al., 2003).

On the other hand, if it is legitimate, an employer's business argument can carry the day. "Is it discrimination to fire someone if it is based on economic foundations?"

asks Bob Smith, Professor of Labor Economics, ILR at Cornell University in Ithaca, New York. "It's not a slam dunk that they've been mistreated just because they say they are. There may be good reasons why they're singled out. They often are paid too much and have shorter time to work, making them a poorer investment. Why should I expect my employer to invest more in me than someone who will be there longer? Just because they complain, doesn't mean there's discrimination" (Smith, 2003).

5. Avoiding scrutiny

Employers' incentives to avoid litigation are compelling from financial and public relations perspectives. Generally, when employers get wind that employees are disgruntled and plan to complain or sue, they move to settle by enticing them into retirement with incentives and buyouts, awarded contingent upon their agreeing to confidentiality clauses that prevent discussion of the situation.

The Older Worker Protection Act clarified for employers what they need to say and do when they reach termination agreements with workers. The act requires an employer to give workers 21 days to consider a buyout proposal, to advise them of their right to seek legal counsel, and even to rescind the agreement 10 days after the fact if they have a change of heart. Until recently, a properly negotiated settlement would foreclose a former employee from further litigation. Now, there has been at least one case where the EEOC has been able to sue on behalf of workers who previously signed releases.

In a typical settlement, the employer denies discrimination, attributing the settlement to "business decisions." In a recent survey by Jury Verdict Research, plaintiffs' lawyers estimated that 84% of their clients' claims were settled, while defense lawyers reported 79% (Jury Verdict Research, 2002).

Often, employees are relieved to accept the face-saving exit. In reality, their options are meager. They are scared if they are still working or owed pensions, and lack money if they have been terminated. According to Howard Eglit, Professor of Law at Chicago-Kent College, it costs, on average, about $50,000 for a lawyer if cases go beyond early negotiations with an employer. Most attorneys will not handle such cases on a contingent basis because they know the chances of winning are slim. Employers, on average, can count on spending $100,000 in legal fees from the time a complaint is filed with the EEOC until trial (Eglit, 2003).

Although the amounts paid to ease workers into retirement or silence complaints are private, high-profile EEOC settlements reveal just how well workers actually do when they press the ADEA to the limit. In March, 2003, the EEOC announced a class action settlement with Gulfstream Aerospace, owned by General Dynamics, on behalf of 66 workers for $2.1 million dollars, an average of approximately $33,000 for each manager the EEOC claimed had been wrongfully terminated. Ninety-three percent, many of whom may never work again full-time, accepted the deal and faded away, careers in shambles.

As meager as the settlement proved to be, there would not have been a case without former Gulfstream Aerospace manager Eddie Cosper of Rincon, Georgia. His role suggests that, behind every major class action, there is an activist who serves as a catalyst in pushing for remediation.

When Gulfstream Aerospace cut more than 200 of its nearly 2000 management employees, most of whom worked in Savannah, it had not bargained on Cosper's pride and persistence. Aged 54 and with the company for 28 years, Eddie Cosper was proud, professional, and still moving up. "I was still ambitious. Every time I put out a fire, I kept getting a promotion," he recalls. However, Cosper reached a dead-end when General Dynamics took over the company in 1999. His seasoning suddenly turned sour. "The VP would tell me, 'You're like father time; you've been here forever. Wouldn't you like to retire and do something different?'" Soon Cosper found himself reassigned to nights, with responsibility for 40 people instead of the 300 he usually had. Then, 30 days later, he was terminated. "My performance reviews were all above average," he says. "I had the highest ranking of all the four managers in my category." How did he feel when his career went up in smoke? "It's like a burning sensation in your gut. You say, why me? I put my whole life into something and it's been taken away for no reason. In the beginning, I felt sorry for myself, then I got angry. I did the numbers and realized I wasn't the only older person being targeted. So I started talking to others and built a network and database." Communication was key. "People who don't have that network have no clue," he says. "Every Joe Blow could get hit cold and not know what's happening. Probably half the people in our suit were along for the ride. If I hadn't reached them, they wouldn't have realized they were discriminated against and would have gotten nothing."

The EEOC's settlement with Footlocker is another example of a remedy that fell short of the mark. When the company settled with 764 former Woolworth employees, the complainants, mostly low-paid hourly workers, walked off with an average of $4,000 per person. Overall, the $3.4 million was a small price to pay for a 40,000-worker retailing giant like Footlocker (EEOC, 2002). A tougher question is why they let the matter fester as long as they did. Many companies buy themselves out of trouble, right or wrong (Eglit, 2003). According to Jury Verdict Research, the median settlement for age cases from 1994 to 2000 was $65,000, $5,000 higher than the median reported for all types of discrimination, age included (Jury Verdict Research, 2002).

6. Complaints grow

If age discrimination had been decreasing throughout the years, even allowing for more people being aware of their right to complain and more older workers proving their

mettle to those who question their ability, it would be reasonable to expect the number of complaints to be trending down. Instead, there are more cases. The EEOC logged 19,921 age discrimination complaints in 2002, an increase of 14.5% from the previous year and accounting for 23.6% of all discrimination claims filed with the agency (U.S. Equal Employment Opportunity Commission, ADEA Charges, 2003).

Some EEOC complainants, either uncertain as to the true basis of the discrimination against them or believing there is more than one basis, file multiple charges. EEOC data reveals that instances of ADEA claimants who alleged an additional type of discrimination are declining. The data suggests there is no move on the part of complainants making their case on some other basis of discrimination (gender, race, religion, or national origin) to add age simply in order to bolster the case, even though it was not thought to be the primary or even substantial basis of the discrimination. For the 3-year period of 1997 to 1999, an average of 17.9% of ADEA claimants made an additional charge. From 2000 to 2003, the average percentage dropped to 15.8%. In addition, states Farber, private lawyers are seeing similar increases in age complaints in proportion to race, gender, and disability (Farber, 2003).

7. Profile

Overall, the majority of claimants tend to be white males, 55 and older at the middle management level. However, the number of women filing claims has doubled in the last few years, a trend that Eglit estimates will continue as women earn more, hold more desirable jobs, and can afford to hire counsel. "The ADEA offers two essential remedies: reinstatement and back pay. If you weren't getting much and your job wasn't worth much, why sue? Now, even with the glass ceiling, women have good jobs and can afford to hire an attorney and sue" (Eglit, 2003) (Table 2).

In 2002, 53% of the cases related to job loss; wrongful discharge, 8,741 and involuntary layoff, 1,463. "They're easier to prove," Eglit says. "If you've been working at a place for 20 years, look around and see five other people

Table 2. Age bias charge filings with EEOC nationwide by age group of charging parties fiscal years 1999–2002[a]

Fiscal year/age	Age 40–49	Age 50–59	Age 60–69
1999	3367	5949	3526
2000	3941	6620	4609
2001	3779	7584	4603
2002	4219	8455	5686

Source: EEOC, Office of Communications and Legislative Affairs (2003).

[a] Note: the three age ranges combined do not comprise the total ADEA charge filings with the EEOC per year, as a small number of charges which are not listed are filed by individuals 70 and older.

Table 3. Age discrimination charge filings with EEOC nationwide fiscal years 1998–2002

Year[a]	FY 1998	FY 1999	FY 2000	FY 2001	FY 2002
Discharge	7054	6733	6851	7376	8741
Harassment	1871	1758	1966	2146	2311
Hiring	1953	1647	1990	3116	4889
Layoff	1036	1149	1128	1107	1810
Promotion	1547	1590	1666	1623	1463
Terms of Employment	2510	2357	2610	3440	3181
TOTAL	15,191	14,141	16,008	17,405	19,921

Source: EEOC, Office of Communications and Legislative Affairs (2003).
[a] Fiscal years run from October 1 through September 30.

fired, you have a case." (Eglit, 2003) It happened in the Woolworth's/Footlocker case, says Michelle Le-Moal-Grey, EEOC attorney. "When they were fired, workers spoke by phone and began to see a pattern forming in their store and beyond" (LeMoal-Grey, 2003).

Of the EEOC claimants between ages 40 and 69, 46% were in their fifties, 31% in their 60s and 23% in their 40s. About 25% of claims were based on failure to hire, an increase of 200% since 1999. As these cases are harder to prove and because damages are limited, it is difficult to find a private attorney for hire without having to pay up-front. "If you're not hired, how do you know what the reason was? It's not so easy to figure it out," Eglit observes (Eglit, 2003).

About 12% of the claimants cited harassment; antagonism, or intimidation, creating a hostile work environment; an increase of 31.5% since 1999. Constructive discharge would be an example, says Dorothy Stubblebine, an expert witness for both plaintiffs and defendants, and President of DJS Associates in Mantua, New Jersey. "Tyically, the older person is pushed out by giving him a really hard time. He's given the worst assignments 'til he can't take it any more" (Stubblebine, 2003) (Table 3).

8. Chances for success

Whatever the claim and whomever the claimant, few gamblers would bet on the probability of prevailing in an ADEA suit. EEOC data reveals that for most claimants, the filing with the EEOC is a dead-end. Last year, of the cases before it, the agency found "reasonable cause" only 4.3% of the time, "no reasonable cause" 52% of the time, and closed cases for "administrative" reasons 33.5% of the time. Only 6.5% of cases were eventually settled. In contrast, for claimants charging all types of discrimination, age included, the EEOC found reasonable cause 7.2% of the time, found no reasonable cause 59.3% of the time, and closed cases for administrative reasons 26% of the time (U.S. Equal Employment Opportunity Commission, 2003) (Tables 4 and Table 5).

For plaintiffs who win at trial, damages are legally limited to reinstatement, loss of pay, or, where there is a finding of willful discrimination, double the lost salary. In contrast, race and gender plaintiffs have the opportunity to be awarded more lucrative punitive damages. "Why shouldn't someone who's old be compensated for pain and suffering just like someone who's fired for their religion, race, or gender?" Miller asks. "There's nothing worse than, after 30 years' service, to be fired at 58" (Miller et al., 2003).

The solution for many attorneys is to bypass the ADEA and, where possible, sue under local or state statutes. "Everybody tries to stay out of Federal Court," Farber says. "Plaintiffs get their audience but they lose before they can get to a jury. It's so bad that a fellow attorney once told me that if I went to Federal Court when there were other options available, I would be guilty of malpractice." Farber says a plaintiff's chances to reach a jury brighten considerably in state or local courts. Virtually everyone on a jury can identify with the plight of an older worker. "Everybody on the jury is getting older and has a mother and father" (Farber, 2003).

If they get to a state or federal jury, Jury Verdict Research in its study, *Employment Practice Liability: Jury Award Trends and Statistics,* reports a 78% success rate overall for age cases in 2000. In Federal District Courts, from 1994 to 2000, the median verdict was $269,350, tops for all types of discrimination. However, the chances of plaintiffs getting there with the EEOC in their corner are limited. The Office of General counsel states that during the 5-year period from 1997 to 2001, the EEOC filed 205 lawsuits based on the ADEA, leaving plaintiffs who push ahead with claims the EEOC determines are without merit with the risk and expense of proceeding toward litigation on their own (Office of General Counsel, 2002). Jury Verdict Research indicates that the median verdict for more numerous privately initiated state cases was about the same (Jury Verdict Research, 2002).

Table 4.   EEOC resolution of ADEA claims fiscal years 1998–2002

	FY 1998	FY 1999	FY 2000	FY 2001	FY 2002
Total ADEA Claims	15,191.	14,141	16,008	17,405	19,921
Settlements (%)	4.7	5.3	7.9	6.6	6.5
Withdrawals with benefits (%)	3.6	3.7	3.8	3.6	3.6
Administrative closures (%)	26.1	23.3	22.0	26.1	33.5
No reasonable cause (%)	61.7	59.4	58.0	55.3	52.1
Reasonable cause (%)	3.9	8.3	8.2	8.2	4.3

Source: EEOC, Office of Research, Information, and Planning (2003).

Table 5.   EEOC resolution of all discrimination claims fiscal years 1998–2002

	FY 1998	FY 1999	FY 2000	FY 2001	FY 2002
Total Claims	79,591	77,444	79,896	80,840	84,442
Settlements (%)	4.6	6.2	8.5	8.1	8.8
Withdrawals with benefits (%)	3.2	3.7	4.0	4.1	4
Administrative closures (%)	26.7	24.1	20.5	20.7	20.6
No reasonable cause (%)	60.9	59.5	58.3	57.2	59.3
Reasonable cause (%)	4.6	6.6	8.8	9.9	7.2

Source: EEOC, Office of Research, Information, and Planning (2003).

9. Justification

Critics point out that there may be valid reasons for determining that older workers are less desirable employees. There is no question that technological changes have significantly altered the way we work, especially in white-collar jobs, explains Camille Olson, Chair of the Labor and Employment Practice Group, Seyfeith Shaw, in Chicago, Illinois. "Persons in their 20s and 30s who are comfortable with technology are more responsive and more adaptable to change. Can people in their 40s and 50s without this background feel that they belong in the workplace? You feel that time has passed you by. Does that affect your motivation, your ability to do things? It does" (Olson, 2003).

"A lot of people who think they've been screwed over have it wrong," agrees AARP's McCann. "Though I'm an advocate, I'd be the first to admit that when someone gets fired or doesn't get promoted, they yell foul. An age discrimination claim is the last resort for older white males. "If you're a 55 year old male who's lost your $70,000 job, what do you do? The odds of finding any job, let alone a comparable job, are slim, so you fight" (McCann, 2003).

"If a person has lost a step or two and doesn't project or have the kind of energy to move forward, the fact that he isn't promoted may show that's where he belongs," explains Ed King, Executive Director of the National Senior Citizen Law Center, a former EEOC mediator in Hawaii. "The question is whether the employer is stereotyping or it is legitimate" (King, 2003).

It is undeniable that age has its advantages; plusses that advocates for older workers tend to downplay. "They do better; get paid more. Their employment rates are high and they get cared for in retirement," Neumark observes. However, he says, it is not all roses and caviar for workers in their 50s or 60s. Once they are unemployed, it is hard for them to find work. They are out of work longer, have difficulty finding jobs with comparable responsibilities and wages, and tend to become disheartened and "retire" (Neumark, 2003).

Adding to the debate is the difference of opinion as to whether age 40, which seemed appropriate in the 1960s, should still be the turning point for providing a person with ADEA coverage. Some experts ask, Why not? There needs to be some beginning point, and 40 is reasonable. Others disagree, arguing that 45 or 50 are more realistic ages when discriminatory treatment is most likely to occur. Whatever the threshold, it has been clear until recently that all people from 40 on up had to be treated similarly, but no longer.

In an opinion issued February 24, 2004, on General Dynamics Land Systems versus Cline, the U.S. Supreme Court held that the ADEA does not prevent an employer from favoring older employees over younger employees. The court upheld an agreement between General Dynamics and the United Auto Workers union that provided for continued retirement health benefits for employees then over 50 years of age but eliminated that benefit for all other employees. The plaintiffs were between the ages of 40 and 50, and were denied the benefits available only to workers over the age of 50.

10. No special treatment

Should an employer invest extra to help support an older worker? Offer more and different training? Provide less stressful assignments? The issue, Olson says, is whether under the ADEA an employer needs to take affirmative efforts to assist individuals who do not naturally have the same skills, while at the same time paying them more. Clearly, Olson says, the law never contemplated affirmative action. The law is there only to make sure older people are not treated differently (Olson, 2003).

"The ADEA is about equal treatment, not about preferential treatment," agrees Lynn Clemens, Attorney, Office of Legal Counsel at EEOC. "There are no affirmative obligations on the employer's part. That notion goes against the act." Regardless, advocates are making the case that there are other benefits to be gained by retaining older workers anyway, although they are paid more and have fewer skills. Olson says she does not buy it unless there is a compelling business case. "The issue is whether you need to invest in targeted training, making older workers more productive because you need them to stick around" (Olson, 2003).

11. Call for action

Meanwhile, William Rothwell, Professor of Workforce Education and Development at Penn State University observes that Bureau of Labor Statistics projections show that while 13 percent of American workers today are 55 and older, that figure will increase to 20% by the year 2015. At the same time, the nation is expected to experience a drop in the percentage of younger workers aged 25 to 44.

With this information in mind, Rothwell says the current economic slump is the calm before the storm. When the economy turns around and there is more demand for products and services, the worker shortage will be the number one issue. "Employers in the U.S. will be forced to go back to their retiree base and deploy it more effectively

than ever before. If we can't get labor from anywhere else, we'll look to the most obvious population who knows everything about our business" (Rothwell, 2003).

Unless we get serious about addressing the stereotypes and focus on reducing the alienation that older workers feel, these workers, as well as retirees, may be unreceptive and unprepared to step up when the market finally swings in their favor. Reforming the ADEA is the first step. To better combat age discrimination, we must move quickly to put more teeth into the law. If we do not, when we go to the well, it may just be dry.

References

AARP. (2003). *Staying ahead of the curve.*

Barrington, L. (2003 April 10). Telephone interview. New York, NY.

Beres M. (2003 April 22). Telephone interview. Rockville, MD.

EEOC Press Release. (2002, November 15). *EEOC settles major age bias suit; foot locker to pay $3.5 million to former Woolworth employees.*

Eglit, H. (2003 April 10). Telephone interview. Chicago, IL.

Farber, M. (2003 April 21). Telephone interview. Rockville, MD.

Jury Verdict Research. (2002). *Employment practice liability verdicts and settlements: Jury award trends and statistics.*

King, E. (2003 April 15). Telephone interview. Washington, D.C.

Klingert, A. (2003 May 1). Telephone interview. Bronx, NY.

LeMoal-Grey, M. (2003 April 28). Telephone interview. New York, NY.

Maurer, T. (2003 April 17). Telephone interview. Atlanta, GA.

McCann, L. (2003 April 17). Telephone interview. Washington, D.C.

Miller, Harlan, Principal, Miller, Billips & Ates. (2003). Atlanta, GA. (18 April).

Neumark, D. (2003 April 8). Telephone interview. San Francisco, CA.

Office of General Counsel. (2002, August 13). The U.S. Equal Employment Opportunity Commission. *Study of the litigation program fiscal years 1997–2001*, Table 2.

Olson, C. (2003 April 10). Telephone interview. Chicago, IL.

Rothwell, W. (2003 April 17). Telephone interview. University Park, PA.

Rubin, J. (2003 April 21). Telephone interview. Rockville, MD.

Smith, B. (2003 April 17). Telephone interview. Ithaca, NY.

Stubblebine, D. (2003 April 4). Telephone interview. Mantua, NJ.

The Age Discrimination in Employment Act of 1967. (1967). Pub. L. 90–202, as amended. Volume 29 of the United States Code beginning at section 621.

The Conference Board. (2002). *Voices of experience: Mature workers in the future workplace.*

United States Supreme Court. (2004, February 24). *General Dynamics Land Systems*, v. cline, No. 02–1080.

U.S. Equal Employment Opportunity Commission. (2003). *Age discrimination in employment act charges*, FY 1992-FY 2002.

From *Business Horizons*, 2005, 48, pp. 71-78. Copyright © 2005 by Elsevier Science Ltd. Reprinted by permission.

Where Are the Women?

Not in the corner office, even after all these years.
Not now. Maybe not ever. So what happened?

By Linda Tischler

Brenda Barnes knows what it takes to hold a top job in a highly competitive company. As president and chief executive of the North American arm of PepsiCo, a place famous for its driven culture, she set a fast pace. Rising at 3:30 a.m., she would blitz through a few hours of work before waking her three children at 7 a.m., then dash off to the office, where she'd grind through an 11- or 12-hour day crammed with meetings, conference calls, and strategy sessions. Then it was home for dinner and bedtime stories before finishing up with phone calls or email before falling into bed. Three nights a week, she was on the road. Seven times, she relocated when the company wanted her in another office. For eight years, she and her husband lived in separate cities, trying valiantly to juggle both job demands and those of marriage and family. And all the effort was paying off: Barnes was widely considered a real contender for the top job at PepsiCo when CEO Roger Enrico retired. But in September 1997, at 43, she suddenly stepped down when the toll of the job began, in her mind, to outstrip its rewards.

Unlike some women executives who have famously dropped out, Barnes did not go home to write her memoirs or devote herself to charity and her children's soccer schedules. She just chose what is for her, a less demanding path: She serves on the board of six major companies, among them Sears, Avon, and The New York Times; she's taught at the Kellogg School of Management, and stepped in as interim president of Starwood Hotels and Resorts in early 2000. Although she's had many offers for other enticing jobs, she's unwilling to consider another gig at the top. "When you talk about those big jobs, those CEO jobs, you just have to give them your life," she says. "You can't alter them to make them accommodate women any better than men. It's just the way it is."

Six years after the fact, Barnes is still happy with her decision. But she admits that despite her considerable post-PepsiCo accomplishments, she's been forever branded as The Woman Who Walked Away. Small wonder. In a workplace where women CEOs of major companies are so scarce that they can be identified, like rock stars, by first name only—Carly and Martha and Andrea and Oprah and Meg—it's shocking each time a contender to join their august ranks steps down.

It wasn't supposed to turn out this way. By 2004, after three decades of the women's movement, when business schools annually graduate thousands of qualified young women, when the managerial pipeline is stuffed with capable, talented female candidates for senior positions, why are there still so few women at the top?

In part, the answer probably still lies in lingering bias in the system. Most women interviewed for this story say that overt discrimination is rare; still, the executive suites of most major corporations remain largely boys' clubs. Catalyst, the women's business group, blames the gap on the fact that women often choose staff jobs, such as marketing and human resources, while senior executives are disproportionately plucked from the ranks of those with line jobs, where a manager can have critical profit-and-loss responsibility. Others fault the workplace itself, saying corporations don't do enough to accommodate women's often more-significant family responsibilities.

All those things are true. But there may be a simpler—and in many ways more disturbing—reason that women remain so underrepresented in the corner office: For the most part, men just compete harder than women. They put in more hours. They're more willing to relocate. They're more comfortable putting work ahead of personal commitments. And they just want the top job more.

Let's be clear: Many, many individual women work at least as hard as men. Many even harder. But in the aggregate, statistics show, they work less, and as long as that remains true, it means women's chances of reaching parity in the corner office will remain remote. Those top jobs have become all-consuming: In today's markets, being CEO is a global, 24-hour-a-day job. You have to, as Barnes says, give it your life. Since women tend to experience work-life conflicts more viscerally than their male peers, they're less likely to be willing to do that. And at the upper reaches of corporate hierarchy, where the pyramid narrows sharply and the game becomes winner-take-all, a moment's hesitation—one important stint in the Beijing office that a woman doesn't take because of a sick child or an unhappy husband—means the odds get a little worse for her and a little better for the guy down the hall.

And let's be clear, too, that we're not talking about women who simply opt out. They've been getting a lot of press and sparking a lot of controversy lately—those young women investment bankers and lawyers who are quitting to become stay-at-home moms (and, really, they're still using those MBA skills on the board of the PTA). That's still a fringe phenomenon affecting relatively few privileged women with high-earning husbands.

Many, many women work at least as hard as men. But the disturbing truth is that *most* women don't compete as hard as *most* men.

No, the women we're talking about here work, want to work, want to continue to work. But not the way you have to work in order to reach the top these days. That's the conclusion that Marta Cabrera finally came to four years ago. By 1999, Cabrera was a vice president at JP Morgan Chase, one of only two women on the emerging-markets trading desk. True, the demands were steep—12-hour days were the norm. But the rewards, at the peak of the boom, were pretty delicious, too: an apartment in Manhattan, a country home, and the chance for an artist husband to pursue his vocation.

Not only was Cabrera at the top of her game, but she had, by all measures, managed to pull off the career woman's trifecta—a great job, a happy marriage, and two beautiful, healthy little daughters—all by age 43. But in October of that year, as she watched her second-grader blow out the candles on her birthday cake, Cabrera had an unsettling realization: She didn't know her own child as well as most of the friends and family who had gathered to celebrate the big event. "I realized seven years had gone by, and I had only seen her and my five-year-old on weekends," she says. No first words. No school plays. No class trips. "I asked myself, 'What the hell am I doing?'" Then she thought about her job. To walk away would mean upheaval. Plus, there was a principal at stake: "I had the sense I was letting down my sex by leaving."

It took another seven months, and much soul-searching, to reach her decision, but in May of 2000, Cabrera quit. Like Barnes, she did not opt out. No 180-degree turn to a life of play dates or book groups. No reconnecting with her inner tennis-lady. Instead, she became executive director of EMPower, a microlender in developing countries. Facing a precipitous drop in income, she and her husband rented out their Manhattan place and moved to the country. Now she works from home three days a week, and is in the city the other two, an arrangement that lets her do rewarding work and still spend time with her kids.

And what did her experience at JP Morgan Chase teach her? "There's a different quality of what men give up versus what women give up" when they attempt to reconcile the demands of a senior job with those of family responsibilities. "The sacrifices for women are deeper, and you must weigh them very consciously if you want to continue," she says. "I didn't want to be the biggest, best, greatest. I didn't feel compelled to be number one."

She was doing what women often do: scaling back on work for the sake of family, with a clear-eyed realization that she was, simultaneously, torpedoing her chances for a climb up the ladder. What's more, she didn't care. It's a choice women often make, with no particular social sanctions. For some, it's even an easy and convenient way to escape an increasingly hostile and unfriendly work world, an out that men simply don't have. But it's also the reason women may continue to be stalled at the lower rungs in organizations and men may continue to rule.

Charles A. O'Reilly III, professor of organizational behavior at Stanford Graduate School of Business, has been particularly interested in women's career attainment and the problem of why, despite notable gains in education and experience, women are still so woefully underrepresented in the top ranks of American corporations. In 1986, he began following a group of University of California, Berkeley MBAs to see if he could isolate those qualities that led to a corner office. His conclusion is starkly simple: Success in a corporation is less a function of gender discrimination than of how hard a person chooses to compete. And the folks who tend to compete the hardest are generally the stereotypical manly men.

Think of careers as a tournament, he says. In the final rounds, players are usually matched pretty equally for ability. At that point, what differentiates winners from losers is effort—how many backhands a tennis player hits in practice, how many calls a sales rep is willing to make. "From an organization's perspective," he says, "those most likely to be promoted are those who both have the skills and are willing to put in the effort. Individuals who are more loyal, work longer hours, and are willing to sacrifice for the organization are the ones who will be rewarded."

Today's women, he says, are equal to their male counterparts in education, experience, and skill. But when it's a painful choice between the client crisis and the birthday party, the long road trip and the middle schooler who needs attention, the employee most likely to put company over family is the traditional, work-oriented male. Interestingly, the women in O'Reilly's study reported levels of career satisfaction equal to those of their more-driven male peers, even if they were not as outwardly successful. In other words, women may be happier not gunning for power positions if it means they can work less and have a life.

After seven years with the big computer leasing company Comdisco, Diane Brandt, for example, left to form a small investment banking firm with two male colleagues. She decided to leave that job, too, when the growing business's hours increased and the moment approached when her only son would leave for college. Recently, she launched a small company, Captio Corp., that offers budgeting and scheduling tools for college students. "I've made choices all through my career," she says from her home in Menlo Park, California, days before heading to Germany to visit her son, who's studying abroad. "I've not pursued promotions in the same way I might have had I not been trying to balance other things in my life. It's been important to me to be home and have dinner with my family. You can't do that and move up the ladder."

Beth Johnson, a banker in Chicago, describes herself as "very ambitious," and says she has always loved business: the deal making, the challenge, the money. But she still remembers when her son was a baby, calculating the percentage of his waking hours that she could, if all went well, actually be present. "I doubt that his father was doing the same," she says dryly.

Recently, when the fund she was managing fell victim to the stock market, she decided to take some time off to help her son negotiate his final precollege year. Her brief attempt to be a "golf lady" didn't pan out. "I just couldn't do it," she confesses. She's now mulling various job offers. While she will go back to work, she knows there are sacrifices she and most other women are less willing to make than men. "People may get mad if I describe women as a group," she says, "but we are relational family beings. We do not have a world that's structured to understand that, to know how to account for it, and I don't know that we ever will."

There's a scene near the end of the 1956 movie *The Man in the Gray Flannel Suit* in which Fredric March, who plays a work-obsessed network president, turns on Gregory Peck, who plays his conflicted speechwriter. "Big, successful companies just aren't built by men like you, nine-to-five and home and family," March says. "They're built by men like me, who give everything they've got to it, who live it body and soul." March, of course, has sacrificed his own happiness to the company, a choice that Peck is unwilling to make.

Not much has changed in 48 years, says David Nadler chairman of Mercer Delta Consulting. Nadler, who advises senior managers, says that because top jobs are typically crushing in their demands, they require a certain psychological type. "I've worked closely with 20 CEOs over the past two decades—both men and women," he says. "All of them are characterized by being driven. Something in them says, 'This is important enough for me to make the sacrifices that are inherent with the job.'"

Certainly, there are women willing and able to compete by those draconian rules. A 2003 Catalyst study found that more than half of the women not yet in senior

average hours worked per week

	Men	Women
Lawyers*	47.5	43.0
Management, business, and financial operations occupations*	46.1	40.4
Doctors (primary care physicians)**	50.0	45.0

Sources: *Bureau of Labor Statistics, Current Population Survey 1989 (lawyers), 2002 (business); ** *Medical Economics*, 2003

leadership positions within their companies aspired to be there (although 26% also said they weren't interested.) And some women want nothing less than a full-throttle engagement with work. "I don't seek balance. I want to work, work, work," Ann Livermore, executive vice president of Hewlett-Packard, told Karin Kauffmann and Peggy Baskin for their book, *Beyond Superwoman* (Carmel, 2003). Or as Kim Perdikou, CIO of Juniper Networks, told the author, "I'm wired 24 hours a day."

But such decisions continue to have consequences that thoughtful women are all too aware of. Asked what advice she would give to a daughter, M.R.C. Greenwood, chancellor of the University of California at Santa Cruz, warns, "Remember that the assumption that one's marriage will remain intact as she moves up is a false assumption. You really have to know yourself and know it will take a toll."

Conversely, there are plenty of men who would like the option to lead saner lives. A recent study of 101 senior human-resource managers found that men are also starting to leave big companies to try to improve the balance between their home lives and their worklives. Still, many more men than women seem to get an adrenaline rush from work that allows them to log long hours, zoom through time zones, and multitask savagely.

As a nation, we now clock more time on the job than any other worker on earth, some 500 hours a year more than the Germans, and 250 hours per year more than the British. But the true heavy lifters in the productivity parade are American men. According to the Bureau of Labor Statistics, men work longer hours in every industry, including those traditionally identified with women. In financial fields, for example, men worked an average of 43.8 hours per week compared with women's 38.7; in management, it was men 47.2, women 39.4; in educational services, men 39.2, women 36.0; in health services, men 43.1, women 36.4.

The same pattern holds true in professions whose elaborate hazing rituals are designed to separate potential chiefs from the rest of the tribe. Young associates at prestigious law firms, for example, often put in 60- to 70-hour weeks for long periods of time. "It's almost an intentional hurdle placed by the firms to weed out those who simply don't have the drive and ambition to do it," says Stanford

University economist Edward Lazear. "It may be excessive, but you select out a very elite few, and those are the ones who make it to partner and make very high salaries."

▼Women are as scarce in the upper reaches of the legal profession as they are in top-tier corporate offices. According to the National Directory of Legal Employers and Catalyst, women represented only 15.6% of law partners nationwide and 13.7% of the general counsels of Fortune 500 companies in 2000 (even though they have accounted for at least 40% of enrollments at top law schools since 1985 and nearly 50% since 2000). Women in these firms say personal or family responsibilities are the top barrier to advancement, with 71% of women in law firms reporting difficulty juggling work and family, and 66% of women in corporate legal departments citing the same struggle.

Depending on the specialty, medical practices can be similarly pitiless. Among doctors, women work 45 hours per week compared with men's 50. Male physicians also see 117 patients per week, compared with 97 for women. And, as with the law, the top rungs of the medical ladder are populated by men who are willing to put work ahead of family, with women doctors concentrated in lower-paying positions in hospitals, HMOs, and group practices.

Meanwhile, back in the executive suite, researchers at Catalyst say some progress has been made. Women made up 15.7% of corporate officers in the *Fortune* 500 in 2002, up from 8.7% in 1995. In 2003, they held 13.6% of board seats in the same companies, up from 12.4% in 2001. But their actual numbers, compared to the percentage of women in the workforce, are still minuscule. This has occasioned much hand-wringing among business organizations and women's advocacy groups. But maybe all that angst is misplaced.

"The higher up you go, jobs get greedier and greedier," says one researcher. "The idea that if only employers would reshape jobs they would be perfectly easy for women to do is just nonsense."

"When a woman gets near the top, she starts asking herself the most intelligent questions," says Warren Farrell, the San Diego-based author of *The Myth of Male Power* (Simon & Schuster, 1993). The fact that few women make it to the very top is a measure of women's power, not powerlessness, he maintains. "Women haven't learned to get their love by being president of a company," he says. "They've learned they can get respect and love in a variety of different ways—from being a good parent, from being a top executive, or a combination of both." Free of the ego needs driving male colleagues, they're likelier to weigh the trade-offs and opt for saner lives.

Mary Lou Quinlan has seen the view from the top and decided it's not worth the price. In 1998, she stepped down as CEO of the big advertising agency N.W. Ayer when she realized she was no longer enjoying a life that had no room for weekends, vacations, or, often, sleep. She went on to found Just Ask a Woman, a New York-based consulting firm that helps big companies build business with women. The decision wasn't driven by guilt over giving family responsibilities short shrift (Quinlan has no children); it was about calibrating the value of work in one's life. Quinlan thinks that calculation is different for women. "The reason a lot of women aren't shooting for the corner office is that they've seen it up close, and it's not a pretty scene," she says. "It's not about talent, dedication, experience, or the ability to take the heat. Women simply say, 'I just don't like that kitchen.'"

Catalyst and other groups have suggested that the heat can be turned down in that kitchen—that senior jobs can be changed to allow for more flexibility and balance, which will in turn help more women to the top of the heap. Catherine Hakim thinks that is bunk. Hakim, a sociologist at the London School of Economics, has been investigating the attitudes toward work among European men and women, and says reengineering jobs won't solve two fundamental problems: First, many women have decidedly mixed feelings about working, and second, top jobs by their very nature will remain relentlessly demanding. In surveys of 4,700 workers in Britain and Spain, she found that only 20% of women considered themselves "work-centered"—they made their careers a primary focus of their lives, and said they would work even if they didn't have to. By contrast, 55% of men said they focused primarily on work. Given those numbers, most top jobs will continue to go to men, she says, despite the equal-opportunity movement and the contraceptive revolution.

That's because work-centered employees are most likely to leap to the tasks that are most disruptive to life. "That's the bottom line, and it's not a sexist bottom line," Hakim says. "Of course, you could say jobs shouldn't be so greedy, but in practice, the higher up you go, by and large, jobs get greedier and greedier. The idea that some people have, that if only employers would reshape jobs they would be perfectly easy for women to do, is just nonsense."

Not surprisingly, the suggestion that the fault lies with women and not with the system drives many women nuts. Margaret Heffernan, the outspoken former CEO of the CMGI company iCast, for example, goes apoplectic at what she calls the perennial "little black dress stories"—tales of how various women have stepped down from their big jobs to spend more time with their families. Their implicit message, she says, is that women can't cut it and would prefer to be back in the kitchen. Indeed, she says, the conclusion we should be drawing is, "Another company just f****d up big time. Another company just trained somebody and made them incredibly skilled and still couldn't keep them."

Heffernan says the hordes of women refusing to play the career-advancement game aren't doing so because

percentage of workers in top jobs

	Men	Women
Lawyers (partner)*	84.4%	15.6%
Corporate officers in the *Fortune* 500**	84.3%	15.7%
Top-earning doctors**	93.4%	6.6%

Sources: *National Directory of Legal Employers, NALP 2000, and 2000 Catalyst Census of Women Corporate Officers and Top Earners; **2002 Catalyst; ***Medical Economics: cardiology, gastroenterology, and orthopedic surgery are top-earning specialities. Percentages of women in those fields calculated from data on doctors (by gender and specialty), from American Medical Association.

they can't hack it, but because they've lost faith in the institutions they've worked for and are tired of cultures driven by hairy-chested notions of how companies must function. Instead, they are founding businesses where they can use the experience in an environment they can better control. "They leave to create companies where they don't have to be the change agents, where they can start from scratch without the fights, without the baggage, and without the brawls," she says.

Stanford's Lazear so envisions a different scenario for women, one in which they wouldn't have to leave corporate America to get the jobs they want. Given the coming labor shortage, which the U.S. Department of Labor predicts will hit by 2010, companies maybe forced to redesign jobs to a talented workers. And that, combined with technology that will let people work from a variety of locations, he says, will make it possible for more women to reach the top. He predicts that 20% of CEOs in top organizations will be women in 15 to 20 years. But total parity? "I don't expect it ever to be equal—ever," he says.

Brenda Barnes thinks as today's business-school students gain power in companies, they will force changes that benefit men and women. When she taught at Kellogg, she asked her students to write a paper describing how they saw their careers playing out. "They were far more focused on having a life than my generation was," she says. "And it wasn't just a female thing. They grew up seeing their parents killing themselves and then being downsized despite their loyalty. How much this generation is willing to give to any enterprise is a totally different ballgame."

We can hope so. Unfortunately, her students' desire for more balance could be one more form of youthful idealism. As a 24-hour global economy makes it ever more difficult to turn off the office, it's hard to imagine a day when the promotions won't go to the worker who makes just a little more effort, who logs on just a little longer. Or to envision a day when there won't be plenty of contenders—maybe most of them men—who will be willing to do just that.

Linda Tischler (ltischler@fastcompany.com) is a FAST COMPANY senior writer.

From *Fast Company*, February 2004, pp. 52, 54-55, 58, 60. Copyright © 2004 by Fast Company (Gruner + Jahr USA). Reprinted by permission.

HOW CORPORATE AMERICA IS BETRAYING WOMEN

Forty years after sex discrimination became illegal, a huge gap in pay and promotions still yawns. Now angry women are suing their employers—and winning. How afraid should you be?

Betsy Morris

THE DELUGE BEGAN LAST MAY. THAT'S WHEN Boeing agreed to cough up as much as $72.5 million to settle a class-action lawsuit brought by female employees; they had asserted that the company paid them less than men and did not promote them as quickly. The next month, in June, a court ruled that a lawsuit charging Wal-Mart with discriminatory pay and promotion practices could proceed as a class action. In July, Morgan Stanley stunned a courtroom jam-packed with Wall Street women by announcing an 11th-hour $54 million settlement to a class-action suit that made similar allegations. Then, in August, an assistant store manager for Costco sued the retailer for denying her a promotion. Her lawyers have asked the court to allow that case, too, to proceed as a class action.

Just because a company is sued doesn't mean it's guilty, but the flood of sex-discrimination headlines is sobering. After all, didn't we get through this long ago? Don't men and women have a pretty level playing field? Aren't women paid basically the same amount as men for doing the same job? And don't women have an equal shot at getting promoted?

Not exactly. For most management jobs it's still not even close. And if men don't know it, women certainly do. They are bringing these cases, and winning big settlements, because it appears that the evidence is overwhelmingly on their side. Forty years after the Civil Rights Act made discrimination on the basis of sex illegal, studies show that women—virtually across all job categories—are still paid less for doing the very same job. And though women now hold about half of all managerial and professional positions, they account for only about 8% of executive vice presidents and above at FORTUNE 500 companies. "Everybody expected a lot more progress by now," says Ilene Lang, president of Catalyst, the research

firm that gathered the data. "There are so many women in the workplace. You just assumed this was a 20th-century battle, and by the 21st century it would be over."

Over a lifetime, the pay gap widens— determining, say, whose kid takes on a boatload of college debt.

Why the explosion in litigation now? Well, just as the economy went south, the market tanked, and stock options dried up, a critical mass of career women began reaching their 40s and 50s and 60s. And they are shouldering way more financial responsibility than ever before: About 62% of all working women are contributing half or more of their household income, according to an AFL-CIO survey of 800 working women earlier this year. A difference of several thousand dollars between a woman's entry-level salary and a man's may not have mattered much at the start of their careers, but over a lifetime, the gap widens—adding up to a world of difference in, say, which worker's kids will be burdened with a boatload of college debt.

Changes in civil rights legislation enacted in 1991 made it easier for women to do something about the problem. The changes allowed for jury trials and substantial compensatory and punitive damages against companies that discriminate by gender. Suddenly those cases became "incredibly lucrative," says one defense lawyer. "Companies settle them because they don't want to go to trial and look like a bigot in front of a jury." What's more, recent technological advances make it easy for plaintiffs lawyers to gather and analyze mountains of data across vast geographies and gather prospective class members. Women can join such cases with the click of a mouse.

> ## Employers are furious, says an employment lawyer. "They say, 'How dare you bite the hand that feeds you!'"

The threat of a sex-discrimination case has become one of corporate America's worst nightmares. When the Houston-based law firm Fulbright & Jaworski surveyed 300 company general counsels last summer, 62% said their biggest area of litigation exposure—and greatest fear—was employment lawsuits, which include suits claiming sex discrimination. The American Bar Association is currently advertising a seminar entitled *Wal-Mart Class Certification: How an Individual Can Take On a Whole Company—And How to Prevent It.* Many legal and human resources experts expect the number of suits to increase dramatically. Nobody knows exactly how costly they'll be to business. But a brief filed recently by the U.S. Chamber of Commerce litigation center in support of Wal-Mart's appeal of the class-action certification of its lawsuit estimates the damage somewhere in the "billions and billions of dollars." One analyst says the potential damages to Wal-Mart alone, if it is found liable, could amount to $2 billion to $4 billion—and that doesn't include what the company would probably have to pay to equalize skewed salaries.

The cases cast a cold, harsh glare on practices corporate America would prefer to keep out of the spotlight: the way it rewards its workers, determines entry-level salaries, makes promotion decisions, and divvies up merit raises. Traditionally those matters have been largely secret and, except in unionized shops, left to the discretion of management. Now, some say, a byproduct of the lawsuits will be to push companies, for defensive reasons if nothing else, to raise some salaries and put pressure on others at a time when extra money is especially hard to come by, and to adopt quotas (though nobody is using that word), making sure they have enough women in all ranks of management to keep them out of trouble. "I have heard corporate executives say, 'We are going to be forced to do this,'" says Robin Conrad, senior VP of the Chamber of Commerce litigation center, who is apoplectic about the implications of the Wal-Mart class action. "Then we're regimented, right? Like the federal government. It sort of flies in the face of a system of meritocracy in this country—that we work hard and should be rewarded for it."

It's no surprise that the lawsuits have stoked workplace distrust. "Employers are pissed. They say, 'How dare you bite the hand that feeds you!'" says Johnny Taylor Jr., an employment lawyer and chair of the Society of Human Resource Management. "Employees already mistrust employers. So each time a case reveals the secret that was never told, employees think, 'Aha! They really are paying men more than women.'" That breeds more cases, more inquiries, more management defensiveness. "The mindset of employers is: 'Which one of my employees is going to sue me tomorrow?'" says John Harper, a partner at Fulbright, which conducted the general counsel survey.

Forty years ago women's biggest battle was simply to get access to the workplace at all. That changed with the Civil Rights Act of 1964, which made it illegal for employers to discriminate on the basis of race, creed, and—as an afterthought—sex. (Congressman Howard Smith of Virginia slipped the gender provision into the bill in a last-ditch effort to kill it.) The law provided for the creation of the Equal Employment Opportunity Commission and required that any company with 100 employees or more file annual accounts of how many women and minorities it had at all levels of the organization.

In the 1970s the EEOC took on the automakers, oil companies, and AT&T—where, in 1971, only 1% of all but the lowliest supervisory jobs were held by women, according to the *New York Times,* even though the company ran on an army of female telephone operators. The big blue chip replied that the commission "failed to recognize that the primary reason the Bell System exists is to provide communications service to the American public, not merely to provide employment to all comers, regardless of ability." But two years and $70 million—plus in settlement costs later, the chastened company agreed to promote more women. It's no coincidence that two of the eight women running FORTUNE 500 companies today—Carly Fiorina at Hewlett-Packard and Pat Russo at Lucent—are both products of the enlightened post-lawsuit AT&T.

In the '80s the EEOC (headed by Clarence Thomas from 1982 to 1990) became less feisty; conservative Reagan-era courts all but eliminated the class-action suit and made it much tougher to prove sex discrimination. But under mounting pressure from civil-rights and women's groups, in 1991 Congress passed the law that made it easier for women to file sex discrimination charges. While the economy was booming, not much happened. But in the latter part of the decade, cases against big companies started trickling in: Mitsubishi settled for $34 million in 1996; Home Depot for $104.5 million in 1997; Merrill Lynch for an undisclosed sum in 1998; American Express for $42 million in 2002. And on to Boeing and Morgan Stanley in 2004.

When the courts pondered whether to give the green light to those class-action suits, they turned to statistical analysis. The courts have said that if data on pay or job levels indicate a pattern that is "two deviations from the norm," then there is a "legal inference" that discrimination is present—and a suit can proceed. The norm is generally defined as what might be expected, say, given the number of women in your workforce.

Calculating a standard deviation can be devilishly complex. But at Wal-Mart and Costco, allege the plaintiffs' lawyers, it wasn't hard to tell that the numbers were out of whack. At Wal-Mart women make up more than 72% of hourly workers and hold only about a third of the store manager jobs, according to charges in *Betty Dukes v. Wal-Mart*. A Wal-Mart spokesperson disputes that figure, saying that 60% of the company's associates are women and more than 40% of its managers and professionals are women—and adding that "Wal-Mart does not tolerate discrimination of any kind." At Costco women make up half the workforce but hold only one in six of the richly paying top management jobs, according to charges in *Ellis v. Costco*. (Costco denies the allegations; a spokesperson didn't return calls asking for comment.) Says the Chamber of Commerce's Conrad of the allegations: "You know how you can play around with statistics. You can make them say anything you want to say. There is an element of junk science in all of this."

To be sure, there are several reasons a pay gap between men and women exists. Biology is one: Working women who have children often take time off, delaying promotions. Preference is another: Some women choose professions that pay less or quit high-powered jobs when they don't seem worth it (see "Power: Do Women Really Want It?" on fortune.com). The oft-quoted Census Bureau statistic—women working full-time earn just 75 ½ cents for every dollar a man earns—doesn't correct for those things.

Women professors earn 75 cents to the male dollar, a study shows. Women lawyers and judges earn 69 cents.

So Hilary Lips, a Radford University psychology professor who has studied the pay gap, recently decided to conduct a study that *did* control for those factors. The study caused quite a stir. She found that only in jobs that pay $25,000 to $30,000 a year do men and women earn roughly the same. The further up the pay scale and the higher the education, the wider the earnings gap. Women psychologists earn 83 cents to the male dollar; women college professors earn 75 cents; women lawyers and judges earn 69 cents (see chart for more examples). Even in "women's industries," women consistently earn less than men: women elementary-school teachers earn 95 cents to the dollar; women bookkeepers earn 94 cents; women secretaries earn 84 cents. Says Lips: "It cannot be explained in any way except that people think that what men do is more important and more valuable than what women do."

A top financial services executive who has appeared on FORTUNE's list of the 50 Most Powerful Women in American Business will never forget the weekend she spent several years ago analyzing the pay scales of her direct reports. She was taken aback to find that time and again the men outearned the women. Her father was visiting her at the time, and she was sitting on the floor of her porch, surrounded by paper, on a Sunday. "Dad, look at this. How can this be?" she asked. "Well," her father replied to his daughter, "maybe women just don't work as hard."

But research shows that women—including women with children—are every bit as hardworking and ambitious as men. Earlier this year Catalyst conducted a survey of 950 top executives, both men and women. Fifty-five percent of the women said they wanted to be CEOs, almost exactly the same as the men. About as many mothers aspired to be CEOs as fathers. Women, like men, believed they needed to outperform expectations, take on big assignments, and work long hours and weekends to get ahead.

So what was the difference? Lack of operational experience accounted for some of it—36% of women in the Catalyst study said it was a problem for them, compared with 25% of men. But the far bigger reasons cited by the women were exclusion from informal networks—the boys' after-dinner drinks, the golf games, the men's clubs—and persistent stereotypes and assumptions their bosses made about their ambitions, their aspirations, and their abilities. Men, for example, may assume a woman wants to cut back or quit when she has a baby. But in a story two years ago on the growing number of women with stay-at-home husbands (see "Trophy Husbands" on fortune.com), FORTUNE found that when the playing field is level for women, they keep working. The decision about which spouse stays home with the kids has little to do with gender. The biggest determinants are serendipity, timing, and, most of all, which parent has the greatest earning potential.

Over a lifetime that earning potential can be significantly affected by seemingly small disparities in pay—Marc Bendick Jr., an economist and expert witness for the Wal-Mart plaintiffs, calls them "micro-inequities." Consider the stories from Boeing. Charles Phillips, a former training manager there, notes that when it was time to dole out annual raises, there was no way to rectify the fact that in the same job category men usually made the most, and women and minorities, the least. Even if you subtracted two percentage points from the 7% raise for the man making $100,000 and added two percentage points to the 7% raise for the deserving woman making $50,000, the man would get $5,000 to the woman's $4,500—widening the gap still further. "There was never enough money to fix the problem," Phillips says. "It was heart-wrenching to figure out how to bring the women up and at the same time not penalize the men. Eventually we just gave up."

If you start out too low, it's almost impossible to catch up. Consider Phillips' wife, Terri, 50. She wanted so badly to have a career at Boeing that she accepted a $13,000 job as a clerk there in 1989, figuring she'd work her way up. Soon after, she was making $27,000; by the time she was laid off in 2003, she was making about $70,000 as a senior manager in HR. At least that's what the org chart reflected, and that's what her boss called her. In payroll, though, she was a Level 1 employee (one step lower than a senior manager) and paid accordingly. When she tried to fix the discrepancy, higher-ups told her she didn't have enough direct reports to be called senior manager; another time she was

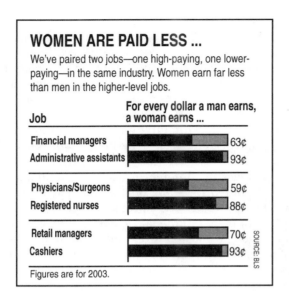

WOMEN ARE PAID LESS ...

We've paired two jobs—one high-paying, one lower-paying—in the same industry. Women earn far less than men in the higher-level jobs.

Job	For every dollar a man earns, a woman earns ...
Financial managers	63¢
Administrative assistants	93¢
Physicians/Surgeons	59¢
Registered nurses	88¢
Retail managers	70¢
Cashiers	93¢

Figures are for 2003.

SOURCE: BLS

told Boeing was afraid that if it corrected the problem, she might sue. When she left the company, she was still making $15,000 to $20,000 less than the other senior managers. She says she figures her gender cost her about $200,000 during her management years. A Boeing spokesperson says that the company "is firmly committed to an environment in which employees are treated fairly," adding that Boeing never admitted wrongdoing.

One explanation for women's lower pay and status is that women don't negotiate as deftly as men, according to economist Linda Babcock, co-author of the 2003 book *Women Don't Ask*. Studies show that women are much more likely to accept a salary offer without quibbling. A study of Carnegie Mellon graduate students reports that men were eight times more likely than women to negotiate an initial salary, resulting in starting pay an average of 7.4%, or $4,000, more than their female classmates.

Many companies argue, in effect, that failing to negotiate is the job candidate's problem, not theirs. "If [a woman] will work for $8 and a guy will hold out for $9," asks one defense lawyer, "is that discrimination, or is it market reality?" Retorts employment lawyer Taylor: "That's like saying, 'If I could hire children to work for $1 an hour in a coal mine, why wouldn't I?' There are a lot of decisions and practices we could justify on the basis of pure market analysis."

Wal-Mart has gotten religion. The retailer has made big changes to its employee practices that one analyst warns could drive up its operational costs. The far greater consequence, though, may be the standard it sets for the rest of corporate America. Recently Wal-Mart began to tie 15% of a manager's bonus (which can amount to 85% of salary for top executives) to meeting diversity goals. What that includes, explains the company's new chief diversity officer, Charlyn Jerrells Porter, is that the sex and race of those promoted closely reflect the percentages of those who apply. This is not a quota system, she says. Only the most quali-

fied are to be promoted. But if the company is recruiting effectively, "at some point, the stats take over" and the percentages naturally match up. Wal-Mart is also taking another bold, possibly precedent-setting step: It has begun to require that new hires with the same experience receive the same starting pay—no matter what their pay was in the past. (This applies to hourly hires; the company is reviewing changes for salaried types.) Says Porter: "We don't bring a female in at $6 and a male in at $7, where both have similar prior work experience, because if you do, then you have an immediate issue."

Of course, gender disparities in pay and promotions aren't always glaring. In companies where the problem is subtler, many people in power tend to think there is no problem. Remember the financial executive whose father thinks women don't work hard enough? Last year she was on a diversity committee made up of herself and white men. She says the men were convinced that women were getting promoted faster than men—until she got them the stats that showed otherwise. Laura Liswood, a senior adviser and former managing partner at Goldman Sachs and head of the Council of Women World Leaders at Harvard's Kennedy School, says that the groups that dominate (usually white men) "tend to think the system is meritocratic, that it works correctly, and that if changes are needed, they're minor." In the exact same organization, she says, women—and minorities—believe the opposite.

That disconnect between what working men and women think underlines the need for transparency about pay and promotions, according to a growing consensus among legal and HR experts and defense lawyers. So far, of course, transparency has been in very short supply. For example, Boeing spent four years and enough legal challenges to fill 31 feet of shelf space, according to the plaintiffs' lawyers, just to keep from having to reveal that it had conducted its own internal studies and found that it was indeed underpaying its women. Boeing settled one day before the start of the trial, which would have forced the company to share those details. Boeing agreed to settle "because it was in the best interests of the company, its employees, and shareholders, and enables the company to move forward and avoid the continued exposure and distraction of protracted litigation," says a spokesman.

One simple solution would be for the EEOC to make public the reams of employment data that companies are required to file every year. But it won't—because, according the 1964 Civil Rights Act, it can't, except in some cases. The EEOC can supply data to be used in certain lawsuits. It also sometimes shares information with academics for research on the condition that no companies be identified. Isn't the EEOC supposed to sniff out discrimination whenever it occurs? Yes, says EEOC chair Cari Dominguez, but it has limited resources. When it comes to litigation, it must pick its shots, such as the Morgan Stanley case settled last summer. "We can't boil the ocean," says Dominguez.

"If a woman will work for $8 and a guy will hold out for $9, asks one lawyer, "is that discrimination, or is it reality?"

For companies that may be vulnerable to sex-discrimination lawsuits, here's the prescription from one defense lawyer handling a high-profile case. Be much more formal in setting up systems for selection and promotion. Define the required competencies. Always post jobs. Be able to justify your selections either for hire or for promotion: Have a good explanation when pay and promotion don't look even-steven. Establish guidelines for how you set pay—both entry-level and raises—so that you are consistent. "Some companies do a good job and some do a terrible job in outlining expectations and being candid about performance," says the defense lawyer. "Make sure that women are getting the explanations and feedback they need to honestly understand the skills they need to advance." Finally, when you deny a woman a promotion, explain why. The companies in which all this is a closed and secret process are the ones that get into trouble.

Taking that kind of action may not eliminate the pay gap or suddenly catapult more women to the top. But at least it might lead to happier and more productive employees. And it would certainly reduce the risk of lawsuits from people like Terri Phillips, the former Boeing manager. "There wasn't anything in my nature to sue," she says. "That's not the way I was taught to deal with things." In the end, though, her reasoning for joining the class-action suit went according to an imprecise formula used by many of the other plaintiffs in sex-discrimination suits: "I don't want to hurt the company. But if companies continue to be run like this, it will end up hurting my granddaughters."

FEEDBACK *bmorris@fortunemail.com*

Reprinted from the January 10, 2005, pp. 64, 66-74 issue of *Fortune*, by Betsy Morris. Copyright © 2005 by Time, Inc. All rights reserved.

50 AND FIRED

Getting fired during your peak earning years has always been scary. You'd scramble for a few months, but you'd find something. Today it's different. Get fired and you can scramble for years—and still find nothing. Welcome to the cold new world of the prematurely, involuntarily retired.

John Helyar

When Zurich Financial let Bob Miller go in February 2003, he wasn't worried. His résumé was impeccable. He had 20 years of experience under his belt and plenty of references describing him as a high-energy, highly accomplished financial-services marketer. From his home base in Chicago, he'd racked up 100,000-plus frequent-flier miles a year, working a vast network of contacts among insurance agents and financial planners to generate millions of dollars of revenue for financial giants like CNA. Sure, it hurt to be let go. It always did. But he'd been there before—five times, in fact. "And in every situation I ended up in a better place," he says.

Two years later he's still looking for that better place. Or any place, for that matter. His wife, a real-estate agent, encourages him to think of his unemployment as a respite between sprints. "Enjoy your downtime," she says. "This is your reward." But since he doesn't know when or how it's going to end, it doesn't feel like one. Money isn't the problem: The Millers have neither kids nor mortgage payments (they paid cash for their downtown Chicago co-op). The problem is Miller's sense of uselessness, which is barely alleviated by his service on nonprofit boards and his occasional pro bono consulting gigs. Miller wants a real job, a sales job—something that gets him back to where his previously scheduled career left off.

So Miller, 55, whiles away the days making phone calls, doing a lot of reading, and mulling what the hell happened. He keeps up with fellow members of MENG (Marketing Executives Networking Group), a national organization of 1,300 members who once held top corporate marketing jobs and now, for the most part, don't. And he sees a lot of people out there like himself, trying desperately to keep up appearances: "You go into upscale suburbs, and what you see is lots of guys with laptops and cellphones, trying to look busy at the Starbucks."

Miller and his peers are members of a flourishing species: the involuntary retiree. When these anxious white-collar exiles aren't trying to look busy, they're going to support groups. Or worrying about the bills. Or reading advice columns about the résumé risk of fudging their age or

taking a sales job at Home Depot. Or hoping that a recent Supreme Court decision on age discrimination will give them some kind of legal recourse to sue the bastards who fired them. Or all of the above, in which case their internal terror alert has hit code red. After Linda Stalely, 52, lost her job as an information-technology manager at an Atlanta pharmaceutical company in 2003, she was all jagged nerves and pent-up energy. At five o'clock one morning toward the end of her 16 months between jobs, Staley's husband got up for a few minutes and came back only to find she'd made the bed. "What are you doing?" he asked, dumbfounded. She was, Staley now realizes, at the breaking point, feeling if she could just get her house in order, maybe her career would follow. "Your self-worth, your self-confidence just takes a nosedive," she says.

> "You go into upscale suburbs, and you see lots of guys with laptops and cellphones, **trying to look busy** at the Starbucks."

In 1991, long before Starbucks became the waiting lounge of the damned, FORTUNE published a story about unemployed executives. "It now takes the average laid-off executive more than eight months to find a new position," we wrote. What's changed over the intervening 14 years is that discarded executives of a certain age may never find that new position. As Bob Miller has discovered, a great many of those jobs simply aren't coming back. Even if you're gainfully employed, uncomfortable questions are probably swimming around in your mind. Are you vulnerable? What would you do if you got the sack and couldn't find a new gig? Plus, your pension has been gutted, your once-rich 401(k) appears to have been converted to Canadian dollars, you keep seeing newspaper headlines about cuts in Social Security. "Of course I'm scared," says a 57-year-old executive vice president of a trade association in New York City. (He didn't want his name used.) "I got laid off in 1989 and again in 1995, so it could happen. There's always an extra layer of stress. I'm always aware that the wheels could come off—and if they did, this time it would be serious."

For millions of people, it already is serious. Bruce Tulgan, a consultant on generational workplace issues, estimates that 3.5 million people between the ages of 40 and 58 vanished from the American workforce from 2001 to 2004. That's about 5% of all baby-boomers. The Bureau of Labor Statistics survey of "displaced workers" (people who lost their jobs for any reason other than for cause) offers a concise litany of the ways middle-aged people get screwed. In the most recent survey, which covers 2001 through 2003, 55- to 64-year-old displaced workers were less likely to find new jobs than 25- to 54-year-olds (57% vs. 69%), and more likely to drop out of the workforce altogether (20% vs. 11%). Of the lucky castoffs who get rehired, older folks take a much bigger pay cut than the young'uns. A 2003 survey by DBM, an outplacement firm, found that only 32% of workers over 57 earned the same or higher pay at their new employer, versus 42% of 38-to-56-year-olds (and 60% of 21-to-37-year-olds). Those data are all a year or two old, but the trends are continuing. "Older white-collar workers quickly become disenfranchised," says Mark Zandi, chief economist of Economy.com. "They have difficulty getting back into the job market, and when they do, their compensation is often significantly reduced."

How did life get so bad for pentagenarians? Age discrimination is part of the problem. Some employers assume that people north of 50 are marking time, or lacking in energy and up-to-date skills. In a survey of 428 HR managers by the Society for Human Resource Management, 53% said older workers "didn't keep up with technology," and 28% characterized them as "less flexible." That certainly rings true for Sam Horgan, 57, a veteran CFO who's spent a lot of time between jobs. A 30-ish job interviewer asked him, "Would you have trouble working with young bright people?" One job interviewer pointedly said to 58-year-old Russ Rakestraw, "You've got a lot of maturity." The former Louisville public administrator didn't take it as a compliment. "Why don't you come out and tell me I'm old?" he silently fumed. "Who's kidding who?"

But another reason is a profound, age-neutral economic transformation. These people had the bad luck to reach their peak earning years during an economic perfect storm. There was the recent recession and its aftermath, of course. Beyond that, there are some forces that have been building for a while, such as the bottom-line demands of Wall Street and the steady rise in health costs. Other pressures have developed more recently—for example, the proliferation of excellent, inexpensive engineers and systems analysts and whatnot in China and India. All those factors have hastened the demise of the safe, secure white-collar job.

"It's a true paradigm shift," says Karen Hochman, chair of the New York City chapter of MENG, all of whose 550 members have held top corporate jobs and half of whom are out of work. "You've got hundreds of thousands of obsolete professionals who can't find employment in positions where they've been successful. These are people living off

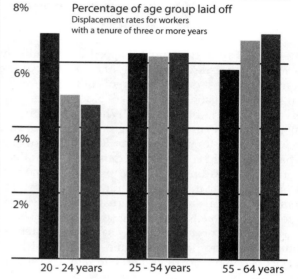

OLDER, WISER, LESS EMPLOYED

It used to be that young folks got laid off first when economic trouble hit. Now, older workers are the first overboard.

Percentage of age group laid off
Displacement rates for workers with a tenure of three or more years

retirement savings 15 years before they were supposed to retire. They don't know what they're going to do."

You don't see many overt signs of panic at gatherings of involuntary retirees. What's most noticeable at support groups and networking meetings is a kind of sustenance through euphemism. No one is unemployed; they're "in transition." But at a recent meeting of the Atlanta chapter of FENG (Financial Executives Networking Group), anxiety surfaces when a facilitator asks each of the dozen middle-aged men in the room to review their past week's job-hunting tactics and confess shortcomings. "Making the phone calls," says the first man on the hot seat. "I hate it." It's just not like middle-aged bean counters to hustle and cold-call. "I remember trying to make calls without standing on my tongue," says chapter vice president Grant Anderson, who landed a new CFO job in March after a year's hiatus. "But you have to get over it, because that's how you network and that's how I got my job. It was an unadvertised blue-plate special." And when you do finally get a job, Anderson advises, keep networking. Today, he says, "being employed is an illusion."

"Seasoned" hasn't always been a code word for "untouchable." When America was an agrarian society, elders were honored for their knowledge of the earth and kept involved in the family farm long into old age. But with the Industrial Revolution, far greater value was placed on speed and productivity. That was the province of younger people. The creation of Social Security in 1935 wasn't just a beneficent gesture to seniors. "From then on we had the cult of youth, the belief that each generation brought more and better and smarter young people than ever," says Ken Dychtwald, president of AgeWave, a demographic consulting firm in San Francisco. "We had to move the old people out."

And if you do finally get a job, one executive advises, keep networking. Today, he says, **"being employed is an illusion."**

By the 1990s the demand for speed and productivity dwarfed anything the industrialists of the 1890s could have imagined. The most devout adherents of the cult of youth are arguably in Silicon Valley, where older workers can be forgiven for feeling blacklisted. "When the [Internet] explosion happened, all these young people were drawn in who were willing to work for six or Running an organization based on truth requires—and demands—the taking of personal risks and time. The perception that time is limited, or the fear that the truth will hurt us, or hurt someone or something we care about, are perhaps the greatest obstacles to organizational truth telling.seven days a week for little pay and a lot of stock options," says Paul Kostek of the Institute of Electrical and Electronics Engineers-USA. "A lot of people who were older and had families said, 'Do I want to take this risk?'" Tech veterans who sat out the bubble bacchanalia couldn't regain positions even after sobriety returned, according to Kostek, a former president of the trade group and an engineer at Boeing. The bubble may have burst, but the industry's belief in the virtues of inexperienced, inexhaustible, inexpensive youth remained. "Technology has taken the position that if you've got gray hair, you're not up to speed," Kostek says. Think he's exaggerating? A November survey of 983 IEEE-USA members, median age 49, found that 42% were unemployed.

Old-economy stalwarts embraced youth almost as zealously in the 1990s. (They almost had to, lest they lose newly recruited MBAs to dot-coms.) General Electric made an obsession of identifying its hottest up-and-comers at tender ages. They were called "high pots," for high potential, and fast-tracked up the corporate ladder. Pity the middle-aged managers who occupied rungs along their route. They were called "blockers," and they had to be removed.

GE devised an elaborate system to weed out blockers and other laggards en masse. Employees were evaluated and placed in three tiers. The top 20% were ranked A— high pots and other hotshots. The middle 70% were solid if not spectacular B players. The bottom 10% were C's, and they were gone. Jack Welch called it "the vitality curve"; those on the receiving end called it "dead man's curve" or "rank and yank." (The generic HR term is "forced ranking.")

Welch being an icon and GE being a management paragon, this system came to be imitated by other companies wishing to ooze youth and vitality. One of them was Capital One, a Richmond financial services company, which promoted a "fun" culture to attract recent college graduates. The company once sent an HR delegation to Welch's Crotonville, N.Y., training facility to learn more about how GE Capital handled its high pots and blockers. According to an age-discrimination complaint, those lessons in the vitality-curve arts came in handy in 2001 when Capital One had to trim payroll by 10%. It used a Welchian system to pick who got the pink slips, according to the suit, and packed the C tier with older workers. That produced such anomalies as a 48-year-old analyst being canned by her 30-year-old boss, even though just seven months earlier she'd gotten a $2,000 raise for stellar performance. The lawsuit was settled out of court in 2003.

"You could tell what they were thinking: 'You've been strategic. But can you still **haul the wood**—and would you want to?'"

What's unusual about the Capital One case is that it was settled. There are tens of thousands of age-discrimination suits filed every year. The Equal Employment Opportunity Commission reported 17,837 age-discrimination cases in 2004, a 26% increase over 1999, though a decline from the peak of 19,921 in 2002. But people who file these complaints rarely win, or even get a cash settlement. In fact, simply avoiding a summary dismissal is an achievement. Less than 1% of the complaints are litigated by the short-staffed EEOC, and in 2004 just 15% of the cases closed by the agency yielded out-of-court settlements. (In the rare instances when age-discrimination cases do go to trial, they yield the highest median damages awards of all employer-discrimination categories, at $255,000, according to Jury Verdict Research of Horsham, Pa.)

The reason it's so hard for plaintiffs to win has to do with the courts' interpretation of the Age Discrimination Employment Act of 1967. While that law makes it illegal for employers to discriminate against people over 40, federal courts have generally come to require that plaintiffs show that the boss had conscious bias. In legalese the plaintiffs must have suffered "disparate treatment." Of course, an enormous number of employer practices can seem neutral on their face but have the effect of harming certain categories of workers—forced ranking being a prime example. This is called "disparate impact," which doesn't clear the bar for most federal judges. Janice Rogers Brown, a California supreme court justice and one of President Bush's controversial nominees to the federal bench, wrote in a 2004 opinion, "Discrimination based on age is *not*…like race and sex discrimination. It does not mark its victim with a 'stigma of inferiority and second-class citizenship'; it is the unavoidable consequence of that universal leveler: time."

But a recent Supreme Court decision may increase plaintiffs' leverage in age-discrimination lawsuits. The court reviewed a case brought by a group of older police officers against the city of Jackson, Miss. The Jackson Police Department's method of determining pay raises, they alleged, favored officers under 40 at the expense of those over 40. (Cops with less than five years' experience were getting most of the raises.) The officers argued that the process had a disparate impact on them. The Supreme Court

WHAT IF IT HAPPENS TO YOU?

Your boss no longer talks to you about the future. Upper management is obsessed with hacking at costs. Everyone getting promoted is younger than you. Sound familiar? If so, your job could be in jeopardy. (For more, take the quiz "How Safe Is Your Job?" at fortune.com/careers.) Here are a few do's and don'ts to help smooth the transition to your next position.

—Anne Fisher

DON'T ...

➤ **bother trying** to negotiate to stay. Says Andrea Waines, a managing director at outplacement powerhouse DBM: "By the time you're told about the decision to let you go, it's irreversible."

➤ **keep your job** loss a secret from family and friends. That will only deprive you of networking opportunities and emotional support, and it's a waste of energy.

➤ **fudge your résumé** to seem younger. "An interviewer will wonder what else you're trying to hide," says Dave Theobald, CEO of Netshare, an online executive job board. "And the résumé goes right in the trash." Ouch.

➤ **rely solely on** the Internet to find your next position. "During a long career, you've accumulated a vast range of great contacts," notes Jean Erickson Walker, author of a book called *The Age Advantage* (Berkeley Books, $12.95). "You need to start using that network."

DO ...

➤ **negotiate** a generous severance package. Federal law gives anyone over 40 the right to mull over a severance deal for 21 days before signing. (For a crash course in severance negotiation, see fortune.com/careers.)

➤ **realize that** it can easily take six to 18 months to find a new job. A financial advisor can help you stretch your severance pay and savings.

➤ **emphasize** to employers your unique experience and skills, says Alan Sklover, author of Fired, Downsized, or Laid Off. "As Tom Peters says, 'If you're not distinct, you're extinct.'"

➤ **job-hunt** in the area (marketing, finance) where you've been working. A study by Right Management Consultants shows that a third of unemployed execs last year took their skills to a new industry, but only 5% found work in a new functional role.

➤ **consider doing** "interim executive" work for a while, through recruiters like Spherion (spherion.com).

➤ **get in touch** with small companies, which are often eager to hire a grownup with a gray hair or two.

➤ **consider suing** if you feel you've been sacked just because of your age. "Age discrimination is a wrong that needs to be righted," says demographer and consultant Ken Dychtwald. "Too many people slink away quietly. That helps no one."

---

ruled against the plaintiffs, by a 5-3 vote. In his majority opinion Justice John Paul Stevens wrote that employers had to show an age-neutral "business necessity" for their actions—which was the case in Jackson, Miss., he found. But by shifting the burden of proof to employers, the court effectively lowered it for plaintiffs. People who think they've been discriminated against on the basis of age now need to show only disparate impact to get in the courthouse door. Laurie McCann, who filed an amicus brief as an attorney for the AARP, was delighted to see the court open the door to "disparate impact" cases. But she's concerned that the opening is no more than a crack. "It's still certainly not going to be an easy road," she says.

The problem for plaintiffs—and the reason most employer-side attorneys aren't overly worried about the Supreme Court ruling—is that there usually is a "business necessity" for dumping workers over 50. The business logic is cold but inescapable: Peter Cappelli, a professor at the Wharton School, says the executive recruiters he talks to don't want older people who have tenured compensation—not when they can hire younger, cheaper people. "It makes economic sense," he says. "It's just hard on the employees. They were hugely valuable yesterday, because they performed valuable specific skills. And now they're tossed on the general labor market, where they're suddenly not worth much."

A number of Cappelli's Wharton students are involuntary retirees looking to claw their way back into the game. They've been ousted from jobs—often good ones—and are in business school to retool their careers. If they're young enough at graduation time, maybe they'll find a nice new employer. If that doesn't work, there's a good chance they'll end up in a category you might call involuntary consultants. They might break out on their own, or they might try something they'd never imagined: temping. This longtime pink-collar niche is now teeming with white-collar staffing agencies like Tatum Partners, a high-end operation in Atlanta. Its 400 operatives are short-stay CFOs and CIOs.

One of Tatum's guns for hire is Sam Horgan, the 57-year-old serial CFO. After working for only two employers up to age 47, he went through six in nine years—and then the job offers stopped. "If I'm between jobs and I'm getting well into my 50s, I'm a leper with executive recruiters," he says. Tatum enabled Horgan to use his skills and make a good living, plus it delivered another benefit: He no longer needed to sit through condescending interviews conducted by 30-year-old twerps. More important, he enjoys his work again. "When I'm in partners meetings, I feel like I'm with peers," he says.

Other out-of-work executives have adopted a "multi—revenue stream" model. Gary Lafferty was fired as a senior vice president at Phillips Consumer Electronics North America in 2001 and couldn't interest any other company in that industry in hiring him. Then 51, Lafferty at first thought they would covet his experience, but "you could tell what they were thinking: 'You've been strategic, you've created the plans, but can you still haul the wood—and would you want to?'"

Employers aren't too worried about the court's ruling because there usually is a "business necessity" for **dumping workers over 50.**

He finally had an epiphany: Nobody wanted to buy him, but maybe they'd *rent* him. Lafferty started haunting trade shows, walking past the big fancy booths like those he once manned for Phillips and making his way back to the little ones in the halls' rear. He'd chat up the proprietors about their fledgling enterprises until he figured out the holes in their business plans. Then he'd offer his services as a consultant or interim executive to fill them. He garnered enough clients to make the rental scheme work—he now typically has three gigs going at a time. It's no cushy corporate job, but financially it's worked out well.

The U.S. economy, amazingly adaptable organism that it is, will eventually figure out a sustainable way to exploit the talent and experience of older workers. By the time today's 35-year-olds hit 55, they may enjoy some entirely new infrastructure of work. If they're lucky, it will be a flexible, meritocratic, and highly liquid labor market. Perhaps standard business practice will be to have a phased retirement in which people can ease out over a number of years, which would be a major change from the all-or-nothing, you're-retired-or-you're-not approach of today.

That kind of liquid labor market is in companies' own best interest. Why? Because they're staring at a major problem: There aren't enough people in the baby-bust cohort to replace all the aging boomers. From 2002 to 2012, the U.S. Bureau of Labor Statistics projects that the number of 35- to 44-year-olds in the labor force will decline by 3.8 million, while the number of available 55- to 64-year-olds will increase by 8.3 million. Ken Dychtwald, the demographer, figures that businesses must roughly double their number of older employees over the next decade. "The managers trying to move everybody in their 50s out the door are taking their companies off a demographic cliff," he says.

That forecast has already begun to come true in some sectors. Georgia Pacific has offered retention incentives to older research Ph.Ds. American oil companies face a serious shortage of petroleum engineers. (The average age in the profession is 50.) But a broader upsurge in demand for older workers is still several years away.

And when we do reach that demographic cliff, no one really knows what kind of jobs companies will be trying to fill. Will recruiters be looking for six-figure middle managers? Or low-five-figure home-health-care aides? And even if the former scenario is the case, who's to say whether all those exiles will want their old jobs back? It may be too late. Gary Lafferty, the former Phillips VP, misses the corporate life but dismisses his occasional fantasies of reentering it. After moving his family six times during his career, he needs only to remember the denouement: "This rock hits you between the eyes."

"You won't be in a high-rise corner office with five secretaries. But it's going to be **a more fun life,** because you're in charge."

John McDorman, an outplacement counselor in Dallas, says more and more of his clients are coming to the realization that they have to move on. McDorman encourages them to abandon their corporate job searches before they ever get started and start or buy their own business—provided they have the requisite cash, skills, and attitude. "You've got to be able to put your ego on the shelf," he says. "You won't be in a high-rise corner office with five secretaries. But it's going to be a more fun life, because you're in charge." McDorman wouldn't put it this way, but he's doing his part to ease people into their next life stage: involuntary entrepreneurship.

One of McDorman's clients is Tom McGoldrick, 54, who was hired as a CIO by Clarke American Checks in 1995 and thought he was doing a great job—the company won the U.S. Commerce Department's Baldrige award for manufacturing excellence in 2001. The next year, says McGoldrick, "I was told my services were no longer required."

He spent the next four months in his house, wallpapering and painting in a cold fury. Upon emerging, his first instinct was to find another CIO job. But McDorman talked him into checking out small businesses for sale, and McGoldrick threw himself into that, reviewing 400 of them in three months. Then serendipity and the family dog, Apollo, led him to The One. The 13-year-old Lab had an enlarged heart and had to be euthanized. McGoldrick had the beloved pet cremated, and got to talking with the crematorium's owner when he picked up Apollo's ashes. It turned out Paws In Heaven was for sale. McGoldrick bought the business, sank $1 million into it, and, along with his wife, immersed himself in its operation. He's improving cremation processes, developing a website, adding pet memorials, and "making more decisions in a day than a CEO makes in a month."

That's the attitude that McDorman likes to see. So does Lynn Guillory. Guillory is the HR chief of Foxworth-Galbraith Lumber in Dallas, and in his spare time he also runs a church jobs ministry. His message to members: Never confuse regaining leverage with returning to what they once knew. "My heart really goes out to the 55-year-olds who can't come to terms with what's happened to them," he says. "They are still looking for the old implied employment agreement: The company would take care of you; all you had to do was work hard." Forget the paycheck, he tells them. Your W-2 days are over. It's a 1099 world now.

FEEDBACK jhelyar@fortunemail.com
Research Associate **Brenda Moore Cherry**

Reprinted from the May 16, 2005, pp. 80, 83-84, 86, 88, 90 issue of *Fortune*, by John Helyar. Copyright © 2005 by Time, Inc. All rights reserved.

INTO THIN AIR

THESE PEOPLE LOST HIGH-TECH JOBS TO LOW-WAGE COUNTRIES. TRY TELL-ING *THEM* THAT OFFSHORING IS A GOOD THING IN THE LONG RUN.

By Jennifer Reingold
with Jena McGregor, Fiona Haley, Michael Prospero, and Carleen Hawn

It was Saddam Hussein who broke the news to Myra Bronstein that her job was *gone forever*.

A 48-year-old senior engineer at WatchMark Corp., a Bellevue, Washington, software company, Bronstein had spent three years running tests and hunting for bugs in the company's software. She knew that things weren't going so well at work; she'd been asked to pull 12- to 18-hour shifts frequently, her boss reiterating that the company's success depended on her "hard work and efforts." So when Bronstein received a brusque email in March 2003 instructing her to come to a 10 a.m. meeting in the boardroom the next day, she began to worry. "No way can that be good," she thought.

Looking for guidance, Bronstein logged on to a Yahoo users' group for WatchMark employees. And there it was, in a post written by "Saddam Hussein": "Here's what's going to happen tomorrow," Bronstein remembers the post read. "For all the quality assurance engineers reading this, your jobs are gone." At that very moment, it said, their replacements were on their way here from India for training. It listed their names, then concluded with sadistic glee: "Make sure on Monday you

welcome your replacements with open arms, because your company has chosen them over you."

Bronstein says she felt an icy chill. "It's a feeling of horror and panic because there's nothing to be done," she says. "Saddam Hussein's" intelligence proved absolutely right. The next morning, a Friday, Bronstein and some 60 others were told that they were being terminated. Some left immediately; others, like Bronstein, were asked to stay on for several weeks to train the new folks. "Our severance and unemployment were contingent on training the replacements," she says. "It was quite explicit." WatchMark's new CEO, John Hansen, says an additional payment beyond the severance was offered to those who stayed on.

And so the next week, Bronstein walked into a room to find her old coworkers on one side and the new group from India on the other. "It was like a sock hop where everyone's lined up against the wall blinking at each other," she says. "People were trying not to cry." In an attempt to lighten the mood, her boss said she would like to introduce the old

staff to the new staff, while the VP of engineering chimed in with familiar words. "We're depending on you to help this company succeed," he said. Bronstein spent the next four weeks training her two replacements who then went back to India—two people whose lives were suddenly bettered in exchange for one whose life had taken an unexpected turn for the worse.

Since leaving WatchMark (now called WatchMark-Comnitel), Bronstein, who made $76,500 plus bonus, has been out of work, making ends meet with unemployment and by cashing out her 401(k). With both of those gone, she's turned to selling her collection of antique women's compacts on eBay. "It's the difference between hopeful and hopeless," she says. "If you're just laid off, you can tell yourself that the economy swings back and forth, but if it's outsourced offshore, it ain't coming back. It still exists, but it just exists in another place. The IT industry in the United States has gone from being a very high-level, well-paying industry to being very low-paying sweatshop labor, and that's an inexorable trend."

Bronstein's story is increasingly common in a global economy where labor is crossing borders almost as freely as capital. Starting decades ago with low-skilled manufacturing jobs in basic industries, followed by textiles, cars, semiconductors, and now, services, the nimbleness of the world's economy has allowed us to reduce costs by moving production to wherever it's least expensive. The benefits to our economy—in increased productivity, lower prices, and greater demand for American products—are touted by corporate America as the only way to remain competitive. "This is the next iteration of the global economy," says Atul Vashistha, CEO of neoIT, an offshore advisory firm. "The story is what would happen to these companies if they did not go offshore."

Whether you believe such dislocations are ultimately good or bad, they're here, they're real, and they're happening at speeds and levels unforeseen just a few years ago. In December 2003, IBM decided to move the jobs of nearly 5,000 programmers to India and China. GE has moved much of its research and development overseas. Microsoft, Dell, American Express, and virtually every major multinational from Accenture to Yahoo has already offshored work or is considering doing so, with 40% of the Fortune 500 expected to have done so by the end of this year, according to the research firm Gartner Inc. The savings are dramatic: Companies can cut 20% to 70% of their labor costs by moving jobs to low-wage nations—assuming that the work is of comparable quality.

Equally dramatic are the displacement, downward mobility, and suffering of the people left behind. So far, at least, that enhanced productivity hasn't translated into jobs at home. Offshoring is steadily eating its way into the educated classes, both in the United States and elsewhere, affecting jobs traditionally considered secure. People whose livelihoods could now be at risk include everyone from

---

Going, Going, GONE?

Offshoring jobs is an old story in the manufacturing sector. Now, service jobs once considered safe are being shipped overseas. Lawyers, accountants, journalists, engineers, take heed. "Any knowledge-worker job is at some risk," says Michael T. Robinson, president of Careerplanner.com. Working with his firm and our own research, we've come up with a list of jobs and their relative vulnerability.

EXTREME RISK Accountant · Industrial Engineer · Production Control Specialist · Quality Assurance Engineer · Call-Center Operator · Help-Desk Specialist · Telemarketer

HIGH OR MODERATE RISK Automotive Engineer · Computer Systems Analyst · Database Administrator · Software Developer · Customer-Service Representative · CAD Technician · Paralegal/Legal Assistant · Medical Trancriptionist · Copy Editor/Journalist · Film Editor · Insurance

LOW RISK Airplane Mechanic · Artist · Carpenter · Civil Engineer · Headhunter · Interior Designer

Data: Careerplanner.com, UC Berkeley Fisher Center for Real Estate and Urban Economics, FAST COMPANY

IT experts to accountants, medical transcriptionists to customer-service representatives. In IT alone, Gartner estimates that another 500,000 positions in the U.S. may leave by the end of this year; in one scenario, as many as 25% of all IT professional jobs could go overseas by 2008. If just 40% of those people never find another job in their field, that could be more than 1 million whose careers are altered forever.

The implications of this colossal transformation are only just beginning to be understood. This time around, these categories cover a much greater share of our economy; manufacturing accounts for just 14% of U.S. output, while services provide 60% and employ two-thirds of all workers. "It's happening much

---

faster [than in manufacturing]," says Cynthia Kroll, senior regional economist at UC Berkeley's Haas School of Business. "There are fewer capital investments required in outsourcing a services job." Kroll cowrote a recent study that pegged the current number of jobs vulnerable in some way to offshoring at a stunning 14 million.

Wait a second. Wasn't it this transition to a service economy that was supposed to give us a lasting edge over our global competition? And weren't technology jobs supposed to offer a secure refuge to other displaced workers? So far, things haven't worked out that way. There are now millions of trained and educated people abroad who can do many of our jobs at a fraction of the price. And this upheaval has many people worried. "Industrialization happened and people moved from farms to factories," says Marcus Courtney, president of the Washington Alliance of Technology Workers. "In this round of globalization, people aren't moving to anything. Skills do not grant one immunity." Some argue that the shift will free resources for the innovations that will create the next big boom; others see it as an admission that our competitive advantage is gone. "More than just outsourcing IT or anyone's job, we're outsourcing the American middle class," says Bronstein.

It's no surprise, then, that offshoring is suddenly one of the hottest topics around. Presidential hopefuls like John Kerry have waded into the debate, and the media have leaped on the subject. Even CNN's Lou Dobbs—hardly a bleeding heart—has jumped in with his "shame on you" list of companies that have moved jobs overseas. Blogs and Web sites such as YourjobisgoingtoIndia.com have sprung up to rail against evil corporate interests, and some antiforeigner groups have seized on this issue as a way to promote their beliefs. Offshoring has re-energized an ugly strain of nativism in the United States, with anti-immigration groups using it to argue against work visas. Other groups, often company-sponsored, use the dirty word "protectionist" against opponents. The din grows louder every day.

Yet much of this discussion is beside the point. Offshoring is here to stay (as long as the cost savings are for real) and there's little point in hand-wringing over whether it should or shouldn't take place. Equally useless—and disingenuous—are the bland, marginally empathetic statements of business leaders alluding to the "short-term pain" as if it were a stubbed toe or a nick from shaving. When contacted, some companies refused comment, while many confirmed that they had moved some jobs overseas or said some losses were simply the result of lay-offs. A Microsoft spokesperson, for example, disputed one person's claim to have been offshored, saying it was just "part of the ebb and flow of business." Drowned out in all the hype are the voices of those on the bleeding edge of the change—the real people caught in the crosswinds of this massive global shift. The macro outlook seems irrelevant when the goal is to pay the rent.

That's the challenge faced by both Rexanna Sieber and Doug Hill every day. They come from different backgrounds—Sieber, 58, was an $11-an-hour keyboarder in Villisca, Iowa, for a company that helped make textbooks, while Hill, 60, worked as a contractor in automotive design at Lear Seating in Dearborn, Michigan, and earned six figures. But both saw their jobs move overseas and neither has found permanent work since. Hill works part-time in the veterans' benefits office of American Indian Health and Family Services; Sieber is unemployed.

"I'm done," says Hill. "I know that. Who's going to hire me? I'm 60. I'm just living one day at a time, and I do a lot of praying." Both Hill and Sieber are philosophical about the offshoring trend, saying that's the way the world works, but they worry about the long-term impact on the middle class. "I believe in free enterprise," says Sieber, "but personally, I think that the government makes it too easy to do it."

Sieber's argument is gaining support among some politicians, who are writing legislation that may make offshoring more difficult. One bill that passed the Indiana Senate on February 2 by a vote of 39–10 would require that any state government work be performed in the U.S. The measure was a reaction to a contract—later canceled by the governor—that gave Tata America International Corp., an American subsidiary of the Indian multinational, $15 million for a computer upgrade of the unemployment insurance program, of all things. It's just one of several initiatives addressing offshoring. "It's a national crisis," says the bill's sponsor, Republican state senator Jeff Drozda.

Even some corporate leaders are looking to the government for guidance. "In the absence of a public policy that tells me what to do," former Intel CEO Andrew Grove told an audience last October, "I have no choice as corporate manager, nor do my colleagues . . . [but to make decisions] that very often involve moves of jobs into other countries."

But most companies see such laws as the worst kind of protectionism. Ultimately, these measures will lead to more job loss, not less, critics say. "A lot of times [offshored people] don't think about people that are still left here," says Hansen, WatchMark's CEO. "What about those companies that didn't survive?" In an economy where "There is no job that is America's God-given right anymore," in the words of Hewlett-Packard CEO Carly Fiorina, they believe that job security is up to the individual.

Fiorina probably never had the chance to meet Debi Null. A 49-year-old former system administrator at Agilent Technologies who worked for the company and its former parent, Hewlett-Packard, for more than 20 years, Null was laid off in January 2002, then was hired for less money as a contract employee to do the same job. When her contract ended last year, Null got the news that her job was moving to Singapore. Although she says Agilent treated her with respect throughout the process, finding a new position in her field has proven impossible. In order to get by and pay her health insurance, which costs some $650 a month for treatment related to a liver transplant, she sold her two cars, cashed out her 401(k), and took on three jobs. One, at Foley's department store, pays $6.50 an hour; a second, as a real estate saleswoman, depends on commission. She has yet to sell a house.

To qualify for benefits, Null has also taken a job as a $12-an-hour call-center operator at T-Mobile. But with call centers one of the most commonly offshored jobs in the country, it's hardly a secure gig. "I'm part of history, I guess," she says resignedly. "I worked for high tech in the glory days, but I would not encourage my kids to go into [it]," she says. "Right now, my oldest son is a furniture salesman and my younger one is an apprentice plumber. I don't think they can send those things overseas yet."

It's easy to argue that people like Null should have seen it coming and ought to have constantly upgraded their skills. But as offshoring eats away at ever more sophisticated jobs, is it safe to assume that there is a skill level or point in the food chain at which jobs can no longer be outsourced? "No one's immune," says Frances Karamouzis, a research director at Gartner. "We as analysts have had internal discussions, [wondering] are we next?"

Job insecurity, of course, is hardly limited to victims of offshoring. And there is less sympathy for well-educated IT workers, many of whom benefited from a dramatic run-up in salaries during the bubble. "The cost of technology inside the U.S. and the salaries along with it are outrageous," says Michael Mullarkey, CEO of Workstream Inc., a Canadian-based tech company. "I'm paying $65,000 Canadian for developers that were making $147,000 [in California], and they're smiling ear to ear. People are a dime a dozen."

With that kind of pressure, even those who keep their jobs are feeling the squeeze: A January 2004 study by Foote Partners shows that IT compensation has fallen for four straight quarters in the areas most vulnerable to outsourcing, dropping an average of 7.6% in 2003 alone. "There's no way to stay competitive, no matter how hard you work, when you can get 8 to 16 heads for the price of one," says Bronstein.

So is there any such thing as a safe refuge? Melissa Charters was a data security administrator in Los Angeles with five kids and a freelancer husband. Her $70,000 job was first outsourced to a local company and then offshored to India in May 2003. It's an increasingly common pattern. Full-time jobs become contract work, without benefits, and then vanish overseas. Thanks to a state-funded program for displaced IT workers, Charters is going back to college—to learn to teach home economics. "I seriously considered going back to school to do data or network security," she says. "But then I thought, how could I invest my own money in a career to have it taken away again? I'm pretty sure teachers can't be offshored, but if I start seeing big-screen TVs in my classes, I am going to be worried."

Charters is lucky to have found some government help. While the Trade Adjustment Assistance Reform Act of 2002 provides federal aid for those whose jobs have moved overseas, it is aimed at manufacturing jobs; most software developers and other white-collar workers aren't eligible. In January, a group of former IBM programmers filed a class action suit against the U.S. government to change that.

Corporations bear some responsibility to the workers they leave behind, argues Ray Lane, the former COO and president of Oracle Corp. and currently a partner at Kleiner Perkins Caufield & Byers. "Take some of your expected profits from offshoring and make your severance

packages higher or retrain the employees … in known growth industries," he says. "But don't kid them. My cousin worked as a bartender for eight years while he waited for his $22-an-hour steel mill job to 'come back.' These jobs never come back."

In an August 2003 report entitled "Offshoring: Is It a Win-Win Game?" McKinsey Global Institute concludes with great specificity that every dollar of offshoring results in 58 cents of savings to the American economy. But even that report acknowledges that 31% of workers who lost their jobs in earlier waves were never fully reemployed, with 80% taking pay cuts. That's the reality for Clifford Paino, a systems analyst whose job moved to Ireland in December 2002. After six months, he found a new job as a contract worker for the same company—earning 40% less, with no job security. "They can tell me they can get rid of me tomorrow," he says.

The situation is particularly acute in certain cities—often the very ones that were a little slice of heaven in the 1990s. In the Colorado Springs area, a thriving IT industry was powered in part by Agilent, the company that was spun off from HP in 1999. The retrenchment that resulted from the decline of the Internet economy has led to the loss of thousands of jobs in the area, many of which went overseas. Agilent won kudos for handling the difficult process as gracefully as possible. Yet its status as part of the original HP—a place once famous for treating its workers with loyalty and respect and for fostering lifelong careers—makes the human impact all the more poignant.

"I walked to work when I was seven months' pregnant in a blizzard and stayed for three more shifts," says Joan Pounds, an IT representative at Agilent who lost her job in July 2003. "I did that because I cared about the company." Pounds wasn't surprised to get the bad news—she'd already survived seven layoffs—but she was surprised to learn that she had to train her replacements in India via teleconference.

One of the Indian replacement workers did, however, congratulate Pounds on her new job. "I said, 'I don't know where that is,' and he said that they had been told we were going on to much better positions," she remembers. "It was emotional on both sides." Shocked to learn that they were, in fact, putting Pounds out of work, both replacement workers tried to back out of the contract, Pounds says. But their employer, a contractor in India, told them they couldn't. As for Pounds, a single mother, she sent out 25 résumés a week with no luck before taking a 13-hour-a-week job as a senior-citizen caregiver. The pay: $7 an hour. She has no medical benefits and must pay the costs of treatment for a son with bipolar disorder. A few months ago, she sold her house at a loss just two days before it was scheduled to be foreclosed.

After his job on Agilent's Windows NT support team ended up in Singapore, William V. Grebenik decided to set up a company that would help smaller companies move offshore. He thought he could help clients with the cultural issues that often create problems, but he blew through his severance before the company could get any traction. "I'm living on one-fourth of what I was making," says Grebenik, who now runs a part-time technical training company. "I've got to make the rent in five days. I'm going to be borrowing it off somebody."

It took courage for people like Grebenik and Pounds to share their stories, because many others whom FAST COMPANY contacted refused, terrified that speaking out would further harm their chances of finding work. "People are really frightened about potential blacklisting," says Natasha Humphries, a former senior software engineer for Palm who was laid off last August. Humphries says she was sent to Bangalore to train some contractors, only to find out later that they were her group's replacements. (Palm disputes Humphries's account, saying her work was split between two local managers.) One man we contacted who had spoken to a local paper about being offshored was told he'd be fired from his new position if he was quoted elsewhere. His wife spoke to us instead.

Many U.S. companies are also doing their best to stay out of the spotlight on this issue—even as they rely increasingly on overseas workers. Rather than loudly proclaiming the benefits—or, alternatively, opting not to shift those jobs overseas—many are simply continuing their offshoring as quietly as possible. "Nobody wants to be the poster child for this," says Vashistha of neoIT, who says publicity-shy clients asked him to take their names down from his Web site. Even McKinsey, which extols offshoring's benefits publicly, didn't respond to a reporter's request to learn more about its own offshoring efforts.

For many multinationals, in fact, offshoring can be a public-relations nightmare at both ends of the pipeline. They fear being associated with the loss of U.S. jobs, of course—but they also worry about offending huge markets if they pull back from employing workers in places such as India, China, and Indonesia. Dell, for example, has tried hard to downplay its decision to bring back some of its call-center operations to the United States from India after criticism about the service quality. According to Barry French, a Dell spokesman, it was "a lot of flurry over something reasonably insignificant. The climate is pretty intense, so what was a small action got blown out of proportion. We remain absolutely committed to India." And at Lehman Brothers, questions about a recent decision to bring back its help desk, which had been outsourced to Indian tech company Wipro Ltd. in January 2003, brought the following clipped response from a spokeswoman: "We're not getting into the details of it. We don't want to be quoted on this. It was a management decision."

The irony is that offshoring is not an American-only concern. In manufacturing, the jobs have trampolined from country to country. In a world where people are treated as any other factor of production, scapegoating one country is pointless. Already, jobs that just five years ago went to Ireland are now done in India; as wages rise there, new, cheaper sources of well-trained workers are springing up in such places as the Philippines and, of course, China. "People in India, of course they're happy, they're getting more money," says Andres Urv, whose job as a quality assurance engineer was offshored in 2003. "But when companies pull out and say, 'Thank you so much but we found someone cheaper,' will they be feeling like we do?"

Where will it all end? Some people believe that population trends make the whole debate a waste of time. Even if the worst-case scenario for offshoring comes true, they say, the departure of boomers from the workforce will create a demographic earthquake so severe that filling, not finding, jobs will pose the biggest challenge.

But other observers see a bleaker prospect ahead. "As centers of skilled high-tech professionals build up in other parts of the world, the U.S.... may no longer dominate the next wave of innovations," a fall 2003 Berkeley study on outsourcing reads. Or perhaps it doesn't matter. "Anyone who is looking at this current debate isn't looking down the road far enough," says Tim Chou, president of Oracle Outsourcing. "The future is HAL [the superintelligent computer in 2001: A Space Odyssey]—a computer sitting in a dark room spitting out money. It won't involve any people, because [computers] are way more repetitive, reliable, and much lower cost than any human."

Perhaps Pounds, formerly of Agilent, sums it up best: "We've had throwaway clothes, throwaway cars, and now we have throwaway people." Is that what globalization was supposed to be all about?

From *Fast Company*, April 2004, pp. 76, 78-82. Copyright © 2004 by Fast Company (Gruner + Jahr USA). Reprinted by permission.

HALL MONITORS IN THE WORKPLACE

Encouraging Employee WHISTLEBLOWERS

Remember the teacher's pet in grade school? Everyone resented the kid who would tattletale on his or her peers. This might explain why we're uncomfortable with employee whistleblowers. Get over it.

BY SHARIE A. BROWN

It's actually in a company's best interests to encourage employee whistleblowers who can uncover problems before they become fodder for front-page news.

Creating an environment in which workers feel safe confiding in management about potential accounting errors, questionable business deals and government compliance oversights could save millions of dollars in the long run. It could even save the company.

In today's world of corporate mistrust, public companies may not realize that they really don't have a choice. With corporate financial and ethic scandals topping the news every day, you can rest assured that if an employee's complaints fall on deaf ears in the office, there will be a line of people on the outside willing to listen.

Government prosecutors are always willing to listen to articulate, disgruntled employees with documents to validate their claims of misconduct. And to make matters worse for misbehaving companies, whistleblowers are being paid huge sums from courts for uncovering problems. They're entitled to as much as one-third of the monetary damages they unearth.

EMPLOYEE HOTLINES

Smart companies know that they should clean their own houses in hopes of preventing Uncle Sam from being asked to do the job. Creating an effective *internal* whistleblower program is one of management's best tools for heading off possible government enforcement actions, unwanted media scrutiny, third-party legal measures and large pay-outs.

Some companies already have internal whistleblower programs of a sort in place—they just call them "employee hotlines" or "helplines." Many organizations even include information about them in mission statements or use employee handbooks to spell out procedures for reporting information.

Even with these existing programs, it is a tough challenge to create an *effective* internal whistleblower program. To begin with, some supervisors are uncomfortable with employees who report the misdeeds of others. They generally don't like their departments or personnel to be painted in a negative light to management.

Management must be willing to virtually guarantee employees that no retaliatory action will be taken against them for coming forward....

AN EFFECTIVE PROGRAM

As organizations begin to build suitable programs, they need to remember that it's no longer enough just to set up a system where employees can expose a problem to a supervisor. Employees have to understand that they won't be harmed because of their honesty. Management must be willing to virtually guarantee employees that no retaliatory action will be taken against them for coming forward—and employees have to believe management.

Once an infraction is reported, the company must also be committed to conducting internal reviews or investigations, taking appropriate actions to correct problems and disciplining the employees at fault. Companies may even decide to refer the offender to law enforcement or regulatory authorities.

Companies must walk the walk as well as talk the talk. Otherwise, employees will see no reason to step forward. Moreover, legal precedence shows that officers and directors who learn of misconduct but fail or refuse to take appropriate action can be held liable.

There's good news for companies that want to do the right thing but are not sure how to begin. There are guidelines that describe many of the attributes that an effective whistleblower program should have.

For instance, we know from sentencing guidelines that courts will consider a program successful if it has standards and procedures that are capable of reducing the prospect of criminal activity.

That's easier said than done. But, it is important to create an internal reporting system where employees feel able to report suspected misconduct without fear of reprisal and with the confidence that appropriate action will be taken. Intended or not,

many workers are intimidated and fear for their jobs if they rock the boat.

THE CORNERSTONE

Fostering comfort and confidence is a cornerstone of a strong internal system. Without those features, frustrated employees might be driven into the arms of eager journalists, government officials or private lawyers.

Another key attribute of a successful program is confidentiality. Your system should ensure that employees can maintain their anonymity and report in a confidential environment to someone other than a direct supervisor, who may be part of the problem. Usually, a worker should be able to report impropriety to senior management, someone from human resources, or counsel from the company's legal department.

And it has to be stressed again: management cannot be vindictive in any way toward the whistleblower—whether it is through a transfer, denial of a bonus, demotion in title or loss of a job.

Retaliation not only destroys trust within the internal program but also leads to criminal charges and jail time. Under the corporate responsibility bill authored by Senator Sarbanes and Congressman Oxley and recently passed by Congress, retaliatory measures can result in up to 10 years in prison for the responsible executives.

Companies can also prevent problems, based on sentencing guidelines, by having their whistleblower programs overseen by high-level personnel. Too often, lower-level personnel oversee these programs, while senior management remains disengaged and uninformed. Officers and directors can be caught off-guard when problems arise, but courts may still view them as being liable.

The helpful level of involvement comes if senior management goes the extra step and *encourages* watchdogs. Today, some companies are actually providing incentives and recognition for workers who catch problems before they get out of hand or become public knowledge.

A whistleblower program is useless without an effective communication and education policy that reaches all levels of employees.

In summary, a responsible company's job doesn't end by taking a whistleblower's report. That's just the first step.

To make sure your system can live up to the government's standards, ask yourself the following two key questions before the Department of Justice does:

1. Do you enforce compliance standards in a *consistent* manner, using appropriate disciplinary measures? There can be no exceptions; punishments must be consistent.

2. Upon detection of the violation, have you taken reasonable steps to respond and to prevent similar offenses in the future? The government and shareholders are quite unforgiving of repeat offenses.

EFFECTIVE COMMUNICATION AND EDUCATION

Now that your system is in place, it's time to tell all of your workers about it. A whistleblower program is useless without an effective communication and education policy that reaches all levels of employees. This is more than just an insert in the employee handbook. It means constant internal communications—tell them early, and tell them often.

When designed correctly, and when encouraged from the top, your employees can be your eyes and ears.

These modern-day hall monitors might not win any office popularity contests among wrongdoing colleagues, but in the long run, they could keep you out of big trouble. MW

Sharie A. Brown is a partner in the Litigation Department of the Washington, D.C., office of Foley & Lardner, where she counsels companies on corporate ethics and compliance. As a senior counsel in Mobil Oil Corporation's legal department, she helped build and oversee one of the nation's most successful internal whistleblower programs.

From *M World,* Winter 2003 pp. 8-11. Copyright © 2003 by American Management Association. Reprinted by permission.

On Witnessing a Fraud

Saying no to the scam was easy, but deciding whether to report it was harder

DON SOEKEN

Skiers in bright parkas swooshed by on the slopes as Joe pushed open the gleaming silver doors of the Highland Ski Club, ready to begin another day as computer technician. It was expensive living in the tourist town of Bastcliff, Colo., but Joe loved it. Little did he know, on this fine November morning, of the emotional storm that approached just inside the doors.

The nightmare began innocently enough, when a supervisor tapped Joe on the shoulder and murmured, "We've had an energy surge in the computer system. Will you check out the damage and report to the club manager?"

"Sure thing," said Joe. "I'll get right on it."

He found a relatively minor problem. The surge had fried a few underground wires and computer circuits, which would have to be replaced at a cost of about $15,000. When Joe reported this to the supervisor and the club manager, their response surprised him. They asked him to dig up nearly all the underground wire and cable, then dispose of it before the insurance adjuster arrived. If that were done, the cost of the repair job paid by the insurance company would come to $600,000.

"Wow, I don't think that's something I want to do," Joe told them. But his superiors assured him that if the scam were discovered, the company would be liable rather than him personally. They also noted the plan would allow the club to install a new computer system, which Joe had been asking for.

"I'm sorry," Joe said. "It's fraud, and I refuse to be part of it."

The club manager scowled angrily, and then shrugged as Joe left the room. Minutes later Joe was dismayed to learn that his fellow employee Todd was on his way to dig up the good wiring and stash it in a dumpster far removed from the clubhouse.

To clear his head, Joe stepped out into the cold bright air. Should he report the scam, he asked himself, or let it go? What should he do?

C. Fred Alford, Professor of Government and Politics, University of Maryland, College Park

Ever since my book on whistleblowing (Whistleblowers: Broken Lives and Organizational Power) was published, I've been contacted once a month from would-be whistleblowers asking what they should do. Usually the cases are complex, both factually and ethically. The first part of this case isn't. Joe is being asked to go along with felony fraud, and he has no choice but to say no. The second part is harder: Should he inform the insurance company and possibly get his friend Todd in trouble?

My advice is yes, he should make that phone call. You can't let something like this go—it's like seeing a traffic accident and not reporting it.

Joe will no doubt be fired, and will have to find new work. But he's in field with a lot of jobs, unlike the field of nuclear engineering, for example, where whistleblowers have little chance to start over. I assume Joe has not been working at the ski club for years and years, since most of these jobs are staffed by young people looking for adventure.

If some or all of this is true, I recommend Joe move to another state, come up with a convincing explanation for the gap in his employment record, and get on with his life. Most whistleblowers want vindication— they want to fight a lawsuit for reinstatement. But it's enough to have done the right thing and move on.

Here my advice is practical rather than moral. Rather than explaining why he was fired, I'm suggesting Joe leave that job out of his resume and make something up to fill the gap. I recommend he lie. Not about having done something bad, but about having done something moral.

Don Soeken's comments

Even at the risk of losing his job, Joe behaved with the ethical integrity he had been taught to value during childhood: he refused to be part of a fraud. Joe did what too many of us are afraid to do, in standing up for what's right.

As for reporting the fraud, I agree that Joe must call the insurance company. Prof. Alford introduces a surprising twist, in suggesting that when Joe loses his job, he should lie to smooth out his employment record. This is a question on which I think good people will disagree. I recommend that Joe keep the resume correct and list someone at the ski club who could help him get another job.

What Actually Happened

Joe reported the $600,000 attempted fraud to the insurance company, and admitted to his bosses he was the whistleblower. He was fired. The ski club received money from the insurance company, which was slow to investigate, and the outcome of that investigation is unknown. No negative consequences happened to Joe's coworker who dug up the cable. Joe later discovered the ski club had defrauded insurance companies on several occasions.

Joe found it hard to get another job, since his personnel file held a negative assessment of his job performance. Several evaluations said he had "problems with authority." Before the whistleblowing, similar evaluations had described Joe's work as superior. Soon, Joe was struggling with clinical depression.

He filed a lawsuit to seek various kinds of compensation—including lost wages. After years of legal wrangling, the judge ordered both mediation and settlement talks. Joe settled for an undisclosed payment. The company did not admit wrongdoing.

Don Soeken (helpline@tidal wave.net) is director of Integrity International, which provides counseling support and expert witness testimony for whistleblowers. See www.whistle blowing.us.

All cases in What Would You Do? are real, though disguised.

From *Business Ethics*, Summer 2004, vol. 18, pp. 14 . Copyright © 2004 by Business Ethics Magazine. Reprinted by permission.

Birth of the Ethics Industry

James C. Hyatt

Board of directors resigning,
My auditor's front page news.
My CFO's calling in from Rio,
I got the Sarbanes-Oxley blues.

—posting by a Denver banking firm.

A lot of companies are singing the compliance blues these days, as they struggle to cope with the complexities of Sarbanes-Oxley legislation, passed in 2002 in the wake of financial scandals. Complaints about the cost and time involved are common, but there's another effect of Sarbanes-Oxley less remarked upon. Corporations are rushing to learn ethics virtually overnight, and as they do so, a vast new industry of consultants and suppliers has emerged. The ethics industry has been born.

Consider a few examples of recent mushrooming attention to ethics. At Goldman Sachs, CEO Hank Paulson will moderate 20 forums this year on ethics, for the bank's entire staff of managing directors. Citigroup is adding annual ethics training for all 300,000 employees, and The New York Times Co. is doing likewise.

Where do such firms turn for help? The New York Times signed a multi-year agreement with LRN, an 11-year-old Los Angeles-based firm that helped advise the U.S. Sentencing Commission on effective compliance programs. LRN will provide a legal and ethics education program, including a customized course on the company's business ethics policy. LRN CEO Dov Seidman says his business has at least doubled in the last two years. Growth is also rapid at EthicsPoint, a five-year-old Portland, Ore. firm that is one of three leading providers of ethics hotline services. Section 301 of Sarbanes-Oxley (SOX, as it's often called) requires board audit committees to create a reporting system to receive complaints and tips. In the past, nearly two out of three companies used internal systems, says EthicsPoint CEO David Childers. "But in the last year, there has been a dramatic wave of going to outside providers," he adds. Studies have found employees are 50 percent more likely to use a hotline managed out of house. "People are afraid of retaliation and that anonymity can be breached," he says. Among EthicsPoint's clients are Ceridian, First Federal Bankshares Inc., and Syracuse University.

The faces behind these ethics services include people like Kevin Kelton, 48, who spent 24 years writing TV scripts for *Saturday Night Live* and *Night Court*, and now is a "content author manager" for LRN. Kelton directs six in-house writers to prepare lessons on a variety of ethical and legal issues for LRN, which offers a web-based education platform with more than 200 modules.

Kelton's new job isn't that different from his old one, he insists. The challenge is to engage audiences, "not so much as entertainment as to keep the user emotionally involved." Thus, the ethics writers might prepare a script on how an executive ran afoul of conflict-of-interest rules, illustrating how such behavior didn't square with ethics rules.

Julie, 24, a recent college graduate, works in a West Coast call center for EthicsPoint, fielding hotline inquiries over the phone and the web, on issues ranging from suspected fraud to sexual harassment. (Her last name remains confidential due to the nature of her job.) "My boss describes it more as 911 dispatch," Julie said. Most calls aren't ethics related, and only 9 to 10 percent are SOX-related. More than half involve human resource issues such as complaints about harassment or workplace conditions.

Callers, she finds, are often upset or angry, not able to tell the full story. It may take her two hours to elicit enough information to forward to a client (while protecting the caller's identity). The hardest part of her job: "Not giving advice."

Recruiting for the ethics army is vigorous. Craigslist— the free community search engine – recently listed 64 jobs in San Francisco and 50 in Boston that included the word "Sarbanes." Monster.com—a broader job search engine —tallies more than 1,000 and, on a recent check, 158 posted in "the last 24 hours."

Not all new "Sarbanes" jobs are directly tied to ethics, since the legislation focuses on accounting control systems, creating a boom in accounting positions. The Public Company Accounting Oversight Board, created by SOX, has a $136 million budget and should have 450 employees by the end of this year.

At major firms, there has been a boom in new ethics officer positions, with such positions being filled recently at the New York Stock Exchange, Marsh & McLennan, Nortel Networks, and Computer Associates International, among many others.

Kerry D. Moynihan, a managing partner at recruiting firm Christian & Timbers, reports "more and more work" helping companies find executives to handle compliance issues, with job titles ranging from chief compliance officer or general counsel to vice president of human relations. At financial companies, in particular, such officials are called upon to be "much more accountable to boards and to federal regulators." And more companies "are creating offices around things like corporate social responsibility officer."

There was a time, he says, when compliance duties landed in the lap of "the green eyeshade people you didn't want as front men. Now they are much more front of the house, three doors down from the chief executive." Wall Street compliance officers that used to make $350,000 to $450,000 a year now can command $750,000 or a million dollars in salary, he reports. And he expects demand to continue. He predicts hedge funds, for instance, will be subject to SEC regulations by 2006. And mutual funds will need help "coming up to speed."

Ethics officers often wear more than one hat. At Lubrizol Corp., in Wyckliffe, Oh., Mark Meister has been vice president for human relations as well as chief ethics officer since 1994. He finds the duties have expanded substantially over the years. Currently, two people work with him on ethics part-time, helping with tasks like posting ethics guidelines in seven languages, and overseeing 27 regional ethics leaders around the world whom employees can contact with questions. The company currently is rolling out its ethics program to 3,000 new employees who've joined Lubrizol, a specialty chemicals company, through an acquisition.

To convince employees it's serious about ethics, Lubrizol frequently notes the experience of CEO James Hambrick. When he oversaw business in the former Soviet Union, "he came back and said basically we can have our business plan or our ethics policy, but not both. We walked away from business as a result," Meister says. The story "lets people know you can make ethical decisions and be successful in this organization."

Venture capital money is flowing into the ethics industry these days, as a result of the boom. The training business Midi Corp. of Princeton, N.J., was acquired a year ago with $7 million in venture capital and "more money has been guaranteed when we need it," said CEO Bette Tomaszewicz. In one year, company employees have grown from 20 to nearly 70.

Midi has developed more than 50 different courses on legal and ethical topics, and is adding 20 courses a year. The material, available as online videos, is designed to "have a long mental shelf life," said Jeffrey M. Kaplan, a Midi vice president. "Nobody ever asks an employee to commit a crime three days after training," he says. "The devil on your shoulder is always pretty big: your boss or a customer in your face. The question is, what is your little angel going to say? We want our training to give the devil a run for his money."

Kaplan says what's driving the ethics boom is not so much the SOX legislation, as the increased tendency of prosecutors and regulators to take ethics programs into account when considering charges. Midi also sees demand for training on the Foreign Corrupt Practices Act, antitrust issues, and harassment.

One Sarbanes-related script Midi produced depicts a sales executive persuading a customer to help inflate sales numbers by accepting goods that can be returned later. The sales person, in turn, asks another employee to help cover up the arrangement. The second employee considers reporting the problem, but doesn't, lies to an FBI agent, threatens a whistleblower, and eventually goes to prison—a chain of events "you're likely to remember for a long time," Kaplan says. Midi's sales, about $2 million last year, are projected to balloon to $8 to $10 million this year, possibly $20 million next year.

In this new era of growth, established ethics-related businesses are re-creating themselves. Global Compliance Services, in Charlotte, N.C.—the largest hotline provider — traces its business to AlertLine, set up in 1981 to help defense contractors identify fraud. The business eventually became part of the Pinkerton security company, and it now provides services to half of the Fortune 500. In 2003, two Pinkerton businesses were purchased in a management buyout, and the new company has embarked on a drive to expand in the current receptive climate. CEO Dennis Muse says AlertLine gets 25,000 calls a month, with topics ranging from ethics charges to a manager's behavior.

Reaching out beyond ethics, Pinkerton recently launched a service called "Stakeholder," providing a way for stakeholders like shareholders, customers, or contractors to voice concerns.

Software companies have found a bonanza in Sarbanes-Oxley. "Last year (2004), we more than tripled our revenue," declares Ed Thomas, product marketing manager for OpenPages, Waltham, Mass., a maker of governance, risk, and compliance management software. He expects similar growth this year.

The company's SOX Express software helps companies automate the compliance process of documenting internal financial controls, a SOX requirement. Next on the horizon: expanding to general risk management issues such as manufacturing and human resources. "Sarbanes is risk management for your financial department," he says.

EMC Corp., the $8 billion-revenue information storage company in Hopkinton, Mass., is also finding opportunities in what a spokesman calls the "emerging trend of records management." In 2003 the firm spent nearly $3 billion to acquire two software companies serving that market. Fueled in part by SOX demands, revenues at those two companies rose more than 20 percent in first quarter 2005. "A lot of the Sarbanes-related activity ended up being about protection and management of information," says Andrew Cohen, director and senior counsel at EMC.

At Iron Mountain Inc., the big Boston record management company, the impact of the current ethics era "has been profound," says Ken Rubin, executive vice president for corporate marketing. The collapse of Arthur Andersen and Enron moved records management "from the back room to the boardroom," he says. "How companies manage records became linked to corporate ethics and, ultimately, to brand reputation and share price." In the new atmosphere, clients "began to treat records as information assets, as footprints of action or inaction."

The price of all this new activity is enormous. AMR Research estimates that organizations this year will spend $6.1 billion on Sarbanes-Oxley; others estimate twice that amount. Large companies dealing with one of the big four accounting firms have seen their annual fees double. Technology research firm Aberdeen Group of Boston reported earlier this year that "for many mid-tier firms, the cost of complying with SOX is temporarily spelling the difference between profit and loss."

The collapse of Arthur Andersen and Enron moved records management from the back room to the boardroom. Companies now treat records as footprints of action or inaction.

At its best, though, the ethics evolution underway is about more than complying with expensive and detailed rules. It's about shifting how firms are managed, to incorporate an ethics focus. Dov Seidman, LRN's founder and CEO, likes to say he was in the ethics business "BE—Before Enron." He began LRN 10 years ago doing legal research for Fortune 500 companies, "putting out fires through expert analysis." But he soon developed a notion of "ethical capitalism as a long-term driver of business success," and launched training programs to establish "do it right cultures." LRN has worked with companies like Johnson & Johnson, Pfizer, and. DuPont for years. "Ethics isn't about games," Seidman says. "Integrity is either there or it's not."

David Gebler, president of Working Values Ltd., a decade-old Boston-based business ethics consulting firm, says in the new climate, "it's often hard for organizations to make the leap to an ethical culture because they are unsure of where to start."

He adds: "It is not enough to merely ask whether controls are in place or if everyone has attended a class or signed a code. The organization has to understand what the drivers of behavior are," and how those align with integrity goals.

Brian Gontarski, director of business development at Working Values, says an organization's code of conduct, its values, and its business goals may be created by separate units. "We strive to find the point where they all intersect," so ethics is seen "as a way of doing business, not just following the company line."

Over time, as boards get more involved, the new focus on ethical behavior will only expand, says Mary Ann Jorgenson, a partner in Cleveland-based Squire, Sanders & Dempsey LLP. "What's changed dramatically is that CEOs are moving away from the inclination to control board discussions," becoming willing to hear other points of view, she says. Her job as an advisor is to "make people comfortable with the exercise of independent judgment and to understand what constructive skepticism is."

It may all be working. There are indications that the focus on ethics is bearing fruit.

The National Benchmark Study by the University of Michigan and research firm Employee Motivation & Performance Assessment looks at a variety of working condition measures, and it found that among 1,000 major companies, the only statistically significant change in 2004 was a jump in companies' scores for "ethics and fairness."

Surveying financial executives, Oversight Systems Inc., Atlanta found that most have seen bottom-line benefits from SOX compliance. Nearly half, 49 percent, say SOX compliance reduced the risk of fraud and errors, and 48 percent say it made financial operations more efficient.

There are always critics, of course, and they're making a buck as well. CafePress, selling customized merchandise online, is offering mugs priced at $15.99 that are emblazoned with the words, "Sox Stinks!"

James C. Hyatt (jchyatt@yahoo.com), a Princeton, N.J., freelance writer, formerly was a reporter and editor for The Wall Street Journal.

From *Business Ethics*, Summer 2005, pp. 20, 22, 26. Copyright © 2005 by Business Ethics Magazine. Reprinted by permission.

Academic Values and the Lure of Profit

By Derek Bok

J OHN LE CARRÉ'S LATEST NOVEL, *The Constant Gardener*, tells of the murder of a young woman in Africa and her husband's valiant efforts to avenge her death. It soon appears that these events all grow out of a major pharmaceutical company's campaign to develop a new drug for combating tuberculosis. Discovered in a Polish laboratory, the drug looks promising at first, raising hopes of earning hundreds of millions of dollars. As tests on human subjects begin in Kenya and other African countries, however, problems start to surface. There are side effects. Patients die.

One of the scientists who discovered the drug has second thoughts and threatens to go public. Frantic, the company tries to suppress the unfavorable evidence and to buy off or intimidate critics. To bolster its case, the company uses money to get help from universities. It contrives to have several well-known professors publish favorable reports about the drug in leading journals without disclosing that the reports were actually written by the company itself and that the purported authors are beneficiaries of lucrative research contracts from the same source. A distant medical school is persuaded to offer the disaffected discoverer of the drug an amply funded post where she can be watched and induced to keep silent. When she finally speaks out, she is quickly vilified and ostracized by colleagues at her university and its affiliated hospital, which just happen to have been promised large donations by... that's right, the drug's manufacturer.

Le Carré takes care to point out that his book is a work of imagination. He makes no claim that pharmaceutical companies resort to beatings and killings to get new drugs to the market. Still, the author does say that his account "draws on several cases, particularly in the North American continent, where highly qualified medical researchers have dared to disagree with their pharmaceutical paymasters and suffered vilification and persecution for their pains."

Is Le Carré correct? Just how far have industrial sponsors actually gone in seeking to use higher-education institutions and professors for their own commercial ends? How willing have universities been to accept money at the cost of compromising values central to the academic enterprise?

To understand what lies behind Le Carré's book, one must appreciate the predicament in which universities find themselves. Now more than ever, they have become the principal source of the three most important ingredients of progress in a modern, industrial society: expert knowledge, highly educated people, and scientific discoveries. At the same time—in a depressed economy, with the federal budget heavily in deficit and state governments cutting investments in higher education—campus officials are confronting a chronic shortage of money to satisfy the demands of students, faculty members, and other constituencies.

As a result, university administrators are under great pressure to become more entrepreneurial. They feel compelled to search more aggressively for novel ways of making profits that can help meet pressing campus needs. Increasingly, one reads of new lucrative ventures launched by one university or another: medical-school consortia to test drugs for pharmaceutical companies; highly advertised executive courses to earn a tidy surplus for their business-school sponsors; alliances with venture capitalists to launch for-profit companies producing Internet courses for far-flung audiences.

The "entrepreneurial university" is the subject of a growing body of scholarly literature and media commentary. Led by resourceful executives, these institutions are often portrayed in books and articles as constantly looking out for new and ingenious ways to serve society's needs while reaping profits with which to scale new pinnacles of excellence and prestige. Reading such accounts, skeptics are quick to assume that such institutions have turned their backs on their academic missions and to criticize them for attempting to bring such businesslike ways into the academy.

Yet profit seeking has undoubtedly helped in some instances to improve academic work and to enhance higher education's value to society. Before Congress made it easy for universities to patent government-financed scientific discoveries and license them to corporations, administrators made little effort to scour campus laboratories for advances that could be turned to practical use to benefit consumers. Today, several hundred institutions have active technology-transfer offices to perform that function, and the number of patents issued to universities has grown more than tenfold. The lure of profit has likewise brought about keener competition to produce more and better-quality training programs for business executives than would have existed otherwise. Similar incentives could conceivably spur a more rapid development of Internet courses that will allow universities to make excellent educational programs available to distant audiences.

But, in their pursuit of moneymaking ventures, universities also risk compromising their essential academic values. To earn a handsome profit from a company, business schools may divert assistant professors from their on-campus duties so that they can teach elementary material to entry-level executives. To win at football, colleges may admit students with grades and scores far below the normal requirements. To profit from the Internet, universities may offer gullible students overseas a chance to take inferior courses that will earn them a dubious certificate of business studies. Once such compromises are made, competitive pressures can cause the questionable practices to spread and eventually become so deeply rooted as to be well nigh irreversible. One can imagine a university of the future tenuring professors because they bring in large amounts of patent royalties, seeking commercial advertisers to sponsor courses on the Internet, and admitting undistinguished students on the quiet understanding that their parents will make substantial gifts.

To avoid those pitfalls, universities need to examine the process of commercialization with greater care than in the past. Otherwise, they may gradually alter their essential character in ways that could eventually forfeit the respect of students and faculty members, and erode the trust of the public.

History offers several lessons about commercialization that are well worth pondering. One conclusion that emerges repeatedly is that rewards from profit-seeking ventures seldom are as great as their university sponsors hoped at the beginning. High-profile athletics teams—the academy's first big commercial venture—have certainly produced revenues. But their costs have risen at least as rapidly, to the point where very few institutions consistently make money from their sports programs. Likewise, patent licensing has brought substantial revenues to a handful of universities, but most institutions do not earn much more than the cost of operating their technology-transfer offices.

Internet courses have been recently touted as the latest El Dorado in the long history of commercial ventures. Not long ago, newspapers were filled with accounts of exciting new schemes offering large potential profits. In the last two years, however, New York and Temple Universities have both shut down for-profit Internet ventures, and Columbia University in January announced the demise of its widely publicized Fathom program after losing millions of dollars in the enterprise.

If disappointing profits were the only problem with moneymaking activities, there would be little reason to lose much sleep over growing commercialization. But profit seeking has already shown disturbing tendencies to get out of hand and threaten far more important matters than expected revenues. In high-profile sports, for example, the prior grades and test scores of freshman athletes and their subsequent academic performance in college have fallen further and further below the levels of their classmates, and scandals have continued to erupt periodically in one university after another.

Commercialization has already taken a toll on the quality of educational programs.

While athletics may be dismissed as an extracurricular activity peripheral to the main academic enterprise, other commercial ventures have begun to strike closer to the core of research and education. In their zeal to build financial support from industry, many universities have signed research agreements with companies that allow more secrecy than is needed to protect the legitimate interests of their sponsors. Many campuses have failed to impose strict conflict-of-interest rules to prevent their scientists from performing experiments on human subjects for companies to which they have significant financial ties. Echoing the events described by John Le Carré, some universities have failed to protect their scientists from corporate pressure to suppress unfavorable research findings. Thomas Bodenheimer, a clinical professor of family and community medicine at the University of California at San Francisco, has even reported that as many as 10 percent of published reports by university researchers on the efficacy of products manufactured by the commercial sponsors of the research are actually ghostwritten by company personnel. As practices of this kind become more widely known, the public's confidence in the credibility and objectivity of university research is bound to suffer.

Commercialization has also taken a toll on the quality of educational programs. Many institutions, seeking to profit from their continuing-education divisions, follow practices in those areas that they would never tolerate in their regular degree programs. They typically offer little or no financial aid, while paying salaries to instructors that are well below the normal university scale. As a result, access to such programs has suffered, along with the quality of teaching.

In medical schools, administrators hoping to extract a greater surplus from continuing-education programs accept substantial subsidies from pharmaceutical companies in exchange for agreeing to choose instructors from company-approved lists and allowing the sponsor to prepare the slides and teaching notes that are used in the lectures. Further harm could result from commercializing Internet programs if universities (and their venture-capital partners) try to maximize profits by attracting large audiences of unwary students with flashy lecture courses taught by famous professors who do not take full advantage of the (more expensive) interactive power that new technology allows to improve the effectiveness of teaching and learning.

HOW SIGNIFICANT are the questionable practices that many universities already tolerate? Because they involve values as well as money, the costs are impossible to quantify. But that does not mean they are unimportant. Far from it. It is vital to uphold admissions standards, preserve the integrity of evaluating faculty scholarship and student papers, maintain the openness and objectivity of scientific inquiry, and sustain other important academic values. These values are essential to maintaining the public's trust in student transcripts and published faculty research. They preserve professors' faith in the academic enterprise and help ensure that they will continue to regard their work as a calling rather than merely a way to make a living.

University officials may insist that they can keep commercial activity from getting out of hand. Yet the long, sorry history of intercollegiate sports clearly shows how far the erosion of values can proceed. Through a series of small steps, many prominent institutions have come to sacrifice the most basic academic standards in their quest for added athletics revenue and visibility. Left unchecked, the chronic need for money could drive universities to similar extremes in more-central programs of education and research.

What can universities do to protect themselves against that danger? Five steps seem especially important.

First, universities should not rely upon presidents alone to protect the institution and its values from the pitfalls of commercialization. Presidents are under enormous pressure to find the money not only to balance the budget but to improve financial aid, build new buildings and laboratories, increase faculty salaries, launch new programs, and hire star professors to enhance the institution's reputation. Trustees judge presidential performance in substantial part by the amount of money that the chief executive raises. Faculty members hold presi-

dents accountable for finding the means to fulfill intellectual ambitions. Students want better residence halls. Boosters insist on winning teams.

In the face of these pressures, if presidents are left by themselves to preserve academic values, questionable compromises are likely to occur. Though none may be glaring by itself, their accumulation will gradually threaten the integrity of the institution. The values of a college or university can be preserved only if boards of trustees make upholding academic standards an integral part of evaluating presidents—and insist on reviewing conflict-of-interest rules, admissions practices for athletes, and other standards that are at risk from commercialization.

The second principle to observe is not to consider commercial opportunities on a case-by-case basis. Rather, institutions should insist on promulgating general rules to govern matters such as secrecy provisions in corporate-research agreements, admissions standards for athletes, and conflicts of interest for scientists. Ad hoc decisions are bound to lead to a gradual erosion of academic values; the cards are almost always stacked in favor of allowing moneymaking schemes to proceed.

When such opportunities present themselves, interested faculty members and administrators are typically those with a stake in having the project move forward; the risks are usually too diffuse to generate opposition. The potential rewards seem tangible and very tempting at the outset, while the dangers will be speculative and hard to quantify. The hoped-for benefits are, for the most part, immediate, whereas the risks loom far in the future.

In addition, the benefits accrue to the institution and its members, but the costs often involve matters, such as a loss of trust in the objectivity of research, that are shared by all universities. Similarly, the blame for turning a project down falls squarely on identifiable university officials, but the responsibility for undermining academic standards and squandering public trust can never be traced to any specific decision or institution. Under such circumstances, in the absence of clear, well-publicized rules, the path of least resistance will almost always lie in approving the questionable project.

A third important principle is to involve the faculty in developing and enforcing all rules that protect academic values. Many administrators have a dangerous habit of regarding the faculty as an irritating obstruction to discussions of commercial ventures. The entrepreneurial university, it is said, must be able to move quickly. It cannot wait for windy faculty debates to run their course lest valuable opportunities be lost in the fast-moving corporate world in which we live.

In fact, there is remarkably little evidence to support this view. Looking back over the checkered history of commercial activity on campuses, one can much more easily point to examples of costly unilateral decisions by impatient administrators, such as ill-advised Internet ventures or grandiose athletics projects, than to valuable opportunities lost through inordinate faculty delays.

That is not to say that existing processes of faculty governance are perfect, or even nearly so. New and streamlined procedures may be needed, with smaller committees staffed by carefully chosen, well-respected, highly knowledgeable professors, in order to deal with conflicts of interest, secrecy, and other complex issues created by emerging commercial opportunities. Still, the essential fact remains that faculty members have the greatest stake in preserving academic values—and hence have a critical role to play in making sure that the quest for revenue does not impair the basic intellectual standards of the institution.

Universities should ponder the sorry history of intercollegiate athletics.

A fourth useful step in safeguarding academic standards is to look for opportunities for universities to agree among themselves on basic rules governing matters such as conflicts of interest in research, the length of time that results can be kept secret under commercially sponsored research agreements, or conference-wide rules protecting academic standards in athletics. The Ivy League agreement setting minimum admissions requirements for athletes is a case in point.

Without such agreements, competition works to erode academic standards. In the struggle for revenue or competitive advantage, a few institutions are bound to succumb to the temptation to undertake highly questionable commercial ventures. Once a few agree, competitive pressures on other universities will cause them to do likewise. Before long, what began as suspect behavior will become accepted practice. Uniform rules, by agreement or by legislation, are often the only defense against such corrosive pressures (although universities need to take pains to avoid the sort of restrictive agreements without a redeeming public purpose that could run afoul of antitrust laws).

Finally, reasonably stable government support is the ultimate guarantee of high academic standards. Faced with a choice between sacrificing academic values and enduring serious cuts in programs, most universities will find a way to choose the former. Fortunately, government support for higher education has been relatively generous over the years. That is one important reason why American universities have achieved such a place of eminence in the world. My point is not to complain or to urge massive increases in public support for higher education. I simply want to make clear that sudden, major cuts, or steady erosion of support over an extended period of time, will put intolerable pressure on universities to sacrifice important academic standards in the hope of gaining badly needed revenue through dubious commercial ventures.

Above all, university leaders, faculty members, and trustees need to recognize the risks involved in pursuing more and more commercial ventures and begin to build sturdier safeguards. To be sure, setting proper limits and providing supportive structures will take a lot of work. Entrepreneurial professors may resist new rules. Boosters may protest athletics reforms. Corporations may balk at strict secrecy limits and refuse to enter into lucrative research contracts.

MEANWHILE, the temptation to push ahead will frequently be great. Most profit-seeking ventures start not with obvious violations of principle but with modest compromises that carry few immediate costs. The problems tend to appear so gradually that their link to commercialization may not even be perceived. Like adolescents experimenting with drugs, campus officials may believe that they can proceed without serious risk.

Before succumbing to such temptations, university leaders should recall the history of intercollegiate athletics and ponder the sobering lessons that it teaches. Once the critical compromises have been made and tolerated long enough, universities will find it hard to rebuild the public's trust, regain the faculty's respect, and return to the happier conditions of earlier times. In exchange for ephemeral gains in the constant struggle for prestige, universities will have sacrificed essential values that are very difficult to restore.

Derek Bok is a university professor and president emeritus of Harvard University. His latest book, Universities in the Marketplace: The Commercialization of Higher Education, *was published April 2003 by Princeton University Press.*

From *The Chronicle of Higher Education,* April 4, 2003 pp. B7, B9. Copyright © 2003 by Derek Bok. Reprinted by permission of the author.

Like the Smoke of a Blazing Room

On the new fraud hotline, a disturbing rumor was reported.

DOUG WALLACE

As Walter Haverford turned his chair to watch the clouds roll in, he thought to himself, How could this have happened? This could blow the company sky high. It was hard to believe, but too many details from too many informants pointed in the same direction. Haverford knew that as general manager of the Munitions Division of Thunderbolt Defense Co., whatever happened next was his call.

The problem had surfaced only a few days ago, though the scene had been set earlier when Haverford installed an ethics hotline. He had taken great pains to make sure all employees knew how important it was to report problems. It was attorney Pat Smith who took the fateful call, late one evening. A finance clerk on the line said he couldn't talk at work but please call him at home. When Smith returned the call, he learned that a troubling rumor was circulating about technicians in the Test Center.

Haverford's division in Kansas City specialized in making small arms ammunition—an area so competitive it was difficult to get the product out the door on time and make a profit. Parts made in K C. were assembled at the plant in Greenwich, Miss., and that's where the problem arose. The plant was under pressure to perform, and it was performing, under the competent hand of Dan White, a no-nonsense, high-performance type with Thunderbolt 30 years. Some had wanted a more human relations oriented manager when White had been hired, but under him, the plant's safety record was exceptional and worker morale was high.

It's no wonder Haverford was puzzled when he heard Smith's news. Rumor had it that several lots of am-munition had been shipped to the Army that were outside government specifications.

After an emergency meeting of the top managers, the director of quality, Sam Mallony, flew to Greenwich to talk to the caller. Apparently, testing technicians may have slightly altered the test procedures, to make the pro-duces pass. Mallony found the techni-cians who surfaced the problem were fearful; they agreed to talk only off-hours and away from the job site.

Haverford found himself remem-bering that when Dan White had as-sumed control of the new facility, he had wanted control of quality testing. Haverford began to wonder whether that function should have reported to division headquarters, to ensure in-dependent reporting.

The atmosphere in Greenwich was different than Kansas City. Green-wich was a depressed town with 10 percent unemployment. People were fearful about their jobs. And the di-rector of testing was known to have family problems, which may have left him unable to cope with the pressured environment.

Haverford asked other senior exec-utives whether the Army should be called. Attorneys advised against it. Another executive pointed out this could be a minor problem. They didn't know how far the ammo was out of specification, how many lots were involved, or whether it was un-safe to use. If misinformation got out, it could ruin the plant and put people out of work.

On the other hand, Haverford said, the technicians could go to the press. Even if nothing was wrong, there would be a lot of explaining to do, and it might force the Army's hand. Haverford gazed out his win-dow at the thunderclouds rolling in. What should he do?

John Rollwagen, former CEO of Cray Research

I would need additional technical data on the specifications that were relaxed and the consequences of us-ing the ammunition. Regardless of what I found, I'd get in touch with the Army and present them with the data, as well as a plan to recall and inspect.

I'd make the actions very visible. To the Army you send a message that you are to be trusted. To employees you communicate that the firm's fi-nancial stability can never involve sacrificing safety. My major concerns are these:

- I need to protect both the infor-mants and Army personnel.
- The production process may be faulty.
- A decision like this by a com-pany veteran reflects a. funda-mental problem because no one lasts 30 years without absorb-ing a set of values that run deep in the company. Above all, how-ever, this is a great opportunity to re-establish critical values.

The technicians were enormously fearful. They agreed to talk only off-hours and away from the job site.

Tom Wyman, former CEO of CBS

When you're talking about human safety, the paramount thing is to re-duce the chance that anybody could be injured. That is more important than the company's future, its employment, or the town's economic welfare.

You have to call the person receiving the material, just as J&J did with Tylenol. It doesn't matter that it may be half the company's business, you need to get the material back. If by informing the customer you lose the next order, maybe that's the way the world should work. If you don't tell them and a problem erupts, they won't buy from you for a thousand years.

You have to ask yourself whether you share in the problem by the pressures exerted in the environment. I'd bring the people together and say something like this: "I am embarrassed by creating an environment that communicated the wrong priorities. I am apologizing to all of you. But you share the burden. At a minimum you should have come to me with this concern. It is not your role to slash safety standards."

You have to hold those responsible who altered the data. I'd probably suspend them for 30 days. With the plant manager, Dan White, it's time to put someone in that job for the next generation. You send the wrong signal by leaving him there.

Doug Wallace's comments

For those who have never worked in the corporate trenches, Thunderbolt's problem may seem simple. But those who have been there know too well the traffic jam pressures that temper a rush to righteous judgment. It's like the difference between breathing the suffocating smoke of a blazing room, or watching it on the 6:00 news. Ethical leadership is not a spectator sport.

Our commentators here have all been there in rooms ablaze. All focused on a few critical themes; 1) Other considerations take a back seat to safety. 2) You must get all the facts: 3) It's critical to be honest with customers and employees. 4) The problem reflects a more fundamental issue about the environment of the company.

> You have to ask yourself whether you share in the problem by the pressures exerted in the company environment.

What Actually Happened?

The case is a real one, though the names have been changed. The real "Walt Haverford" didn't believe the out-of-spec ammunition represented a safety hazard. But if there was any doubt, his first obligation was to soldiers' safety.

Haverford called the Army and told them what he knew. He set up a team to investigate. He suspended and eventually replaced both the plant manager and the director of testing. In discussions with the whistleblowing technicians, he uncovered the original and valid test data—which led to the early identification of the exact lots for recall. Because of the prompt, candid, and voluntary action by Thunderbolt, the Army cooperated. All ammunition in question was replaced. The Army assessed penalties in the hundreds of thousands of dollars, but Thunderbolt did not lose the contract nor suffer a great deal financially.

This column originally appeared in the April/May 1989 issue of Business Ethics. *Writer Doug Wallace, now retired, was formerly the vice president for social policy at Norwest Bank (which today is Wells Fargo).*

All cases in What Would You Do? Are real, though disguised.

From *Business Ethics,* Winter 2004, pp. 6-7, 2004, pp. 6-7. Copyright © 2004 by Business Ethics Magazine. Reprinted by permission.

The Parable of the Sadhu

After encountering a dying pilgrim on a climbing trip in the Himalayas, a businessman ponders the differences between individual and corporate ethics.

by Bowen H. McCoy

This article was originally published in the September–October 1983 issue of HBR. For its republication as an HBR Classic, Bowen H. McCoy has written the commentary "When Do We Take a Stand?" to update his observations.

Last year, as the first participant in the new six-month sabbatical program that Morgan Stanley has adopted, I enjoyed a rare opportunity to collect my thoughts as well as do some traveling. I spent the first three months in Nepal, walking 600 miles through 200 villages in the Himalayas and climbing some 120,000 vertical feet. My sole Western companion on the trip was an anthropologist who shed light on the cultural patterns of the villages that we passed through.

During the Nepal hike, something occurred that has had a powerful impact on my thinking about corporate ethics. Although some might argue that the experience has no relevance to business, it was a situation in which a basic ethical dilemma suddenly intruded into the lives of a group of individuals. How the group responded holds a lesson for all organizations, no matter how defined.

The Sadhu

The Nepal experience was more rugged than I had anticipated. Most commercial treks last two or three weeks and cover a quarter of the distance we traveled.

My friend Stephen, the anthropologist, and I were halfway through the 60-day Himalayan part of the trip when we reached the high point, an 18,000-foot pass over a crest that we'd have to traverse to reach the village of Muklinath, an ancient holy place for pilgrims.

Six years earlier, I had suffered pulmonary edema, an acute form of altitude sickness, at 16,500 feet in the vicinity of Everest base camp—so we were understandably concerned about what would happen at 18,000 feet. Moreover, the Himalayas were having their wettest spring in 20 years; hip-deep powder and ice had already driven us off one ridge. If we failed to cross the pass, I feared that the last half of our once-in-a-lifetime trip would be ruined.

The night before we would try the pass, we camped in a hut at 14,500 feet. In the photos taken at that camp, my face appears wan. The last village we'd passed through was a sturdy two-day walk below us, and I was tired.

During the late afternoon, four backpackers from New Zealand joined us, and we spent most of the night awake, anticipating the climb. Below, we could see the fires of two other parties, which turned out to be two Swiss couples and a Japanese hiking club.

To get over the steep part of the climb before the sun melted the steps cut in the ice, we departed at 3:30 A.M. The New Zealanders left first, followed by Stephen and myself, our porters and Sherpas, and then the Swiss. The Japanese lingered in their camp. The sky was clear, and we were confident that no spring storm would erupt that day to close the pass.

At 15,500 feet, it looked to me as if Stephen were shuffling and staggering a bit, which are symptoms of altitude sickness. (The initial stage of altitude sickness brings a headache and nausea. As the condition worsens, a climber may encounter difficult breathing, disorientation, aphasia, and paralysis.) I felt strong—my adrenaline was flowing—but I was very concerned about my ultimate ability to get across. A couple of our porters were also suffering from the height, and Pasang, our Sherpa sirdar (leader), was worried.

Just after daybreak, while we rested at 15,500 feet, one of the New Zealanders, who had gone ahead, came staggering down toward us with a body slung across his shoulders. He dumped the almost naked, barefoot body of an Indian holy man—a sadhu—at my feet. He had found the pilgrim lying on the ice, shivering and suffering from hypothermia. I cradled the sadhu's head and laid him out on the rocks. The New Zealander was angry. He wanted to get across the pass before the bright sun melted the snow. He said, "Look, I've done what I can. You have porters and Sherpa guides. You care for him. We're going on!" He turned and went back up the mountain to join his friends.

I took a carotid pulse and found that the sadhu was still alive. We figured he had probably visited the holy shrines at Muklinath and was on his way home. It was fruitless to question why he had chosen this desperately high route instead of the safe, heavily traveled caravan route through the Kali Gandaki gorge. Or why he was shoeless and almost naked, or how long he had been lying in the pass. The answers weren't going to solve our problem.

Stephen and the four Swiss began stripping off their outer clothing and opening their packs. The sadhu was soon clothed from head to foot. He was not able to walk, but he was very much alive. I looked down the mountain and spotted the Japanese climbers, marching up with a horse.

When I reached them, Stephen glared at me and said, "How do you feel about contributing to the death of a fellow man?"

Without a great deal of thought, I told Stephen and Pasang that I was concerned about withstanding the heights to come and wanted to get over the pass. I took off after several of our porters who had gone ahead.

On the steep part of the ascent where, if the ice steps had given way, I would have slid down about 3,000 feet, I felt vertigo. I stopped for a breather, allowing the Swiss to catch up with me. I inquired about the sadhu and Stephen. They said that the sadhu was fine and that Stephen was just behind them. I set off again for the summit.

Stephen arrived at the summit an hour after I did. Still exhilarated by victory, I ran down the slope to congratulate him. He was suffering from altitude sickness—walking 15 steps, then stopping, walking 15 steps, then stopping. Pasang accompanied him all the way up. When I reached them, Stephen glared at me and said: "How do you feel about contributing to the death of a fellow man?"

I did not completely comprehend what he meant. "Is the sadhu dead?" I inquired.

"No," replied Stephen, "but he surely will be!"

After I had gone, followed not long after by the Swiss, Stephen had remained with the sadhu. When the Japanese had arrived, Stephen had asked to use their horse to transport the sadhu down to the hut. They had refused. He had then asked Pasang to have a group of our porters carry the sadhu. Pasang had resisted the idea, saying that the porters would have to exert all their energy to get themselves over the pass. He believed they could not carry a man down 1,000 feet to the hut, reclimb the slope, and get across safely before the snow melted. Pasang had pressed Stephen not to delay any longer.

The Sherpas had carried the sadhu down to a rock in the sun at about 15,000 feet and pointed out the hut another 500 feet below. The Japanese had given him food and drink. When they had last seen him, he was listlessly throwing rocks at the Japanese party's dog, which had frightened him.

We do not know if the sadhu lived or died.

For many of the following days and evenings, Stephen and I discussed and debated our behavior toward the sadhu. Stephen is a committed Quaker with deep moral vision. He said, "I feel that what happened with the sadhu is a good example of the breakdown between the individual ethic and the corporate ethic. No one person was willing to assume ultimate responsibility for the sadhu. Each was willing to do his bit just so long as it was not too inconvenient. When it got to be a bother, everyone just passed the buck to someone else and took off. Jesus was relevant to a more individualistic stage of society, but how do we interpret his teaching today in a world filled with large, impersonal organizations and groups?"

I defended the larger group, saying, "Look, we all cared. We all gave aid and comfort. Everyone did his bit. The New Zealander carried him down below the snow line. I took his pulse and suggested we treat him for hypothermia. You and the Swiss gave him clothing and got him warmed up. The Japanese gave him food

and water. The Sherpas carried him down to the sun and pointed out the easy trail toward the hut. He was well enough to throw rocks at a dog. What more could we do?"

"You have just described the typical affluent Westerner's response to a problem. Throwing money—in this case, food and sweaters—at it, but not solving the fundamentals!" Stephen retorted.

I asked, "Where is the limit of our responsibility in a situation like this?"

"What would satisfy you?" I said. "Here we are, a group of New Zealanders, Swiss, Americans, and Japanese who have never met before and who are at the apex of one of the most powerful experiences of our lives. Some years the pass is so bad no one gets over it. What right does an almost naked pilgrim who chooses the wrong trail have to disrupt our lives? Even the Sherpas had no interest in risking the trip to help him beyond a certain point."

Stephen calmly rebutted, "I wonder what the Sherpas would have done if the sadhu had been a well-dressed Nepali, or what the Japanese would have done if the sadhu had been a well-dressed Asian, or what you would have done, Buzz, if the sadhu had been a well-dressed Western woman?"

"Where, in your opinion," I asked, "is the limit of our responsibility in a situation like this? We had our own well-being to worry about. Our Sherpa guides were unwilling to jeopardize us or the porters for the sadhu. No one else on the mountain was willing to commit himself beyond certain self-imposed limits."

Stephen said, "As individual Christians or people with a Western ethical tradition, we can fulfill our obligations in such a situation only if one, the sadhu dies in our care; two, the sadhu demonstrates to us that he can undertake the two-day walk down to the village; or three, we carry the sadhu for two days down to the village and persuade someone there to care for him."

"Leaving the sadhu in the sun with food and clothing—where he demonstrated hand-eye coordination by throwing a rock at a dog—comes close to fulfilling items one and two," I answered. "And it wouldn't have made sense to take him to the village where the people appeared to be far less caring than the Sherpas, so the third condition is impractical. Are you really saying that, no matter what the implications, we should, at the drop of a hat, have changed our entire plan?"

The Individual Versus the Group Ethic

Despite my arguments, I felt and continue to feel guilt about the sadhu. I had literally walked through a classic moral dilemma without fully thinking through the consequences. My excuses for my actions include a high adrenaline flow, a superordinate goal, and a once-in-a-lifetime opportunity—common factors in corporate situations, especially stressful ones.

Real moral dilemmas are ambiguous, and many of us hike right through them, unaware that they exist. When, usually after the fact, someone makes an issue of one, we tend to resent his or her bringing it up. Often, when the full import of what we have done (or not done) hits us, we dig into a defensive position from which it is very difficult to emerge. In rare circumstances, we may contemplate what we have done from inside a prison.

Had we mountaineers been free of stress caused by the effort and the high altitude, we might have treated the sadhu differently. Yet isn't stress the real test of personal and corporate values? The instant decisions that executives make under pressure reveal the most about personal and corporate character.

As a group, we had no process for developing a consensus. We had no sense of purpose or plan.

Among the many questions that occur to me when I ponder my experience with the sadhu are: What are the practical limits of moral imagination and vision? Is there a collective or institutional ethic that differs from the ethics of the individ-

ual? At what level of effort or commitment can one discharge one's ethical responsibilities?

Not every ethical dilemma has a right solution. Reasonable people often disagree; otherwise there would be no dilemma. In a business context, however, it is essential that managers agree on a process for dealing with dilemmas.

Our experience with the sadhu offers an interesting parallel to business situations. An immediate response was mandatory. Failure to act was a decision in itself. Up on the mountain we could not resign and submit our résumés to a headhunter. In contrast to philosophy, business involves action and implementation—getting things done. Managers must come up with answers based on what they see and what they allow to influence their decision-making processes. On the mountain, none of us but Stephen realized the true dimensions of the situation we were facing.

One of our problems was that as a group we had no process for developing a consensus. We had no sense of purpose or plan. The difficulties of dealing with the sadhu were so complex that no one person could handle them. Because the group did not have a set of preconditions that could guide its action to an acceptable resolution, we reacted instinctively as individuals. The cross-cultural nature of the group added a further layer of complexity. We had no leader with whom we could all identify and in whose purpose we believed. Only Stephen was willing to take charge, but he could not gain adequate support from the group to care for the sadhu.

Some organizations do have values that transcend the personal values of their managers. Such values, which go beyond profitability, are usually revealed when the organization is under stress. People throughout the organization generally accept its values, which, because they are not presented as a rigid list of commandments, may be somewhat ambiguous. The stories people tell, rather than printed materials, transmit the organization's conceptions of what is proper behavior.

For 20 years, I have been exposed at senior levels to a variety of corporations and organizations. It is amazing how quickly an outsider can sense the tone and style of an organization and, with that, the degree of tolerated openness and freedom to challenge management.

Organizations that do not have a heritage of mutually accepted, shared values tend to become unhinged during stress, with each individual bailing out for himself or herself. In the great takeover battles we have witnessed during past years, companies that had strong cultures drew the wagons around them and fought it out, while other companies saw executives—supported by golden parachutes—bail out of the struggles.

Because corporations and their members are interdependent, for the corporation to be strong the members need to share a preconceived notion of correct behavior, a "business ethic," and think of it as a positive force, not a constraint.

As an investment banker, I am continually warned by well-meaning lawyers, clients, and associates to be wary of conflicts of interest. Yet if I were to run away from every difficult situation, I wouldn't be an effective investment banker. I have to feel my way through conflicts. An effective manager can't run from risk either; he or she has to confront risk. To feel "safe" in doing that, managers need the guidelines of an agreed-upon process and set of values within the organization.

After my three months in Nepal, I spent three months as an executive-in-residence at both the Stanford Business School and the University of California at Berkeley's Center for Ethics and Social Policy of the Graduate Theological Union. Those six months away from my job gave me time to assimilate 20 years of business experience. My thoughts turned often to the meaning of the leadership role in any large organization. Students at the seminary thought of themselves as antibusiness. But when I questioned them, they agreed that they distrusted all large organizations, including the church. They perceived all large organizations as impersonal and opposed to individual values and needs. Yet we all know of organizations in which people's values and beliefs are respected and their expressions encouraged. What makes the difference? Can we identify the difference and, as a result, manage more effectively?

WHEN DO WE TAKE A STAND?

by Bowen H. McCoy

I wrote about my experiences purposely to present an ambiguous situation. I never found out if the sadhu lived or died. I can attest, though, that the sadhu lives on in his story. He lives in the ethics classes I teach each year at business schools and churches. He lives in the classrooms of numerous business schools, where professors have taught the case to tens of thousands of students. He lives in several casebooks on ethics and on an educational video. And he lives in organizations such as the American Red Cross and AT&T, which use his story in their ethics training.

As I reflect on the sadhu now, 15 years after the fact, I first have to wonder, What actually happened on that Himalayan slope? When I first wrote about the event, I reported the experience in as much detail as I could remember, but I shaped it to the needs of a good classroom discussion. After years of reading my story, viewing it on video, and hearing others discuss it, I'm not sure I myself know what actually occurred on the mountainside that day!

I've also heard a wide variety of responses to the story. The sadhu, for example, may not have wanted our help at all—he may have been intentionally bringing on his own death as a way to holiness. Why had he taken the dangerous way over the pass instead of the caravan route through the gorge? Hindu businesspeople have told me that in trying to assist the sadhu, we were being typically arrogant Westerners imposing our cultural values on the world.

I've learned that each year along the pass, a few Nepali porters are left to freeze to death outside the tents of the unthinking tourists who hired them. A few years ago, a French group even left one of their own, a young French woman, to die there. The difficult pass seems to demonstrate a perverse version of Gresham's law of currency: The bad practices of previous travelers have driven out the values that new travelers might have followed if they were at home. Perhaps that helps to explain why our porters behaved as they did and why it was so difficult for Stephen or anyone else to establish a different approach on the spot.

Our Sherpa sirdar, Pasang, was focused on his responsibility for bringing us up the mountain safe and sound. (His livelihood and status in the Sherpa ethnic group depended on our safe return.) We were weak, our party was split, the porters were well on their way to the top with all our gear and food, and a storm would have separated us irrevocably from our logistical base.

The fact was, we had no plan for dealing with the contingency of the sadhu. There was nothing we could do to unite our multicultural group in the little time we had. An ethical dilemma had come upon us unexpectedly, an element of drama that may explain why the sadhu's story has continued to attract students.

I am often asked for help in teaching the story. I usually advise keeping the details as ambiguous as possible. A true ethical dilemma requires a decision between two hard choices. In the case of the sadhu, we had to decide how much to sacrifice ourselves to take care of a stranger. And given the constraints of our trek, we had to make a group decision, not an individual one. If a large majority of students in a class ends up thinking I'm a bad person because of my decision on the mountain, the instructor may not have given the case its due. The same is true if the majority sees no problem with the choices we made.

Any class's response depends on its setting, whether it's a business school, a church, or a corporation. I've found that younger students are more likely to see the issue as black-and-white, whereas older ones tend to see shades of gray. Some have seen a conflict between the different ethical approaches that we followed at the time. Stephen felt he had to do everything he could to save the sadhu's life, in accordance with his Christian ethic of compassion. I had a utilitarian response: do the greatest good for the greatest number. Give a burst of aid to minimize the sadhu's exposure, then continue on our way.

The basic question of the case remains, When do we take a stand? When do we allow a "sadhu" to intrude into our daily lives? Few of us can afford the time or effort to take care of every needy person we encounter. How much must we give of ourselves? And how do we prepare our organizations and institutions so they will respond appropriately in a crisis? How do we influence them if we do not agree with their points of view?

We cannot quit our jobs over every ethical dilemma, but if we continually ignore our sense of values, who do we become? As a journalist asked at a recent conference on ethics, "Which ditch are we willing to die in?" For each of us, the answer is a bit different. How we act in response to that question defines better than anything else who we are, just as, in a collective sense, our acts define our institutions. In effect, the sadhu is always there, ready to remind us of the tensions between our own goals and the claims of strangers.

The word *ethics* turns off many and confuses more. Yet the notions of shared values and an agreed-upon process for dealing with adversity and change— what many people mean when they talk about corporate culture—seem to be at the heart of the ethical issue. People who are in touch with their own core beliefs and the beliefs of others and who are sustained by them can be more comfortable living on the cutting edge. At times, taking a tough line or a decisive stand in a muddle of ambiguity is the only ethical thing to do. If a manager is indecisive about a problem and spends time trying to figure out the "good" thing to do, the enterprise may be lost.

Business ethics, then, has to do with the authenticity and integrity of the enterprise. To be ethical is to follow the business as well as the cultural goals of the corporation, its owners, its employees, and its customers. Those who cannot serve the corporate vision are not authentic businesspeople and, therefore, are not ethical in the business sense.

At this stage of my own business experience, I have a strong interest in organizational behavior. Sociologists are keenly studying what they call corporate stories, legends, and heroes as a way organizations have of transmitting value systems. Corporations such as Arco have even hired consultants to perform an audit of their corporate culture. In a company, a leader is a person who understands, interprets, and manages the corporate value system. Effective managers, therefore, are action-oriented people who resolve conflict, are tolerant of ambiguity, stress, and change, and have a strong sense of purpose for themselves and their organizations.

If all this is true, I wonder about the role of the professional manager who moves from company to company. How can he or she quickly absorb the values and culture of different organizations? Or is there, indeed, an art of management that is totally transportable? Assuming that such fungible managers do exist, is it proper for them to manipulate the values of others?

What would have happened had Stephen and I carried the sadhu for two days back to the village and become involved with the villagers in his care? In four trips to Nepal, my most interesting experience occurred in 1975 when I lived in a Sherpa home in the Khumbu for five days while recovering from altitude sickness. The high point of Stephen's trip was an invitation to participate in a family funeral ceremony in Manang. Neither experience had to do with climbing the high passes of the Himalayas. Why were we so reluctant to try the lower path, the ambiguous trail? Perhaps because we did not have a leader who could reveal the greater purpose of the trip to us.

Why didn't Stephen, with his moral vision, opt to take the sadhu under his personal care? The answer is partly because Stephen was hard-stressed physically himself and partly because, without some support system that encompassed our involuntary and episodic community on the mountain, it was beyond his individual capacity to do so.

I see the current interest in corporate culture and corporate value systems as a positive response to pessimism such as Stephen's about the decline of the role of the individual in large organizations. Individuals who operate from a thoughtful set of personal values provide the foundation for a corporate culture. A corporate tradition that encourages freedom of inquiry, supports personal values, and reinforces a focused sense of direction can fulfill the need to combine individuality with the prosperity and success of the group. Without such corporate support, the individual is lost.

That is the lesson of the sadhu. In a complex corporate situation, the individual requires and deserves the support of the group. When people cannot find such support in their organizations, they don't know how to act. If such support is forthcoming, a person has a stake in the success of the group and can add much to the process of establishing and maintaining a corporate culture. Management's challenge is to be sensitive to individual needs, to shape them, and to direct and focus them for the benefit of the group as a whole.

For each of us the sadhu lives. Should we stop what we are doing and comfort him; or should we keep trudging up toward the high pass? Should I pause to help the derelict I pass on the street each night as I walk by the Yale Club en route to Grand Central Station? Am I his brother? What is the nature of our responsibility if we consider ourselves to be ethical persons? Perhaps it is to change the values of the group so that it can, with all its resources, take the other road.

Bowen H. McCoy retired from Morgan Stanley in 1990 after 28 years of service. He is now a real estate and business counselor, a teacher and a philanthropist.

Reprinted with permission from *Harvard Business Review*, May/June 1997, pp. 54–56, 58–60, 62, 64. © 1997 by the President and Fellows of Harvard College. All rights reserved.

UNIT 3

Business and Society: Contemporary Ethical, Social, and Environmental Issues

Unit Selections

Key Points to Consider

- How well are organizations responding to issues of work and family schedules, day care, and telecommuting?

- Should corporations and executives face criminal charges for unsafe products, dangerous working conditions, or industrial pollution? Why or why not?

- What ethical dilemmas is management likely to face when conducting business in foreign environments?

Student Website

www.mhcls.com/online

Internet References

Further information regarding these websites may be found in this book's preface or online.

National Immigrant Forum
http://www.immigrationforum.org

Sympatico: Workplace
http://sympatico.workopolis.com

United Nations Environment Programme (UNEP)
http://www.unep.ch

United States Trade Representative (USTR)
http://www.ustr.gov

Both at home and abroad, there are social and environmental issues that have potential ethical consequences for management. Incidents of insider trading, deaths resulting from unsafe products or work environments, AIDS in the workplace, and the adoption of policies for involvement in the global market are a few of the issues that need to be seriously addressed by management.

This unit investigates the nature and ramifications of prominent ethical, social, and environmental issues facing management today. The unit articles are grouped into three sections. The first article, "Does it Pay to be Good" covers why corporate citizenship is a diffuse concept for many. The next article scrutinizes the importance of companies gaining and maintaining trust in the marketplace. The last three articles in this subsection provide some thoughtful insight on ways women approach management and leadership differently than men, the contribution of older Americans to organizations and the economy, and why the pharmaceutical industry is due for fundamental reform.

The first article in the second subsection addresses the controversial issue of eminent domain. The second article in this subsection addresses the current debate over violence in video games.

The subsection **Global Ethics** concludes this unit with readings that provide helpful insight on ethical issues and dilemmas inherent in multinational operations. They describe adapting ethical decisions to a global marketplace and offer guidelines for helping management deal with ethical issues in international markets as well as revealing the extent that the global counterfeit business has gone out of control.

Does It **PAY** To Be **GOOD?**

Yes, say advocates of corporate citizenship, who believes their time has come—finally.

By A.J. Vogl

Corporate citizenship: For believers, the words speak of the dawning of a new era of capitalism, when business, government, and citizen groups join forces for the greater good, to jointly tackle such problems as water shortages and air pollution, to do something about the 1.2 billion people who live on less than a dollar a day.

Corporate citizenship: For critics of today's capitalism, the words smack of hypocrisy, big business' cynical response to charges of greed and corruption in high places, intended to mollify those who say corporations have too much power and that they wield it shamelessly. Critics charge that corporate citizenship is a placebo to the enemies of globalization, a public-relations smoke screen, capitalism's last-ditch attempt to preserve itself by co-opting its opposition.

Corporate citizenship: For many, it remains a diffuse concept, but generally it speaks to companies voluntarily adopting a triple bottom line, one that takes into account social, economic, and environmental considerations as well as financial results. Though some associate corporate citizenship with charity and philanthropy, the concept goes further—it embraces a corporate *conscience* above and beyond profits and markets. David Vidal, who directs research in global corporate citizenship at The Conference Board, comments, "Citizenship is not, as some critics charge, window dressing for the corporation. It deals with primary business relationships that are part of a company's strategic vision, and a good business case can be made for corporate citizenship."

Whether you are a critic or believer, however, there is no question that corporate citizenship—a term that embraces corporate social responsibility (CSR) and sustainability—is no longer a concept fostered by idealists on the fringe. It has entered the mainstream.

But why *now*? Though the era of corporate citizenship was ushered in with the fall of the Berlin Wall and the rise of market capitalism worldwide, current sentiment against big business has given new weight to the cause. Virtually every opinion survey shows that people think corporations have too much power, and that they will do anything in the pursuit of profits. And now, to add to public distrust, we have a flagging economy, a shambolic stock market, and what have been called "pornographic" CEO salaries. These circumstances have given citizenship's champions new planks for their platform, such as accounting and compensation practices. At the same time, attacks on the very nature of business have sent corporate leaders searching for a bright spot, and that spot may very well be the concept of corporate citizenship.

But that makes corporate enthusiasm for citizenship sound like a calculated, even cynical stance that is likely to last only as long as the environment remains hostile. There are grounds for believing that it is more than that, that it speaks to deeper changes in the greater world that make it *necessary* for large corporations to do good. Some of these changes include:

Tightening regulatory pressures. France, for instance, requires all companies listed on the Paris Stock Exchange to include information about their social and environmental performance within their financial statements; the Johannesburg Stock Exchange requires compliance with a CSR-based code of conduct; and the United Kingdom (the first nation with a minister for corporate social responsibility) requires pension-fund managers to disclose the degree to which social and environmental criteria are part of their investment decisions.

Will there be more national legislation? "If you had asked me that three or four years ago, I would have answered, 'Unclear, or probably not,'" says Allen White. White is acting chief executive of Global Reporting Initiative, an Amsterdam-based organization that has developed uniform guidelines for CSR reporting. "But in 2002 we've seen developments that could not have been anticipated several years ago, developments that have challenged companies to reconstruct or restore credibility, challenges to markets to demonstrate to investors that available information is accurate. Governments have taken note and are considering legislative and regulatory action."

Changing demographics. A socially engaged and better-educated population demands that the companies with which they do business—as consumers, employees, or investors—conform to higher standards. Both consumers and employees tell researchers that they prefer to purchase from and work for a company that is a good corporate citizen. On the investor front, activists—including individuals, socially responsible mutual funds, public pension funds, and religious groups—submitted 800 resolutions in 2002, according to Meg Voorhes, director of the social-is-

Investors Are Listening

For companies in sectors not considered exemplars of corporate citizenship—munitions, pornography, gambling, and tobacco (yes); liquor (probably); and oil (maybe)—there's good news: The market hasn't penalized them for their supposed lack of citizenship. For companies at the opposite end of the spectrum, there's also good news: Investors haven't penalized them for their expenditures on social causes.

On balance, the better news is for the socially responsible companies, who have long labored under the assumption that the investor automatically pays a price for investing in a socially responsible company or mutual fund—the price, of course, being a company or fund that doesn't perform as well as its peers that don't fly the socially-responsible banner.

Investors appear to be listening. According to Financial Research Corp., investors added $1.29 billion of new money into socially responsible funds during the first half of 2002, compared to $847.1 million added during all of 2001. Over the year ending July 31, the average mutual fund—including stock, bond, and balanced funds—was down 13 percent, while comparable socially responsible funds were down 19 percent. But advocates point out that different indices—particularly the Domini Social Index, a capitalization-weighted market index of 400 common stocks screened according to social and environmental criteria, and the Citizen's Index, a market-weighted portfolio of common stocks representing ownership in 300 of the most socially responsible U.S. companies, have outperformed the S&P 500 over the last one, three, and five years.

While the $13 billion invested in socially responsible funds (according to Morningstar) comprises only about 2 percent of total fund assets, advocates expect this percentage to climb to 10 percent by 2012, says Barbara Krumsiek, chief executive of the Bethesda, Md.-based Calvert Group, a mutual-fund complex specializing in socially responsible investing. And others' tallies are far higher: The nonprofit Social Investment Forum counts more than $2 trillion in total assets under management in portfolios screened for socially concerned investors, including socially screened mutual funds and separate accounts managed for socially conscious institutions and individual investors.

Plus, recent corporate scandals may have raised many investors' consciousness: In the first half of 2002, socially responsible mutual funds saw their assets increase by 3 percent, while conventional diversified funds lost 9.5 percent in total assets. People may have decided that if their mutual-fund investments were going to lose money, it might as well be for a good cause.

—A.J.V.

---

sues department at Investor Responsibility Research Center, a Washington, D.C.-based organization that tracks proxies.

More opportunity for investors to back their convictions with money. Socially aware investors can choose among some 230 mutual funds, and, according to Steven J. Schueth of the nonprofit Social Investment Forum, more than 800 independent asset managers identify themselves as managers of socially responsible portfolios for institutional investors and high-net-worth individuals. (See "Investors Are Listening.") Indexes of social and environmental performance—like the Dow Jones Sustainability World Indexes and FTSE4Good—are becoming significant market factors in screening for good citizenship. These indexes have teeth in them: They will and do drop companies that fail to meet social-responsibility standards.

Pressure from nongovernmental organizations. Not only are international NGOs growing in number—at last count, there were 28,000 worldwide—their visibility and credibility are on the rise. Last year, PR executive Richard Edelman told the World Economic Forum, "NGOs are now the Fifth Estate in global governance—the true credible source on issues related to the environment and social justice." While Americans generally trust corporations more than NGO "brands," the

opposite is true in Europe. A study conducted by Edelman's firm found that Amnesty International, the World Wildlife Fund, and Greenpeace outstripped by a margin of nearly two to one the four highest-rated corporations in Europe: Microsoft, Bayer, Shell, and Ford. As in other areas, it appears, European public opinion affirming social responsibility is ahead of that of the United States.

The most prominent corporate citizens rarely receive commensurate rewards.

Greater transparency. If good news travels fast, bad news moves faster. The Internet has given a platform to critics who, if they existed before, could be ignored; now they will be heard. There is the by-now-classic story of MIT graduate student Jonah Peretti, who submitted the word *sweatshop* to Nike's personalize-your-shoes iD program. Nike refused the order, terming the word "inappropriate slang."

Peretti replied, "I have decided to order the shoes with a different iD, but I would like to make one small request. Could you please send me a color snapshot of the ten-year-old Vietnamese girl who makes my shoes?" His e-mail correspondence was forwarded around the world and picked up by the mass media. Nike, in its first annual "corporate responsibility report," responded convincingly to charges that it exploited workers—indeed, the company is generally known as a CSR innovator—but inevitably sounded defensive.

All of these factors have led to increasing corporate acceptance of the importance of citizenship. Every three years, Bearing-Point, the consultancy formerly known as KPMG Consulting, surveys global *Fortune* 250 companies on corporate-responsibility issues. The latest survey found that 45 percent of the 250 companies surveyed issued environmental, social, and/or sustainability reports in 2001, up from 35 percent in 1998, and the number of U.S. companies that issued such reports increased 14 percent over the same period. Today, too, two-thirds of the world's largest companies use their Websites to trumpet their social and environmental activities.

Which is not to say that all these corporations have become true believers. "[W]e have to acknowledge," writes Steve Hilton, a British CSR consultant, "that fear of

Bringing Standards Up to Code

In May 2000, the International Chamber of Commerce counted more than 40 codes, existing or in preparation, intended to govern the activities of global corporations; among the most prominent are those of the OECD, the U.N. Global Compact, and the International Labor Organization.

Companies may be forgiven for having been confused over which set of guidelines to follow.

That confusion appears to be on the way to being lifted through the "2002 Sustainability Reporting Guidelines," introduced at the World Summit in Johannesburg by the Global Reporting Initiative. The guidelines are not another code. Rather, they are an attempt to create a generally accepted reporting framework for social responsibility. The outcome of two years of work by GRI, the guidelines are a rejoinder to the "deep scepticism" that "the creation of new wealth ... will do anything to decrease social inequities," as the document's introduction states. In nearly 100 pages, the guidelines cover such issues as transparency, sustainability, auditability, and comparability.

The last of these issues is critical, argues Eric Israel, a partner at BearingPoint, the consultancy formerly known as KPMG Consulting. "The meaning of citizenship for one particular company can be completely different than for another," he says. "So how do you benchmark an organization and compare it to others in the same industry? Up to now, there's been no equivalent of GAAP for social responsibility. That's where GRI comes in with its guidelines."

How does one verify that GRI guidelines have been met? Since the advent of CSR codes, companies have hired organizations, ranging from consultancies like BearingPoint to single-issue nonprofits, to verify their compliance for onlookers' eyes. Some monitor the companies themselves and attest that standards are being met—for instance, Chiquita Brands International has partnered with the Rainforest Alliance, which sends inspectors to each farm and offers its Better Bananas seal of approval to products from those farms that pass muster.

Other firms simply verify companies' CSR reports, the public face of compliance with codes. Considering the many codes in circulation and the range of organizations hired to verify compliance, it's not easy to put any particular report in broader context. That's where another organization, London-based AccountAbility, enters the picture.

Last June, AccountAbility issued something called the AA1000S Assurance Standard, which outlines principles around verification and CSR auditing—and which the firm hopes will become the gold standard of CSR verification standards. AccountAbility has credibility because of its governing constituencies—businesses, nonprofits, accountancies, researchers and academics, and consultancies—and its endorsement of GRI's reporting guidelines will likely give a boost to acceptance of both. "What we do is entirely complementary to what GRI does," says AccountAbility COO Mike Peirce. "It's a marriage made in heaven." In future, then, expect to see more annual reports that cite GRI guidelines verified by accountants using AccountAbility standards.

But the existence of these codes and organizations is only a first step; there's still a long way to go. According to a recent OECD survey, only one in five companies with codes of conduct share compliance information with the public, and third-party auditing remains the exception rather than the rule.

—A.J.V.

---

exposure and the need for compliance are the most powerful forces galvanizing the majority of active corporate citizens."

No Good Deed Goes Unpunished

As necessary as corporate citizenship may be, it still faces challenges from both inside and outside the corner office. Perhaps the most disheartening of these hurdles is that the most prominent corporate citizens rarely receive rewards commensurate with their prominence. As Hilton and Giles Gibbons, co-authors of the pro-CSR *Good Business: Your World Needs You*, point out, "Curiously, the companies whose hearts are most visibly fixed to their pinstriped sleeves tend to be the ones that attract the most frequent and venomous attacks from anti-business critics." Is this because critics feel that devious agendas lie behind the enlightened policies? Noreena Hertz, a British critic of corporate citizenship, wonders whether Microsoft, by

putting computers in schools today, will determine how children learn tomorrow.

Is it that corporations haven't gotten their stories across properly, or that they *have*—and are still being vilified? The experience of McDonald's in this arena is revealing. Last April, the fast-food chain published its first social-responsibility report, composed of 46 pages summarizing its efforts in four categories: community, environment, people, and marketplace. Those efforts have been rewarded in some courts of public opinion: In 2000 and 2001 *Financial Times*/PricewaterhouseCoopers surveys of media and NGOs, McDonald's placed 14th among the world's most respected companies for environmental performance.

At the same time, few corporations have been attacked as savagely as McDonald's for its "citizenship." It has been portrayed as an omnivorous monster that destroys local businesses and culture, promotes obesity, treats its employees badly, and despoils the environment. McDonald's goes to great lengths to answer

these charges in its social-responsibility report—which was itself widely criticized—but, like Nike, it can't help looking defensive. It will take a great deal more than a report of its good works to diminish the Golden Arches as a symbol of "capitalist imperialism" in the eyes of antiglobalists or to stanch the vitriol on such Websites as Mcspotlight.

There's no question that the bar is set exceedingly high in the arena of corporate social involvement. Philip Morris Cos. spends more than $100 million a year, most conspicuously in a series of TV commercials, on measures to discourage underage smoking—and still critics charge that the Philip Morris campaign is a cynical PR stunt that actually *encourages* kids to smoke. The company has been accused of having "a profound conflict of interest that cannot be overcome."

Another tobacco company, BAT, the world's second-largest, put some members of the social-responsibility establishment in an uncomfortable position when, last July, it became the industry's first company to publish a social-responsibility report. Few knew what to think upon reading the tobacco company's blunt rhetoric—"[T]here is no such thing as a 'safe' cigarette.... We openly state that, put simply, smoking is a cause of certain serious diseases"—and the 18 pages devoted to the risks of smoking. BAT even had its report audited by an independent verifier. All this wasn't nearly enough to satisfy antismoking groups, of course—they continue to view the company with deep suspicion. Would anyone have predicted otherwise?

When accused of being overly suspicious, critics point to one company that, over the last six years, won numerous awards for its environmental, human rights, anti-corruption, anti-bribery, and climate-change policies; a company prominent on "most admired" and "best companies to work for" lists; a company that issued a report on the good deeds that supported its claim to be a top corporate citizen. That company was Enron.

No one would argue that Enron is typical, yet its debacle has tainted other companies. It also raises a difficult question about CSR: What is the link between how a company is managed—corporate governance—and corporate citizenship? Steve Hilton, speaking from London, says that the link is not really understood in the United Kingdom: "People here have not made the connection between the corporate-governance, executive-compensation, and accounting-fraud issues in the United States and operational issues that come under the heading of corporate citizenship. I would argue they're all part of the same thing."

So would Transparency International's Frank Vogl, co-founder of the anti-corruption NGO. He believes that CSR has been undermined because it has been disconnected from corporate-conduct issues. "Foreign public trust in Corporate America has been diminished," he said, "and there is scant evidence that U.S. business leaders recognize the global impact of the U.S. scandals."

Vogl says that, for most countries in the world, corruption is much more of a social-responsibility issue than either the environment or labor rights. "What U.S. businesspeople see as a facilitating payment may be seen in developing countries as a bribe," he comments, "and I think that provides some insight into why the United States ranks behind 12 other countries on the Transparency International Bribe Payers Index. To me, corporate citizenship means you don't bribe foreign officials. That's the worst kind of hypocrisy."

Will They Be Good in Bad Times?

The specter of hypocrisy raises its head in another quarter as well: Do employees of companies claiming to be good corporate citizens see their employer's citizenship activities as a diversion or cover-up to charges of bad leadership and poor management practices? Certainly, if recent surveys are a guide, top management needs to restore its credibility with employees. In a recent Mercer Human Resource Consulting study, only a third of the 2,600 workers surveyed agreed with the statement, "I can trust management in my organization to always communicate honestly." And a Walker Information survey of employees found that only 49 percent believe their senior leaders to be "people of high personal integrity." If CSR is perceived by employees merely as puffery to make top management look good, it will not get under an organization's cultural skin.

"Businesses needn't apologize for making products that other Americans want to buy."

Even if there is a genuine management commitment, corporations have other obligations that may take precedence, begging the question: Will corporations be good citizens in bad times as well as good? The experience of Ford Motor Co. brings the question to earth. In August, Ford issued its third annual corporate-citizenship report. Previous reports had drawn plaudits from environmentalists, but this one, coming at a time when the automaker faced financial difficulties, was attacked by the same environmentalists for failing to set aggressive goals for reducing greenhouse-gas emissions or improving gas mileage. Sierra Club's executive director called it "a giant step in the wrong direction for Ford Motor Co., for American consumers, and for the environment."

Lingering tough economic conditions may impel other companies to take their own "giant steps" backward. An old business saw has it that when times get tough and cuts have to be made, certain budgets are at the top of the list for cutbacks—advertising for one, public relations for another. For companies in which corporate

citizenship is seen as an extension of public relations, of "image building" or "reputation management," it may suffer this fate.

Which is as it should be, say some critics. As *The Wall Street Journal* lectured CEO William Ford on its editorial page: "We also hope Mr. Ford has learned from his mistake of ceding the moral and political high ground to environmentalists.... Businesses needn't apologize for making products that other Americans want to buy. Their first obligation is to their shareholders and employees and that means above all making an honest profit."

Does the "Business Case" Really Have a Case?

But hold on: What about the so-called business case for corporate citizenship—that it contributes to making "an honest profit"? Unfortunately, it's difficult to quantify in cost-benefit terms what that contribution is. Not something to be concerned about, says Simon Zadek, CEO of AccountAbility, a London-based institute that has established CSR verification standards. (See "Bringing Standards Up to Code.") "It is a fact that the vast majority of day-to-day business decisions are taken without any explicit cost-benefit analysis," he says, pointing to employee training as an example of a corporate expenditure that is difficult to quantify in cost-benefit terms. What he doesn't mention is that, when business is suffering, training is usually among the expenditures to be cut back or eliminated.

Ultimately, Zadek concedes that, in strictly quantifiable terms, one cannot make a cost-benefit case for corporate citizenship. "Although the question 'Does corporate citizenship pay?' is technically right, it is misleading in practice," he says. "Rephrasing the core question as 'In what ways does corporate citizenship contribute to achieving the core business strategy?' is far preferable."

To some hardheaded corporate types, Zadek's reasoning may seem disingenuous, but even the hardheads can't be dismissive—at least publicly. Moreover, they would probably acknowledge that corporate citizenship, in concept and practice, has come too far to be ignored. In the future, it may well become what Steve Hilton calls a "hygiene factor," a condition of doing business. Hilton's firm, Good Business, consults with firms on citizenship issues. "I think business leaders are coming to realize CSR's potential to go beyond

Attacked From All Sides

While many skeptics criticize the ways in which corporate social responsibility is enacted, some take matters a step further by asking if the concept should exist at all. Who would object to the idea of a company doing good, of moving beyond the traditional and literal bottom line, to take a larger view of the reason for its existence? You may be surprised: There are many critics, and they come from various and sometimes unpredictable directions.

First is a group that says corporate social responsibility is flawed at its heart because it's doing the right thing for the wrong reason. The right thing, they believe, is doing the right thing because it is right, as a matter of principle—not because it advances the firm's business interests. The rejoinder, of course, is that if a larger social or environmental good is met, we should not quibble about motivation. As corporate-governance activist Robert A.G. Monks points out: "You can get backing from institutional investors only if you talk a commercial idiom."

Next is a group of dissimilar critics who believe that, in attempting to pursue goals of corporate citizenship, companies are doing things that are none of their business. Paradoxically, these critics come from both the right and the left.

The right feels that the business of business should be business: As Michael Prowse argues in the *Financial Times*, the role of the corporation "is to provide individuals with the means to be socially responsible. Rather than trying to play the role of social worker, senior executives should concentrate on their statutory obligations. We should not expect benevolence of them, but we should demand probity: the socially responsible chief executive is the one who turns a profit without lying, cheating, robbing or defrauding anyone."

The left, on the other hand, feels that corporations are usurping the powers of government, to the detriment of the citizenry and democracy itself. Noreena Hertz, the British academic and broadcaster who wrote of *The Silent Takeover: Global Capitalism and the Death of Democracy*, is not only dubious about business taking over responsibilities that she feels properly belong to government—she is skeptical about business' ability to handle them: "[M]anagers of multinationals operating in the third world are often overwhelmed by the social problems they encounter, and understandably find it difficult to know which causes to prioritize.... Their contributions can be squandered, or diverted through corruption."

And what happens, she asks, when a corporation decides to pull out, if government has allowed private industry to take over its role? Worse still, she worries about situations in which a socially responsible corporation could use its position "to exact a stream of IOUs and quid pro quos, to demand ever more favorable terms and concessions from host governments."

Then there is a group of critics who see corporate citizenship as a diversionary ploy to placate a public outraged at dubious corporate practices. They will concede that Enron, WorldCom, and Tyco are egregious exceptions, but are other companies exemplars of probity? Hardly. Can companies be considered good corporate citizens when they move their headquarters to Bermuda to avoid taxes (and enrich their CEOs in the process)? Can companies like General Electric, Monsanto, Merck, SmithKline Beecham, and Chiquita Brands International claim the moral high ground when they have cut employee benefits in connection with mergers and spinoffs? And what of such companies as Wyeth, Wal-Mart, McKesson, and Merrill Lynch? Can they, ask the critics, be considered high-minded citizens when the top executives accumulate pots of money in their deferred-compensation accounts? This may be why PR *eminence grise* John Budd says, "For at least the next 18 post-Enron months, I certainly would not counsel any CEO to magically appear publicly as an enlightened champion of social responsibility. The circumstances make it automatic that it would be perceived as spinning."

Last, there is a group of critics that says that simply doing more good than we're doing now is not enough, that we have to rethink the nature of the beast—capitalism itself. Steven Piersanti, president of Berrett-Koehler Publishers, is in the thick of this intellectual contretemps. Last fall, his firm published two books that took divergent views on the issue. The first, *Walking the Talk*, was written by Swiss industrialist Stephan Schmidheiny, along with two colleagues at the World Business Council for Sustainable Development, Chad Holliday of DuPont and Philip Watts of Royal Dutch/Shell. "It advances a reformist view that major changes are needed in our business world," says Piersanti, "but that these changes can best be achieved by reforms within our existing economic structures, institutions, and systems." The second book, *Alternatives to Economic Globalization: A Better World Is Possible*, presents "an activist view that existing economic structures are insufficient and that new structures, institutions, and systems are needed in the world."

It's likely that doubts about the nature and purpose of corporate citizenship will continue to be raised from all quarters. But with social-responsibility reporting and verification initiatives in place and likely government regulation down the road, there's reason to think that their voices will become more isolated.

—A.J.V.

a compliance/risk-management issue into a genuine business tool," he says. "That's been the rhetoric all along, but the reality has been that it's been a slightly marginal issue. With few exceptions, it's been seen as an add-on, without being incorporated into core business decision-making."

This is Zadek's point when he argues the case for what he calls "third-generation corporate citizenship." The first generation is defined by cause-related marketing and short-term reputation management. The second occurs when social and environmental objectives become a core part of long-term business strategy; as an example, he points to automakers competing in the arena of emission controls. The third generation is based on collective action, where corporations join with competitors, NGOs, and government "to change the un-derlying rules of the game to ensure that business delivers adequate social and environmental results."

Changing the rules means, for one thing, a more level playing field. "In CSR," says AccountAbility COO Mike Peirce, "companies that are leaders might suffer a penalty if there's a big gap between themselves and laggards in the field, so they'd like everybody ticking along at at least a basic level." In other words, a socially responsible company does not want to be penalized financially for being socially responsible. Of course, a cynic might reply that if CSR indeed provides the competitive advantage that its proponents insist it does, then it is the laggards that should suffer the severest financial penalty.

Expect citizenship proponents to make corporate governance itself the issue.

To convince doubters, efforts are being made to schematically quantify corporate social responsibility. In a recent *Harvard Business Review* article titled "The Virtue Matrix: Calculating the Return on Corporate Responsibility," Roger L. Martin makes a point of treating corporate responsibility as a product or service like any other. According to Martin, who is dean of the University of Toronto's Rotman School of Management, his matrix can help companies sort out such questions as whether a citizenship initiative will erode a company's competitive position.

Even if Martin's formula seems overly clinical, it supports the trend toward closer analysis of what social responsibility means and what it brings to corporations practicing it. But analysis will take you only so far. "[I]t is impossible to prove the direction of the flow of causality," writes Chad Holliday, chairman and CEO of Du-Pont and co-author of *Walking the Talk: The Business Case for Sustainable Development.* "Does a company become profitable and thus enjoy the luxury of being able to worry about environmental and social issues or does the pursuit of sustainability make a company more profitable?"

But for large public companies, the question of whether it truly pays to be good will be asked less and less; for them, it will be *necessary* to be good, if only to avoid appearing Neanderthal. That means that corporate social responsibility, itself nothing less than a growth industry today, will become "normalized" into corporate cultures.

Yes, there will be an effort to level the playing field in CSR, but, further, expect citizenship proponents to attempt to raise the field to a higher level by making corporate governance itself the issue. "Unless we make basic structural changes," says Marjorie Kelly, the editor of *Business Ethics* magazine and a frequent critic of CSR, "it'll be nothing but window dressing. The corporate scandals have given a real-world demonstration that business without ethics collapses, and that has given us an extraordinary opportunity to change the way we do business."

A.J. VOGL is editor of *Across the Board.* He wrote "Worry About the Details" in the Sept/Oct issue.

From *Across the Board,* January/February 2003, pp. 17-23. Copyright © 2003 by Conference Board, Inc. Reprinted by permission.

TRUST
IN THE
MARKETPLACE

John E. Richardson and
Linnea Bernard McCord

Traditionally, ethics is defined as a set of moral values or principles or a code of conduct.

> ... Ethics, as an expression of reality, is predicated upon the assumption that there are right and wrong motives, attitudes, traits of character, and actions that are exhibited in interpersonal relationships. Respectful social interaction is considered a norm by almost everyone.
> ... the overwhelming majority of people perceive others to be ethical when they observe what is considered to be their genuine kindness, consideration, politeness, empathy, and fairness in their interpersonal relationships. When these are absent, and unkindness, inconsideration, rudeness, hardness, and injustice are present, the people exhibiting such conduct are considered unethical. A genuine consideration of others is essential to an ethical life. (Chewning, pp. 175–176).

An essential concomitant of ethics is of trust. Webster's Dictionary defines trust as "assured reliance on the character, ability, strength or truth of someone or something." Businesses are built on a foundation of trust in our free-enterprise system. When there are violations of this trust between competitors, between employer and employees, or between businesses and consumers, our economic system ceases to run smoothly. From a moral viewpoint, ethical behavior should not exist because of economic pragmatism, governmental edict, or contemporary fashionability—it should exist because it is morally appropriate and right. From an economic point of view, ethical behavior should exist because it just makes good business sense to be ethical and operate in a manner that demonstrates trustworthiness.

Robert Bruce Shaw, in *Trust in the Balance*, makes some thoughtful observations about trust within an organization. Paraphrasing his observations and applying his ideas to the marketplace as a whole:

1. Trust requires consumers have confidence in organizational promises or claims made to them. This means that a consumer should be able to believe that a commitment made will be met.

2. Trust requires integrity and consistency in following a known set of values, beliefs, and practices.

3. Trust requires concern for the well-being of others. This does not mean that organizational needs are not given appropriate emphasis—but it suggests the importance of understanding the impact of decisions and actions on others—i.e. consumers. (Shaw, pp. 39–40)

Companies can lose the trust of their customers by portraying their products in a deceptive or inaccurate manner. In one recent example, a Nike advertisement exhorted golfers to buy the same golf balls used by Tiger Woods. However, since Tiger Woods was using custom-made Nike golf balls not yet available to the general golfing public, the ad was, in fact, deceptive. In one of its ads, Volvo represented that Volvo cars could withstand a physical impact that, in fact, was not possible. Once a company is "caught" giving inaccurate information, even if done innocently, trust in that company is eroded.

Companies can also lose the trust of their customers when they fail to act promptly and notify their customers of problems that the company has discovered, especially where deaths may be involved. This occurred when Chrysler dragged its feet in replacing a safety latch on its Minivan (Geyelin, pp. A1, A10). More recently, Firestone and Ford had been publicly brought to task for failing to expeditiously notify American consumers of tire defects in SUVs even though the problem had occurred years earlier in other countries. In cases like these, trust might not just be eroded, it might be destroyed. It could take years of painstaking effort to rebuild trust under these circumstances, and some companies might not have the economic ability to withstand such a rebuilding process with their consumers.

A *20/20* and *New York Times* investigation on a recent *ABC 20/20* program, entitled "The Car Dealer's Secret" revealed a sad example of the violation of trust in the marketplace. The investigation divulged that many unsuspecting consumers have had hidden charges tacked on by some car dealers when purchasing a new car. According to consumer attorney Gary Klein, "It's a dirty little secret that the auto lending industry has not owned up to." (*ABC News 20/20*)

The scheme worked in the following manner. Car dealers would send a prospective buyer's application to a number of lenders, who would report to the car dealer what interest rate the lender would give to the buyer for his or her car loan. This interest rate is referred to as the "buy rate." Legally a car dealer is not required to tell the buyer what the "buy rate" is or how much the dealer is marking up the loan. If dealers did most of the loans at the buy rate, they only get a small fee. However, if they were able to convince the buyer to pay a higher rate, they made considerably more money. Lenders encouraged car dealers to charge the buyer a higher rate than the "buy rate" by agreeing to split the extra income with the dealer.

David Robertson, head of the Association of Finance and Insurance Professionals—a trade group representing finance managers—defended the practice, reflecting that it was akin to a retail markup on loans. "The dealership provides a valuable service on behalf of the customer in negotiating these loans," he said. "Because of that, the dealership should be compensated for that work." (*ABC News 20/20*)

Careful examination of the entire report, however, makes one seriously question this apologetic. Even if this practice is deemed to be legal, the critical issue is what happens to trust when the buyers discover that they have been charged an additional 1–3% of the loan without their knowledge? In some cases, consumers were led to believe that they were getting the dealer's bank rate, and in other cases, they were told that the dealer had shopped around at several banks to secure the best loan rate they could get for the buyer. While this practice may be questionable from a legal standpoint, it is clearly in ethical breach of trust with the consumer. Once discovered, the companies doing this will have the same credibility and trustworthiness problems as the other examples mentioned above.

The untrustworthiness problems of the car companies was compounded by the fact that the investigation appeared to reveal statistics showing that black customers were twice as likely as whites to have their rate marked up—and at a higher level. That evidence—included in thousands of pages of confidential documents which *20/20* and *The New York Times* obtained from a Tennessee court—revealed that some Nissan and GM dealers in Tennessee routinely marked up rates for blacks, forcing them to pay between $300 and $400 more than whites. (*ABC News 20/20*)

This is a tragic example for everyone who was affected by this markup and was the victim of this secret policy. Not only is trust destroyed, there is a huge economic cost to the general public. It is estimated that in the last four years or so, Texas car dealers have received approximately $9 billion of kickbacks from lenders, affecting 5.2 million consumers. (*ABC News 20/20*)

Let's compare these unfortunate examples of untrustworthy corporate behavior with the landmark example of Johnson & Johnson which ultimately increased its trustworthiness with consumers by the way it handled the Tylenol incident. After seven individuals, who had consumed Tylenol capsules contaminated by a third party died, Johnson & Johnson instituted a total product recall within a week costing an estimated $50 million after taxes. The company did this, not because it was responsible for causing the problem, but because it was the right thing to do. In addition, Johnson & Johnson spearheaded the development of more effective tamper-proof containers for their industry. Because of the company's swift response, consumers once again were able to trust in the Johnson & Johnson name. Although Johnson & Johnson suffered a decrease in market share at the time because of the scare, over the long term it has maintained its profitability in a highly competitive market. Certainly part of this profit success is attributable to consumers believing that Johnson & Johnson is a trustworthy company. (Robin and Reidenbach)

The e-commerce arena presents another example of the importance of marketers building a mutually valuable relationship with customers through a trust-based collaboration process. Recent research with 50 e-businesses reflects that companies which create and nurture trust find customers return to their sites repeatedly. (Dayal.... p. 64)

In the e-commerce world, six components of trust were found to be critical in developing trusting, satisfied customers:

- State-of-art reliable security measures on one's site
- Merchant legitimacy (e.g., ally one's product or service with an established brand)
- Order fulfillment (i.e. placing orders and getting merchandise efficiently and with minimal hassles)
- Tone and ambiance—handling consumers' personal information with sensitivity and iron-clad confidentiality
- Customers feeling that they are in control of the buying process
- Consumer collaboration—e.g., having chat groups to let consumers query each other about their purchases and experiences (Dayal..., pp. 64–67)

Additionally, one author noted recently that in the e-commerce world we've moved beyond brands and trademarks to "trustmarks." This author defined a trustmark as a

> … (D)istinctive name or symbol that emotionally binds a company with the desires and aspirations of its customers. It's an emotional connection—and it's much bigger and more powerful than the uses that we traditionally associate with a trademark.... (Webber, p. 214)

Certainly if this is the case, trust—being an emotional link—is of supreme importance for a company that wants to succeed in doing business on the Internet.

It's unfortunate that while a plethora of examples of violation of trust easily come to mind, a paucity of examples "pop up" as noteworthy paradigms of organizational courage and trust in their relationship with consumers.

In conclusion, some key areas for companies to scrutinize and practice with regard to decisions that may affect trustworthiness in the marketplace might include:

- Does a company practice the Golden Rule with its customers? As a company insider, knowing what you know about the product, how willing would you be to purchase it for yourself or for a family member?
- How proud would you be if your marketing practices were made public.... shared with your friends....

or family? (Blanchard and Peale, p. 27)

- Are bottom-line concerns the sole component of your organizational decision-making process? What about human rights, the ecological/environmental impact, and other areas of social responsibility?
- Can a firm which engages in unethical business practices with customers be trusted to deal with its employees any differently? Unfortunately, frequently a willingness to violate standards of ethics is not an isolated phenomenon but permeates the culture. The result is erosion of integrity throughout a company. In such cases, trust is elusive at best. (Shaw, p. 75)
- Is your organization not only market driven, but also value-oriented? (Peters and Levering, Moskowitz, and Katz)
- Is there a strong commitment to a positive corporate culture and a clearly defined mission which is frequently and unambiguously voiced by upper-management?
- Does your organization exemplify trust by practicing a genuine relationship partnership with your customers—*before, during, and after* the initial purchase? (Strout, p. 69)

Companies which exemplify treating customers ethically are founded on a covenant of trust. There is a shared belief, confidence, and faith that the company and its people will be fair, reliable, and ethical in all its dealings. *Total trust is the belief that a company and its people will never take opportunistic advantage of customer vulnerabilities*. (Hart and Johnson, pp. 11–13)

References

ABC News 20/20, "The Car Dealer's Secret," October 27, 2000.

Blanchard, Kenneth, and Norman Vincent Peale, *The Power of Ethical Management*, New York: William Morrow and Company, Inc., 1988.

Chewning, Richard C., *Business Ethics in a Changing Culture* (Reston, Virginia: Reston Publishing, 1984).

Dayal, Sandeep, Landesberg, Helen, and Michael Zeissner, "How to Build Trust Online," *Marketing Management*, Fall 1999, pp. 64–69.

Geyelin, Milo, "Why One Jury Dealt a Big Blow to Chrysler in Minivan-Latch Case," *Wall Street Journal*, November 19, 1997, pp. A1, A10.

Hart, Christopher W. and Michael D. Johnson, "Growing the Trust Relationship," *Marketing Management*, Spring 1999, pp. 9–19.

Hosmer, La Rue Tone, *The Ethics of Management*, second edition (Homewood, Illinois: Irwin, 1991).

Kaydo, Chad, "A Position of Power," *Sales & Marketing Management*, June 2000, pp. 104–106, 108ff.

Levering, Robert; Moskowitz, Milton; and Michael Katz, *The 100 Best Companies to Work for in America* (Reading, Mass.: Addison-Wesley, 1984).

Magnet, Myron, "Meet the New Revolutionaries," *Fortune*, February 24, 1992, pp. 94–101.

Muoio, Anna, "The Experienced Customer," *Net Company*, Fall 1999, pp. 025–027.

Peters, Thomas J. and Robert H. Waterman Jr., *In Search of Excellence* (New York: Harper & Row, 1982).

Richardson, John (ed.), *Annual Editions: Business Ethics 00/01* (Guilford, CT: McGraw-Hill/Dushkin, 2000).

_____, *Annual Editions: Marketing 00/01* (Guilford, CT: McGraw-Hill/Dushkin, 2000).

Robin, Donald P., and Erich Reidenbach, "Social Responsibility, Ethics, and Marketing Strategy: Closing the Gap Between Concept and Application," *Journal of Marketing*, Vol. 51 (January 1987), pp. 44–58.

Shaw, Robert Bruce, *Trust in the Balance*, (San Francisco: Jossey-Bass Publishers, 1997).

Strout, Erin, "Tough Customers," *Sales Marketing Management*, January 2000, pp. 63–69.

Webber, Alan M., "Trust in the Future," *Fast Company*, September 2000, pp. 209–212ff.

Dr. John E. Richardson is Professor of Marketing in the Graziadio School of Business and Management at Pepperdine University, Malibu, California

Dr. Linnea Bernard McCord is Associate Professor of Business Law in the Graziadio School of Business and Management at Pepperdine University, Malibu, California

© 2000 by John E. Richardson and Linnea Bernard McCord. Reprinted by permission of the authors.

HOW WOMEN ARE CHANGING CORPORATE AMERICA

"I hate golfing, shoulder pads look horrible and I hate man ties,"
says Michelle Peluso, CEO of Travelocity. "I don't feel pressure to act like the guys."

By Yoji Cole

The American work force has changed dramatically in the past several decades. Where women once were the "girls in the office" even if they were in their 60s, they now are CEOs and presidents as well as just about everything else. Yet they aren't just female clones of male executives. Women approach management and leadership differently, emphasizing relationship-building and attentiveness to employee needs, both of which focus a team on common goals.

What most women do not do now is wear those dreaded man ties.

"It's not like we make up half of the country's CEOs, but now we're doing it our own way," says Peluso, 33.

As more women rise in the ranks of corporate America, smart companies are noticing their distinctive leadership qualities and rewarding them. Among DiversityInc's Top 10 Companies for Executive Women, the advancement of female employees is taken so seriously that nine out of 10 link managers' pay to diversity initiatives for women. At these companies, women are visible, powerful and supported with programs that balance their lives in the office and at home.

The numbers tell the story. The Top 10 Companies for Executive Women hire more females than males and employ a quarter more women in management than the typical American employer. Almost a third of their top 10 percent of highest-paid employees are women, 14 percent more than at the Top 50 Companies for Diversity.

Additionally, the Top 10 Companies for Executive Women outperform the Fortune 500's percentage of female board directors by a third.

Why do some companies surpass others when it comes to advancing women? Many claim that their inclusiveness is a deeply ingrained part of their culture dating back many years. But even the top companies had to start somewhere, and change usually begins with leadership.

Peluso and the other executives in this story are a snapshot of corporate America's women leaders. They are GenXers, they are baby boomers, and they are CEOs, CFOs and senior vice presidents. Some of them entered corporate America when male CEOs thought married men were the best employees, when women could not become vice presidents and when survival meant assimilating dress and management tactics to male mores.

The personal leadership styles of the four women here represent the promise of greater inclusiveness as corporate America evolves.

In addition to Peluso, *DiversityInc* spoke with Diane Parks, 53, senior vice president and general manager, specialty biotherapeutics and managed care for Genentech; Sallie Krawcheck, 39, CFO and head of strategy at Citigroup; and Amy S. Butte, 37, CFO of the New York Stock Exchange (NYSE). They all have brought value to their respective organizations through their business acumen

and effort to build morale through inclusive management tactics.

"Its important to reach out to people who make us intellectually uncomfortable," says Krawcheck. "You have to lead people who are independent self-starters."

Krawcheck, after joining Citigroup in 2002 as the chairman and CEO of "Smith Barney—Citigroup's private wealth-management and equity-research unit—guided the restructuring of Smith Barneys equity-research business and strengthened the quality and transparency of its research.

Krawcheck attributes her success to a practice of purposely seeking out assignments that forced her to stretch her abilities. Women, she says, should be "unflinching and open-eyed about [their] strengths and weaknesses and not just accepting of critiques but asking for them and acting upon them."

Parks, as the senior member of the group interviewed, recalls the days when women executives were passed over for promotion simply because they were women. At the outset of her career in the mid-1970s, Parks worked at a Kansas City-based pharmaceutical company called Marion Laboratories, now Aventis. Women at that time mostly were relegated to sales-support functions. That's where Parks found herself, even though she had wanted to be a product manager. She believes that married men were preferred because the management believed they were motivated to provide for their families.

So Parks, not wanting to leave her hometown of Kansas City, dealt with the limiting corporate culture by trying her hand at as many jobs as possible. She made lateral moves working in therapeutics, wound care, cardiovascular medicine and other areas.

In the 1980s, Marions management decided it was time to include more women in its sales department and launched a rotational training program that placed candidates in different areas of the business for six months at a time. Parks joined.

"[These lateral moves] enabled me to show I could do other things, learn other things and have a broad line of experience," says Parks.

Training programs such as these are the first step in transforming a company into a diversity leader. Nine of the Top 10 Companies for Executive Women have employee-resource groups and seven of the 10 offer official mentoring and training programs.

The experience Parks gained helped her to move up the corporate ladder. In 1998, she beat three male candidates out of a vice-presidential position at the pharmaceutical company. She contends that lateral moves do not always spell doom.

"I see some women not being flexible and [not] taking lateral moves because they're so focused on 'upward' they don't see the benefit in broadening their experience," says Parks.

Parks left the company for Genentech in 1999, where her presence sends a signal to aspiring female recruits that their gender won't impede their upward mobility. Before a company can become a top company for women, it must open its upper ranks to them.

Butte, by noticing the unnoticed, created a more inclusive corporate culture at the NYSE. "People in the [NYSE] finance department would point to the fact that my presence has made a difference in terms of how we operate and changing the expectations," says Butte.

She joined the NYSE as an executive vice president in February 2004 and the following April was named its CFO. Throughout her career, she's been a producer, she says, "whether it was a client relationship, sale[s], [or as] an analyst building coverage and attracting clients to the firm. And today I'm viewed as someone who produces by setting our mission and meeting objectives."

One of her objectives has been to recognize talented employees in the NYSE's financial department.

"It's important to reach out to people who make us intellectually uncomfortable."
Salle Krawcheck, Citigroup

Since becoming CFO of the NYSE, Butte has used her position to promote financial services as a career choice for women. She's also proud of the role she played in promoting Rae Amen, a 29-year NYSE veteran who was moved up from manager to assistant controller of operations, and 26-year NYSE veteran Doreen Bloise, who was promoted to manager of collection from collection coordinator.

"They are an example of women I've seen come alive and are making a difference," says Butte.

Women executives, like men, want to be valued members of their organizations. Like men, women report that they are frustrated with a lack of mentor programs and having to navigate through office politics.

One of the traits that set top companies apart is the degree to which they create formal development opportunities for women. Marriott, which ranks No. 9 on the Top 10 Companies for Women, for example, hosts regional women's leadership councils so that women can gain visibility in the organization. SBC Communications, which ranks No. 8, offers a three-year leadership-development program that prepares women for greater responsibility.

While none of the executives in this story benefited from formal mentoring programs, they all endorsed mentoring and are themselves mentors. For example, Krawcheck partners with Citigroups employee network groups to organize a leadership-training program for women executives. Citigroup ranks No. 7 on the Top 10 Companies for Executive Women list and No. 2 on the Top 50 Companies for Diversity.

Another result of the influx of women into corporate America is choices.

"I see women who are 25 and are saying by the time they're 40, they want to be a CEO somewhere, and I see women who love what they're doing and move on when they've accomplished their goals," says Parks, before adding with a laugh: "And I have a 21-year-old daughter who says she doesn't want to work, period."

Such choices are the result of progressive companies, such as those on the Top 50 Companies for Diversity list, which have created diversity programs and/or women's initiatives to augment male-dominated corporate cultures to ensure women are included in succession planning and other high-profile activities.

As a result, progressive companies have reaped financial rewards. In studying companies that appeared on the Fortune 500 between 1996 and 2000, the women's research organization Catalyst found that companies with the highest percentage of women on their top management teams had better financial performance than those companies with the lowest representation—total return to shareholders was 34 percent higher and return on equity was 35.1 percent higher.

Despite stereotypes that women aren't aggressive enough to run major companies, the reality is that entrepreneurialism runs strong in executive women.

Since becoming Travelocity's CEO in December 2003, Peluso has overseen the company's effort to diversify its revenue streams in an attempt to reclaim its position as the No. 1 online travel Web site, a position currently held by Expedia. Under Pelusos direction, Travelocity developed technology that provides a direct connection to hotels and allows consumers to build their own vacation packages. This diverted the company's focus away from bookings.

"It was risky," says Peluso, who during her tenure as Travelocity's vice president of hotels and COO increased annual gross bookings by 11.6 percent in 2003 to $3.9 billion. "But that's how you differentiate who you are," she says.

"Women tend to be good at interpersonal relationships."

Sallie Krawcheck, Citigroup

TOP 10 COMPANIES FOR EXECUTIVE WOMEN

TOP 10 RANK	Company
1	AstraZeneca
2	Merck & Company
3	PricewaterhouseCoopers
4	Abbot Laboratories
5	Prudential Financial
6	Thompson Hospitality
7	Citigroup
8	SBC Communications
9	Marriott International
10	KPMG

Peluso is also trying to differentiate Travelocity in the minds of diverse consumers. She expects to dedicate more effort to attracting diverse travelers in the upcoming year. In April, the company launched a section on its site for gay and lesbian travelers.

Peluso attributes her success at Travelocity to her staff more than she does herself and in doing so does not do her management techniques justice. She, like the other women in this story, seeks to build team unity by paying attention to her employees' personal and professional needs.

"Work should feel like a mission and not a job".

Michelle Peluso, Travelocity

"Women understand what its like to get pregnant and still want your job. Women understand what its like to be in a meeting where you're the only one. I think we think about those issues a little harder or differently [than male leaders] because we have the experience base," says Peluso.

Krawcheck agrees: "Women tend to be good at interpersonal relationships."

To further build a collegial, interpersonal atmosphere at Travelocity, Peluso has organized parties using the company's theme of making over its product. One party called "extreme makeover day" had employees come to work as their alter egos. Peluso took the lead in this as well, showing up to work dressed in an army-fatigue skirt and T-shirt with an anarchy symbol. She has also been known to dance on stage at company parties, is a practical joker and will e-mail phrases to employees who win a prize if they can guess who said the phrase.

"Work should feel like a mission and not a job," says Peluso.

Thinking of work as a mission might come easier for women since each time a woman sits in a meeting or boardroom, moves upstairs to a corner office or has her name etched on the company's front door, it is not only a personal success but a success shared by other women. It is a success won by trudging through corporate and gender politics, and while it is getting easier, as exemplified by the experiences of Peluso, Butte, Krawcheck and Parks, it still is difficult.

From *Diversity Inc.*, March 2005, pp. 26-27, 30. Copyright © 2005 by Diversity Inc. Reprinted by permission.

OLD. SMART. PRODUCTIVE.

Surprise! The graying of the workforce is better news than you think

Peter Coy

EMMA SHULMAN IS A DYNAMO. THE VETERAN SOCIAL WORKER WORKS up to 50 hours a week recruiting people for treatment at an Alzheimer's clinic at New York University School of Medicine. Her boss, psychiatrist Steven H. Ferris, dreads the day she decides to retire: "We'd definitely have to hire two or three people to replace her," he says. Complains Shulman: "One of my problems is excess energy, which drives me nuts."

Oh, one more thing about Emma Shulman. She's nearly 93 years old.

Shulman is more than one amazing woman. She just might be a harbinger of things to come as the leading edge of the 78 million-strong Baby Boom generation approaches its golden years. Of course, nobody's predicting that boomers will routinely work into their 90s. But Shulman—and better-known oldsters like investor Kirk Kerkorian, 87, and Federal Reserve Chairman Alan Greenspan, 79—are proof that productive, paying work does not have to end at 55, 60, or even 65.

Old. Smart. Productive. Rather than being an economic deadweight, the next generation of older Americans is likely to make a much bigger contribution to the economy than many of today's forecasts predict. Sure, most people slow down as they get older. But new research suggests that boomers will have the ability—and the desire—to work productively and innovatively well beyond today's normal retirement age. If society can tap their talents, employers will benefit, living standards will be higher, and the financing problems of Social Security and Medicare will be easier to solve. The logic is so powerful that it is likely to sweep aside many of the legal barriers and corporate practices that today keep older workers from achieving their full productive potential.

INTERNET MEMORY TOOLS

In coming years, more Americans reaching their 60s and 70s are going to want to work, at least part-time. Researchers are finding that far from wearing people down, work can actually help keep them mentally and physically fit. Many highly educated and well-paid workers—lawyers, physicians, architects—already work to advanced ages because their skills are valued. Boomers, with more education than any generation in history, are likely to follow that pattern. And today's rapid obsolescence

of knowledge can actually play to older workers' advantage: It used to be considered wasteful to train people near retirement. But if training has to be refreshed every year, then companies might as well retrain old employees as young ones.

"One of my problems is excess energy, which drives me nuts"

Equally important, high-level work is getting easier for the old. Thanks to medical advances, people are staying healthy, enabling them to work longer than before. Fewer jobs require physically demanding tasks such as heavy lifting. And technology—from memory-enhancing drugs to Internet search engines that serve as auxiliary memories—will help senior workers compensate for the effects of aging. "Assuming that the improved health trends continue, boomers should be able to work productively into their late 70s" if they choose to, says Elizabeth Zelinski, dean of the Leonard Davis School of Gerontology at the University of Southern California.

But realizing that potential requires that government and business discard the outdated rules, practices, and prejudices that prematurely retire people who would prefer to keep working. In many corporations, there's an unspoken assumption that older workers are much less capable than their younger counterparts. So in addition to ensuring older workers get their fair share of training, CEOs may also need to directly confront unintended age discrimination.

Society will also have to grapple with the tricky question of how to change the Social Security system to suit an aging but healthier population. A balanced approach might be to increase the Social Security retirement age at a more rapid clip while beefing up the Social Security disability program—which now covers 8 million disabled workers and dependents.

This optimistic vision of aging in America stands in sharp contrast to the conventional wisdom, which looks ahead with dread to the 60th birthday parties of the first boomers in 2006. Pessimistic pundits expect that boomers will retire in droves soon after hitting 60, as their predecessors did, while those who do keep working will dial back to less challenging and less productive jobs. The fear is that boomers will finally heed Timothy

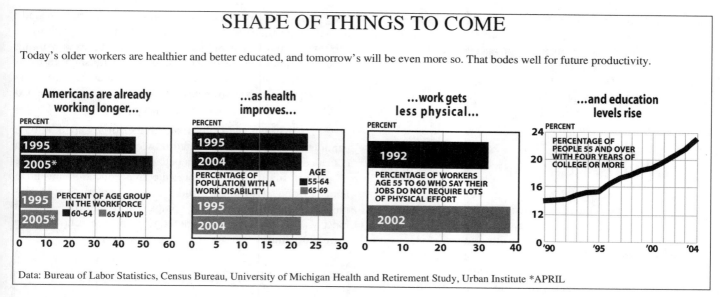

SHAPE OF THINGS TO COME

Today's older workers are healthier and better educated, and tomorrow's will be even more so. That bodes well for future productivity.

Data: Bureau of Labor Statistics, Census Bureau, University of Michigan Health and Retirement Study, Urban Institute *APRIL

Leary's call, dropping out (of the workforce) and turning on (the TV). "This explosion in the number of elderly Americans will place an unprecedented economic burden on working-age adults," investment banker Peter G. Peterson wrote last year in his latest book, *Running on Empty*.

But the burden won't be nearly so heavy if people's productive careers stretch out in synch with their extended lifetimes. How much could the economy benefit from people working longer and better?

An analysis by *BusinessWeek* finds that increased productivity of older Americans and higher labor-force participation could add 9% to gross domestic product by 2045, on top of what it otherwise would have been. (This assumes, for example, that over the next 40 years better health and technology reduce the productivity gap between older workers and their younger counterparts.) This 9% increase in gross domestic product would add more than $3 trillion a year, in today's dollars, to economic output.

The added growth would be a pure win for government finances, since a bigger economy with more productive workers yields higher tax revenues. And there's little doubt that encouraging people to work longer in step with longer life spans would do much to guarantee the solvency of Social Security.

The idea that citizens of a wealthy nation such as the U.S. would choose to work extra years is still a little new. For most of the 20th century, retirement ages fell as life spans grew. The trend seemed unstoppable: While in 1950, 46% of men 65 and older were in the labor force, by 1985 the fraction had plummeted to 16%. An influx of women into the labor force only partially offset the overall decline.

But starting in the mid-1980s, something highly unexpected began to happen: The trend reversed, and more older Americans chose to keep working. The upsurge accelerated even in the weak labor markets of recent years. The share of men 65 and over in the labor force is back up to almost 20%—the highest since the 1970s.

In part, of course, the latest uptick in working ages can be blamed on the stock market's drop from its 2000 peak, which

dented retirement savings. Also, fewer workers have good defined-benefit pension plans, which would allow them to retire young. But financial need can't be the whole reason older Americans are working more. Federal Reserve surveys show that older families have been getting richer, not poorer. The average net worth of families headed by 55- to 64-year-olds soared by 74% from 1992 to 2001, after adjusting for inflation, and likely has gone up since then.

At least as important is that many institutional barriers to working longer have been removed. In 1986, in the name of equal rights, Congress banned mandatory retirement for all but a handful of workers, such as airline pilots. And 401(k) plans, which are gradually replacing defined-benefit plans, don't induce people to retire at a certain age.

YOUNG AS YOU FEEL

Better yet, work doesn't feel like a burden to today's fit, older Americans. Many people over 60 don't think of themselves as old. A good example is Theodora Emiko "Teddy" Yoshikami, 61, who organizes cultural programs at New York's American Museum of Natural History. In her spare time, she whacks big drums in a Japanese percussion group. "People are always surprised to hear how old I am," says the former dancer.

The Baby Boom generation is even fitter for its age and more determined to stay active. Two-thirds of the people surveyed last year by the Employee Benefit Research Institute, a company-backed organization, said they expect to work for pay in retirement. A survey of boomers by AARP in January found that two in five workers age 50 to 65 were interested in a gradual, "phased" retirement instead of an abrupt cessation of work—and nearly 80% of those said that availability of phased retirement programs at work would encourage them to keep working longer. While it's likely that many boomers won't stick to those brave resolutions, the trend in work is clearly up.

Good health will help. The share of 65- to 69-year-olds with a disability affecting their ability to work fell from nearly 28% in 1995 to less than 22% last year. Advances in medicine are curing many of the problems that once forced older workers into retirement. For example, Genentech Inc. announced on May 23 that a drug undergoing trials for treatment of macular generation improves eyesight in the elderly. And better health is coinciding with less strenuous work, thanks to automation and the shrinkage of manufacturing. The share of workers 55 to 60 who said their jobs did not require lots of physical effort rose from 32% in 1992 to 38% in 2002, according to an Urban Institute study.

TRIAL AND ERROR

Mental health appears to be improving as well. USC's Zelinski has discovered that heart disease, hypertension, and diabetes directly impair brain functioning—and she sees evidence that modern medicine is getting a better handle on those diseases. As a result, memory and other functions are improving among the elderly. Emma Shulman's boss at NYU Medical Center, Steven Ferris, expects further gains for older workers from the spreading use of memory-enhancing drugs and technological aids such as personal digital assistants and search engines. Says Ferris: "I remember my father with little scraps of paper to remember things. People don't have to do that anymore."

"Once I got gray hair, people actually listened to me. This is working really well"

Older workers who thrive tend to have skills that are prized in the workplace, even if they can't easily be measured by standard tests. What matters most, according to psychologist Regina Colonia-Willner, president of consultancy Practical Intelligence at Work Inc. in Boca Raton, Fla., is the ability to solve ill-defined business problems using rules of thumb that can't be put down on paper. Example: how to deal with a difficult boss. In a study of 200 banking executives, she found that the ones who exhibited the highest "practical intelligence" were as likely to be old as young—and the older among them excelled even though their scores on traditional intelligence tests were no better than average for their age. "Practical intelligence stays with you," says Colonia-Willner. "You don't lose it when you get older."

The rap that older workers are inflexible and uncreative is also overstated. Research by economists David W. Galenson of the University of Chicago and Bruce A. Weinberg of Ohio State University finds that the innovations of older people are more likely to be "experimental," vs. the break-the-mold "conceptual" innovations of younger types. The conceptual types tend to have a bolt from the blue, whereas the experimenters build new ideas from a lifetime of observation, trial, and error. Among the "experimental" innovators who produced some of their best work later in life: painters Henri Matisse and Paul Cézanne, author Fyodor Dostoevsky, and architect Frank Lloyd Wright.

Some enlightened companies are catching on to all of this. They're hiring or retaining older workers with flexible work schedules and ample training. United Technologies Corp. spends more than $60 million a year on its Employee Scholar Program, which pays the costs of workers of any age who study in their spare time. At UTC's Hamilton Sundstrand facility in Miramar, Fla., 61-year-old lead mechanic Ed Perez is working on a bachelor's degree in legal studies. He finished an associate's degree in aviation-maintenance management two years ago and hopes to go to law school. "If I don't run out of time and UTC doesn't run out of money, I'll keep going," he says.

UTC Chairman and Chief Executive George David, at 63 a candidate himself for discounted movie tickets, argues that an educated worker like Perez is a better worker, regardless of age or area of study. What's more, the free education incentive tends to appeal to UTC's most skilled and motivated employees, so it's a way for the company to retain the people it most wants. Retention rates among "employee scholars" are about 20% higher than for regular U.S. workers.

OLDER AND WISER

Businesses often act as if older workers are a liability in an economy that prizes productivity, flexibility, and innovation. But research suggests that they are underestimating these employees.

TWO KINDS OF INNOVATION

Creativity isn't just for the young. Economist David Galenson of the University of Chicago has identified two types of innovators. Break-the-mold **"conceptual" innovators** (like Vietnam Veterans Memorial designer Maya Lin), **do their best work when young.** In contrast, **"experimental" innovators** (novelist Fyodor Dostoevsky, sculptor Auguste Rodin) **do their best work at older ages,** drawing on a lifetime of observation, trial, and error.

SOUND BODIES

University of Southern California gerontologist Elizabeth Zelinski has found that ailments such as **high blood pressure, diabetes, and heart disease are key factors depressing brain function among the elderly.** The ease with which we can treat these conditions now helps reduce the apparent cognitive handicap of older workers. In short, medicine is postponing mental decline.

PROBLEM SOLVING

Conventional measures of mental function don't capture abilities important in business, such as accumulated knowledge or judgment. Psychologist Regina Colonia-Willner of Practical Intelligence at Work Inc. found that **managers who are successful at older ages are masters at solving ill-defined problems,** even though they do no better than other older workers on standard psychometric tests.

COMPENSATION

Speed, reasoning, and memory decline steadily after age 20, while vocabulary increases to age 50. University of Virginia psychologist Timothy Salthouse found that **older workers make up for their shortfalls with clever coping strategies.** For example, older typists gain an edge by looking farther ahead in to-be-typed text during pauses, presumably to compensate for the slowdown in their ability to type words as read. **Data:** *Business Week*

HOLDING ON TO EXPERIENCE

Consolidated Edison Inc., a New York power company with an aging workforce, is trying to hang on to its valuable older workers with benefits like an elder-care referral service and career-long training. It wants to retain the experience of workers like Frederick R. Simms, 67, an emergency field manager who has seen just about everything in his 49 years with the company, from water main breaks to the collapse of the World Trade Center. In a job where trust and rapport are vital, Simms is on a first-name basis with Fire Dept. officials and other emergency workers all over Manhattan. Con Ed recently sent him for a two-day "working people-smart" class. "I don't have the zip I used to have, but I'm good enough to work 16 hours if I had to today," says Simms, adding: "I know the company likes having me around."

It's common these days to find older workers on the sales floor of retailers like Home Depot Inc. and CVS Corp., but what's new is the growing presence of older workers in high-pay, high-productivity careers. MITRE Corp., a research and development outfit in Bedford, Mass., is worried about losing its expertise in fields such as radar, which is something of a lost art for young engineers. So it brings back retirees on what it calls a "part-time, on-call" basis. The Energy Dept.'s National Energy Technology Laboratory in Morgantown, W. Va., also recognizes the value of older workers with technical expertise. It has clung to chemical engineer Hugh D. Guthrie, 86, as a full-time technical adviser in part because he has ideas that younger engineers might never think of. Says Guthrie: "My experience gives me a perspective on questions, which may not always be right but nearly always will be different. The greatest service I provide is in stimulating the thinking of people involved in a project."

Unfortunately, many other companies haven't gotten the message. The Society for Human Resource Management, an association of personnel execs, says 59% of members surveyed don't actively recruit older workers and 65% don't do anything specific to retain older workers. The Bureau of Labor Statistics found in 1995, the last time it looked, that workers age 55 and up got only one-third as many hours of formal training as workers 45 to 54. Marian Stoltz-Loike, CEO of SeniorThinking LLC, a consultancy, says executives often aren't even aware that older workers are getting a subtle message that training isn't for them.

Economists have found that businesses are missing an opportunity by giving less training to their older workers. Research shows that they tend to operate information technology more slowly but with fewer errors. Research on displaced workers who got retraining in community colleges in Washington State found that the pay gains were just as big for older workers who took training as for younger ones—indicating that the training they got took hold.

Will longer-working boomers block the advancement of younger workers? Maybe. But what worries employers more is the opposite—labor shortages that could emerge if boomers retire en masse and there aren't enough people to take their place. The Congressional Budget Office is forecasting that labor-force growth will slow by almost half over the next 10 years.

The U.S. takes better advantage of the potential of its older citizens than does most of Europe, where extremely early retirement is routine because of rich retirement benefits. Six in 10 Americans are still working at ages 55 to 64, vs. just four in 10 in the European Union.

Smart policy choices, such as the abolition of most mandatory retirement rules, have helped put the U.S. in a position to tap the ability and energy of older people. Since 2000, Social Security recipients have been allowed to receive their full benefits no matter how much they earn from working after age 65. The Internal Revenue Service has proposed rules, starting next year, to allow people 59½ and older to receive part of their pensions even while they are still working. Because people would not have to retire outright to get a pension, more are likely to remain on the job, experts predict. The proposed rules are a step in the right direction, although employer groups are complaining that there's too much red tape involved.

CREATING INCENTIVES

What more can be done to tap the productivity potential of older workers? The goal is to introduce more flexibility into pay and retirement systems, to create more options as workers age. Consultant Ken Dychtwald, author of **Age Wave,** recommends the example of Deloitte Consulting LLC, which lures highly valued older employees to stay by designating them "senior leaders" and giving them incentives such as flexible hours and work location, special projects, and opportunities for mentoring and research.

Another possibility is to allow companies to convert traditional defined-benefit pensions, which encourage retirement as early as age 55, to cash-balance plans, which have no built-in incentives to retire. Such conversions have been frozen since 1999 over legitimate age-discrimination concerns, though the Bush Administration has proposed legislation that would break the logjam. It's prudent to make sure that switching to cash-balance plans doesn't harm older workers, but such caution is also preserving a system that lures people into retiring when they still have much to contribute in the working world.

Perhaps the most controversial idea is to break the typical link between pay and seniority. As more people work into their late 60s and 70s, pay should be adjusted to match how much people work and what they accomplish on the job.

It's also critical to rethink the role of Social Security in an economy where incomes—and life spans—are rising. In theory, Social Security should provide a secure safety net for those who are truly too old to work and lack savings, while encouraging the huge boomer generation to stay employed and productive for the good of themselves and the economy.

"The greatest service I provide is in stimulating the thinking of people involved in a project."

The logical conclusion: raise Social Security's normal retirement age incrementally to 70. From then on, peg further increases to gains in longevity. It's also essential to increase the age, now 62, at which people can first choose to take early retirement. Research suggests that many take the official early retirement age as a signal that it's O.K. to drop out of the workforce, even though they will get much smaller checks for the rest of their lifetimes. Raising the early retirement age would signal that 62 is too young for most people to quit in an era of marathon-running septuagenarians.

Increasing Social Security's early retirement age would be hard on workers with health problems, or whose jobs require more physical exertion. A possible solution is to liberalize the qualifications for Social Security's disability insurance program. The extra expense of disability payments to aging laborers would be far outweighed by the savings from raising the normal and early retirement ages in tandem.

There's no dispute that America is graying. But the solution to the demographic shift is staring us in the face. As Urban Institute senior fellow C. Eugene Steuerle told the House Ways & Means Committee in May: "People in their late 50s, 60s, and 70s have now become the largest underutilized pool of human resources in the economy." By working longer—and more productively—boomers will help the U.S. economy thrive even as their personal odometers keep clicking forward.

—With Diane Brady in New York

Reprinted by special permission from *Business Week,* June 27, 2005, pp. 78, 80-84, 86. Copyright © 2005 by The McGraw-Hill Companies, Inc.

The Truth About the Drug Companies

Marcia Angell

1.

Every day Americans are subjected to a barrage of advertising by the pharmaceutical industry. Mixed in with the pitches for a particular drug—usually featuring beautiful people enjoying themselves in the great outdoors—is a more general message. Boiled down to its essentials, it is this: "Yes, prescription drugs are expensive, but that shows how valuable they are. Besides, our research and development costs are enormous, and we need to cover them somehow. As 'research-based' companies, we turn out a steady stream of innovative medicines that lengthen life, enhance its quality, and avert more expensive medical care. You are the beneficiaries of this ongoing achievement of the American free enterprise system, so be grateful, quit whining, and pay up." More prosaically, what the industry is saying is that you get what you pay for.

Is any of this true? Well, the first part certainly is. Prescription drug costs are indeed high—and rising fast. Americans now spend a staggering $200 billion a year on prescription drugs, and that figure is growing at a rate of about 12 percent a year (down from a high of 18 percent in 1999).[1] Drugs are the fastest-growing part of the health care bill—which itself is rising at an alarming rate. The increase in drug spending reflects, in almost equal parts, the facts that people are taking a lot more drugs than they used to, that those drugs are more likely to be expensive new ones instead of older, cheaper ones, and that the prices of the most heavily prescribed drugs are routinely jacked up, sometimes several times a year.

Before its patent ran out, for example, the price of Schering-Plough's top-selling allergy pill, Claritin, was raised thirteen times over five years, for a cumulative increase of more than 50 percent—over four times the rate of general inflation.[2] As a spokeswoman for one company explained, "Price increases are not uncommon in the industry and this allows us to be able to invest in R&D."[3] In 2002, the average price of the fifty drugs most used by senior citizens was nearly $1,500 for a year's supply. (Pricing varies greatly, but this refers to what the companies call the average wholesale price, which is usually pretty close to what an individual without insurance pays at the pharmacy.)

Paying for prescription drugs is no longer a problem just for poor people. As the economy continues to struggle, health insurance is shrinking. Employers are requiring workers to pay more of the costs themselves, and many businesses are dropping health benefits altogether. Since prescription drug costs are rising so fast, payers are particularly eager to get out from under them by shifting costs to individuals. The result is that more people have to pay a greater fraction of their drug bills out of pocket. And that packs a wallop.

Many of them simply can't do it. They trade off drugs against home heating or food. Some people try to string out their drugs by taking them less often than prescribed, or sharing them with a spouse. Others, too embarrassed to admit that they can't afford to pay for drugs, leave their doctors' offices with prescriptions in hand but don't have them filled. Not only do these patients go without needed treatment but their doctors sometimes wrongly conclude that the drugs they prescribed haven't worked and prescribe yet others—thus compounding the problem.

The people hurting most are the elderly. When Medicare was enacted in 1965, people took far fewer prescription drugs and they were cheap. For that reason, no one thought it necessary to include an outpatient prescription drug benefit in the program. In those days, senior citizens could generally afford to buy whatever drugs they needed out of pocket. Approximately half to two thirds of the elderly have supplementary insurance that partly covers prescription drugs, but that percentage is dropping as employers and insurers decide it is a losing proposition for them. At the end of 2003, Congress passed a Medicare reform bill that included a prescription drug benefit scheduled to begin in 2006, but as we shall see later, its benefits are inadequate to begin with and will quickly be overtaken by rising prices and administrative costs.

For obvious reasons, the elderly tend to need more prescription drugs than younger people—mainly for chronic conditions like arthritis, diabetes, high blood pressure, and elevated cholesterol. In 2001, nearly one in four seniors reported that they skipped doses or did not fill prescriptions because of the cost. (That fraction is almost certainly higher now.) Sadly, the frailest are the least likely to have supplementary insurance. At an average cost of $1,500 a year for each drug, someone without supplementary insurance who takes six different prescription drugs—and this is not rare—would have to spend $9,000 out of pocket. Not many among the old and frail have such deep pockets.

Furthermore, in one of the more perverse of the pharmaceutical industry's practices, prices are much higher for precisely the people who most need the drugs and can least afford them. The industry charges Medicare recipients without supplementary insurance much more than it does favored customers, such as large HMOs or the Veterans Affairs (VA) system. Because the latter buy in bulk, they can bargain for steep discounts or rebates. People without insurance have no bargaining power; and so they pay the highest prices.

In the past two years, we have started to see, for the first time, the beginnings of public resistance to rapacious pricing and other dubious practices of the pharmaceutical industry. It is mainly because of this resistance that drug companies are now blanketing us with public relations messages. And the magic words, repeated over and over like an incantation, are *research, innovation,* and *American.* Research. Innovation. American. It makes a great story.

But while the rhetoric is stirring, it has very little to do with reality. First, research and development (R&D) is a relatively small part of the budgets of the big drug companies—dwarfed by their vast expenditures on marketing and administration, and smaller even than profits. In fact, year after year, for over two decades, this industry has been far and away the most profitable in the United States. (In 2003, for the first time, the industry lost its first-place position, coming in third, behind "mining, crude oil production," and "commercial banks.") The prices drug companies charge have little relationship to the costs of making the drugs and could be cut dramatically without coming anywhere close to threatening R&D.

Second, the pharmaceutical industry is not especially innovative. As hard as it is to believe, only a handful of truly important drugs have been brought to market in recent years, and they were mostly based on taxpayer-funded research at academic institutions, small biotechnology companies, or the National Institutes of Health (NIH). The great majority of "new" drugs are not new at all but merely variations of older drugs already on the market. These are called "me-too" drugs. The idea is to grab a share of an established, lucrative market by producing something very similar to a top-selling drug. For instance, we now have six statins (Mevacor, Lipitor, Zocor, Pravachol, Lescol, and the newest, Crestor) on the market to lower cholesterol, all variants of the first. As Dr. Sharon Levine, associate executive director of the Kaiser Permanente Medical Group, put it,

If I'm a manufacturer and I can change one molecule and get another twenty years of patent rights, and convince physicians to prescribe and consumers to demand the next form of Prilosec, or weekly Prozac instead of daily Prozac, just as my patent expires, then why would I be spending money on a lot less certain endeavor, which is looking for brand-new drugs?[4]

Third, the industry is hardly a model of American free enterprise. To be sure, it is free to decide which drugs to develop (me-too drugs instead of innovative ones, for instance), and it is free to price them as high as the traffic will bear, but it is utterly dependent on government-granted monopolies—in the form of patents and Food and Drug Administration (FDA)–approved exclusive marketing rights. If it is not particularly innovative in discovering new drugs, it is highly innovative— and aggressive—in dreaming up ways to extend its monopoly rights.

And there is nothing peculiarly American about this industry. It is the very essence of a global enterprise. Roughly half of the largest drug companies are based in Europe. (The exact count shifts because of mergers.) In 2002, the top ten were the American companies Pfizer, Merck, Johnson & Johnson, Bristol-Myers Squibb, and Wyeth (formerly American Home Products); the British companies GlaxoSmithKline and AstraZeneca; the Swiss companies Novartis and Roche; and the French company Aventis (which in 2004 merged with another French company, Sanofi Synthelabo, putting it in third place).[5] All are much alike in their operations. All price their drugs much higher here than in other markets.

Since the United States is the major profit center, it is simply good public relations for drug companies to pass themselves off as American, whether they are or not. It is true, however, that some of the European companies are now locating their R&D operations in the United States. They claim the reason for this is that we don't regulate prices, as does much of the rest of the world. But more likely it is that they want to feed on the unparalleled research output of American universities and the NIH. In other words, it's not private enterprise that draws them here but the very opposite—our publicly sponsored research enterprise.

Over the past two decades the pharmaceutical industry has moved very far from its original high purpose of discovering and producing useful new drugs. Now primarily a marketing machine to sell drugs of dubious benefit, this industry uses its wealth and power to co-opt every institution that might stand in its way, including the US Congress, the FDA, academic medical centers, and the medical profession itself. (Most of its marketing efforts are focused on influencing doctors, since they must write the prescriptions.)

If prescription drugs were like ordinary consumer goods, all this might not matter very much. But drugs are different. People depend on them for their health and even their lives. In the words of Senator Debbie Stabenow (D-Mich.), "It's not like buying a car or tennis shoes or peanut butter." People need to know that there are some checks and balances on this industry, so that its quest for profits doesn't push every other consideration aside. But there aren't such checks and balances.

2.

What does the eight-hundred-pound gorilla do?
Anything it wants to.

What's true of the eight-hundred-pound gorilla is true of the colossus that is the pharmaceutical industry. It is used to doing pretty much what it wants to do. The watershed year was 1980. Before then, it was a good business, but afterward, it was a stupendous one. From 1960 to 1980, prescription drug sales were fairly static as a percent of US gross domestic product, but from 1980 to 2000, they tripled. They now stand at more than $200 billion a year.[6] Of the many events that contributed to the industry's great and good fortune, none had to do with the quality of the drugs the companies were selling.

The claim that drugs are a $200 billion industry is an understatement. According to government sources, that is roughly how much Americans spent on prescription drugs in 2002. That figure refers to direct consumer purchases at drugstores and mail-order pharmacies (whether paid for out of pocket or not), and it includes the nearly 25 percent markup for wholesalers, pharmacists, and other middlemen and retailers. But it does not include the large amounts spent for drugs administered in hospitals, nursing homes, or doctors' offices (as is the case for many cancer drugs). In most analyses, they are allocated to costs for those facilities.

Drug company revenues (or sales) are a little different, at least as they are reported in summaries of corporate annual reports. They usually refer to a company's worldwide sales, including those to health facilities. But they do not include the revenues of middlemen and retailers.

Perhaps the most quoted source of statistics on the pharmaceutical industry, IMS Health, estimated total worldwide sales for prescription drugs to be about $400 billion in 2002. About half were in the United States. So the $200 billion colossus is really a $400 billion megacolossus.

The election of Ronald Reagan in 1980 was perhaps the fundamental element in the rapid rise of big pharma—the collective name for the largest drug companies. With the Reagan administration came a strong pro-business shift not only in government policies but in society at large.

And with the shift, the public attitude toward great wealth changed. Before then, there was something faintly disreputable about really big fortunes. You could choose to do well or you could choose to do good, but most people who had any choice in the matter thought it difficult to do both. That belief was particularly strong among scientists and other intellectuals. They could choose to live a comfortable but not luxurious life in academia, hoping to do exciting cutting-edge research, or they could "sell out" to industry and do less important but more remunerative work. Starting in the Reagan years and continuing through the 1990s, Americans changed their tune. It became not only reputable to be wealthy, but something close to virtuous. There were "winners" and there were "losers," and the winners were rich and deserved to be. The gap between the rich and poor, which had been narrowing since World War II, suddenly began to widen again, until today it is a chasm.

The pharmaceutical industry and its CEOs quickly joined the ranks of the winners as a result of a number of business-friendly government actions. I won't enumerate all of them, but two are especially important. Beginning in 1980, Congress enacted a series of laws designed to speed the translation of tax-supported basic research into useful new products—a process sometimes referred to as "technology transfer." The goal was also to improve the position of American-owned high-tech businesses in world markets.

The most important of these laws is known as the Bayh-Dole Act, after its chief sponsors, Senator Birch Bayh (D-Ind.) and Senator Robert Dole (R-Kans.). Bayh-Dole enabled universities and small businesses to patent discoveries emanating from research sponsored by the National Institutes of Health, the major distributor of tax dollars for medical research, and then to grant exclusive licenses to drug companies. Until then, taxpayer-financed discoveries were in the public domain, available to any company that wanted to use them. But now universities, where most NIH-sponsored work is carried out, can patent and license their discoveries, and charge royalties. Similar legislation permitted the NIH itself to enter into deals with drug companies that would directly transfer NIH discoveries to industry.

Bayh-Dole gave a tremendous boost to the nascent biotechnology industry, as well as to big pharma. Small biotech companies, many of them founded by university researchers to exploit their discoveries, proliferated rapidly. They now ring the major academic research institutions and often carry out the initial phases of drug development, hoping for lucrative deals with big drug companies that can market the new drugs. Usually both academic researchers and their institutions own equity in the biotechnology companies they are involved with. Thus, when a patent held by a university or a small biotech company is eventually licensed to a big drug company, all parties cash in on the public investment in research.

These laws mean that drug companies no longer have to rely on their own research for new drugs, and few of the large ones do. Increasingly, they rely on academia, small biotech startup companies, and the NIH for that.[7] At least a third of drugs marketed by the major drug companies are now licensed from universities or small biotech companies, and these tend to be the most innovative ones.[8] While Bayh-Dole was clearly a bonanza for big pharma and the biotech industry, whether its enactment was a net benefit to the public is arguable.

The Reagan years and Bayh-Dole also transformed the ethos of medical schools and teaching hospitals. These nonprofit institutions started to see themselves as "partners" of industry, and they became just as enthusiastic as any entrepreneur about the opportunities to parlay their discoveries into financial gain. Faculty researchers were encouraged to obtain patents on their work (which were assigned to their universities), and they shared in the royalties. Many medical schools and teaching hospitals set up "technology transfer" offices to help in this activity and capitalize on faculty discoveries. As the entrepreneurial spirit grew during the 1990s, medical school faculty entered into other lucrative financial arrangements with drug companies, as did their parent institutions.

One of the results has been a growing pro-industry bias in medical research—exactly where such bias doesn't belong. Faculty members who had earlier contented themselves with what was once referred to as a "threadbare but genteel" lifestyle began to ask themselves, in the words of my grandmother, "If you're so smart, why aren't you rich?" Medical schools and teaching hospitals, for their part, put more resources into searching for commercial opportunities.

Starting in 1984, with legislation known as the Hatch-Waxman Act, Congress passed another series of laws that were just as big a bonanza for the pharmaceutical industry. These laws extended monopoly rights for brand-name drugs. Exclusivity is the lifeblood of the industry because it means that no other company may sell the same drug for a set period. After exclusive marketing rights expire, copies (called generic drugs) enter the market, and the price usually falls to as little as 20 percent of what it was.[9] There are two forms of monopoly rights—patents granted by the US Patent and Trade Office (USPTO) and exclusivity granted by the FDA. While related, they operate somewhat independently, almost as backups for each other. Hatch-Waxman, named for Senator Orrin Hatch (R-Utah) and Representative Henry Waxman (D-Calif.), was meant mainly to stimulate the foundering generic industry by short-circuiting some of the FDA requirements for bringing generic drugs to market. While successful in doing that, Hatch-Waxman also lengthened the patent life for brand-name drugs. Since then, industry lawyers have manipulated some of its provisions to extend patents far longer than the lawmakers intended.

In the 1990s, Congress enacted other laws that further increased the patent life of brand-name drugs. Drug companies now employ small armies of lawyers to milk these laws for all they're worth—and they're worth a lot. The result is that the effective patent life of brand-name drugs increased from about eight years in 1980 to about fourteen years in 2000.[10] For a blockbuster—usually defined as a drug with sales of over a billion dollars a year (like Lipitor or Celebrex or Zoloft)—those six years of additional exclusivity are golden. They can add billions of dollars to sales—enough to buy a lot of lawyers and have plenty of change left over. No wonder big pharma will do almost anything to protect exclusive marketing rights, despite the fact that doing so flies in the face of all its rhetoric about the free market.

As their profits skyrocketed during the 1980s and 1990s, so did the political power of drug companies. By 1990, the industry had assumed its present contours as a business with unprecedented control over its own fortunes. For example, if it didn't like something about the FDA, the federal agency that is supposed to regulate the industry, it could change it through direct pressure or through its friends in Congress. The top ten drug companies (which included European companies) had profits of nearly 25 percent of sales in 1990, and except for a dip at the time of President Bill Clinton's health care reform proposal, profits as a percentage of sales remained about the same for the next decade. (Of course, in absolute terms, as sales mounted, so did profits.) In 2001, the ten American drug companies in the Fortune 500 list (not quite the same as the top ten worldwide, but their profit margins are much the same) ranked far above all other American industries in average net return, whether as a percentage of sales (18.5 percent), of assets (16.3 percent), or of shareholders' equity (33.2 percent). These are astonishing margins. For comparison, the median net return for all other industries in the Fortune 500 was only 3.3 percent of sales. Commercial banking, itself no slouch as an aggressive industry with many friends in high places, was a distant second, at 13.5 percent of sales.[11]

In 2002, as the economic downturn continued, big pharma showed only a slight drop in profits—from 18.5 to 17.0 percent of sales. The most startling fact about 2002 is that the combined profits for the ten drug companies in the Fortune 500 ($35.9 billion) were more than the profits for all the other 490 businesses put together ($33.7 billion).[12] In 2003 profits of the Fortune 500 drug companies dropped to 14.3 percent of sales, still well above the median for all industries of 4.6 percent for that year. When I say this is a profitable industry, I mean really profitable. It is difficult to conceive of how awash in money big pharma is.

Drug industry expenditures for research and development, while large, were consistently far less than profits. For the top ten companies, they amounted to only 11 percent of sales in 1990, rising slightly to 14 percent in 2000. The biggest single item in the budget is neither R&D nor even profits but something usually called "marketing and administration"—a name that varies slightly from company to company. In 1990, a staggering 36 percent of sales revenues went into this category, and that proportion remained about the same for over a decade.[13] Note that this is two and a half times the expenditures for R&D.

These figures are drawn from the industry's own annual reports to the Securities and Exchange Commission (SEC) and to stockholders, but what actually goes into these categories is not at all clear, because drug companies hold that information very close to their chests. It is likely, for instance, that R&D includes many activities most people would consider marketing, but no one can know for sure. For its part, "marketing and administration" is a gigantic black box that probably includes what the industry calls "education," as well as advertising and promotion, legal costs, and executive salaries—which are whopping. According to a report by the non-profit group Families USA, the former chairman and CEO of Bristol-Myers Squibb, Charles A. Heimbold Jr., made $74,890,918 in 2001, not counting his $76,095,611 worth of unexercised stock options. The chairman of Wyeth made $40,521,011, exclusive of his $40,629,459 in stock options. And so on.[14]

3.

If 1980 was a watershed year for the pharmaceutical industry, 2000 may very well turn out to have been another one—the year things began to go wrong. As the booming economy of the late 1990s turned sour, many successful businesses found themselves in trouble. And as tax revenues dropped, state governments also found themselves in trouble. In one respect, the pharmaceutical industry is well protected against the downturn, since it has so much wealth and power. But in another respect, it is peculiarly vulnerable, since it depends on employer-sponsored insurance and state-run Medicaid programs for much of its revenues. When employers and states are in trouble, so is big pharma.

And sure enough, in just the past couple of years, employers and the private health insurers with whom they contract have started to push back against drug costs. Most big managed care plans now bargain for steep price discounts. Most have also instituted three-tiered coverage for prescription drugs—full coverage for generic drugs, partial coverage for useful brand-name drugs, and no coverage for expensive drugs that offer no added benefit over cheaper ones. These lists of preferred drugs are called formularies, and they are an increasingly important method for containing drug costs. Big pharma is feeling the effects of these measures, although not surprisingly, it has become adept at manipulating the system—mainly by inducing doctors or health plans to put expensive, brand-name drugs on formularies.

State governments, too, are looking for ways to cut their drug costs. Some state legislatures are drafting measures that would permit them to regulate prescription drug prices for state employees, Medicaid recipients, and the uninsured. Like managed care plans, they are creating formularies of preferred drugs. The industry is fighting these efforts—mainly with its legions of lobbyists and lawyers. It fought the state of Maine all the way to the US Supreme Court, which in 2003 upheld Maine's right to bargain with drug companies for lower prices, while leaving open the details. But that war has just begun, and it promises to go on for years and get very ugly.

Recently the public has shown signs of being fed up. The fact that Americans pay much more for prescription drugs than Europeans and Canadians is now widely known. An estimated one to two million Americans buy their medicines from Canadian drugstores over the Internet, despite the fact that in 1987, in response to heavy industry lobbying, a compliant Congress had made it illegal for anyone other than manufacturers to import prescription drugs from other countries.[15] In addition, there is a brisk traffic in bus trips for people in border states, particularly the elderly, to travel to Canada or Mexico to buy prescription drugs. Their resentment is palpable, and they constitute a powerful voter block—a fact not lost on Congress or state legislatures.

The industry faces other, less familiar problems. It happens that, by chance, some of the top-selling drugs —with combined sales of around $35 billion a year—are scheduled to go off patent within a few years of one another.[16] This drop over the cliff began in 2001, with the expiration of Eli Lilly's patent on its blockbuster antidepressant Prozac. In the same year, AstraZeneca lost its patent on Prilosec, the original "purple pill" for heartburn, which at its peak brought in a stunning $6 billion a year. Bristol-Myers Squibb lost its best-selling diabetes drug, Glucophage. The unusual cluster of expirations will continue for another couple of years. While it represents a huge loss to the industry as a whole, for some companies it's a disaster. Schering-Plough's blockbuster allergy drug, Claritin, brought in fully a third of that company's revenues before its patent expired in 2002.[17] Claritin is now sold over the counter for much less than its prescription price. So far, the company has been unable to make up for the loss by trying to switch Claritin users to Clarinex—a drug that is virtually identical but has the advantage of still being on patent.

Even worse is the fact that there are very few drugs in the pipeline ready to take the place of blockbusters going off patent. In fact, that is the biggest problem facing the industry today, and its darkest secret. All the public relations about innovation is meant to obscure precisely this fact. The stream of new drugs has slowed to a trickle, and few of them are innovative in any sense of that word. Instead, the great majority are variations of oldies but goodies—"me-too" drugs.

Of the seventy-eight drugs approved by the FDA in 2002, only seventeen contained new active ingredients, and only seven of these were classified by the FDA as improvements over older drugs. The other seventy-one drugs approved that year were variations of old drugs or deemed no better than drugs already on the market. In other words, they were me-too drugs. Seven of seventy-eight is not much of a yield. Furthermore, of those seven, not one came from a major US drug company.[18]

For the first time, in just a few short years, the gigantic pharmaceutical industry is finding itself in serious difficulty. It is facing, as one industry spokesman put it, "a perfect storm." To be sure, profits are still beyond anything most other industries could hope for, but they have recently fallen, and for some companies they fell a lot. And that is what matters to investors. Wall Street doesn't care how high profits are today, only how high they will be tomorrow. For some companies, stock prices have plummeted. Nevertheless, the industry keeps promising a bright new day. It bases its reassurances on the notion that the mapping of the human genome and the accompanying burst in genetic research will yield a cornucopia of important new drugs. Left unsaid is the fact that big pharma is depending on government, universities, and small biotech companies for that innovation. While there is no doubt that genetic discoveries will lead to treatments, the fact remains that it will probably be years before the basic research pays off with new drugs. In the meantime, the once-solid foundations of the big pharma colossus are shaking.

The hints of trouble and the public's growing resentment over high prices are producing the first cracks in the industry's formerly firm support in Washington. In 2000, Congress passed legislation that would have closed some of the loopholes in Hatch-Waxman and also permitted American pharmacies, as well as individuals, to import drugs from certain countries where prices are lower. In particular, they could buy back FDA-approved drugs from Canada that had been exported there. It sounds silly to "reimport" drugs that are marketed in the United States, but even with the added transaction costs, doing so is cheaper than buying them here. But the bill required the secretary of health and human services to certify that the practice would not pose any "added risk" to the public, and secretaries in both the Clinton and Bush administrations, under pressure from the industry, refused to do that.

The industry is also being hit with a tidal wave of government investigations and civil and criminal lawsuits. The litany of charges includes illegally overcharging Medicaid and Medicare, paying kickbacks to doctors, engaging in anticompetitive practices, colluding with generic companies to keep generic drugs off the market, illegally promoting drugs for unapproved uses, engaging in misleading direct-to-consumer advertising, and, of course, covering up evidence. Some of the settlements have been huge. TAP Pharmaceuticals, for instance, paid $875 million to settle civil and criminal charges of Medicaid and Medicare fraud in the marketing of its prostate cancer drug, Lupron.[19] All of these efforts could be summed up as increasingly desperate marketing and patent games, activities that always skirted the edge of legality but now are sometimes well on the other side.

How is the pharmaceutical industry responding to its difficulties? One could hope drug companies would decide to make some changes—trim their prices, or at least make them more equitable, and put more of their money into trying to discover genuinely innovative drugs, instead of just talking about it. But that is not what is happening. Instead, drug companies are doing more of what got them into this situation. They are marketing their me-too drugs even more relentlessly. They are pushing even harder to extend their monopolies on top-selling drugs. And they are pouring more money into lobbying and political campaigns. As for innovation, they are still waiting for Godot.

The news is not all bad for the industry. The Medicare prescription drug benefit enacted in 2003, and scheduled to go into effect in 2006, promises a windfall for big pharma since it forbids the government from negotiating prices. The immediate jump in pharmaceutical stock prices after the bill passed indicated that the industry and investors were well aware of the windfall. But at best, this legislation will be only a temporary boost for the industry. As costs rise, Congress will have to reconsider its industry-friendly decision to allow drug companies to set their own prices, no questions asked.

This is an industry that in some ways is like the Wizard of Oz—still full of bluster but now being exposed as something far different from its image. Instead of being an engine of innovation, it is a vast marketing machine. Instead of being a free market success story, it lives off government-funded research and monopoly rights. Yet this industry occupies an essential role in the American health care system, and it performs a valuable function, if not in discovering important new drugs at least in developing them and bringing them to market. But big pharma is extravagantly rewarded for its relatively modest functions. We get nowhere near our money's worth. The United States can no longer afford it in its present form.

Clearly, the pharmaceutical industry is due for fundamental reform. Reform will have to extend beyond the industry to the agencies and institutions it has co-opted, including the FDA and the medical profession and its teaching centers. In my forthcoming book, *The Truth About the Drug Companies,* I discuss the major reforms that will be necessary.

For example, we need to get the industry to focus on discovering truly innovative drugs instead of turning out me-too drugs (and spending billions of dollars to promote them as though they were miracles). The me-too business is made possible by the fact that the FDA usually approves a drug only if it is better than a placebo. It needn't be better than an older drug already on the market to treat the same condition; in fact, it may be worse. There is no way of knowing, since companies generally do not test their new drugs against older ones for the same conditions at equivalent doses. (For obvious reasons, they would rather not find the answer.) They should be required to do so.

The me-too market would collapse virtually overnight if the FDA made approval of new drugs contingent on their being better in some important way than older drugs already on the market. Probably very few new drugs could meet that test. By default, then, drug companies would have to concentrate on finding truly innovative drugs, and we would finally find out whether this much-vaunted industry is turning out better drugs. A welcome by-product of this reform is that it would also reduce the incessant and enormously expensive marketing necessary to jockey for position in the me-too market. Genuinely important new drugs do not need much promotion (imagine having to advertise a cure for cancer).

A second important reform would be to require drug companies to open their books. Drug companies reveal very little about the most crucial aspects of their business. We know next to nothing about how much they spend to bring each drug to market or what they spend it on. (We know that it is *not* $802 million, as some industry apologists have recently claimed.) Nor do we know what their gigantic "marketing and administration" budgets cover. We don't even know the prices they charge their various customers. Perhaps most important, we do not know the results of the clinical trials they sponsor—only those they choose to make public, which tend to be the most favorable findings. (The FDA is not allowed to reveal the results it has.) The industry claims all of this is "proprietary" information. Yet, unlike other businesses, drug companies are dependent on the public for a host of special favors—including the rights to NIH-funded research, long periods of market monopoly, and multiple tax breaks that almost guarantee a profit. Because of these special favors and the importance of its products to public health, as well as the fact that the government is a major purchaser of its products, the pharmaceutical industry should be regarded much as a public utility.

These are just two of many reforms I advocate in my book. Some of the others have to do with breaking the dependence of the medical profession on the industry and with the inappropriate control drug companies have over the evaluation of their own products. The sort of thoroughgoing changes required will take government action, which in turn will require strong public pressure. It will be tough. Drug companies have the largest lobby in Washington, and they give copiously to political campaigns. Legislators are now so beholden to the pharmaceutical industry that it will be exceedingly difficult to break its lock on them.

But the one thing legislators need more than campaign contributions is votes. That is why citizens should know what is really going on. Contrary to the industry's public relations, they don't get what they pay for. The fact is that this industry is taking us for a ride, and there will be no real reform without an aroused and determined public to make it happen.

Notes

1. There are several sources of statistics on the size and growth of the industry. One is IMS Health (www.imshealth.com), a private company that collects and sells information on the global pharmaceutical industry. See www.imshealth.com/ims/portal/front/articleC/0,2777,6599_3665_41336931,00.html for the $200 billion figure. For further sources on this and other matters, see my book *The Truth About the Drug Companies: How They Deceive Us and What to Do About It* (to be published in August by Random House), from which this article is drawn.
2. For a full picture of the special burden of rising drug prices on senior citizens, see Families USA, "Out-of-Bounds: Rising Prescription Drug Prices for Seniors" (www.familiesusa .org/site/PageServer?pagename=Publications_Reports).
3. Sarah Lueck, "Drug Prices Far Outpace Inflation," *The Wall Street Journal*, July 10, 2003, p. D2.
4. On ABC Special with Peter Jennings, "Bitter Medicine: Pills, Profit, and the Public Health," May 29, 2002.
5. For the top ten companies and their recent mergers as of 2003, see www.oligopolywatch.com/2003/05/25.html.
6. These figures come from the US Centers for Medicare & Medicaid Services, Office of the Actuary, National Health Statistics Group, Baltimore, Maryland. They were summarized in Cynthia Smith, "Retail Prescription Drug Spending in the National Health Accounts," *Health Affairs*, January–February 2004, p. 160.
7. For excellent summaries of public contributions to drug company research, see Public Citizen Congress Watch, "Rx R&D Myths: The Case Against the Drug Industry's R&D 'Scare Card,'" July 2001 (www.citizen.org); and NIHCM, "Changing Patterns of Pharmaceutical Innovation," May 2002 (www.nihcm.org).
8. This is probably an underestimate. One source that indicates it is at least this is CenterWatch, www.centerwatch.com, a private company owned by Thomson Medical Economics, which provides information to the clinical trial industry. See *An Industry in Evolution*, third edition, edited by Mary Jo Lamberti (CenterWatch, 2001), p. 22.
9. Families USA, "Out-of-Bounds: Rising Prescription Drug Prices for Seniors."
10. Public Citizen Congress Watch, "Rx R&D Myths."
11. "The Fortune 500," *Fortune*, April 15, 2002, p. F26.
12. Public Citizen Congress Watch, "Drug Industry Profits: Hefty Pharmaceutical Company Margins Dwarf Other Industries," June 2003 (www.citizen .org/documents/Pharma_Report.pdf). The data are drawn mainly from the Fortune 500 list in *Fortune*, April 7, 2003, and drug company annual reports.
13. Henry J. Kaiser Family Foundation, "Prescription Drug Trends," November 2001 (www.kff.org).
14. FamiliesUSA, "Profiting from Pain: Where Prescription Drug Dollars Go," July 2002 (www.familiesusa.org/site/DocServer/PReport.pdf?docID= 249).
15. Patricia Barry, "More Americans Go North for Drugs," *AARP Bulletin*, April 2003, p. 3.
16. Chandrani Ghosh and Andrew Tanzer, "Patent Play," *Forbes*, September 17, 2001, p. 141.
17. Gardiner Harris, "Schering-Plough Is Hurt by Plummeting Pill Costs," *The New York Times*, July 8, 2003, p. C1.
18. For key information about the numbers and kinds of drugs approved each year, see the Web site of the US Food and Drug Administration (FDA), www.fda.gov/cder/rdmt/pstable.htm.
19. Alice Dembner, "Drug Firm to Pay $875M Fine for Fraud," *The Boston Globe*, October 4, 2001, p. A13.

From *The New York Review*, July 15, 2004, pp. 52–58. Copyright © 2004 by New York Review of Books. Reprinted by permission.

Eminent Domain:
Is It Only Hope For Inner Cities?

RYAN CHITTUM

EAST ST. LOUIS, Ill.
This city doesn't scream "build here" to most real-estate developers. One of the poorest urban areas in the U.S., its median household income is $21,324, and nearly 32% of families live below the poverty line, more than triple the national average.

Jim Koman looks at the numbers another way. He sees a city, like many other downtrodden places, with few quality stores to serve its residents. East St. Louis has just 3 square feet of retail space per person, compared with the national average of 20 square feet.

In 1999, after pharmacy chain Walgreen Co. came to him looking for retail space, Koman Properties Inc., of Clayton, Mo., built the city's first new shopping center in several decades. Now, amid street after street of trash-strewn lots and broken-down buildings, it is a commercial oasis stretching for several blocks, including a grocery-anchored strip mall with a beauty salon, a Foot Locker, an Auto Zone and other chains. About 95% of the shopping center's workers are from East St. Louis, bringing the city much-needed, if low-paying, jobs.

When the Walgreen's opened, then-President Clinton showed up to visit. The State Street Shopping Center "is night and day for these people that don't have anything," Mr. Koman says.

But to build in an urban area like East St. Louis, Mr. Koman must rely on eminent domain—the government's power to force a landowner to sell property at what is considered a fair price. The State Street project wouldn't have happened if the city hadn't used the threat of eminent domain to clear about 40 houses and a gas station, Mr. Koman says. Of those properties, only two owners held out for long periods, and one of those buildings was condemned and appropriated through eminent domain after the owner refused to settle.

Such cases have received new attention following the Supreme Court decision in June upholding the use of eminent domain to seize property for private use. Opponents of the eminent-domain doctrine have pointed to high-profile cases such as arenas and other big urban-development projects as evidence of abuse. But situations such as Mr. Koman's are far more common and in some ways knottier.

Many builders say eminent domain is the only way to bring services and jobs to areas like East St. Louis. Mr. Koman says

he wants to show a different side of the "big, bad developer." But to the people who are losing their homes and their businesses, Mr. Koman is exactly that.

He is currently involved in several disputes with property owners. Across the Mississippi River, on the north side of St. Louis, another struggling area, Mr. Koman plans to expand a shopping center he owns, with a regional urban-wear store, a fish-and-chicken restaurant and a men's hair salon committed to going in. But he is running into local opposition.

To get the land he needs, Mr. Koman wants to buy a trash-strewn lot and an old brick building that are located across the street. The building is owned by St. Louis Housing and Service Corp., a nonprofit group that bought it for $1 a few years back. "They have a business plan, and we have a business plan," says the group's chairwoman, Leeora Daniels, a 63-year-old retired schoolteacher. Mr. Koman's plan "is a strip mall. Our building has social programs along with storefronts to support what we're trying to do." The group plans to house day-care centers for children and adults among other social services, she says, adding that her group has hired a lawyer to fight the developer.

Mr. Koman says the roof is caving in and the building is a hazard. He contends there was no activity there until he came around looking to purchase it. The mayor's office agrees with him. "I think this would clearly qualify as blighted under pretty much anybody's definition," says Barbara Geisman, the mayor's executive director for development in St. Louis.

Next door, Mr. Koman is facing a fight over a postage-stamp-size vacant lot appraised at $7,000. The sale is being held up by one of six heirs to the property, who lives in Atlanta and wants $50,000 for his share alone. "It's all about greed," Mr. Koman says. "How much free money can I get from this developer?" The holdout didn't show up in court recently and couldn't be reached for comment.

Situations such as this, rather than those in which people are pushed out of their homes, make up a large percentage of cases in which St. Louis uses eminent domain, Ms. Geisman says. "There are always going be those poster children, but the reality is a whole lot more complicated than that. We can't let one person hold up something that the entire city wants and needs." It wouldn't be possible to do widespread redevelopment in an old, historic city like St. Louis if the Supreme Court hadn't upheld eminent-domain rules in its Kelo v. New London decision, Ms. Geisman adds.

Eminent-domain opponents, such as the Institute for Justice, the Washington nonprofit law firm that represented the homeowner in the Kelo case, beg to differ. "The idea that private development in cities can't happen without eminent domain is crazy," says Dana Berliner, senior attorney at the institute. "Private development happens all the time without eminent domain. People buy the property: If it's difficult to buy the property, they work around that person or they buy another property."

Why get involved in messy development battles? Mr. Koman doesn't deny it is a way to make a good profit, although he declines to say how much money he has made in the East St. Louis development. His properties there are 100%-occupied, and he hasn't had a tenant go out of business since opening. "Please come invest in the inner city," he says. "We are making money in East St Louis."

Mr. Koman's background, however, lends ammunition to critics who say eminent domain often benefits the powerful at the expense of the less well-off. Mr. Koman's father, Bill, played pro football for the old St. Louis Cardinals in the 1950s and '60s and then went into development. Jim Koman and his brother followed their father into the business. Now, the brother has a separate company that builds offices, and Jim handles retail development. He currently has 18 shopping centers under construction within 180 miles of St. Louis. Six of them may require the use of eminent domain to get the necessary land, including a big cornfield in Troy, Ill, just outside St. Louis.

Mr. Koman isn't averse to using hardball tactics. He tells people who don't want to settle that he will take them to court, where they will get much less than what he is offering. As he drives through a trailer park he is currently trying to buy out, he mocks the people who fight his efforts. "Oh my God, you're ruining my life!" he quotes them as saying. "But half these people can't even find jobs or are alcoholics or whatever," he adds. "Most people are just ecstatic [with the buyouts]."

In East St. Louis, Mr. Koman wants to expand his shopping center but has run into opposition from the owner of a beauty salon who has refused to give up his lease on a neighboring property. Tony Ngo, who owns U.S. Nails, has strong feelings about eminent domain. "Eminent domain is a horrible law...I feel that it's a little bit worse than communism," he says. "The communists—you know they're going to come in and they're going to take. This is a business that I plan to grow."

He is negotiating with Mr. Koman, and the two sides appear to be close to a deal. "The question is, Is it faster for me to buy this guy off, or quicker to go to court and condemn it?" Mr. Koman says.

---

*Write to **Ryan Chittum** at ryan.chittum@wsj.com*

From *The Wall Street Journal*, October 5, 2005, pp. B1, B6. Copyright © 2005 by Dow Jones & Company, Inc. Reprinted by permission of Dow Jones & Company, Inc. via the Copyright Clearance Center.

Debate Flares Anew Over Violence in Video Games

State lawmakers try to regulate the sale of some titles, but the industry contends such efforts amount to censorship.

Alex Pham, Times Staff Writer

As the video game industry gears up to release a new generation of consoles that allow even sharper graphics and more realistic action, lawmakers nationwide are considering bans on the sale or rental of violent titles to minors.

In California, for instance, Gov. Arnold Schwarzenegger has until midnight Thursday to act on a bill that would ban the sale to minors of games that "depict serious injury to human beings in a manner that is especially heinous, atrocious or cruel."

That worries the $25-billion global game industry, which fears that its wares would be the only form of entertainment other than pornography subject to such heavy regulation.

But it's welcome news to Mary Gilbertson, who yanked "Grand Theft Auto: San Andreas" from her 16-year-old son once she realized the game was about more than fast cars.

Her son argued that it was just a game, but "it still disturbed me that he found it entertaining," the Minnesota preschool teacher said of the title, which allows players to shoot cops, run over pedestrians and have sex with prostitutes, then beat them senseless.

In the weeks since publisher Take-Two Interactive Software Inc. acknowledged that some versions of "San Andreas" also included a hidden sex scene, the game has renewed and intensified longtime concerns over excessive sex and violence in video games.

The debate over violence in one of the fastest-growing segments of the entertainment industry ebbs and flows. There's disagreement over whether virtual violence breeds real violence, but the video game industry has for years churned out increasingly graphic titles that rile its critics.

"The topic tends to resurface every few years," said American McGee, a veteran game developer. "Some of it has to do with the improvements in game graphics. People who never play video games see how visceral it is, and they freak out."

In addition to the California bill, Michigan last month passed a similar law, set to take effect Dec. 1, to ban the sale of "ultra-violent explicit video games" to minors under 17. And an Illinois law, set to take effect Jan. 1, prohibits the sale or rental of violent or sexually explicit games to minors.

The Entertainment Software Assn. has filed suit in Michigan and Illinois seeking to block the laws, contending that they amount to censorship.

"The graphics [are] too shocking, too realistic not to have an effect on children," said Assemblyman Leland Yee (D-San Francisco), a child psychologist who sponsored the bill now before Schwarzenegger. "These games are very intense.... You have children scoping targets, pulling the trigger, blowing people's heads off and burning people to a crisp."

Some social scientists say the criticisms lodged against video games parallel the scrutiny that faced other new forms of media—including comic books in the 1950s and television in the 1960s.

"With just about any new medium, there has been concern about the negative effects it might have on young people," said Karen Sternheimer, a lecturer in sociology at USC. "From movies to television to comic books to music and now video games, society tends to project its fears onto newer forms of pop culture. There's a generational divide that makes people on the other side nervous."

In 1957, for instance, when a 21-year-old Elvis Presley gave his trademark, hip-swiveling performance on "The Ed Sullivan Show," cameramen were ordered to shoot him from the waist up to appease offended advertisers.

Four years earlier, a Senate subcommittee led by Sen. Estes Kefauver of Tennessee held hearings on the corruptive influence of comic books, citing a book written by Frederic Wertham called "Seduction of the Innocent," which tried to link comic book reading with murder.

"There was this belief that comic books led young people to kill," Sternheimer said. "The parallels between video games and comic books are eerie."

That argument does little to appease critics of the video game industry. They contend that video games differ from traditional media because games require active participation.

"A violent game is not going to affect a 15-year-old the same way it affects a 30-year-old," said David Walsh, a psychologist and president and founder of the National Institute on Media and the Family in Minneapolis. "Adolescents are much more impulsive. They're predisposed to anger. So you put a 15-year-old in front of a violent video game for hours and hours, and you get a kid who becomes much more aggressive."

The American Psychological Assn. agreed. In August, the Washington-based group said a review of existing studies indicated that "exposure to violence in video games increases aggressive thoughts, aggressive behavior and angry feelings among youth." As a result, it adopted a resolution recommending a reduction in violence in games.

But Dmitri Williams, assistant professor of speech communication at the University of Illinois at Urbana-Champaign, said the studies on which the association based its conclusions were few and flawed.

"There are about 30 studies in all that look at this issue," Williams said. "That's really not a lot of studies, and they don't all agree with one another."

Besides, game industry executives and retailers contend, the sale of violent games to minors is already restricted under a voluntary system established by the Entertainment Software Rating Board, an industry organization that rates nearly all video games sold by major retailers.

Under the system, games are given one of six ratings, ranging from "early childhood" to "adults only." In addition to the ratings, each game is given brief descriptions. "Grand Theft Auto: San Andreas," for example, is rated "mature" and is described as having "blood and gore, intense violence, strong language, strong sexual content, use of drugs."

"We now have nine descriptions for violence alone," said Patricia Vance, president of the rating board. "You have everything from cartoon violence and fantasy violence to intense violence and blood and gore."

Although it isn't mandatory, retailers such as Wal-Mart Stores Inc. and Best Buy Co. have voluntarily agreed to restrict the sale of mature-rated games to those 17 years and older. Many stores don't sell games rated adults only.

"Today, 90% of retailers are committed to checking the age of their customers," said Doug Lowenstein, president of the Entertainment Software Assn. "They're getting better and better at it."

In a study released last fall by the National Institute on Media and the Family, retailers prevented the sale of mature-rated video games to minors 66% of the time.

Others in the video game industry argue that there are no laws restricting the sale of R-rated DVD movies and that the same standard should be true of video games.

"Why single out games?" said Jason Della Rocca, executive director of the International Game Developer Assn. "No other form of entertainment is regulated in this way."

Part of the problem, Della Rocca said, is that games are seen as children's toys, not as an entertainment medium for a broad range of audiences, including adults.

"If your mental image of a game is that of a toy and you're presented with 'Grand Theft Auto,' it's understandable that you'd be shocked," he said. "It's as if you expected TV to be 'Sesame Street,' and you're shown 'Sex and the City.' But that would be absurd.

"Likewise, no one in the movie industry expects children to watch 'The Godfather' or 'Kill Bill.' It's the same with 'GTA.' It was never created for children."

Brooks Brown of Littleton, Colo., who was a student at Columbine High School in 1999 when Dylan Klebold and Eric Harris went on a killing spree, has a different take on video games. Brown, now 25, used to play "Duke Nukem" with Klebold and Harris—that is until Harris threatened to kill Brown, a year before the shootings occurred.

"I look at video games the same way I look at advertisements," Brown said. "They're not designed to make you do anything you're not inclined to do. My guess is that 99.9% of people who play games have absolutely no inclination to kill people.

"Video games, like advertising, only push you to kill if you're already inclined to do that anyway," Brown added. "Dylan and Eric were already very, very violent people. We know that now from Eric's diary. They just weren't taught how to deal with stress and frustration."

From *The Chicago Tribune,* October 5, 2005, pp. C1, C9. Copyright © 2005 by The Chicago Tribune Company. All rights reserved. Used with permission.

Values in Tension: Ethics Away from Home

When is different just different, and when is different wrong?

by Thomas Donaldson

When we leave home and cross our nation's boundaries, moral clarity often blurs. Without a backdrop of shared attitudes, and without familiar laws and judicial procedures that define standards of ethical conduct, certainty is elusive. Should a company invest in a foreign country where civil and political rights are violated? Should a company go along with a host country's discriminatory employment practices? If companies in developed countries shift facilities to developing nations that lack strict environmental and health regulations, or if those companies choose to fill management and other top-level positions in a host nation with people from the home country, whose standards should prevail?

Even the best-informed, best-intentioned executives must rethink their assumptions about business practice in foreign settings. What works in a company's home country can fail in a country with different standards of ethical conduct. Such difficulties are unavoidable for businesspeople who live and work abroad.

But how can managers resolve the problems? What are the principles that can help them work through the maze of cultural differences and establish codes of conduct for globally ethical business practice? How can companies answer the toughest question in global business ethics: What happens when a host country's ethical standards seem lower than the home country's?

Competing Answers

One answer is as old as philosophical discourse. According to cultural relativism, no culture's ethics are better than any other's; therefore there are no international rights and wrongs. If the people of Indonesia tolerate the bribery of their public officials, so what? Their attitude is no better or worse than that of people in Denmark or Singapore who refuse to offer or accept bribes. Likewise, if Belgians fail to find insider trading morally repugnant, who cares? Not enforcing insider-trading laws is no more or less ethical than enforcing such laws.

The cultural relativist's creed—When in Rome, do as the Romans do—is tempting, especially when failing to do as the locals do means forfeiting business opportunities. The inadequacy of cultural relativism, however, becomes apparent when the practices in question are more damaging than petty bribery or insider trading.

In the late 1980s, some European tanneries and pharmaceutical companies were looking for cheap waste-dumping sites. They approached virtually every country on Africa's west coast from Morocco to the Congo. Nigeria agreed to take highly toxic polychlorinated biphenyls. Unprotected local workers, wearing thongs and shorts, unloaded barrels of PCBs and placed them near a residential area. Neither the residents nor the workers knew that the barrels contained toxic waste.

We may denounce governments that permit such abuses, but many countries are unable to police transnational corporations adequately even if they want to. And in many countries, the combination of ineffective enforcement and inadequate regulations leads to behavior by unscrupulous companies that is clearly wrong. A few years ago, for example, a group of investors became interested in restoring the SS *United States*, once a luxurious ocean liner. Before the actual restoration could begin, the ship had to be stripped of its asbestos lining. A bid from a U.S. company, based on U.S. standards for asbestos removal, priced the job at more than $100 million. A company in the Ukranian city of Sevastopol offered to do the work for less than $2 million. In October 1993, the ship was towed to Sevastopol.

The Culture and Ethics of Software Piracy

Before jumping on the cultural relativism bandwagon, stop and consider the potential economic consequences of a when-in-Rome attitude toward business ethics. Take a look at the current statistics on software piracy: In the United States, pirated software is estimated to be 35% of the total software market, and industry losses are estimated at $2.3 billion per year. The piracy rate is 57% in Germany and 80% in Italy and Japan; the rates in most Asian countries are estimated to be nearly 100%.

There are similar laws against software piracy in those countries. What, then, accounts for the differences? Although a country's level of economic development plays a large part, culture, including ethical attitudes, may be a more crucial factor. The 1995 annual report of the Software Publishers Association connects software piracy directly to culture and attitude. It describes Italy and Hong Kong as having "'first world' per capita incomes, along with 'third world' rates of piracy." When asked whether one should use software without paying for it, most people, including people in Italy and Hong Kong, say no. But people in some countries regard the practice as *less* unethical than people in other countries do. Confucian culture, for example, stresses that individuals should share what they create with society. That may be, in part, what prompts the Chinese and other Asians to view the concept of intellectual property as a means for the West to monopolize its technological superiority.

What happens if ethical attitudes around the world permit large-scale software piracy? Software companies won't want to invest as much in developing new products, because they cannot expect any return on their investment in certain parts of the world. When ethics fail to support technological creativity, there are consequences that go beyond statistics—jobs are lost and livelihoods jeopardized.

Companies must do more than lobby foreign governments for tougher enforcement of piracy laws. They must cooperate with other companies and with local organizations to help citizens understand the consequences of piracy and to encourage the evolution of a different ethic toward the practice.

A cultural relativist would have no problem with that outcome, but I do. A country has the right to establish its own health and safety regulations, but in the case described above, the standards and the terms of the contract could not possibly have protected workers in Sevastopol from known health risks. Even if the contract met Ukranian standards, ethical businesspeople must object. Cultural relativism is morally blind. There are fundamental values that cross cultures, and companies must uphold them. (For an economic argument against cultural relativism, see the insert "The Culture and Ethics of Software Piracy.")

At the other end of the spectrum from cultural relativism is ethical imperialism, which directs people to do everywhere exactly as they do at home. Again, an understandably appealing approach but one that is clearly inadequate. Consider the large U.S. computer-products company that

in 1993 introduced a course on sexual harassment in its Saudi Arabian facility. Under the banner of global consistency, instructors used the same approach to train Saudi Arabian managers that they had used with U.S. managers: the participants were asked to discuss a case in which a manager makes sexually explicit remarks to a new female employee over drinks in a bar. The instructors failed to consider how the exercise would work in a culture with strict conventions governing relationships between men and women. As a result, the training sessions were ludicrous. They baffled and offended the Saudi participants, and the message to avoid coercion and sexual discrimination was lost.

The theory behind ethical imperialism is absolutism, which is based on three problematic principles. Absolutists believe that there is a single list of truths, that they can be expressed only with one set of concepts, and that they call for exactly the same behavior around the world.

The first claim clashes with many people's belief that different cultural traditions must be respected. In some cultures, loyalty to a community—family, organization, or society—is the foundation of all ethical behavior. The Japanese, for example, define business ethics in terms of loyalty to their companies, their business networks, and their nation. Americans place a higher value on liberty than on loyalty; the U.S. tradition of rights emphasizes equality, fairness, and individual freedom. It is hard to conclude that truth lies on one side or the other, but an absolutist would have us select just one.

The second problem with absolutism is the presumption that people must express moral truth using only one set of concepts. For instance, some absolutists insist that the language of basic rights provide the framework for any discussion of ethics. That means, though, that entire cultural traditions must be ignored. The notion of a right evolved with the rise of democracy in post-Renaissance Europe and the United States, but the term is not found in either Confucian or Buddhist traditions. We all learn ethics in the context of our particular cultures, and the power in the principles is deeply tied to the way in which they are expressed. Internationally accepted lists of moral principles, such as the United Nations' Universal Declaration of Human Rights, draw on many cultural and religious traditions. As philosopher Michael Walzer has noted, "There is no Esperanto of global ethics."

The third problem with absolutism is the belief in a global standard of ethical behavior. Context must shape ethical practice. Very low wages, for example, may be considered unethical in rich, advanced countries, but developing nations may be acting ethically if they encourage investment and improve living standards by accepting low wages. Likewise, when people are malnourished or starving, a government may be wise to use more fertilizer in order to improve crop yields, even though that means settling for relatively high levels of thermal water pollution.

When cultures have different standards of ethical behavior—and different ways of handling unethical behavior—a company that takes an absolutist approach may find itself making a disastrous mistake. When a manager at a large U.S. specialty-products company in China caught an employee stealing, she followed the company's practice and turned the employee over to the provincial authorities, who executed him. Managers cannot operate in another culture without being aware of that culture's attitudes toward ethics.

If companies can neither adopt a host country's ethics nor extend the home country's standards, what is the answer? Even the traditional litmus test—What would people think of your actions if they were written up on the front page of the newspaper?—is an unreliable guide, for there is no international consensus on standards of business conduct.

What Do These Values Have in Common?

Non-Western	Western
Kyosei (Japanese): Living and working together for the common good.	Individual liberty
Dharma (Hindu): The fulfillment of inherited duty.	Egalitarianism
Santutthi (Buddhist): The importance of limited desires.	Political participation
Zakat (Muslim): The duty to give alms to the Muslim poor.	Human rights

Balancing the Extremes: Three Guiding Principles

Companies must help managers distinguish between practices that are merely different and those that are wrong. For relativists, nothing is sacred and nothing is wrong. For absolutists, many things that are different are wrong. Neither extreme illuminates the real world of business decision making. The answer lies somewhere in between.

When it comes to shaping ethical behavior, companies must be guided by three principles.

• Respect for core human values, which determine the absolute moral threshold for all business activities.
• Respect for local traditions.
• The belief that context matters when deciding what is right and what is wrong.

Consider those principles in action. In Japan, people doing business together often exchange gifts—sometimes expensive ones—in keeping with long-standing Japanese tradition. When U.S. and European companies started doing a lot of business in Japan, many Western businesspeople thought that the practice of gift giving might be wrong rather than simply different. To them, accepting a gift felt like accepting a bribe. As Western companies have become more familiar with Japanese traditions, however, most have come to tolerate the practice and to set different limits on gift giving in Japan than they do elsewhere.

Respecting differences is a crucial ethical practice. Research shows that management ethics differ among cultures; respecting those differences means recognizing that some cultures have obvious weaknesses—as well as hidden strengths. Managers in Hong Kong, for example, have a higher tolerance for some forms of bribery than their Western counterparts, but they have a much lower tolerance for the failure to acknowledge a subordinate's work. In some parts of the Far East, stealing credit from a subordinate is nearly an unpardonable sin.

People often equate respect for local traditions with cultural relativism. That is incorrect. Some practices are clearly wrong. Union Carbide's tragic experience in Bhopal, India, provides one example. The company's executives seriously underestimated how much on-site management involvement was needed at the Bhopal plant to compensate for the country's poor infrastructure and regulatory capabilities. In the aftermath of the disastrous gas leak, the lesson is clear: companies using sophisticated technology in a developing country must evaluate that country's ability to oversee its safe use. Since the incident at Bhopal, Union Carbide has become a leader in advising companies on using hazardous technologies safely in developing countries.

Some activities are wrong no matter where they take place. But some practices that are unethical in one setting may be acceptable in another. For instance, the chemical EDB, a soil fungicide, is banned for use in the United States. In hot climates, however, it quickly becomes harmless through exposure to intense solar radiation and high soil temperatures. As long as the chemical is monitored, companies may be able to use EDB ethically in certain parts of the world.

Defining the Ethical Threshold: Core Values

Few ethical questions are easy for managers to answer. But there are some hard truths that must guide managers' actions, a set of what I call *core human values*, which define minimum ethical standards for all companies.[1] The right to good health and the right to economic advancement and an improved standard of living are two core human values. Another is what Westerners call the Golden Rule, which is recognizable in every major religious and ethical tradition around the world. In Book 15 of his *Analects*, for instance, Confucius counsels people to maintain reciprocity, or not to do to others what they do not want done to themselves.

Although no single list would satisfy every scholar, I believe it is possible to articulate three core values that incorporate the work of scores of theologians and philosophers around the world. To be broadly relevant, these values must include elements found in both Western and non-Western cultural and religious traditions. Consider the examples of values in the insert "What Do These Values Have in Common?"

At first glance, the values expressed in the two lists seem quite different. Nonetheless, in the spirit of what philosopher John Rawls calls *overlapping consensus*, one can see that the seemingly divergent values converge at key points. Despite important differences between Western and non-Western cultural and religious traditions, both express shared attitudes about what it means to be human. First, individuals must not treat others simply as tools; in other words, they must recognize a person's value as a human being. Next, individuals and communities must treat people in ways that respect people's basic rights. Finally, members of a community must work together to support and improve the institutions on which the community depends. I call those three values *respect for human dignity, respect for basic rights*, and *good citizenship*.

Those values must be the starting point for all companies as they formulate and evaluate standards of ethical conduct at home and abroad. But they are only a starting point. Companies need much more specific guidelines, and the first step to developing those is to translate the core human values into core values for business. What does it mean, for example, for a company to respect human dignity? How can a company be a good citizen?

I believe that companies can respect human dignity by creating and sustaining a corporate culture in which employees, customers, and suppliers are treated not as means to an end but as people whose intrinsic value must be acknowledged, and by producing safe products and services in a safe workplace. Companies can respect basic rights by acting in ways that support and protect the individual rights of employees, customers, and surrounding communities, and by avoiding relationships that violate human beings' rights to health, education, safety, and an adequate standard of living. And companies can be good citizens by supporting essential social institutions, such as the economic system and the education system, and by working with host governments and other organizations to protect the environment.

The core values establish a moral compass for business practice. They can help companies identify practices that are acceptable and those that are intolerable—even if the practices are compatible with a host country's norms and laws. Dumping pollutants near people's homes and accepting inadequate standards for handling hazardous materials are two examples of actions that violate core values.

Similarly, if employing children prevents them from receiving a basic education, the practice is intolerable. Lying about product specifications in the act of selling may not affect human lives directly, but it too is intolerable because it violates the trust that is needed to sustain a corporate culture in which customers are respected.

Sometimes it is not a company's actions but those of a supplier or customer that pose problems. Take the case of the Tan family, a large supplier for Levi Strauss. The Tans were allegedly forcing 1,200 Chinese and Filipino women to work 74 hours per week in guarded compounds on the Mariana Islands. In 1992, after repeated warnings to the Tans, Levi Strauss broke off business relations with them.

Creating an Ethical Corporate Culture

The core values for business that I have enumerated can help companies begin to exercise ethical judgment and think about how to operate ethically in foreign cultures, but they are not specific enough to guide managers through actual ethical dilemmas. Levi Strauss relied on a written code of conduct when figuring out how to deal with the Tan family. The company's Global Sourcing and Operating Guidelines, formerly called the Business Partner Terms of Engagement, state that Levi Strauss will "seek to identify and utilize business partners who aspire as individuals and in the conduct of all their businesses to a set of ethical standards not incompatible with our own." Whenever intolerable business situations arise, managers should be guided by precise statements that spell out the behavior and operating practices that the company demands.

Many companies don't do anything with their codes of conduct; they simply paste them on the wall.

Ninety percent of all *Fortune* 500 companies have codes of conduct, and 70% have statements of vision and values. In Europe and the Far East, the percentages are lower but are increasing rapidly. Does that mean that most companies have what they need? Hardly. Even though most large U.S. companies have both statements of values and codes of conduct, many might be better off if they didn't. Too many companies don't do anything with the documents; they simply paste them on the wall to impress employees, customers, suppliers, and the public. As a result, the senior managers who drafted the statements lose credibility by proclaiming values and not living up to them. Companies such as Johnson & Johnson, Levi Strauss, Motorola, Texas Instruments, and Lockheed Martin, however, do a great deal to make the words meaningful. Johnson & Johnson, for example, has become well known for its Credo Challenge sessions, in which managers discuss ethics in the context of their current business problems and are invited to criticize the company's credo and make suggestions for changes. The participants' ideas are passed on to the company's senior managers. Lockheed Martin has created an innovative site on the World Wide Web and on its local network that gives employees, customers, and suppliers access to the company's ethical code and the chance to voice complaints.

If a company declared all gift giving unethical, it wouldn't be able to do business in Japan.

Codes of conduct must provide clear direction about ethical behavior when the temptation to behave unethically is strongest. The pronouncement in a code of conduct that bribery is unacceptable is useless unless accompanied by guidelines for gift giving, payments to get goods through customs, and "requests" from intermediaries who are hired to ask for bribes.

Motorola's values are stated very simply as "How we will always act: [with] constant respect for people [and] uncompromising integrity." The company's code of conduct, however, is explicit about actual business practice. With respect to bribery, for example, the code states that the "funds and assets of Motorola shall not be used, directly or indirectly, for illegal payments of any kind." It is unambiguous about what sort of payment is illegal: "the payment of a bribe to a public official or the kickback of funds to an employee of a customer...." The code goes on to prescribe specific procedures for handling commissions to intermediaries, issuing sales invoices, and disclosing confidential information in a sales transaction—all situations in which employees might have an opportunity to accept or offer bribes.

Codes of conduct must be explicit to be useful, but they must also leave room for a manager to use his or her judgment in situations requiring cultural sensitivity. Host-country employees shouldn't be forced to adopt all home-country values and renounce their own. Again, Motorola's code is exemplary. First, it gives clear direction: "Employees of Motorola will respect the laws, customs, and traditions of each country in which they operate, but will, at the same time, engage in no course of conduct which, even if legal, customary, and accepted in any such country, could be deemed to be in violation of the accepted business ethics of Motorola or the laws of the United States relating to business ethics." After laying down such absolutes, Motorola's code then makes clear when individual judgment will be necessary. For example, employees may sometimes accept certain kinds of small gifts "in rare circumstances, where the refusal to accept a gift" would injure Motorola's "legitimate business interests." Under certain circumstances, such gifts "may be accepted so long as the gift inures to the benefit of Motorola" and not "to the benefit of the Motorola employee."

Striking the appropriate balance between providing clear direction and leaving room for individual judgment makes crafting corporate values statements and ethics codes one of the hardest tasks that executives confront. The words are only a start. A company's leaders need to refer often to their organization's credo and code and must themselves be credible, committed, and consistent. If senior managers act as though ethics don't matter, the rest of the company's employees won't think they do, either.

Conflicts of Development and Conflicts of Tradition

Managers living and working abroad who are not prepared to grapple with moral ambiguity and tension should pack their bags and come home. The view that all business practices can be categorized as either ethical or unethical is too simple. As Einstein is reported to have said, "Things should be as simple as possible—but no simpler." Many business practices that are considered unethical in one setting may be ethical in another. Such activities are neither black nor white but exist in what Thomas Dunfee and I have called *moral free space*.[2] In this gray zone, there are no tight prescriptions for a company's behavior. Managers must chart their own courses—as long as they do not violate core human values.

Many activities are neither good nor bad but exist in *moral free space*.

Consider the following example. Some successful Indian companies offer employees the opportunity for one of their children to gain a job with the company once the child has completed a certain level in school. The companies honor this commitment even when other applicants are more qualified than an employee's child. The perk is extremely valuable in a country where jobs are hard to find, and it reflects the Indian culture's belief that the West has gone too far in allowing economic opportunities to break up families. Not surprisingly, the perk is among the most cherished by employees, but in most Western countries, it would be branded unacceptable nepotism. In the United States, for example, the ethical principle of equal opportunity holds that jobs should go to the applicants with the best qualifications. If a U.S. company made such promises to its employees, it would violate regulations established by the Equal Employment Opportunity Commission. Given this difference in ethical attitudes, how should U.S. managers react to Indian nepotism? Should they condemn the Indian companies, refusing to accept them as partners or suppliers until they agree to clean up their act?

Despite the obvious tension between nepotism and principles of equal opportunity, I cannot condemn the practice for Indians. In a country, such as India, that emphasizes clan and family relationships and has catastrophic levels of

The Problem with Bribery

Bribery is widespread and insidious. Managers in transnational companies routinely confront bribery even though most countries have laws against it. The fact is that officials in many developing countries wink at the practice, and the salaries of local bureaucrats are so low that many consider bribes a form of remuneration. The U.S. Foreign Corrupt Practices Act defines allowable limits on petty bribery in the form of routine payments required to move goods through customs. But demands for bribes often exceed those limits, and there is seldom a good solution.

Bribery disrupts distribution channels when goods languish on docks until local handlers are paid off, and it destroys incentives to compete on quality and cost when purchasing decisions are based on who pays what under the table. Refusing to acquiesce is often tantamount to giving business to unscrupulous companies.

I believe that even routine bribery is intolerable. Bribery undermines market efficiency and predictability, thus ultimately denying people their right to a minimal standard of living. Some degree of ethical commitment—some sense that everyone will play by the rules—is necessary for a sound economy. Without an ability to predict outcomes, who would be willing to invest?

There was a U.S. company whose shipping crates were regularly pilfered by handlers on the docks of Rio de Janeiro. The handlers would take about 10% of the contents of the crates, but the company was never sure which 10% it would be. In a partial solution, the company began sending two crates—the first with 90% of the merchandise, the second with 10%. The handlers learned to take the second crate and leave the first untouched. From the company's perspective, at least knowing which goods it would lose was an improvement.

Bribery does more than destroy predictability; it undermines essential social and economic systems. That truth is not lost on businesspeople in countries where the practice is woven into the social fabric. CEOs in India admit that their companies engage constantly in bribery, and they say that they have considerable disgust for the practice. They blame government policies in part, but Indian executives also know that their country's business practices perpetuate corrupt behavior. Anyone walking the streets of Calcutta, where it is clear that even a dramatic redistribution of wealth would still leave most of India's inhabitants in dire poverty, comes face-to-face with the devastating effects of corruption.

standards not only are different but also seem lower than the home country's. Managers must recognize that when countries have different ethical standards, there are two types of conflict that commonly arise. Each type requires its own line of reasoning.

In the first type of conflict, which I call a *conflict of relative development*, ethical standards conflict because of the countries' different levels of economic development. As mentioned before, developing countries may accept wage rates that seem inhumane to more advanced countries in order to attract investment. As economic conditions in a developing country improve, the incidence of that sort of conflict usually decreases. The second type of conflict is a *conflict of cultural tradition*. For example, Saudi Arabia, unlike most other countries, does not allow women to serve as corporate managers. Instead, women may work in only a few professions, such as education and health care. The prohibition stems from strongly held religious and cultural beliefs; any increase in the country's level of economic development, which is already quite high, is not likely to change the rules.

To resolve a conflict of relative development, a manager must ask the following question: Would the practice be acceptable at home if my country were in a similar stage of economic development? Consider the difference between wage and safety standards in the United States and in Angola, where citizens accept lower standards on both counts. If a U.S. oil company is hiring Angolans to work on an offshore Angolan oil rig, can the company pay them lower wages than it pays U.S. workers in the Gulf of Mexico? Reasonable people have to answer yes if the alternative for Angola is the loss of both the foreign investment and the jobs.

Consider, too, differences in regulatory environments. In the 1980s, the government of India fought hard to be able to import Ciba-Geigy's Entero Vioform, a drug known to be enormously effective in fighting dysentery but one that had been banned in the United States because some users experienced side effects. Although dysentery was not a big problem in the United States, in India, poor public sanitation was contributing to epidemic levels of the disease. Was it unethical to make the drug available in India after it had been banned in the United States? On the contrary, rational people should consider it unethical not to do so. Apply our test: Would the United States, at an earlier stage of development, have used this drug despite its side effects? The answer is clearly yes.

But there are many instances when the answer to similar questions is no. Sometimes a host country's standards are inadequate at any level of economic development. If a country's pollution standards are so low that working on an oil rig would considerably increase a person's risk of developing cancer, foreign oil companies must refuse to do business there. Likewise, if the dangerous side effects of a drug treatment outweigh its benefits, managers should not accept health standards that ignore the risks.

unemployment, the practice must be viewed in moral free space. The decision to allow a special perk for employees and their children is not necessarily wrong—at least for members of that country.

How can managers discover the limits of moral free space? That is, how can they learn to distinguish a value in tension with their own from one that is intolerable? Helping managers develop good ethical judgment requires companies to be clear about their core values and codes of conduct. But even the most explicit set of guidelines cannot always provide answers. That is especially true in the thorniest ethical dilemmas, in which the host country's ethical

When relative economic conditions do not drive tensions, there is a more objective test for resolving ethical problems. Managers should deem a practice permissible only if they can answer no to both of the following questions: Is it possible to conduct business successfully in the host country without undertaking the practice? And Is the practice a violation of a core human value? Japanese gift giving is a perfect example of a conflict of cultural tradition. Most experienced businesspeople, Japanese and non-Japanese alike, would agree that doing business in Japan would be virtually impossible without adopting the practice. Does gift giving violate a core human value? I cannot identify one that it violates. As a result, gift giving may be permissible for foreign companies in Japan even if it conflicts with ethical attitudes at home. In fact, that conclusion is widely accepted, even by companies such as Texas Instruments and IBM, which are outspoken against bribery.

Does it follow that all nonmonetary gifts are acceptable or that bribes are generally acceptable in countries where they are common? Not at all. (See the insert "The Problem with Bribery.") What makes the routine practice of gift giving acceptable in Japan are the limits in its scope and intention. When gift giving moves outside those limits, it soon collides with core human values. For example, when Carl Kotchian, president of Lockheed in the 1970s, carried suitcases full of cash to Japanese politicians, he went beyond the norms established by Japanese tradition. That incident galvanized opinion in the United States Congress and helped lead to passage of the Foreign Corrupt Practices Act. Likewise, Roh Tae Woo went beyond the norms established by Korean cultural tradition when he accepted $635.4 million in bribes as president of the Republic of Korea between 1988 and 1993.

Guidelines for Ethical Leadership

Learning to spot intolerable practices and to exercise good judgment when ethical conflicts arise requires practice. Creating a company culture that rewards ethical behavior is essential. The following guidelines for developing a global ethical perspective among managers can help.

Treat corporate values and formal standards of conduct as absolutes. Whatever ethical standards a company chooses, it cannot waver on its principles either at home or abroad. Consider what has become part of company lore at Motorola. Around 1950, a senior executive was negotiating with officials of a South American government on a $10 million sale that would have increased the company's annual net profits by nearly 25%. As the negotiations neared completion, however, the executive walked away from the deal because the officials were asking for $1 million for "fees." CEO Robert Galvin not only supported the executive's decision but also made it clear that Motorola would neither accept the sale on any terms nor do business with those government officials again. Retold over the decades, this story demonstrating Galvin's resolve has

helped cement a culture of ethics for thousands of employees at Motorola.

Design and implement conditions of engagement for suppliers and customers. Will your company do business with any customer or supplier? What if a customer or supplier uses child labor? What if it has strong links with organized crime? What if it pressures your company to break a host country's laws? Such issues are best not left for spur-of-the-moment decisions. Some companies have realized that. Sears, for instance, has developed a policy of not contracting production to companies that use prison labor or infringe on workers' rights to health and safety. And Bank-America has specified as a condition for many of its loans to developing countries that environmental standards and human rights must be observed.

Allow foreign business units to help formulate ethical standards and interpret ethical issues. The French pharmaceutical company Rhône-Poulenc Rorer has allowed foreign subsidiaries to augment lists of corporate ethical principles with their own suggestions. Texas Instruments has paid special attention to issues of international business ethics by creating the Global Business Practices Council, which is made up of managers from countries in which the company operates. With the overarching intent to create a "global ethics strategy, locally deployed," the council's mandate is to provide ethics education and create local processes that will help managers in the company's foreign business units resolve ethical conflicts.

In host countries, support efforts to decrease institutional corruption. Individual managers will not be able to wipe out corruption in a host country, no matter how many bribes they turn down. When a host country's tax system, import and export procedures, and procurement practices favor unethical players, companies must take action.

Many companies have begun to participate in reforming host-country institutions. General Electric, for example, has taken a strong stand in India, using the media to make repeated condemnations of bribery in business and government. General Electric and others have found, however, that a single company usually cannot drive out entrenched corruption. Transparency International, an organization based in Germany, has been effective in helping coalitions of companies, government officials, and others work to reform bribery-ridden bureaucracies in Russia, Bangladesh, and elsewhere.

Exercise moral imagination. Using moral imagination means resolving tensions responsibly and creatively. Coca-Cola, for instance, has consistently turned down requests for bribes from Egyptian officials but has managed to gain political support and public trust by sponsoring a project to plant fruit trees. And take the example of Levi Strauss, which discovered in the early 1990s that two of its suppliers in Bangladesh were employing children under the age of 14—a practice that violated the company's principles but was tolerated in Bangladesh. Forcing the suppliers to fire the children would not have ensured that the children received an education, and it would have caused serious hardship for the families depending on the children's wages. In a creative arrangement, the suppliers agreed to pay the children's regular wages while they attended school and to offer each child a job at age 14. Levi Strauss, in turn, agreed to pay the children's tuition and provide books and uniforms. That arrangement allowed Levi Strauss to uphold its principles and provide long-term benefits to its host country.

Many people think of values as soft; to some they are usually unspoken. A South Seas island society uses the word *mokita*, which means, "the truth that everybody knows but nobody speaks." However difficult they are to articulate, values affect how we all behave. In a global business environment, values in tension are the rule rather than the exception. Without a company's commitment, statements of values and codes of ethics end up as empty plati-

tudes that provide managers with no foundation for behaving ethically. Employees need and deserve more, and responsible members of the global business community can set examples for others to follow. The dark consequences of incidents such as Union Carbide's disaster in Bhopal remind us how high the stakes can be.

Notes

1. In other writings, Thomas W. Dunfee and I have used the term *hypernorm* instead of *core human value*.
2. Thomas Donaldson and Thomas W. Dunfee, "Toward a Unified Conception of Business Ethics: Integrative Social Contracts Theory," *Academy of Management Review*, April 1994; and "Integrative Social Contracts Theory: A Communitarian Conception of Economic Ethics," *Economics and Philosophy*, spring 1995.

Reprinted with permission from *Harvard Business Review*, September/October 1996, pp. 48–62. © 1996 by the President and Fellows of Harvard College. All rights reserved.

Managing ethically with global stakeholders:
A present and future challenge

Archie B. Carroll

In the early 2000s, the era of corporate fraud and corruption defined by the ethical wrongdoing of Enron, World-Com, Tyco, Arthur Andersen, and HealthSouth captured the world's attention as never before. It soon became clear, however, that the U. S. had not cornered the market on questionable ethics. The Dutch firm Ahold and Italy's Parmalat quickly shared center stage with scandals of their own. Domestic business ethics will continue to be a top priority. But global business ethics will demand cutting-edge thinking and practice as companies strive to expand their products, services, sales, and operations throughout the world. Regardless of what is happening in individual countries, whether at home or abroad, the primary venue for ethical debates in the future will more and more be the world stage.

The primary venue for ethical debates in the future will more and more be the world stage.

Globalization characterizes the international setting of business transactions in which U. S. and world multinational corporations (MNCs) will increasingly participate over the next several decades. Despite setbacks such as the attacks upon the World Trade Center in 2001 and the anti-globalization backlash that continues to be seen at major international meetings of the World Trade Organization, International Monetary Fund, and global summits such as the G8 summits, the global economy is irresistible to MNCs, and little will impede the trend toward global capitalism.

The explosive growth of MNCs has set the stage for global business ethics to be one of the highest priorities over the coming decades. Recent data shows that of the 100 largest "economies" in the world, only 47 of them are nation states. The other 53 are MNCs. Exxon Mobil Corporation, for example, has annual revenues that exceed the GDP of all but 20 of the world's 220 nations.[1] Clearly, then, the MNCs' operations throughout the world will constitute a primary arena for business ethics thinking and applications.

The focus in this discussion will be on how businesses and managers can deal with the topic of business ethics vis-à-vis their global stakeholders. As Princeton professor of bioethics Peter Singer recently said, "How well we come through the era of globalization will depend on how we respond ethically to the idea that we live in one world."[2]

Business's major stakeholders include consumers, employees, owners, the community, government, competitors, and the natural environment. There are many others, but we will focus primarily on the community and government. In the context of global ethics, the community is the community of host nations in which the firm is doing business, and the government represents all the separate sovereign nations that serve as "hosts" to investing MNCs. This makes for a much more complex situation than, for example, a U.S. MNC doing business in the U. S. It also represents a most-likely scenario in world affairs that doing business in others' countries will become more of the norm. It is estimated, for example, that while the economies of China and India are much smaller than that of the U. S. now, China is likely to overtake and India to equal the U.S. economy in size by 2050. The world's economic center of gravity is shifting toward Asia, and U.S. preeminence will undoubtedly diminish though its participation in the global economy is expected to grow. The current controversy over the outsourcing of U. S. jobs is one of the latest debate points in the trend.

Some Current Knowledge about Global Ethics

We know so little for sure about global business ethics. Even so, a number of experts testify to its importance. Tichy and McGill declare that "it is difficult to think of a more important basic business ethical commitment than to be a good citizen in the world of your business—with real involvement of your people, as well as your money."[3] As a practical matter, Sir Philip Watts, the chairman of Royal Dutch/Shell, recently has worked hard to recast his once reviled company as a compassionate corporate citizen.[4]

We do know that there is a pressing need for more empirical research on global business ethics, but most of the work to date has been quite contingent. Much business ethics research depends upon many factors, including the ubiquitous issue of culture. The extension of business ethics concepts and thinking to the global arena has probably raised more questions than it has answered. Though textbooks have been available for years on the subject of international business ethics,[5] we are still in the formative stages of providing conceptual models and applications that readily translate into effective practices for business executives.

There is a pressing need for more empirical research on global business ethics.

In global ethics decision-making, so much focus is on the extent to which the manager uses home-country ethical standards versus host-country ethical standards in making decisions and shaping practices. One typology of global types that has been helpful is that of Georges Enderle. He has observed and categorized at least four different types of global firms with respect to their use of home-country versus host-country ethical standards. Enderle's purpose in this typology is to identify and illustrate the various mixtures or combinations of home- and host-country standards that a business operating in the global sphere might adopt.[6]

Through description and example, Enderle helps us to understand different options available and their consequences. He would likely reject the "Foreign Country Type," which simply conforms to local customs and ethics, as being too relativistic. At the other extreme, the "Global Type" strives to abstract from all regional differences and seek ethical principles that would be more globally acceptable. In between these two extremes, he presents the "Empire Type" that applies home-country ethics without any attempt at cultural adaptation and the "Interconnection Type" that blurs national identities and seeks a posture that transcends international boundaries but "connects" with selected clusters, such as the European Union or NAFTA. Though Enderle stops short of offering prescriptive guidelines, the Global model seems preferable to the Foreign Country model as companies seek exemplars.

Another major contribution has been Tom Donaldson and Thomas Dunfee's Integrative Social Contracts Theory (ISCT) as an approach to navigating cross-national cultural differences.[7] Their model is depicted as a series of concentric circles representing various ethical norms that might be held by corporations, industries, or economic cultures. At the center of the circles are *hypernorms*, which represent desired transcultural values. These might include fundamental human rights common to most cultures and countries. Moving out from the center,

one would next find *consistent norms*. These are more culturally specific but are consistent with hypernorms. The next circle is *moral free space*. Here, one finds norms that are inconsistent with at least some other legitimate norms existing in other economic cultures. These represent strongly held cultural beliefs in particular countries. Thus, Buddhist communities may develop norms that reflect their cultures, and Koreans might develop norms regarding work behavior that reflect their culture.[8] Finally, in the outer circle are *illegitimate norms,* which are norms that are incompatible with hypernorms. An example of these might be the practice of exposing workers to unacceptable levels of carcinogens.

In short, ISCT uses the principles of moral free space and adherence to hypernorms as positions that need to be balanced in navigating global international waters. While honoring hypernorms, companies do not have to simply adopt a "do in Rome as the Romans do" philosophy. However, they do need to be sensitive to the transcultural value implications of their actions. In turn, the concept of moral free space makes them ever vigilant of the need to precede judgment with an attempt to understand the local host-country culture. The result is the reality that moral tensions will be an everyday part of doing business in the global sphere.[9] ISCT is a contingency model of ethical decision-making as are most constructs that might be useful in global applications.

The Timeliness of Corporate Social Responsibility and Ethics

Executives want a useful framework for thinking about global business ethics, and the concept of corporate social responsibility, a concept that has endured for decades in the U.S. and is growing exponentially in Europe, fills the bill. This is because companies in diverse industries are conclusively seeing that the public insists that they balance profits with corporate citizenship. According to *The Economist,* the corporate social responsibility (CSR) movement flowered in the decade of the 1990s and is carrying forward into the 2000s. As recently as the World Economic Forum that gathered in Davos, Switzerland in January 2004, the corporate chieftains in attendance were expressing the conviction that global corporate responsibility and citizenship were the order of the day.[10]

The literature of CSR has produced many definitions and many concepts over the past half century since its emergence and formalization on the business scene.[11] In terms of thinking about a concept or model of CSR that would have global applicability, I began considering how the CSR framework earlier developed[12] and then reformulated into a Pyramid of CSR[13] would stand up in application to global CSR and business ethics. The basic definition of CSR is as follows: "The social responsibility of business encompasses the economic, legal, ethical, and discretionary (philanthropic) expectations that society has of organizations at a given point in time."[14] This no-

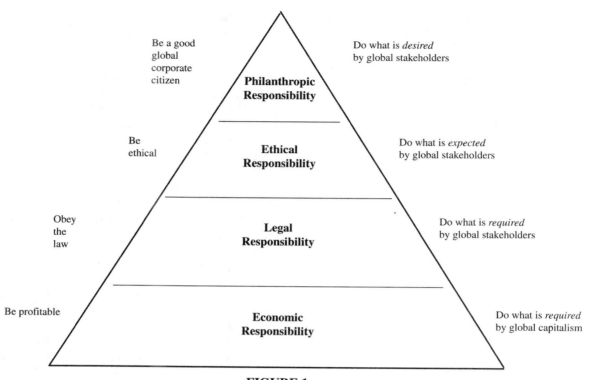

FIGURE 1
Pyramid of Global Corporate Social Responsibility and Performance

tion of CSR is both a stakeholder model and a contingency model. It is a stakeholder model in the sense that various stakeholder groups each send expectations to management about what they expect the organization to do under the banner of economics (profits), law, ethics, and philanthropy. It is a contingency model in several respects, but the most important is that society's views or expectations of business performance change and evolve over time. The expectation that firms will be good corporate citizens in the global sphere is one of the latest mandates of CSR.

A Pyramid of Global CSR as a Framework

Having a framework and context for business's social and ethical responsibilities to global stakeholders is an initial best practice. The Pyramid of Global Corporate Social Responsibility (see Figure 1) is presented as a helpful way to graphically depict the four kinds of social responsibility that business has with respect to global business stakeholders. The pyramid portrays the four components of global CSR, beginning with the basic building block of economic performance. At the same time, business is expected to obey the law because law is every country's codification of acceptable and unacceptable practices. Business also is expected to be ethical. At its most basic level, this is the obligation to do what is right, just, and fair and to avoid or minimize harm to stakeholders. Finally, business is expected to be a good corporate citizen

through its philanthropy. Firms today are expected to contribute financial and human resources to the global community and to "give back" so that the quality of life may be enhanced and sustained.

No metaphor is perfect, and the Global Pyramid of CSR is no exception. It is intended to illustrate that the global social responsibility of business is composed of four definite components that, when taken together, define what business should be doing in the international sphere. These four components are not mutually exclusive. They are treated separately for discussion purposes and are overlapping to some extent and in frequent tension with one another. A brief explanation of each CSR component is appropriate because these categories dictate corporate actions.

The *economic responsibilities* of the firm, whether domestic or global, remain the bedrock foundation for business. Global companies are expected to produce goods and services and sell them at a profit. Sound strategic management offers guidelines as to how and where this may be achieved in a global setting. At this level, consensus is easy to reach about the economic expectations of business firms. What may vary by country or region of the world is the question of what constitutes an acceptable rate of return or growth rate. Companies functioning in hypercompetitive conditions might look upon this question differently than those operating in developing countries. Therefore, this aspect of the framework is contingent upon local and regional expectations found in financial markets but remains foundational to survival and growth.

Legal responsibilities of management and MNCs also are vital. Just as countries have sanctioned economic systems, they also sanction legal systems. The social contract between business firms and host countries varies by country and, thus, legal systems and expectations vary as well. At this level, we observe significant differences in legal systems and responsibilities by countries and regions of the world. For example, we know that Chinese labor laws often are not enforced[15] and that foreign investors are finding that China's legal system resolves few disputes.[16] We also know that the absence of a legal system is inhibiting foreign investment in post-war Iraq.[17] One thing is clear, however: The legal responsibility does exist and is found in developed, developing, and less developed countries alike.

Ethical responsibilities are essential because laws are not adequate and companies and executives care deeply about their reputations, as well as about "doing the right thing." As long as publications such as *Multinational Monitor* publish their annual lists of the "ten worst corporations" in global business, executives will find justifiable and practical reasons to care about ethics.[18] Ethical responsibilities embrace those activities and practices that are expected or prohibited by society even though they may not be codified into law. Ethical responsibilities encompass the full scope of norms, standards, and expectations that reflect a belief in what employees, consumers, shareholders, and the global community regard as fair, just, and consistent with the respect for and protection of stakeholders' moral rights. Superimposed on the host country's expectations of ethics are the implied levels of ethical performance suggested by a consideration of the great ethical principles of moral philosophy, such as justice, rights, and utilitarianism.

Ethical responsibilities embrace those activities and practices that are expected or prohibited by society even though they may not be codified into law.

The ethical category is where divergent views traceable to different cultures are likely to be most significant. In a real sense, global business ethics is about the reconciliation of home- and host-country ethical standards and the identification of norms that will satisfy both. The practice of *moral relativism,* wherein companies simply adapt to local norms, creates an often untenable situation because many countries, especially developing ones, do not have articulated ethical standards that protect vulnerable stakeholders. Bowie recommends *moral universalism* as a principle that would create a moral standard that is accepted by all cultures.[19] Moral universalism is the identification of ethical standards that would have broad, in-

ternational support, such as the U.N. Global Compact or the Global Reporting Initiative.

Philanthropic responsibilities reflect global society's expectations that business will engage in social activities that are not mandated by law nor generally expected of business in an ethical sense. Though sometimes imbued with an ethical thread of rationale, philanthropy today is more often than not strategic in nature, with business expected to play an active role in global corporate citizenship. As in the case of law and ethics, philanthropic expectations vary widely by country of the world, and the wise executive will carefully research expectations of the host countries in this category. While presenting this idea in Helsinki, Finland, for example, I found that the Finns do not regard philanthropy highly because in their system, high taxes are thought by business to more than take care of these kinds of citizenship expectations.

The Global Pyramid of CSR provides a conceptual framework for thinking through the multitude of expectations that may fall on the MNC or global manager. It is intended to illustrate the total social responsibility of global businesses. Although the component parts have been separated for discussion, they are not mutually exclusive and are not to be filled in this sequence. The pyramid intends to suggest the building-block relationship of the four responsibilities with economic at the base, because without it the others are beside the point. The pyramid depicts the full range of responsibilities that global firms and managers are expected to fulfill simultaneously.

Stated in more practical and performance-oriented terms, the Global CSR Pyramid suggests that the MNC should strive to:

- *Make a profit* consistent with expectations for international businesses;
- *Obey the law* of host countries as well as international law;
- *Be ethical in its practices,* taking host-country and global standards into consideration;
- *Be a good corporate citizen,* especially as defined by the host country's expectations.

The Global Pyramid of CSR and Performance will help managers think through in a systematic way the different stakeholder expectations placed on their organizations. It should be recognized that responsibility implies performance. Previous research does support the contention that managers see the importance of their responsibilities as following this sequence of priorities: economic, legal, ethical, and philanthropic.[20]

Other Best Practices for Global Ethics

Having a useful model for framing responsibilities to global stakeholders is a first, and necessary, best practice. What are some other practices that global managers and organizations can best adopt to be responsive to the pressures and demands of international stakeholders? How can managers respond to the ethical responsibility depicted in the Global Pyramid of CSR?

Many global business ethics issues dominate the news today. It has been argued that the ethical issues surrounding MNCs or transnational corporations fall into at least eight major categories: bribery and sensitive payments, employment issues, marketing practices, impact on the economy and development of host countries, effects on the natural environment, cultural impacts of operations, relations with host governments, and relations with home countries.[21]

Flowing from a desire to address these eight categories of issues by fulfilling the responsibilities emanating from the Global Pyramid of CSR or another popular concept, the "triple bottom line" (which is a less detailed version in that it categorizes issues into economic, social, and environmental),[22] companies may pursue several major strategies. At a strategic level, companies should develop both *global corporate codes of conduct* and subscribe to global codes that have been developed by independent international bodies. Well-thought-out corporate codes are illustrated by those developed and adopted by Mattel and Caterpillar Tractor. Examples of respected independent global codes developed by international organizations include the UN Global Compact, the Global Reporting Initiative, OECD Guidelines for Multinational Enterprises, the Caux Principles, and the Principles for Global Corporate Responsibility developed by the Interfaith Center on Corporations.[23]

Companies should develop both global corporate codes of conduct and subscribe to global codes that have been developed by independent international bodies.

In a similar vein, the *integration of ethical principles* into strategic decision-making is another best practice. In this connection, the embracing of a set of fundamental international rights, such as those articulated by Tom Donaldson, will allow the corporation to integrate business ethics into its corporate strategy. Examples of his ten fundamental human rights include rights that should be given to employees and other stakeholders such as freedom from torture, a fair trial, physical security, speech and association, and subsistence. These rights are regarded as moral minimums for all international economic agents.[24]

A strong complement to these international rights are Richard DeGeorge's seven moral guidelines for firms operating globally. According to DeGeorge, MNCs should do no intentional, direct harm; produce more good than bad for the host country; contribute to the host country's development; respect human rights; pay their fair share of taxes; respect the local culture; and cooperate with the host government in developing ethical background institutions (e.g., health and safety standards).[25]

A company striving to develop universal ethical standards for its operations in 66 countries is ING, the multinational Dutch financial group. In an elaborate program based upon getting input from its 250 top international managers, ING has developed a global ethics code and is training its 83,000 worldwide staff via an interactive CD-ROM linked to the Internet to apply the company's ethics principles consistently around the globe. ING's vicechair of the executive board, Ewald Kist, has said, "This is supposed to be common ground that all our cultures can live with."[26]

With respect to the natural environment of host countries, the concept of "sustainable strategic management" sets the standard high. According to W. Edward Stead and Jean Garner Stead, this refers to strategic management processes that seek competitive advantages consistent with a core value of environmental sustainability. With this enterprise-level strategy, firms base their corporate strategies on an analysis of the ecological issues they face, the values they hold that support sustainability, and the ecological interests of their stakeholders.[27] The Paris-based oil company Total, the world's fourth largest oil company, is striving to embrace ethics and environmentalism in its sustainability quest. To establish credibility with its stakeholders, Total created a high-level ethics committee. Two of its European rivals, Shell and BP, are also making ethics a focal point of their environmental practices.[28]

Toward the Future: Much Research Is Needed

Much research is needed in global business ethics. If there is need for research in one particular area, it is in the reconciliation of home-country and host-country ethical standards such that international business ethics moves toward universal ethical standards or norms. Global stakeholders will best be served, as national borders fall, by the creation, implementation, and sustainability of a set of universal ethical guidelines that the developed economies of the world can use in transactions with each other and with the developing economies. The best practices described above will move MNCs toward this goal.

Endnotes

1. Melloan, G. Feeling the muscles of the multinationals. *Wall Street Journal,* 6 January 2004.

2. Singer, P. Navigating the ethics of globalization. *The Chronicle of Higher Education,* 11 October 2002, B8.

3. Tichy, N. M., & McGill, A. R. "Corporate global citizenship: The ethical path for business," in Tichy, N. M., & McGill, A. R., *The ethical challenge: How to lead with unyielding integrity.* San Francisco: Jossey-Bass, 2003, 248.

4. Becker, E. At Shell, grades for citizenship. *New York Times,* 30 November 2003, 2BU.

5. DeGeorge, R. *Competing with integrity in international business.* New York: Oxford University Press, 1993; Donaldson, T. *The ethics of international business.* New York: Oxford University Press, 1989.

6. Enderle, G. What is international? A typology of international spheres and its relevance for business ethics. Paper presented at the International Association for Business and Society, Vienna, Austria, 1995.

7. Donaldson, T., and Dunfee, T. 1999. When ethics travel: The promise and perils of global business ethics. *California Management Review,* 41 (4): 48–49.

8. Fritzsche, D. J. 2004. *Business ethics: A global and managerial perspective.* New York: McGraw-Hill, 56–57.

9. Ibid.

10. Two-faced capitalism. *The Economist,* 22 January 2004.

11. Carroll, A. B. 1999. Corporate social responsibility: Evolution of a definitional construct. *Business and Society,* 38 (3): 268–295.

12. Carroll, A. B. 1979. A three-dimensional conceptual model of corporate social performance. *Academy of Management Review,* 4: 497–505.

13. Carroll, A. B. 1991. The pyramid of corporate social responsibility: Towards the moral management of organizational stakeholders. *Business Horizons,* July-August: 42. An alternative to the pyramid is a Venn-diagram model presented in M. S. Schwartz & A. B. Carroll. 2003. Corporate social responsibility: A three-domain approach. *Business Ethics Quarterly,* 13(4): 503–530.

14. Carroll, 1979.

15. Pan, P. P. Worked to death: Chinese labor laws are rarely enforced. *The Washington Post National Weekly Edition,* 17–23 June 2002, 15.

16. Dolven, B. Foreign investors find that China's legal system resolves few disputes. *Wall Street Journal,* 8 April 2003, A14.

17. King, N., Jr. Iraq's business elite gropes in the dark. *Wall Street Journal,* 25 June 2003, A4.

18. Mokhiber, R., & Weissman, R. 2003. Multiple corporate personality disorder: The 10 worst corporations of 2003. *Multinational Monitor,* December: 9–20.

19. Bowie, N. 1987. The moral obligations of multinational corporations. In S. Luper-Foy (ed.), *Problems of International Justice.* New York: Westview Press, 97–113.

20. Aupperle, K. E., Carroll, A. B., & Hatfield, J. D. 1985. An empirical examination of the relationship between corporate social responsibility and profitability. *Academy of Management Journal,* 28(2): 446–463; Pinkston, T. S., & Carroll, A. B. 1994. Corporate citizenship perspectives and foreign direct investment in the U.S. *Journal of Business Ethics,* 13: 157–169.

21. Donaldson, T. 1997. International business ethics. In P. H. Werhane & R. E. Freeman (eds.), *The Blackwell Dictionary of Business Ethics.* Malden, MA: Blackwell Publishers, 346–348.

22. *http://www.sustainability.com/philosophy/triple-bottom/tblintro. asp.*

23. *Comparison of Selected CSR Standards.* San Francisco: Business for Social Responsibility, November 2000: 10–11.

24. Donaldson, 1989, 81.

25. DeGeorge, 1993.

26. Maitland, A. Common principles in a diverse world. *Financial Times,* 26 August 1999.

27. Stead, W. E., & Stead, J. G. 2004. *Sustainable strategic management.* Armonk, NY: M. E. Sharpe.

28. Gumbel, P. Total clean up. *Time,* 26 January 2004, A10–A12.

Archie B. Carroll holds the Robert W. Scherer Chair of Management in the Terry College of Business, University of Georgia, where he also serves as director of the Nonprofit Management & Community Service Program. He is co-author of *Business & Society: Ethics & Stakeholder Management,* 5th Edition, 2003. His interests span global business ethics, stakeholder management, and business- and-society. He received his doctorate in management from The Florida State University. Contact: *acarroll@terry. uga.edu.*

From *Academy of Management Executive,* 2004, pp. 114-120. Copyright © 2004 as conveyed via the Copyright Clearance Center. Reprinted by permission.

FAKES!

The global counterfeit business is out of control, targeting everything from computer chips to life-saving medicines. It's so bad that even China may need to crack down.

Frederik Balfour

A year and a half ago, Pfizer Inc. got a disturbing call on its customer hotline. A woman who had been taking its cholesterol-lowering drug Lipitor complained that a new bottle of tablets tasted bitter. She sent the suspicious pills to the company, which tested them at a lab in Groton, Conn. The white oblong tablets looked just like the real thing—and even contained some of the active ingredient in Lipitor. But Pfizer soon determined that they were counterfeits. Over the next two months, distributors yanked some 16.5 million tablets from warehouses and pharmacy shelves nationwide.

An isolated case? Hardly. Last October, Brazilian police got a tip-off about a hoard of bogus Hewlett-Packard Co. inkjet cartridges and seized more than $1 million worth of goods. Chinese police last year conducted raids confiscating everything from counterfeit Buick windshields to phony Viagra. In Guam, the Secret Service in July uncovered a network selling bogus North Korean-made pharmaceuticals, cigarettes, and $100 bills. In June, French customs seized more than 11,000 fake parts for Nokia Corp. cell phones—batteries, covers, and more. In January, U.S. Commerce Secretary Donald Evans blasted the Chinese on a visit to Beijing, demanding they step up efforts to police intellectual-property violations. Evans singled out the case of a General Motors Corp. subsidiary that is suing Chinese carmaker Chery Automotive for ripping off the design of its Chevrolet Spark minicar. The uncanny resemblance between the two cars, said Evans, "defies innocent explanation."

Critical Mass

Kiwi shoe polish, Callaway Golf clubs, Intel computer chips, Bosch power drills, BP oil. Pick any product from any well-known brand, and chances are there's a counterfeit version of it out there. Of course, as anyone who has combed the back alleys of Hong Kong, Rio, or Moscow knows, fakes have been around for decades. Only the greenest rube would actually believe that the $20 Rolex watch on Silom Road in Bangkok or the $30 Louis Vuitton bag on New York's Canal Street is genuine.

But counterfeiting has grown up—and that's scaring the multinationals. "We've seen a massive increase in the last five years, and there is a risk it will spiral out of control," says Anthony Simon, marketing chief of Unilever Bestfoods. "It's no longer a cottage industry." The World Customs Organization estimates counterfeiting accounts for 5% to 7% of global merchandise trade, equivalent to lost sales of as much as $512 billion last year—though experts say this is only a guess. Seizures of fakes by U.S. customs jumped by 46% last year as counterfeiters boosted exports to Western markets. Unilever Group says knockoffs of its shampoos, soaps, and teas are growing by 30% annually. The World Health Organization says up to 10% of medicines worldwide are counterfeited—a deadly hazard that could be costing the pharmaceutical industry $46 billion a year. Bogus car parts add up to $12 billion worldwide. "Counterfeiting has gone from a local nuisance to a global threat," says Hanns Glatz, DaimlerChrysler's point man on intellectual property.

The scale of the threat is prompting new efforts by multinationals to stop, or at least curb, the spread of counterfeits. Companies are deploying detectives around the globe in greater force than ever, pressuring governments from Beijing to Brasília to crack down, and trying everything from electronic tagging to redesigned products to aggressive pricing in order to thwart the counterfeiters. Even some Chinese companies, stung by fakes themselves, are getting into the act. "Once Chinese companies start to sue other Chinese companies, the situation will become more balanced," says Stephen Vickers, chief executive of International Risk, a Hong Kong-based brand-protection consultant.

China is key to any solution. Since the country is an economic gorilla, its counterfeiting is turning into quite the beast as well—accounting for nearly two-thirds of all the fake and pirated goods worldwide. Daimler's Glatz figures phony Daimler parts—from fenders to engine blocks—have grabbed 30% of the market in China, Taiwan, and Korea. And Chinese counterfeiters make millions of motorcycles a year, with knockoffs of Honda's workhorse CG125—selling for about $300, or less than half the cost of a real Honda—especially popular. It's tales like this that prompt some trade hawks in the U.S. to call for a World Trade Organization action against China related to counterfeits and intellectual-property rights violations in general. Such pressure is beginning to have some effect. "The Chinese government is starting to take things more seriously because of the unprecedented uniform shouting coming from the U.S., Europe, and Japan," says Joseph Simone, a lawyer specializing in IPR issues at Baker & McKenzie in Hong Kong.

Yet slowing down the counterfeiters in China and elsewhere will take heroic efforts. That's because counterfeiting thrives on the whole process of globalization itself. Globalization, after all, is the spread of capital and knowhow to new markets, which in turn contribute low-cost labor to create the ideal export machine, manufacturing first the cheap stuff, then moving up the value chain. That's the story of Southeast Asia. It's the story of China. Now it's the story of fakes. Counterfeiting packs all the punch of skilled labor, smart distribution, and product savvy without getting bogged down in costly details such as research and brand-building.

The result is a kind of global industry that is starting to rival the multinationals in speed, reach, and sophistication. Factories in China can copy a new model of golf club in less than a week, says Stu Herrington, who oversees brand protection for Callaway Golf Co. "The Chinese are extremely ingenious, inventive, and scientifically oriented, and they are becoming the world's manufacturer," he says. The company has found counterfeiters with three-dimensional design software and experience cranking out legitimate clubs for other brands, so "back-engineering a golf club is a piece of cake" for them, he says. And counterfeiters are skilled at duplicating holograms, "smart" chips, and other security devices intended to distinguish fakes from the genuine article. "We've had sophisticated technology that took years to develop knocked off in a matter of months," says Unilever marketing boss Simon.

The ambition of the counterfeiters just keeps growing. In China, recent raids have turned up everything from fake Sony PlayStation game controllers to Cisco Systems router interface cards. "If you can make it, they can fake it," says David Fernyhough, director of brand protection at investigation firm Hill & Associates Ltd. in Hong Kong. Don't believe him? Shanghai Mitsubishi Elevator Co. discovered a counterfeit elevator after a building owner asked the company for a maintenance contract. "It didn't look like our product," says Wang Chung Heng, a lawyer for Shanghai Mitsubishi. "And it stopped between floors."

Many fakes, though, are getting so good that even company execs say it takes a forensic scientist to distinguish them from the real McCoy. Armed with digital technology, counterfeiters can churn out perfect packaging—a key to duping unwitting distributors and retail customers. GM has come across fake air filters, brake pads, and batteries. "We had to cut them apart or do chemical analysis to tell" they weren't real, says Alexander Theil, director of investigations at General Motors Asia Pacific.

The parts might last half as long as the real thing, but that's not apparent until long after the sale.

The counterfeiters even ape the multinationals by diversifying their sourcing and manufacturing across borders. Last August, Philippine police raided a cigarette factory in Pampanga, two hours outside of Manila. What they found was a global operation in miniature. The factory was producing fake Davidoffs and Mild Sevens for export to Taiwan. The $6 million plant boasted a state-of-the-art German cigarette-rolling machine capable of producing some 3 billion fake smokes, worth $600 million, annually. The top-quality packaging came from a printer in Malaysia. The machinery itself was manned by 23 Chinese brought in by a Singapore-based syndicate, says Josef Gueta, director of Business Profiles Inc., a Manila firm that tracks counterfeit rings for multinationals. "They have shipping, warehousing, and the knowledge and network to move things around easily," he says.

As such counterfeiters get more entrenched and more global, they will be increasingly hard to eradicate. Financing comes from a variety of sources, including Middle East middlemen, local entrepreneurs, and organized crime. Sometimes the counterfeiters are fly-by-night operations, but just as often they're legitimate companies that have a dark side. In fact, many are licensed producers of brand-name goods that simply run an extra, unauthorized shift and sell out the back door. Or they are former licensees who have kept the molds and designs that allow them to go into business for themselves. Shoemaker New Balance Athletic Shoe Inc. is suing a former contract manufacturer in Guangdong province for selling unauthorized New Balance sneakers that have turned up as far away as Australia and Europe. In the Philippines, semiconductor distributor Sardido Industries says it has been burned by counterfeiters that have sold it microprocessors rejected by inspectors from the likes of Intel and Advanced Micro Devices. These are doctored with logos and serial numbers to look like genuine parts and sold off cheaply as returns or production overruns. Other counterfeiters are generic manufacturers who moonlight as makers of fakes. Yamaha Corp. has licensed five plants in China to make its motorcycles, but almost 50 factories have actually produced bikes branded as Yamaha.

It's easy to find the counterfeiters, too. The Ziyuangang market in the sprawling city of Guangzhou, two hours north of Hong Kong, looks pretty much like any recently built Chinese shopping mall. But venture inside, and you'll find row upon row of shops offering bogus Gucci, Versace, Dunhill, Longines, and more. Each shop has just a few dozen samples but offers vast catalogs of goods that can be made and delivered in less than a week. At one outlet, a clerk offers counterfeit Louis Vuitton bags in various sizes. "Even fakes have many grades of quality, and these fakes are really, really good," she boasts. Exports? She's happy to arrange shipping to the country of your choice.

Once those goods leave China, they can sneak into the legitimate supply chain just about anywhere. Sometimes, phony components get used in authentic products. Last year, for example, Kyocera Corp., had to recall a million cell-phone batteries that turned out to be counterfeit, costing the company at least $5 million. Unscrupulous wholesalers will fob off fakes on small auto-repair shops, office-supply stores, or independent pharmacies by saying they have bargain-priced—but not suspiciously cheap—oil filters, printer cartridges, or bottles of shampoo that another retailer returned, or which are close to their sell-by date. Some traders mix phonies in with authentic goods. "It's easy to slide a stack of fake Levis under the real ones," says one investigator based in Shanghai. "Most inspectors and buyers can't tell the difference."

Counterfeiters can also disguise their wares before they reach their final destination. Some ship unmarked counterfeit parts in several consignments to be assembled and labeled at their destination. And last May, Shanghai customs officials were inspecting a Dubai-bound shipment of 67 100cc motorcycles labeled with the brand name Honling. But when they peeled back stickers on the machines' crank cases, they found "Yamaha" engraved on the casting. "They are very sneaky and cunning, and that's very frustrating," laments Masayuki Hosokawa, chief representative of Yamaha Motor Co. in Beijing.

Strategic Defense

They are also making big bucks. Counterfeiting has become as profitable as trading illegal narcotics, and is a lot less risky. In most countries, convicted offenders get off with a slap on the wrist and a fine of a few thousand dollars. Counterfeiters, after all, don't have to cover research and development, marketing, and advertising costs, and most of the expense goes into making goods look convincing, not performing well. Fake Marlboros that cost just pennies a pack to make in China could end up selling for $7.50 in Manhattan. Phony New Balance shoes can be stitched together for about $8 a pair and retail for as much as $80 in Australia, while real ones cost between $11 and $24 to make, and sell for up to $120. Gross margins for knockoff printer cartridges are north of 60%. Counterfeiters "use low-paid employees and cut corners on safety," says Richard K. Willard, general counsel for Gillette Co., which turns up hundreds of thousands of imitation Duracell batteries every week. "If they can push them off as a high-quality product, there is a big margin for them."

While the counterfeiters are piling up profits, the multinationals are spending ever more on stopping them. Luxury house LVMH Möet Hennessy Louis Vuitton spent more than $16 million last year on investigations, busts, and legal fees. GM has seven full-time staffers sleuthing the globe, and Pfizer has five people working in Asia alone. Last September, Nokia started making batteries with holographic images and 20-digit identification codes that can be authenticated online. Cigarette maker JT International has boosted its anti-counterfeiting budget from $200,000 to $15 million in the past six years, spending the money on a network of investigators, lawyers, and informants in factories suspected of making fakes.

Pfizer will soon introduce radio-frequency ID tags on all Viagra sold in the U.S., which will enable it to track drugs all the way from the laboratory to the medicine cabinet. Other companies simply try to make life as difficult as possible for manufacturers and distributors by raiding factories and warehouses or by slightly altering the look of products, making it tough for counterfeiters to keep up with the changes. JT International—which sells Camels and Winstons outside the U.S.—sometimes digs through dumpsters at suspect factories looking for counterfeit packaging. Callaway patrols the Web looking for suspiciously cheap clubs bearing its brand—though as soon as it shuts one dealer down, another is sure to pop up. "Getting rid of the problem altogether is too much to ask," says Callaway's Herrington. "We just try to do our best and give the counterfeiters a really bad day."

One tactic is to outwit the counterfeiters in the marketplace. Anheuser-Busch Cos., for instance, was plagued by knockoff Budweiser in China. A big problem was that counterfeiters were refilling old Bud bottles, so the company started using expensive imported foil on the bottles that was very hard to find in China. The company also added a temperature-sensitive label that turned red when cold. The result: "We've been able to keep [counterfeiting] at a pretty low level," says Stephen J. Burrows, chief executive and president of Anheuser-Busch International. Yamaha, meanwhile, overhauled the way it manufactures and designs motorcycles to lower costs. Now it charges $725 for its cheapest bikes in China, down from about $1,800. To stay competitive, counterfeiters have since lowered their prices from around $1,000 to roughly half that.

The biggest challenge is getting cooperation from China. For years, Chinese authorities turned a blind eye to the problem, largely because most of the harm was inflicted on foreign brand owners and most counterfeiting was seen as a victimless offense. The only time China got tough on counterfeiters was when there was a clear danger to Chinese. Last year, for example, 15 infants died from phony milk powder. The ringleader was sentenced to eight years in prison. But when the victim is a company not an individual, the courts are far less severe. Last June, a Guangdong businessman was found guilty of producing fake windshields under 15 different brand names, including General Motors, DaimlerChrysler, and Mitsubishi Motors. He was fined just $97,000 and given a suspended sentence. It's unclear just how much he made selling fakes, but GM gumshoe Theil says "there is no way the fine is commensurate with the profits he made."

But more Chinese corporate interests have seen profits hit because of counterfeiting—which may lead to a tougher response from Beijing. Li-Ning Co., China's No. 1 homegrown athletic footwear and apparel company, has gotten the ultimate compliment from counterfeiters: They're faking its shoes. So today, Li-Ning has three full-time employees who track counterfeiters. The state tobacco monopoly is conducting joint raids with big international tobacco companies, since counterfeiters have started cranking out Double Happiness, Chunghwa, and other Chinese smokes. The crackdown, investigators believe, has forced some cigarette counterfeiters to decamp to Vietnam and Burma. And the government is finally realizing that piracy—which accounts for 92% of all software used in the mainland—isn't just setting back the likes of Microsoft Corp. "Piracy is a big problem for the development of the local software industry," says Victor Zhang, senior representative for China of the Business Software Alliance, an industry group. Some fear that Western companies may cut research spending in China if the mainland doesn't crack down.

Now, China is toughening its legal sanctions. In December, Beijing lowered the threshold for criminal prosecution of counterfeiters. Prior to the changes, an individual needed to have $12,000 worth of goods on hand before police could prosecute. It was easy to skirt that rule by spreading the wares around. Today, that threshold stands at $6,000 for counterfeiters caught with one brand and $3,600 for those with two or more. And in late January, Beijing began the trial of two Americans who are accused of selling $840,000 in knockoff CDs and DVDs made in China over the Internet. The two could face up to 15 years in jail if convicted.

One big problem: Too many scammers have ties to local officials, who see counterfeit operations as a major source of employment and pillars of the local economy. "Two or three of our raids have failed because of local protection," says Joseph Tsang, chairman of Marksman Consultants Ltd., a Hong Kong-based company that has helped conduct raids on behalf of Titleist and Nike Golf. Take the example of a raid last August in Fujian province. The police found a dirt-covered hatch hiding a stairway that led into a pitch-black cave. Inside was a rolling machine, cigarette paper, and a die for stamping Marlboros and Double Happiness packaging. But the counterfeiters themselves had cleared out and taken the smokes with them. "They knew we were coming," sighs a Hong Kong-based investigator who participated in the raid.

Embattled Beijing

Beijing says it's doing what it can. The government has raised intellectual-property issues to the highest levels: Trade czar and Vice-Premier Wu Yi, for instance, has held regular meetings with the Quality Brands Protection Committee since 2003. "China customs is taking the fight seriously," says Meng Yang, director general for the Policy & Legal Affairs Dept. of the General Administration of Chinese Customs. The agency in November held a conference in Shanghai with brand owners and customs officers from around the world to map out strategies. But delegates acknowledged their biggest challenge is finding the funds to fight counterfeiting, as most governments are more concerned with preventing the smuggling of drugs and arms.

Could the U.S. apply stronger pressure to get China to crack down? "The answer is for the Administration to bring a WTO case against the Chinese," says one leader of the intellectual-property bar in Washington. The challenge is to secure evidence from U.S. companies, which desperately want relief but don't want to anger Beijing. More calls for a WTO action may come soon, after the U.S. Trade Representative's office finishes a review of IPR in China in March.

Hard as it is, there's every reason to try to keep up the fight to stop counterfeiting. One is safety. Novartis says counter-

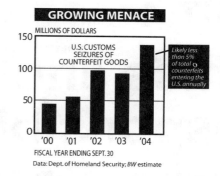

GROWING MENACE

MILLIONS OF DOLLARS

U.S. CUSTOMS SEIZURES OF COUNTERFEIT GOODS

Likely less than 5% of total counterfeits entering the U.S. annually

FISCAL YEAR ENDING SEPT. 30
Data: Dept. of Homeland Security; *BW* estimate

feiters have used yellow highway paint to get the right color match for fake painkillers. And in some African countries, counterfeit or illegal medicines account for as much as 40% of the drugs on the market. "You even have antibiotics without the ingredients," says Daniel L. Vasella, chairman of Novartis. Pfizer says police and regulators in Asia uncovered more than 1.5 million counterfeit doses of its hypertension drug Norvasc in 2003. "You are seeing counterfeiters exploit a loose supply chain and moving from lifestyle drugs to life-saving drugs," says Pfizer's vice-president for global security, John Theriault. "That should make people nervous."

The other reason to mount an offensive against the counterfeits is, obviously, the hit to corporate profits—and the likelihood developed markets will one day be seriously contaminated. It's already happening. In June, 2003, Tommy Hilfiger Corp. successfully sued Goody's Family Clothing Inc. for $11 million for carrying fake shirts. The incidence of fake prescription drugs in the U.S., though small, is rising sharply. The U.S. Food & Drug Administration began 58 investigations of counterfeit drugs in its fiscal 2004, up from 22 in 2003.

More alarming, say police, is counterfeiting's connection to the underworld. "Organized crime thrives on counterfeiting," says Ronald K. Noble, Secretary General of Interpol. So does terrorism. Noble says profits from pirated CDs sold in Central America have funded Hezbollah in the Middle East. One cigarette executive estimates North Korea earns $100 million per year in fees from pirates producing there. That kind of activity proves that buying fakes "isn't innocent, and it's not a game," says Bernard Arnault, chairman of luxury goods maker LVMH.

The counterfeiting scourge, meanwhile, continues to spread. Pakistan and Russia are huge producers of fake pharmaceuticals, while in Italy an estimated 10% of all designer clothing is fake, much of it produced domestically. Gangs in Paraguay funnel phony cosmetics, designer jeans, and toys from China to the rest of South America. Bulgarians are masters at bootlegging U.S. liquor brands. This is one fight that will take years to win.

*—With **Carol Matlack**, in Paris; **Amy Barrett**, in Philadelphia;*
***Kerry Capell**, in London; **Dexter Roberts**, in Beijing;*
***Jonathan Wheatley**, in São Paulo; **William**
***C. Symonds**, in Boston; **Paul Magnusson**, in Washington*
*and **Diane Brady**, in New York*

Reprinted by special permission from *Business Week*, February 7, 2005, pp. 54-58, 60. 62. Copyright © 2005 by The McGraw-Hill Companies, Inc.

UNIT 4

Ethics and Social Responsibility in the Marketplace

Unit Selections

Key Points to Consider

- What responsibility does an organization have to reveal product defects to consumers?

- Given the competitiveness of the business arena, is it possible for marketing personnel to behave ethically and both survive and prosper? Explain. Give suggestions that could be incorporated into the marketing strategy for firms that want to be both ethical and successful.

- Name some organizations that make you feel genuinely valued as a customer. What are the characteristics of these organizations which distinguish them from their competitors? Explain.

- Which area of marketing strategy is most subject to public scrutiny in regard to ethics—product, pricing, place, or promotion? Why? Give some examples of unethical techniques or strategies involving each of these four areas.

Student Website

www.mhcls.com/online

Internet References

Further information regarding these websites may be found in this book's preface or online.

Business for Social Responsibility (BSR)
http://www.bsr.org/

Total Quality Management Sites
http://www.nku.edu/~lindsay/qualhttp.html

U.S. Navy
http://www.navy.mil

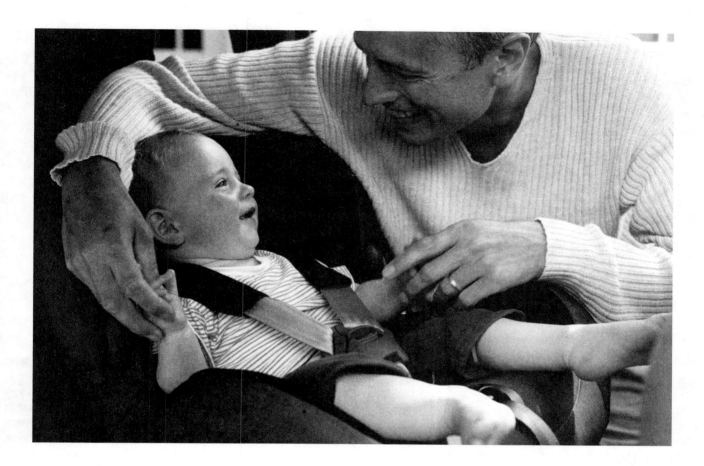

From a consumer viewpoint, the marketplace is the "proof of the pudding" or the place where the "rubber meets the road" for business ethics. In other words, what the company has promulgated about the virtues of its product or service has little meaning if the company's actual marketing practices and its treatment of the consumer contradict its claims.

At its core, marketing has a very noble and moral purpose: to satisfy human needs and wants and to help people through the exchange process. Marketing involves the coordination of the variables of product, price, place, and promotion to effectively and efficiently address the needs of consumers. Unfortunately, at times the unethical marketing practices of some firms have cast a shadow of suspicion over marketing in general. Since marketing is the aspect of business that is most visible to the public, it has perhaps taken a disproportionate share of the criticism directed toward the free-enterprise system.

This unit takes a careful look at the strategic process and practice of incorporating ethics into the marketplace. The first subsection, **Marketing Strategy and Ethics**, contains articles describing how marketing strategy and ethics can be integrated into the marketplace. The first article reflects why a number of companies have discovered how difficult it is to do well by doing good. The next article wrestles with the question: "Is Marketing Ethics an Oxymoron?" "Truth in Advertising" evaluates the promotional and educational effect direct-to-consumer advertising of prescription drugs can have on consumers. The last article in this subsection scrutinizes if Wal-Mart is a good corporate citizen or a bad influence.

In the next subsection, **Ethical Practices in the Marketplace,** the first article delineates the importance of having an organizational culture which encourages and supports sound ethical behavior and socially responsible business practices. The next selection suggests ways to equip salespeople to deal with ethical dilemmas? "The Right Balance" points to the importance of salespeople ethically treating the growing mature market. The last article elucidates how Patagonia is endeavoring to convince corporate America of the significance of environmental issues.

The Perils of Doing the Right Thing

By Andrew W. Singer

At a May 11 press conference, Ford Motor Co. released its first-ever "corporate citizenship" report. In the 98-page document, titled "Connecting With Society," the company acknowledged serious concerns about its highly profitable sport utility vehicles. Not only do SUVs pollute the air and guzzle gas at rates far higher than conventional automobiles, the report conceded, they may be hazardous to other drivers.

Ford's was an unusual announcement. SUVs, after all, contribute about half of the company's earnings. The public's taste for these vehicles has shown no sign of waning. And even though they're three times as likely as cars to kill the other driver in a crash, the government has yet to declare these vehicles inherently unsafe.

What, then, was the company doing announcing that it had problems with these immensely popular, high-margin vehicles?

The front page of the next day's *New York Times* noted that Ford scion and chairman William Clay Ford Jr., whose family controls 40 percent of the company's voting shares, "has been active in environmental causes since his days at prep school and at Princeton" and was now worried "that car makers could get reputations like those of tobacco companies" if they ignored these problems. (The company did *not* pledge to stop producing SUVs, however.)

The company has been lauded for its candor. Veteran automobile-industry analyst Mary Ann Keller, now an executive with Priceline.com Inc., calls the announcement a "welcome instance of leadership." Norman Bowie, Dixons Professor of Business Ethics and Social Responsibility at London Business School, describes Ford's decision as "significant and courageous."

What makes the company's action noteworthy is that it carries real risks. According to Bowie, the biggest danger is a "backlash" among current and prospective SUV owners, who could begin to think the cars dangerous.

"Public tastes are fickle," says Brock Yates, editor-at-large of *Car and Driver*. "No one anticipated the surge in interest in SUVs, and like all fads it could disappear." And credit agency Standard & Poor's has warned that "[t]he automaker's stability could be affected if the sport-utility market slumped."

Before one proclaims a new era of social responsibility, then—as some did in the wake of the Ford press conference—one would do well to pause. Good corporate citizenship is praiseworthy, of course. But it isn't always easy. Indeed, if one looks at the experiences of other companies once acclaimed as "leaders," it is a decidedly mixed history. For all their high promise and initial acclaim, many firms later emerged scarred and chastened, victims of public derision, consumer boycotts, shareholder rebellion, and even bankruptcy.

If Ford does follow through on its exemplary course, it might do well to consider some of the lessons learned by other companies—often the hard way:

Lesson No. 1: Make sure what you are doing is really leadership— and not just self-adulation.

When asked about Ford's quandary—financial dependence on a product that carries potential environmental and safety problems—Bentley College business ethicist W. Michael Hoffman responds, "You can be ethical, and smart too."

Hoffman recalls a story recounted at a 1977 Bentley ethics conference, about a small paper company located on a polluted

New England stream. At a celebration of the first Earth Day, the mill's owner "got religion." He spent $2.5 million in an effort to clean up the company's effluent and, several months later, went broke, since he couldn't compete with other paper companies that didn't follow his example. He was unrepentant, though, "encased in a kind of angelic halo as he spoke of the necessity of clean water and sacrificing material things for spiritual ends." When it was pointed out that the water was no cleaner overall, he said, "Well, that's those other 17 fellows upstream."

"He went out of business, and he put 500 people out of work," Hoffman says. "But he felt ethically pure. That's just crazy." He describes the mill owner's attempt to "do it on his own" as a typically individualistic, American response.

Ford Motor could behave like the mill owner—act alone—and simply stop making SUVs. But that could be financially disastrous. "Ford's executives can do other things," Hoffman continues. "If they are truly concerned about a product but know they can't disarm unilaterally, then they have to work diligently within their industry and with government."

Cornell University economist Robert H. Frank says that the fact that Ford is concerned "is a positive thing." But this is "a collective-action problem," he says. "It's not a matter of Ford breaking any law." The solution Frank suggests: William Clay Ford should sit down with the U.S. secretary of transportation and work something out; a possible solution might involve instituting new passenger-vehicle taxes based on weight, emission levels, and fuel economy.

In late July, Ford took another step, announcing that it had decided to increase the fuel economy of its SUVs by 25 percent over the next five years. Its main competitor, General Motors, bristled: Vice chairman Harry Pearce expressed annoyance at Ford's claim of being "somehow the environmental leader." GM, he insisted, is and will be far superior to Ford in the area of fuel economy. On the other hand, the company is proceeding with full production of the 7,000-plus-pound Hummer, a version of the Humvee, a military transport made famous in the Gulf War.

Lesson No. 2: Be prepared to be attacked by virtue of your virtue.

H.B. Fuller Co., a Minneapolis-based adhesives manufacturer, enjoyed a reputation as one of America's most socially responsible companies. It endowed a chair in the study of business ethics at the University of Minnesota and established a charitable foundation dedicated to the environment, the arts, and social programs. Minnesotans regarded longtime president Elmer L. Andersen so highly that they elected him governor in 1960.

But beginning in the late 1980s, the company was dogged by reports that one of its adhesives, Resistol, had become the drug of choice for glue-sniffing street kids in Central America.

H.B. Fuller seemed unprepared for the furor that arose over the abuse of one of its products. "It's a social problem. It's not a product problem," the company argued. Still, it pulled the product off retail shelves in Guatemala and Honduras.

That didn't stop activists from protesting Fuller's continued marketing of Resistol to industrial customers, and to retailers in neighboring countries. Activists picketed annual shareholder meetings and brought wrongful-death suits against the company. "At risk are millions of dollars and the reputations of the company's top leaders," noted the Minneapolis *Star Tribune*.

How could such a well-regarded company become ensnared in such a circumstance? After all, Fuller's competitors were manufacturing and marketing glue in Latin America at the time, and impoverished street kids were abusing their products too. "But no one expected much of those companies," says Bowie. Social critics mostly gave them a free pass.

Unfortunately, "If you do something ethical, and then market it, and there's a little failure, you get hammered," says Bowie, who adds that company leaders were perhaps not as "proactive as they should have been."

Michael G. Daigneault, president of the nonprofit Ethics Resource Center in Washington, D.C., observes, "There are risks inherent in being perceived as, or fostering the perception of being, an exceptionally ethical or socially responsible organization. People will hold you to that standard."

This isn't to say that such a reputation is not positive. But it can backfire, particularly if a company is "overzealous" in promoting itself in this area. Daigneault says that companies that have made absolute statements—like Wal-Mart Stores Inc. claiming that all of its products are made in the United States, or Tom's of Maine Inc. insisting that all of its products are "natural"—have sometimes invited criticism. "The irony," he says, "is that a lot of these organizations have the best intentions, and many actually walk the talk—99 percent of the time." But the 1 percent of the time that they slip up, someone will be waiting for them.

Lesson No. 3: Expect to have your motives questioned and your leadership credentials challenged.

"The only thing good without qualification is a good will," wrote Immanuel Kant. In business, however, it's often difficult to distinguish goodwill from economic self-interest.

Consider the case of Smith & Wesson, the nation's largest handgun manufacturer. In March, the company entered into an agreement with federal, state, and local governments to restrict the sale of handguns. The company agreed to sell only to "authorized dealers and distributors" that would conform to a code of conduct. Among other things, this required dealers to conduct background checks on buyers at gun shows, and it put some restrictions on multiple gun sales. No other gun manufacturer signed the agreement.

On some fronts, Smith & Wesson was celebrated for its commitment. President Clinton observed that "it took a lot of courage" for the company to sign the agreement in the face of industry resistance. Housing and Urban Development secretary Andrew Cuomo described the settlement as "the most important announcement" during his tenure at HUD, and added, "The principles of the agreement will provide a framework for a new, enlightened gun policy for this nation."

Target of Criticism

"No loaded firearms or live ammunition beyond this point," reads the sign on the front door of Smith & Wesson's headquarters in Springfield, Mass.—a reminder that this is not your average business. Nor was there anything quite ordinary about the industry reaction to the firearms manufacturer's decision to accept some restrictions on its handgun sales.

Smith & Wesson CEO Edward Shultz says he wasn't surprised by the response to the firm's March 17 settlement announcement. "When you take this sort of step, you don't do it without a lot of thought. Certainly, it would have been easier to go with the crowd."

The National Rifle Association denounced Smith & Wesson, the nation's largest gun maker, for surrendering to the Clinton administration. NRA president Charlton Heston asserted that Smith & Wesson's British owner, Tomkins PLC, places less value on the Second Amendment right to bear arms than Americans do. The attorney general of Connecticut warned of "extreme elements that want to punish [Smith & Wesson] or retaliate against it for doing the right thing."

Why such a strong reaction? "We're dealing with the most anti-gun administration in recent history," says Shultz. The fact that S&W is even talking to the Clinton administration "irritates folks."

Still, Shultz says, he hadn't counted on the breadth of the detractors. The majority of S&W customers agree with the company's actions, he asserts. But its move seems to have "had an impact on anyone who owns a firearm." It's as if an automaker had installed safety air bags before any of its competitors and "it angered not just its customers but anyone who owned a car."

Shultz says he understands the emotions of the critics. As a boy in eastern Iowa, he "grew up with guns as a part of [his] daily life. But my head says that the world is changing and we will have to get in harmony with it."

Lawsuits against gun makers—who are being held partly responsible for bloodshed like that which rocked Columbine High School last year—will continue for the next five to 10 years, he predicts. "When you have the federal government after you, and the states, and lots of the cities, it's hard to say that all these people are wrong and you're right."

Will the company be stronger in the long run for signing the agreement? "Our belief was that if we didn't make this decision, we would go out of business," due to ceaseless, costly litigation. "This way, we can still prosper."

Significantly, perhaps, when New York became the first state to take the firearms-manufacturing industry to court in late June, Smith & Wesson was not named in the lawsuit. Local governments have since dropped S&W from lawsuits, too. Meanwhile, though, "The rest of the industry has held fast," noted *The New York Times*. No other gun maker signed the agreement, which requires manufacturers to take steps such as installing safety locks on guns.

Shultz has been working in the consumer-goods sector for 37 years, the last nine of which he has spent in the firearms industry. "I came from the outside to make a change here" because the company was in some financial trouble in 1992. At that time, "I never dreamed of the things that we face today in the legal and political arena."

He says that what S&W is doing is viewed as a huge compromise because it's voluntary, rather than mandated by laws and regulations. Inevitably, though, the firearms industry has to go through change. "Change is expensive, it's painful, and it involves some risk," he says.

"I've spent most of my career dealing with conflicts relating to change," Shultz says. "If I retire, it will probably be from one change too many."

—A.W.S.

Reaction was somewhat less approving in other quarters, however. The National Rifle Association and the National Shooting Sports Foundation (NSSF) denounced Smith & Wesson for "selling out" the industry and called for an immediate boycott of the company's products. (See "Target of Criticism.")

Still, Smith & Wesson CEO Edward Shultz says he's comfortable with his decision. Standards of social responsibility change, he says: "We can't operate as we did in 1935 or 1955 or 1975 and still be described as responsible." In 1955, a customer could order a gun out of a catalog, and the weapon would be delivered to that person's house. "Today, that would be viewed as totally irresponsible," he says.

"From a pure business standpoint, it makes sense to find a solution," Shultz continues. "To understand what's going on, you have to get in a conversation with the people trying to put you out of business," like anti-handgun groups. It also made sense to "settle," given the numbers of lawsuits being brought against the firearms industry in the wake of the Columbine shooting and other acts of carnage. "Rather than go out of business paying for lawsuits, if we go out of business, it will be because customers refuse to buy our products," he says.

Opposition to the company's position proved more lasting and damaging than anticipated. Some dealers refused to sell S&W products, incensed by the code of conduct that the manufacturer imposed on them. In June, Smith & Wesson announced nat it was suspending firearms manufacturing at two New England factories for three weeks. It acknowledged that a contributing factor was "the reaction of some consumers to the greement Smith & Wesson signed with federal, state and local overnment entities."

"I don't think they anticipated the severity of the response," ays Robert Delfay, president and CEO of the NSSF, the largest irearms-industry trade group. Many members saw it as an inringement of their Second Amendment right to bear arms.

Also, inevitably, some critics saw the firm's actions as a natter of sheer expediency. "I don't view what Smith & Vesson did as leadership," Delfay says. "We think it was capitlation to strong-arm tactics by government officials." As he ees it, the gun makers showing real leadership are those that aven't "capitulated to government blackmail."

"Was that a decision of conscience?" asks ethicist Mark astin, president of the Council of Ethics Organizations in Alxandria, Va., of the S&W action. "Or a response to what the narket demands of the company?"

Consultant Eileen Shapiro, author of *The Seven Deadly Sins f Business*, insists that Smith & Wesson's decision *did* represent a leadership position, because it involved real action: They did something that matched their rhetoric."

It's not exceptional that some ambiguity attends the gun naker's action. Few business actions, after all, are ethically pure." Most are a kind of double helix: one strand virtue, the ther economic self-interest. It is almost impossible to disenngle the two.

Shapiro, for one, disputes that Ford Motor took any leaderhip position with its May announcement. Ford isn't redeloying any of its assets. It will still build SUVs. Moreover, she ays, "This guy [William Ford] actually drives an SUV!"

A week after the Ford press conference, automobile-industry vatcher Brock Yates said, "Internally, we're hearing a lot of oncern and confusion. It's seen as a hollow gesture. The randest gesture would have been to cancel the Excursion, vhich has become a paradigm for SUV evil."

In sum, even when a company takes a socially responsible tance, it should still expect to have its moral bona fides quesoned. Ed Shultz speaks from experience: "Leadership is never ery popular, particularly if decisions are made to change and o move forward."

Lesson No. 4: Circumstances beyond your control—including public hysteria—can undermine your position.

In the early 1990s, chemicals manufacturer Monsanto Co. laced a big bet on an exciting new business: sustainable agriulture. It committed its resources to developing seemingly miaculous genetically altered crops—cotton that could be grown vithout pesticides, tomatoes altered to ripen slowly, potatoes nat were insect-resistant.

"Monsanto is in a unique position to contribute to the global uture," gushed prominent biodiversity advocate Peter Raven at

a "global forum" in 1995. "Because of your skills, your dedication, and your understanding, you are equal to the challenge."

The first breakthrough had come two years earlier, in November 1993. After nine years of investigation, the FDA approved the use of Monsanto's bovine growth hormone (marketed under the name of Posilac), which when injected into a cow's pituitary gland increased milk output by 25 percent.

Monsanto spent $1 billion to develop Posilac, with Wall Street's approval. Posilac, after all, was the first of perhaps dozens of genetically altered agricultural products to be introduced in years ahead. The profits anticipated would fill company coffers.

The company's CEO, Robert B. Shapiro, was acclaimed as a visionary. "Bob Shapiro displayed enormous vision in committing the company to sustainable business practices" that neither deplete the world of resources nor damage the environment, noted Robert H. Dunn, president of Business for Social Responsibility, a San Francisco-based membership organization.

Only a few years later, however, things had gone terribly wrong with Monsanto's new direction. A wave of protesters had arisen to campaign against Posilac, and foreign governments were beginning to pay attention. In 1998, a British researcher declared on television that eating genetically modified (GM) potatoes could stunt rats' growth. A Cornell University study contended that pollen from GM corn harmed butterflies.

Europe resisted the U.S.-dominated GM crop business; supermarket chains rejected foods containing GM ingredients. France, citing the precautionary principle, ordered the destruction of hundreds of hectares of rapeseed that had been accidentally planted with seeds containing GM material. Brazil sent out police to burn GM crops. U.S. food processors, such as Archer Daniels Midland Co., advised suppliers to segregate GM from non-GM crops.

Environmentalists turned on Monsanto. Greenpeace told the European Union that it "cannot continue to let GMOs [genetically modified organisms] contaminate our food and environment."

All of this battered the company's share price. Early this year, one analyst noted that "investors have valued Monsanto's $5 billion-a-year agricultural-business unit at less than zero dollars during the past week."

What happened? "In ethics, some stands look appropriate at the time," Bowie observes. But then circumstances change, or science changes, "or people get hysterical—so what looked like a good decision at one time no longer looks like a good decision."

When Bowie asked his London students this past summer why the reaction against GM foods was so severe—why the "hysteria"—they answered: "We don't trust the government." In part, this was because of the British government's belated response to the dangers of "mad cow" disease, which it long downplayed. Asks Bowie: "How could Monsanto anticipate that students wouldn't trust their government because of mad cow disease?"—and by extension, that they wouldn't believe the government when it insisted that GM foods were safe?

"You can't rationalize emotions," says one analyst who follows the company but asked not to be identified in this article.

"[Robert] Shapiro felt that the Green Movement didn't have a rational case," and so the company was reluctant to modify its position. "They should have been more sensitive to the perception of these bold moves. They didn't lay the groundwork."

Ironically, in June, the Paris-based Organization for Economic Cooperation and Development—once at the heart of the GM opposition—announced that genetically modified crops approved for human consumption are as safe as other foods. The announcement may have come a bit late, however, for Robert Shapiro and Monsanto. The company was acquired by Pharmacia & Upjohn Inc. last December—for a price considerably lower than what it could have fetched a few years earlier. Robert Shapiro was slated to be "non-executive" chairman of the merged company for 18 months, and then give way to a successor.

"In the end, Shapiro was a trailblazer," concludes the analyst. One day, the world may view positively the company's technological achievement, the medical applications, the improved yields from these crops. "There is a future, but perhaps the market wasn't ready for them."

Given the costs that some of the companies mentioned here—H.B. Fuller, Monsanto, Smith & Wesson, the New England mill owner—have paid, one might well ask: Does social responsibility pay? Does it make economic sense to take a leadership position where the environment or corporate citizenship is involved?

For years, many have asserted that good ethics is good business, Pastin observes. "But there were no examples. Now there are examples, but they are hard to interpret." There has never been systemic, credible evidence that good ethics indeed leads to good financial results, he notes.

That said, some view Ford Motor's May announcement as evidence of a new era of social responsibility. "Ford has definitely demonstrated leadership as one of the first large, global companies to file a social report as a companion to its financial report," says Dunn of Business for Social Responsibility. The company "instilled in the report a spirit of candor, acknowledging the issues it must address."

Ford has "obviously learned the lesson" of the last 20 years regarding such matters—namely, "that companies that are honest and forthright are forgiven by the public, but those that stonewall earn the public's enmity," says Booz-Allen & Hamilton leadership consultant James O'Toole, whose guess is

that Ford has enough data to conclude that the safety and environmental problems regarding SUVs are real. Moreover, the automaker might have a similar problem to that of the tobacco industry: By sitting on the data, it risks lawsuits later.

By acting in an honest, straightforward manner, the companies expect to be treated accordingly by the public. "Ford is trying to establish its credentials, give itself credibility," O'Toole says. "Young William Ford is laying the foundation of trust."

"I think we're entering a new age of corporate citizenship in which candor will be rewarded," says veteran PR executive Robert Dilenschneider. "Younger people—young CEOs—are willing to stick their necks out farther than the older generation. Bill Ford is a perfect example."

Others note a certain irony here. "It's interesting that it's the Ford Motor Co. that has seen fit to come forward to talk about some safety and environmental problems with SUVs," says Bentley College's Hoffman. "Maybe it has something to do with the lessons learned from the business-ethics movement."

One of the landmark cases in that movement, after all, was the 1979 Ford Pinto case, in which the state of Indiana indicted Ford on charges of criminal homicide after a rear-ended Pinto burst into flames, killing a passenger. "It made world headlines and sent reverberations through Corporate America," Hoffman says.

Even though Ford was eventually acquitted, it "was found guilty in the court of public opinion, as well as in civil cases," particularly when it was disclosed that the company had conducted a cost-benefit analysis to determine whether it should improve safety by adding a $5.08 bladder to fuel tanks—and opted not to do so. The negative public reaction "sent a message to Corporate America," Hoffman says, "that the American public would be watching corporations more carefully in terms of their social responsibility and ethical commitment."

Given the history of other companies that took a lead in "doing the right thing," though, Ford shouldn't expect an unhindered path toward an enlightened future. There are real risks with tampering with the SUV business model: risks to the company's profits, its share price, and its reputation.

ANDREW W. SINGER is publisher and co-editor of Ethikos, *a Mamaroneck, N.Y.-based publication that examines ethical and compliance issues in business. He is writing a book on the perils of corporate leadership. His last article was a review of* When Pride Still Mattered *in the February issue.*

From *Across the Board*, October 2000, pp. 14-19. © 2000 by Andrew W. Singer. Reprinted by permission of the author.

Is Marketing Ethics an Oxymoron?

Philip Kotler

Every profession and business has to wrestle with ethical questions. The recent wave of business scandals over inaccurate reporting of sales and profits and excessive pay and privileges for top executives has brought questions of business ethics to the fore. And lawyers have been continuously accused of "ambulance chasing," jury manipulation, and inflated fees, leaving the plaintiffs with much less than called for in the judgment. Physicians have been known to recommend certain drugs as more effective while receiving support from pharmaceutical companies.

Marketers are not immune from facing a whole set of ethical issues. For evidence, look to Howard Bowen's classic questions from his 1953 book, *Social Responsibilities of the Businessman:*

"Should he conduct selling in ways that intrude on the privacy of people, for example, by door-to-door selling? Should he use methods involving ballyhoo, chances, prizes, hawking, and other tactics which are at least of doubtful good taste? Should he employ 'high pressure' tactics in persuading people to buy? Should he try to hasten the obsolescence of goods by bringing out an endless succession of new models and new styles? Should he appeal to and attempt to strengthen the motives of materialism, invidious consumption, and keeping up with the Joneses?" (Also see Smith, N. Craig and Elizabeth Cooper-Martin (1997), "Ethics and Target Marketing: The Role of Product Harm and Consumer Vulnerability," *Journal of Marketing,* July, 1-20.)

The issues raised are complicated. Drawing a clear line between normal marketing practice and unethical behavior isn't easy. Yet it's important for marketing scholars and those interested in public policy to raise questions about practices that they may normally endorse but which may not coincide with the public interest.

We will examine the central axiom of marketing: Companies that satisfy their target customers will perform better than those that don't. Companies that satisfy customers can expect repeat business; those that don't will get only one-time sales. Steady profits come from holding onto customers, satisfying them, and selling them more goods and services.

This axiom is the essence of the well-known marketing concept. It reduces to the formula "Give the customer what he wants." This sounds reasonable on the surface. But notice that it carries an implied corollary: "Don't judge what the customer wants."

Marketers have been, or should be, a little uneasy about this corollary. It raises two public interest concerns: (1) What if the customer wants something that isn't good for him or her? (2) What if the product or service, while good for the customer, isn't good for society or other groups?

When it comes to the first question, what are some products that some customers desire that might not be good for them? These would be products that can potentially harm their health, safety, or well-being. Tobacco and hard drugs such as cocaine, LSD, or ecstasy immediately come to mind.

As for the second question, examples of products or services that some customers desire that may not be in the public's best interest include using asbestos as a building material or using lead paint indiscriminately. Other products and services where debates continue to rage as to whether they are in the public's interest include the right to own guns and other weapons, the right to have an abor-

EXECUTIVE briefing

Marketers should be proud of their field. They have encouraged and promoted the development of many products and services that have benefited people worldwide. But this is all the more reason that they should carefully and thoughtfully consider where they stand on the ethical issues confronting them today and into the future. Marketers are able to take a stand and must make the effort to do so in order to help resolve these issues.

tion, the right to distribute hate literature, and the right to buy large gas guzzling and polluting automobiles.

We now turn to three questions of interest to marketers, businesses, and the public:

1. Given that expanding consumption is at the core of most businesses, what are the interests and behaviors of companies that make these products?

2. To what extent do these companies care about reducing the negative side effects of these products?

3. What steps can be taken to reduce the consumption of products that have questionable effects and is limited intervention warranted?

Expanding Consumption

Most companies will strive to enlarge their market as much as possible. A tobacco company, if unchecked, will try to get everyone who comes of age to start smoking cigarettes. Given that cigarettes are addictive, this promises the cigarette company "customers for life." Each new customer will create a 50-year profit stream for the cigarette company if the consumer continues to favor the same brand—and live long enough. Suppose a new smoker starts at the age of 13, smokes for 50 years, and dies at 63 from lung cancer. If he spends $500 a year on cigarettes, he will spend $25,000 over his lifetime. If the company's profit rate is 20%, that new customer is worth $5,000 to the company (undiscounted). It is hard to imagine a company that doesn't want to attract a customer who contributes $5,000 to its profits.

The same story describes the hard drug industry, whose products are addictive and even more expensive. The difference is that cigarette companies can operate legally but hard drug companies must operate illegally.

Other products, such as hamburgers, candy, soft drinks, and beer, are less harmful when consumed in moderation, but are addictive for some people. We hear a person saying she has a "sweet tooth." One person drinks three Coca-Colas a day, and another drinks five beers a day. Still another consumer is found who eats most of his meals at McDonald's. These are the "heavy users." Each company treasures the heavy users who account for a high proportion of the company's profits.

All said, every company has a natural drive to expand consumption of its products, leaving any negative consequences to be the result of the "free choice" of consumers. A high-level official working for Coca-Cola in Sweden said that her aim is to get people to start drinking Coca-Cola for breakfast (instead of orange juice). And McDonald's encourages customers to choose a larger hamburger, a larger order of French fries, and a larger cola drink. And these companies have some of the best marketers in the world working for them.

Reducing Side Effects

It would not be a natural act on the part of these companies to try to reduce or restrain consumption of their products. What company wants to reduce its profits? Usually some form of public pressure must bear on these companies before they will act.

The government has passed laws banning tobacco companies from advertising and glamorizing smoking on TV. But Philip Morris' Marlboro brand still will put out posters showing its mythical cowboy. And Marlboro will make sure that its name is mentioned in sports stadiums, art exhibits, and in labels for other products.

Tobacco companies today are treading carefully not to openly try to create smokers out of young people. They have stopped distributing free cigarettes to young people in the United States as they move their operations increasingly into China.

Beer companies have adopted a socially responsible attitude by telling people not to over-drink or drive during or after drinking. They cooperate with efforts to prevent underage people from buying beer. They are trying to behave in a socially responsible manner. They also know that, at the margin, the sales loss resulting from their "cooperation" is very slight.

McDonald's has struggled to find a way to reduce the ill effects (obesity, heart disease) of too much consumption of their products. It tried to offer a reduced-fat hamburger only to find consumers rejecting it. It has offered salads, but they weren't of good quality when originally introduced and they failed. Now it's making a second and better attempt.

Limited Intervention

Do public interest groups or the government have the right to intervene in the free choices of individuals? This question has been endlessly debated. On one side are people who resent any intervention in their choices of products and services. In the extreme, they go by such names as libertarians, vigilantes, and "freedom lovers." They have a legitimate concern about government power and its potential abuse. Some of their views include:

- The marketer's job is to "sell more stuff." It isn't the marketer's job to save the world or make society a better place.

- The marketer's job is to produce profits for the shareholders in any legally sanctioned way.

- A high-minded socially conscious person should not be in marketing. A company shouldn't hire such a person.

On the other side are people concerned with the personal and societal costs of "unregulated consumption." They are considered do-gooders and will document that Coca-Cola delivers six teaspoons of sugar in every bottle or can. They will cite statistics on the heavy health costs of obesity, heart disease, and liver damage that are caused by failing to reduce the consumption of some of these products. These costs fall on everyone through higher medical costs and taxes. Thus, those who don't consume questionable products are still harmed through the unenlightened behavior of others.

Ultimately, the problem is one of conflict among different ethical systems. Consider the following five:

Ethical egoism. Your only obligation is to take care of yourself (Protagoras and Ayn Rand).

Government requirements. The law represents the minimal moral standards of a society (Thomas Hobbes and John Locke).

Personal virtues. Be honest, good, and caring (Plato and Aristotle).

Utilitarianism. Create the greatest good for the greatest number (Jeremy Bentham and John Stuart Mill).

Universal rules. "Act only on that maxim through which you can at the same time will that it should become a universal law" (Immanuel Kant's categorical imperative).

Clearly, people embrace different ethical viewpoints, making marketing ethics and other business issues more complex to resolve.

Let's consider the last two ethical systems insofar as they imply that some interventions are warranted. Aside from the weak gestures of companies toward self-regulation and appearing concerned, there are a range of measures that can be taken by those wishing to push their view of the public interest. They include the following six approaches:

1. Encouraging these companies to make products safer. Many companies have responded to public concern or social pressure to make their products safer. Tobacco companies developed filters that would reduce the chance of contracting emphysema or lung cancer. If a leaf without nicotine could give smokers the same satisfaction, they would be happy to replace the tobacco leaf. Some tobacco companies have even offered information or aids to help smokers limit their appetite for tobacco or curb it entirely.

> Every company has a natural drive to expand consumption of its products, leaving any negative consequences to be the result of the "free choice" of consumers.

Food and soft drink companies have reformulated many of their products to be "light," "nonfat," or "low in calories." Some beer companies have introduced nonalcoholic beer. These companies still offer their standard products but provide concerned consumers with alternatives that present less risk to their weight or health.

Auto companies have reluctantly incorporated devices designed to reduce pollution output into their automobiles. Some are even producing cars with hybrid fuel systems to further reduce harmful emissions to the air. But the auto companies still insist on putting out larger automobiles (such as Hummers) because the "public demands them."

What can we suggest to Coca-Cola and other soft drink competitors that are already offering "light" versions of their drinks? First, they should focus more on developing the bottled water side of their businesses because bottled water is healthier than sugared soft drinks. Further, they should be encouraged to add nutrients and vitamins in standard drinks so these drinks can at least deliver more health benefits, especially to those in undeveloped countries who are deprived of these nutrients and vitamins. (Coca-Cola has some brands doing this now.)

What can we suggest to McDonald's and its fast food competitors? The basic suggestion is to offer more variety in its menu. McDonald's seems to forget that, while parents bring their children to McDonald's, they themselves usually prefer to eat healthier food, not to mention want their children eating healthier foods. How about a first-class salad bar? How about moving more into the healthy sandwich business? Today more Americans are buying their meals at Subway and other sandwich shops where they feel they are getting healthier and tastier food for their dollar.

There seems to be a correlation between the amount of charity given by companies in some categories and the category's degree of "sin." Thus, McDonald's knows that over-consumption of its products can be harmful, but the company is very charitable. A cynic would say that McDonald's wants to build a bank of public goodwill to diffuse potential public criticism.

2. Banning or restricting the sale or use of the product or service. A community or nation will ban certain products where there is strong public support. Hard drugs are banned, although there is some debate about whether the ban should include marijuana and lighter hard drugs. There are even advocates who oppose banning hard drugs, believing that the cost of policing and criminality far exceed the cost of a moderate increase that might take place in hard drug usage. Many people today believe that the "war on drugs" can never be won and is creating more serious consequences than simply dropping the ban or helping drug addicts, as Holland and Switzerland have done.

Some products carry restrictions on their purchase or use. This is particularly true of drugs that require a doctor's prescription and certain poisons that can't be purchased without authorization. Persons buying guns must be free of a criminal record and register their gun ownership. And certain types of guns, such as machine guns, are banned or restricted.

3. Banning or limiting advertising or promotion of the product. Even when a product isn't banned or its purchase restricted, laws may be passed to prevent producers from advertising or promoting the product. Gun, alcohol, and tobacco manufacturers can't advertise on TV, although they can advertise in print media such as magazines and newspapers. They can also inform and possibly promote their products online.

Manufacturers get around this by mentioning their brand name in every possible venue: sports stadiums, music concerts, and feature articles. They don't want to be forgotten in the face of a ban on promoting their products overtly.

4. Increasing "sin" taxes to discourage consumption. One reasonable alternative to banning a product or its promotion is to place a "sin" tax on its consumption. Thus, smokers pay hefty government taxes for cigarettes. This is supposed to have three effects when done right. First, the higher price should discourage consumption. Second, the tax revenue could be used to finance the social costs to health and safety caused by the consumption of the product. Third, some of the tax revenue could be used to counter-advertise the use of the product or support public education against its use. The last effect was enacted by California when it taxed tobacco companies and used the money to "unsell" tobacco smoking.

5. Public education campaigns. In the 1960s, Sweden developed a social policy to use public education to raise a nation of non-smokers and non-drinkers. Children from the first grade up were educated to understand the ill effects of tobacco and alcohol. Other countries are doing this on a less systematic and intensive basis. U.S. public schools devote parts of occasional courses to educate students against certain temptations with mixed success. Girls, not boys, in the United States seem to be more prone to taking up smoking. The reason often given by girls is that smoking curbs their appetite for food and consequently helps them avoid becoming overweight, a problem they consider more serious than lung cancer taking place 40 years later.

Sex education has become a controversial issue, when it comes to public education campaigns. The ultra-conservative camp wants to encourage total abstinence until marriage. The more liberal camp believes that students should be taught the risks of early sex and have the necessary knowledge to protect themselves. The effectiveness of both types of sex education is under debate.

6. Social marketing campaigns. These campaigns describe a wide variety of efforts to communicate the ill effects of certain behaviors that can harm the person, other persons, or society as a whole. These campaigns use techniques of public education, advertising and promotion, incentives, and channel development to make it as easy and attractive as possible for people to change their behavior for the better. (See Kotler, Philip, Eduardo Roberto, and Nancy Lee (2002), *Social Marketing: Improving the Quality of Life,* 2nd ed. London: Sage Publications.) Social marketing uses the tools of commercial marketing—segmentation, targeting, and positioning, and the four Ps (product, price, place, and promotion)—to achieve voluntary compliance with publicly endorsed goals. Some social marketing campaigns, such as family planning and anti-littering, have achieved moderate to high success. Other campaigns including anti-smoking, anti-drugs ("say no to drugs"), and seat belt promotion have worked well when supplemented with legal action.

Social Responsibility and Profits

Each year *Business Ethics* magazine publishes the 100 best American companies out of 1,000 evaluated. The publication examines the degree to which the companies serve seven stakeholder groups: shareholders, communities, minorities and women, employees, environment, non-U.S. stakeholders, and customers. Information is gathered on lawsuits, regulatory problems, pollution emissions, charitable contributions, staff diversity counts, union relations, employee benefits, and awards. Companies are removed from the list if there are significant scandals or improprieties. The research is done by Kinder, Lydenberg, Domini (KLD), an independent rating service. (For more details see the Spring 2003 issue of *Business Ethics.*)

The 20 best-rated companies in 2003 were (in order): General Mills, Cummins Engine, Intel, Procter & Gamble, IBM, Hewlett-Packard, Avon Products, Green Mountain Coffee, John Nuveen Co., St. Paul Companies, AT&T, Fannie Mae, Bank of America, Motorola, Herman Miller, Expedia, Autodesk, Cisco Systems, Wild Oats Markets, and Deluxe.

The earmarks of a socially responsible company include:

- Living out a deep set of company values that drive company purpose, goals, strategies, and tactics

- Treating customers with fairness, openness, and quick response to inquiries and complaints

- Treating employees, suppliers, and distributors fairly

- Caring about the environmental impact of its activities and supply chain

- Behaving in a consistently ethical fashion

The intriguing question is whether socially responsible companies are more profitable. Unfortunately, different research studies have come up with different results. The correlations between financial performance (FP) and social performance (SP) are sometimes positive, sometimes negative, and sometimes neutral, depending on the study. Even when FP and SP are positively related, which causes which? The most probable finding is that high FP firms invest slack resources in SP and then discover the SP leads to better FP, in a virtuous circle. (See Waddock, Sandra A. and Samuel B. Graves (1997), "The Corporate

Social Performance-Financial Performance Link," *Strategic Management Journal*, 18 (4), 303-319.)

Marketers' Responsibilities

As professional marketers, we are hired by some of the aforementioned companies to use our marketing toolkit to help them sell more of their products and services. Through our research, we can discover which consumer groups are the most susceptible to increasing their consumption. We can use the research to assemble the best 30-second TV commercials, print ads, and sales incentives to persuade them that these products will deliver great satisfaction. And we can create price discounts to tempt them to consume even more of the product than would normally be healthy or safe to consume.

But, as professional marketers, we should have the same ambivalence as nuclear scientists who help build nuclear bombs or pilots who spray DDT over crops from the airplane. Some of us, in fact, are independent enough to tell these clients that we will not work for them to find ways to sell more of what hurts people. We can tell them that we're willing to use our marketing toolkit to help them build new businesses around substitute products that are much healthier and safer.

But, even if these companies moved toward these healthier and safer products, they'll probably continue to push their current "cash cows." At that point, marketers will have to decide whether to work for these companies, help them reshape their offerings, avoid these companies altogether, or even work to oppose these company offerings.

Remember Marketing's Contributions

Nothing said here should detract from the major contributions that marketing has made to raise the material standards of living around the world. One doesn't want to go back to the kitchen where the housewife cooked five hours a day, washed dishes by hand, put fresh ice in the ice box, and washed and dried clothes in the open air. We value refrigerators, electric stoves, dishwashers, washing machines, and dryers. We value the invention and diffusion of the radio, the television set, the computer, the Internet, the cellular phone, the automobile, the movies, and even frozen food. Marketing has played a major role in their instigation and diffusion. Granted, any of these are capable of abuse (bad movies or TV shows), but they promise and deliver much that is good and valued in modern life.

Marketers have a right to be proud of their field. They search for unmet needs, encourage the development of products and services addressing these needs, manage communications to inform people of these products and services, arrange for easy accessibility and availability, and price the goods in a way that represents superior value delivered vis-à-vis competitors' offerings. This is the true work of marketing.

Author's Note: The author wishes to thank Professor Evert Gummesson of the School of Business, Stockholm University, for earlier discussion of these issues.

Philip Kotler is S.C. Johnson and Son Distinguished Professor of International Marketing, Kellogg School of Management, Northwestern University. He may be reached at pkotler@nwu.edu.

From *Marketing Management*, November/December 2004. Copyright © 2004 by American Marketing Association. Reprinted by permission.

TRUTH in Advertising

Rx Drug Ads Come of Age

Carol Rados

You may have seen the advertisement: A melodrama of crime and corruption, conflict and emotion, centering on indoor hit men like dust and dander, and outdoor hit men such as pollen and ragweed, all threatening to offend a young and very beautiful woman's nose. The 45-second broadcast ad covers everything from talking to your doctor to the possible side effects that people can expect. Then the narrator mentions "Flonase."

> ## According to the U.S. General Accounting Office ... pharmaceutical manufacturers spend $2.7 billion on DTC advertising in 2001 alone.

Entertaining though it may be, the Food and Drug Administration says this promotional piece about nasal allergy relief also has all the elements of a well-crafted, easy-to-understand prescription drug advertisement directed at consumers, and it meets agency requirements for these ads.

Direct-to-consumer (DTC) advertising of prescription drugs in its varied forms—TV, radio, magazines, newspapers—is widely used throughout the United States. DTC advertising is a category of promotional information about specific drug treatments provided directly to consumers by or on behalf of drug companies. According to the U.S. General Accounting Office—the investigational arm of Congress—pharmaceutical manufacturers spent $2.7 billion on DTC advertising in 2001 alone.

The Controversy

Whether it's a 1940s, detective-style film noir of unusual allergy suspects or a middle-aged man throwing a football through a tire swing announcing that he's "back in the game," the DTC approach to advertising prescription drugs has been controversial. Some say that DTC promotion provides useful information to consumers that results in better health outcomes. Others argue that it encourages overuse of prescription drugs and use of the most costly treatments, instead of less expensive treatments that would be just as satisfactory.

There seems to be little doubt that DTC advertising can help advance the public health by encouraging more people to talk with health care professionals about health problems, particularly undertreated conditions such as high blood pressure and high cholesterol.

DTC advertising also can help remove the stigma that accompanies; diseases that in the past were rarely openly discussed, such as erectile dysfunction or depression. DTC ads also can remind patients to get their prescriptions refilled and help them adhere to their medication regimens.

On the other hand, ads that are false or misleading do not advance—and may even threaten—the public health. While the FDA encourage DTC advertisements that contain accurate information, the agency also has the job of making sure that consumers are not misled or deceived by advertisements that violate the law.

"The goal here is getting truthful, non-misleading information to consumers about safe and effective therapeutic products so they can be partners in their own health care" says Peter Pitts, the FDA's associate commissioner for external relations. "Better-informed consumers are empowered to choose and use the products we regulate to improve their health."

How Ads Affect Consumers

The FDA surveyed both patients and physicians about their attitudes and experiences with DTC advertising between 1999 and 2002. The agency summarized the findings of these surveys in January 2003 in the report, *Assessment of Physician and Patient Attitudes Toward Direct-to-Consumer Promotion of Prescription Drugs.*

DTC advertising appears to influence certain types of behavior. For example, the FDA surveys found that among patients who visited doctors and asked about a prescription drug by brand name because of an ad they saw, 88 percent actually had the condition the drug treats. This is important, Pitts says, because physician visits that

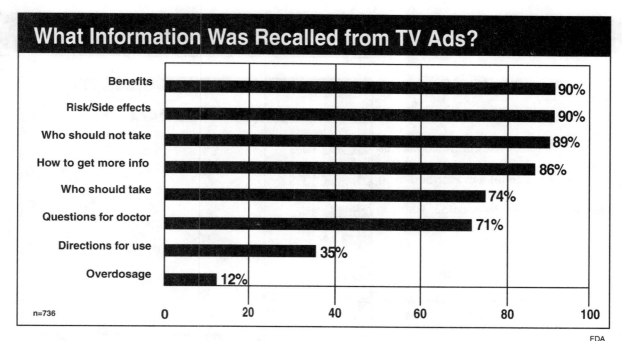

What Information Was Recalled from TV Ads?

Benefits	90%
Risk/Side effects	90%
Who should not take	89%
How to get more info	86%
Who should take	74%
Questions for doctor	71%
Directions for use	35%
Overdosage	12%

n=736

0   20   40   60   80   100

FDA

In three FDA surveys conducted in 1999 and 2002, patients reported recalling this information from TV ads.

result in earlier detection of a disease, combined with appropriate treatment, could mean that more people will live longer, healthier, more productive lives without the risk of future costly medical interventions.

With the number of ailments Patricia A. Sigler lives with—diabetes, fibromyalgia, high blood pressure, high cholesterol, nerve damage, and a heart defect called mitral valve prolapse—the 64-year-old small business owner in Jefferson, Md., says that she's always on the lookout for medicines that might improve her quality of life, and that she pays attention to DTC ads for prescription drugs.

Some Doctors Don't Agree

Michael S. Wilkes, M.D., vice dean of the medical school at the University of California, Davis, says that two reasons he doesn't like DTC advertising are that patients may withhold information from their doctors or try to treat themselves. Aiming prescription drug ads at consumers can affect the "dynamics of the patient-provider relationship," and ultimately, the patient's quality of care, Wilkes says. DTC advertising can motivate consumers to seek more information about a product or disease, but physicians need to help patients evaluate health-related information they obtain from DTC advertising, he says.

"DTC advertising may cultivate the belief among the public that there is a pill for every ill and contribute to the medicalization of trivial ailments, leading to an even more overmedicated society," Wilkes says. "Patients need to trust that I've got their best interest in mind."

Others who favor DTC ads say that consumer-directed information can be an important educational tool in a time when more patients want to be involved in their own health care. Carol Salzman, M.D., Ph.D., an internist in Chevy Chase, Md., emphasizes, however, that physicians still need to remain in control of prescribing medications.

"Doctors shouldn't feel threatened by their patients asking for a medicine by name," she says, "but at the same time, patients shouldn't come in expecting that a drug will be dispensed just because they asked for it."

Salzman says she finds it time-consuming "trying to talk people out of something they have their hearts set on." Wilkes agrees. Discussions motivated by ads that focus on specific drugs or trivial complaints, he says, could take time away from subjects such as a patient's symptoms, the range of available treatments, and specific details about a patient's illness.

Education or Promotion?

At least one patient advocacy group is concerned about what it says are the downsides of advertising prescription drugs directly to consumers, claiming that DTC ads often masquerade as educational tools, but provide more promotion than education. The ads, they say, provide little access to unbiased information.

"People need to be careful with ads that it isn't just hype that they're going to feel better, with no objectivity of the downsides," says Linda Golodner, president of the National Consumers League in Washington, D.C. Although all DTC advertisements must disclose risk information, she says what is typically communicated is a brand name, a reason to use the product, and an impression of the product. Golodner wants all offices within the FDA that have a responsibility for any aspect of DTC ad-

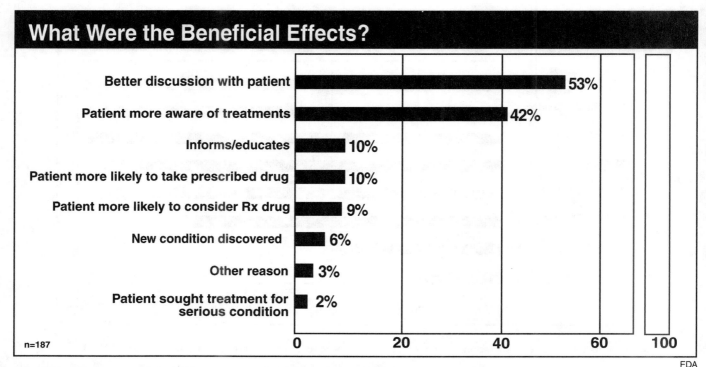

What Were the Beneficial Effects?

Better discussion with patient	53%
Patient more aware of treatments	42%
Informs/educates	10%
Patient more likely to take prescribed drug	10%
Patient more likely to consider Rx drug	9%
New condition discovered	6%
Other reason	3%
Patient sought treatment for serious condition	2%

n=187

FDA

Physicians reported that DTC ads had these beneficial effects for patients.

vertising to work together. "There's a lot of the same information out there, so why not bring it all together so that consumers can understand it better?"

Truth in Advertising

The FDA has regulated the advertising of prescription drugs since 1962, under the Federal Food, Drug, and Cosmetic Act and related regulations. The regulations establish detailed requirements for ad content. Most other advertising, including that of over-the-counter drugs, is regulated by the Federal Trade Commission under a different set of rules.

The FDA's Division of Drug Marketing, Advertising, and Communications (DDMAC) oversees two types of promotion for prescription drugs: promotional labeling and advertising. Advertising includes commercial messages broadcast on television or radio, communicated over the telephone, or printed in magazines and newspapers. Prescription drug ads must contain information in a "brief summary" relating to both risks and benefits. Recognizing the time constraints of broadcast ads, FDA regulations provide that a broadcast advertisement may include, instead of a brief summary information relating to the major risks. The ad must also make "adequate provision" for distributing the FDA-approved labeling in connection with the broadcast ad. This refers to the concept of providing ways for consumers to find more complete information about the drug.

Most ads fulfill this requirement by including a toll-free telephone number, a Web site address, or a link to a concurrently running print ad. They also encourage consumers to talk to their health care providers. Both print and broadcast ads directed at consumers may only make claims that are supported by scientific evidence.

DDMAC oversight helps ensure that pharmaceutical companies accurately communicate the benefits and risks of an advertised drug. The regulations require that advertising for prescription drugs must disclose certain information about the product's uses and risks.

In addition, advertisements cannot be false or misleading and cannot omit material facts. FDA regulations also call for "fair balance" in product claim ad. This means that the risks and benefits must be presented with comparable scope, depth, and detail, and that information relating to the product's effectiveness must be fairly balanced by risk information.

The FDA does not generally require prior approval of DTC ads, although companies are required to submit their ads to the FDA at the time they begin running. The agency, therefore, routinely examines these commercials and published DTC ads after they become available to the public. FDA, however, also is happy to review proposed ads if a drug company makes a request.

"We look at a lot of DTC ads before they run," says Kathryn J. Aikin, Ph.D., a social scientist in DDMAC. "Manufacturers typically want to be sure they're getting started on the right foot."

DTC Ads at a Glance

Product-claim ads:

- mention a drug by name
- make representations about the drug, such as its safety and effectiveness
- must have fair balance of information about effectiveness and risks
- are required to disclose risks in a "brief summary" of benefits and risks (for print ads)
- are required to give a "major statement" of risks and "adequate provision" for finding out more, such as a toll-free number (for broadcast ads).

Reminder ads:

- provide the name of the medication
- may provide other minimal information, such as cost and dosage form
- do not make a representation about the drug, such as the drug's use, effectiveness, or safety
- are not required to provide risk information.

Help-seeking ads:

- educate consumers about a disease or medical condition
- let people know that treatments exist for a medical condition
- don't name a specific drug
- are not required to provide risk information.

The Trouble With Ads

Of the three types of DTC advertisements, the first and most common—product-claim ads—mention a drug's name and the condition it is intended to treat, and describe the risks and benefits associated with taking the drug. Some manufacturers have decided not to present this much information and instead, have made use of two other kinds of ads. "Reminder" ads give only the name of the product, but not what it is used for, and "help-seeking" ads contain information about a disease, but do not mention a specific drug. These help-seeking—or disease-awareness—ads can be extremely informative and, because they name no drug, they are not regulated by the FDA. Examples of help-seeking ads are those that mention high cholesterol or diabetes, and then direct you to ask your doctor about treatments. Reminder ads call attention to a drug's name, but say nothing about the condition it is used to treat, its effectiveness, or safety information. A reminder ad is not required to include risk information.

There has been a great deal of discussion about the brief summary that accompanies DTC print ads. The typical brief summary is not brief and uses technical language. This is because it reprints all of the risk information from the physician labeling. People have complained that the brief summary cannot be understood by consumers. Aikin says, "Patients do not typically read the brief summary in DTC print ads unless they're interested in the product. "Even then, she says, much information is likely glanced at, rather than fully read.

Public input and the FDA's own experiences with DTC promotion prompted the agency to publish two new draft guidances in February 2004: one on the brief summary, and one on help-seeking ads. These guidances are designed to encourage more informative, understandable ads.

Advertising Guidance

The draft guidance on the brief summary encourages companies to use consumer-friendly language and formats to convey prescription drug risk information—through a "less is more" approach. This approach focuses on the most serious and the most common risks of a drug, rather than listing every risk from the physician labeling. "Even though the information currently in the brief summary is complete, accurate, and in compliance," says Pitts, "it does not mean that patients are deriving the maximum benefit from it."

Sometimes marketers combine help-seeking ads with perceptually similar reminder ads in a way that causes the audience to perceive the two pieces as one advertisement. Appearing individually, these ads are exempted by regulation from the risk disclosure requirement. Combined, however, both ads can, in some cases, make a product-claim advertisement that requires risk disclosure.

The agency's recent draft guidance on help-seeking ads explains that help-seeking and reminder ads must appear distinct to avoid coming under the regulations for a product-claim ad. The draft guidance also address's the separation needed between the two types of ads—in space for print ads, and in time for TV ads.

Those in Violation

For companies that don't follow the rules, DDMAC's possible actions include two types of letters—"untitled" and "warning." These letters address advertisements that make misleading claims about a drug's effectiveness—violations such as overstating the effectiveness of the drug, suggesting a broader range of indicated uses than the drug has been approved for, and lack of risk information. In both types of letters, DDMAC asks that the advertisement be withdrawn.

Warning letters, which are sent to companies that have violated the law repeatedly or that have committed serious regulatory violations in their advertising, typically request corrective advertisements to assure that the audience that received the original false or misleading information also receives truthful and accurate information.

Untitled letters are usually, but not always, sent to companies for first-time offenses or for less serious violations.

For example, the 60-second DTC broadcast television ad featuring "Digger," the well-known animated dermatophyte microorganism touting Lamisil (terbinafine), a treatment for nail fungus, was initially found to be false or misleading. The FDA sent an untitled letter to the makers of Lamisil for overstating the drug's effectiveness, minimizing its risk information, and making an unsubstantiated superiority claim. As a result, the manufacturer, Novartis Pharmaceuticals Corp., stopped running that ad.

DDMAC recently sent a warning letter to Bristol-Myers Squibb Co. about false or misleading promotional materials for Pravachol (pravastatin sodium), a drug approved to lower cholesterol in people with high cholesterol, to help prevent heart attacks in people with high cholesterol or heart disease, and to help prevent stroke in people with heart disease. One of the company's ads misleadingly suggested that the drug had been proven to help prevent stroke in all people worried about having a stroke, regardless of whether or not they had heart disease.

Another ad, directed at diabetes patients, misleadingly suggested that Pravachol had been proven to help prevent heart attacks and stroke in people with diabetes. Following the warning letter, the company created a corrective ad campaign acknowledging that Pravachol had not been approved for these indications.

Assessing DTC advertising is an on-going process for the FDA. As more research surfaces, the agency will continue to evaluate DTC drug promotion and will take additional measures as appropriate to protect the public health.

From *FDA Consumer*, July/August 2004. Copyright © 2004 by FDA Consumer. Reprinted by permission.

Rejuvenating Wal-Mart's reputation

Thomas A. Hemphill

Abstract Wal-Mart, the world's largest retailer, was named by *Fortune* as the "most admired company in America" for the years 2003 and 2004. However, these and other accolades have not quieted a chorus of critics, including organized labor, feminists, human rights activists, environmentalists, local businesses, and antisprawl activists, all of whom revile the retail giant for its business practices, resulting in a growing negative consumer perception of Wal-Mart's corporate citizenship. Wal-Mart has instituted a comprehensive nonmarket strategy to counter this criticism, employing a proactive combination of social, political, and legal strategies to manage a contentious environment that could threaten its future growth and financial success.

1. Wal-Mart: good corporate citizen, or bad influence?

Wal-Mart Stores is the world's largest company, with 1.5 million employees worldwide, net sales of $256.3 billion, and a return on equity of 21.3% in fiscal year 2004. Since its founding in 1962, Wal-Mart has embraced the three basic principles enunciated by its founder, Sam Walton: (1) provide value and service to customers by offering quality merchandise at low prices every day; (2) corporate dedication to a partnership between the company's associates (employees), ownership, management, and vendors; and (3) a commitment by Wal-Mart to the United States and the communities in which its stores and distribution centers are located. Each week, over 140 million shoppers visit Wal-Mart stores to avail themselves of the company's "everyday low prices." In the U.S. alone, Wal-Mart reports that, as of January 31, 2004, it operates 1478 discount stores, 1471 Supercenters (that include food retailing), 538 Sam's Club warehouse stores, and 64 smaller Neighborhood Markets, accounting for 8% of total retail sales in America. Adding in its 1355 stores located in nine other countries, Wal-Mart will shortly be opening its 5000th store. In February 2003, *Fortune* magazine, in its annual survey, named Wal-Mart the "most admired company in America." In 2004, Wal-Mart reclaimed that same title.

In the arena of public opinion, Wal-Mart has garnered recent awards and accolades attesting to its laudable corporate citizenship (Wal-Mart, 2004a). In 2002, Wal-Mart received the Ron Brown Award for Corporate Citizenship, named after the late Secretary of Commerce, for its *Good Works* community involvement program. *Good Works* awards more than 160,000 grants each year to organizations supporting local activities and totaled to $71 million contributed in 2001. In the Spring of 2003, Wal-Mart was applauded by Christian groups for banning

Maxim and other racy magazines from its shelves. In November 2003, it received from the Employer Support for the Guard and Reserve nonprofit organization the prestigious *Corporate Patriotism Award*, which is presented annually to a company that exhibits dedication to raising awareness of and support of U.S. service members and their families. Given this litany of favorable news and press coverage, one might believe that all is well with Wal-Mart's corporate reputation, especially among consumers. However, this is not the case.

"Reputation," as defined by Fombrun (1996), is "a perceptual representation of a company's past actions and future prospects that describe the firm's overall appeal to all its key constituents when compared to other leading rivals." Corporate reputation is a combination of both reality (i.e., economic and social performance) and perception (i.e., such performance has been noted). Roberts and Dowling (2002), using statistical regression models measuring the interaction effects of longitudinal financial and reputational data, recently found correlative evidence supporting the proposition that superior-performing firms (i.e., profitable firms) have a greater chance of sustaining their profitability over time if they also possess relatively good reputations. This dynamic study complements the static analysis studies that have associated expected benefits with good corporate reputation.

The results of a January 2004 "Voices of the Leaders Survey" of 132 delegates attending the World Economic Forum in Switzerland revealed that more than 77% believe that corporate reputation has become more important to corporations over the last 2 years (World Economic Forum, 2004). In addition, 59% of survey respondents estimated that corporate brand or reputation represents more than 40% of a company's market capitalization. In the first Annual Department Store and Discount Retailing Industries

Reputation Report, a multidimensional survey based on interviews with senior retail industry executives and retail industry financial analysts, Wal-Mart was ranked highest among all major American retailers (Resnick, 2002). Interestingly, Wal-Mart received its lowest score on the "ethics" dimension; there is some indication that this negative feedback is from competitors, who responded to the cost advantage the company achieves due to the considerable purchasing power it exerts over suppliers.

Like other major corporate managers worldwide, Wal-Mart executives are aware of the importance of their company's corporate reputation. In its 2003 Annual Report, Wal-Mart executives acknowledge that, as the company "has grown to become one of the most successful and visible companies in the world, our good name and reputation have drawn increased scrutiny." In 2002, Wal-Mart initiated comprehensive surveys focused on gathering information from several key company stakeholders, including consumers, investors, local community leaders, suppliers, and employees. According to Wal-Mart's 2003 Annual Report, the survey results will not only assist management "to understand better how they (stakeholders) feel about Wal-Mart, not only as a retailer, but as a responsible employer and good corporate citizen." Results of the surveys revealed that consumers mistrusted the company's labor practices and its impact on the community (Schneider, 2004). This feedback, of course, will also provide Wal-Mart executives with the basis for a strategic response that will address the concerns of these important stakeholder groups via a recently established "reputation taskforce."

Wal-Mart has been the target of many special interest groups over the years, including organized labor (unionization), feminists (gender discrimination in employment practices), human rights activists (overseas working conditions and wages in overseas apparel "sweatshops"), environmentalists, local businesses, and other antisprawl activists (new Wal-Mart stores), all of which have had a cumulative impact on consumer perceptions of Wal-Mart's corporate citizenship. To provide a better understanding of the issues that are adversely impacting the Wal-Mart reputation among consumers, the following will address three critical and troublesome stakeholders for the company: employees, community, and suppliers.

2. Employee stakeholders: the state of associates

Wal-Mart employs some 1.5 million men and women worldwide, with 1.2 million of these employees in the U.S. While providing wages, benefits, and training to many people with limited education and marketable skills, Wal-Mart, concludes Business Week, "is widely blamed for the sorry state of retail wages in America" (Bianco & Zellner, 2003). According to documents filed in a lawsuit pending against the company, Wal-Mart "associates" earned, on average, $8.23 per hour in 2001,

or $13,861 a year. At the time of the court filing, the U.S. federal poverty line for a family of three was $14,630. While Wal-Mart employees begin at the same salary level as unionized employees in the retail industry, they, on average, make 25% less than unionized retail workers after 2 years on the job.

After years of trying to organize Wal-Mart employees, the United Food and Commercial Workers union has been successful in only a single department of 10 butchers/meatpackers in one Jacksonville, Texas location. Following the 7–3 successful vote for union representation, Wal-Mart announced that meat cutting would end at 180 of its Supercenters, with prepackaged meats being delivered instead. In 10 separate cases, the National Labor Relations Board (NLRB) has ruled that Wal-Mart repeatedly broke the law by interrogating workers, confiscating union literature, and firing union supporters. The NLRB has accumulated some 250 allegations of union-busting activities by Wal-Mart. International efforts at unionization of Wal-Mart's 330,000 non-U.S. employees also remain unsuccessful, although they are vigorously pursued in Canada and Great Britain. An industry publication, Retail Forward, estimates that, for every new Supercenter Wal-Mart opens, two supermarkets, whose employees are usually represented by the United Food and Commercial Workers, close. Wal-Mart's union position is explained in the following company statement:

At Wal-Mart, we respect the individual rights of our associates and encourage them to express their ideas, comments, and concerns. Because we believe in maintaining an environment of open communications, *we do not believe there is a need for third-party representation.* (Wal-Mart, 2004b)

Wal-Mart executives argue that they pay their employees a competitive wage, referring to a company-sponsored wage survey that found the company met or exceeded wages paid to retail employees by rival competitors in 50 U.S. markets (Bianco & Zellner, 2003). According to Wal-Mart, it offers its employees a range of benefits without the need for union representation, including (Wal-Mart, 2004c):

- competitive wages
- profit sharing
- a 401 (k) plan
- stock ownership/stock loan program
- paid vacation and holidays
- a discount card
- medical and dental coverage
- life insurance
- accidental death and dismemberment coverage
- short- and long-term disability insurance
- free confidential and professional counseling and assistance
- scholarship bonuses
- child-care discounts

To qualify as a full-time employee, however, one must work a minimum of 28 h per week; approximately 70% of

- *Corporate 100: The Top 100 Companies Providing the Most Opportunities to Hispanics:* Named by *Hispanic Magazine* in 2004.
- *National Hispana Leadership Award:* Awarded in 2002 by the National Hispana Leadership Institute for Wal-Mart's support of leadership and development programs for Latinas
- *Community Commitment Corporate Award:* Awarded in 2002 by the National Action Network in recognition of Wal-Mart's community involvement and diversity practices
- *Corporate Partner of the Year Award:* Awarded in 2002 by the Hispanic National Bar Association to Wal-Mart for its consistent support and best practices in the area of diversity
- *The Organization of Chinese Americans:* Appointed Wal-Mart in 2002 to its Corporate Advisory Board
- *Top 25 Diversity Recruitment Programs:* Wal-Mart named by *Hispanic Business Magazine* in 2001 for its aggressive program to hire and promote Latinos and Latinas
- *Blue Ribbon Award:* Wal-Mart named by Catalyst, a national established organization that works with the business sector to advance women in management, in 1996, 1998, and 2000, for having two women on its board of directors

Figure 1 Wal-Mart employment diversity awards/appointment. Source: http://www.walmartstores.com. Accessed on February 28, 2004.

Wal-Mart workers meet this minimum. Of those employees qualifying for health insurance, only 38% purchase it, possibly because employees are responsible for 35% of the overall cost, which is double the U.S. average for employee copayment. By keeping its deductibles high (the company does not cover flu shots, child vaccinations, or contraception, which many other firms include in their health care coverage), Wal-Mart spends 30% less per employee on health care than its competitors. Giant and Safeway, unionized supermarket chains, estimate that, for every $3 they spend on health care for employees, Wal-Mart spends an average of $1. Furthermore, new fulltime employees wait for 6 months to be eligible for its health care plan and the company does not cover any health care benefits for retirees. Under the Wal-Mart stock ownership plan, the company matches 15% of the first $1800 in stock purchases. However, most employees cannot afford to purchase stock, and not one in 50 employees has amassed as much as $50,000 through the stockownership pension plan. According to surveys conducted by Wal-Mart, the company's 44% annual turnover among employees in the first year is attributable to a lack of recognition and inadequate pay, which could be a problem in the immediate future: from 2004 to 2008, the company plans to add 800,000 new positions, including 47,000 managers.

Yet, when it comes to diversity and opportunity in employment, Wal-Mart Stores is the leading employer of minorities in the U.S. (Wal-Mart, 2004d). More than 160,000 African–American associates and more than 105,000 Hispanic associates work for Wal-Mart stores, Sam's Clubs, and Wal-Mart logistics facilities nationwide. In the 2002 annual poll undertaken by *Careers for the Disabled* magazine, Wal-Mart was named first among all U.S. companies in providing opportunities and a positive working environment for people with disabilities. Furthermore, Wal-Mart is one of the leading employers of senior citizens in the United States, employing more than 164,000 associates 55 years and older. Of the 15-member Wal-Mart board of directors, two Latinos sit along side two women. Attesting to its diverse workforce, Wal-Mart has been awarded a number of diversity employment awards over the last few years (see Fig. 1).

But Wal-Mart is confronted with a plethora of employment-related legal problems. An internal audit covering 1 week of activity in July 2000 found more than 1300 instances of minors working during school hours or later than labor laws permit as well as more than 60,000 instances of workers not taking scheduled breaks. In December 2002, a federal jury found Wal-Mart guilty of forcing employees at 18 Oregon stores to work overtime without pay from 1994 through 1999, and the company also faces nearly 40 additional lawsuits charging management with forcing employees to work overtime without pay. On January 18, 2004, it was reported by the national media that Wal-Mart managers had been locking in late-shift workers for security reasons, with many employees unhappy with this arrangement.

Sex discrimination and employment of illegal aliens are also legal issues that continue to plague Wal-Mart executives. The Equal Employment Opportunity Commission has reported that it has sued Wal-Mart 48 times since 1990, mostly for discriminatory hiring practices, acquiring $8.6 million for the aggrieved and changes in policy and training from Wal-Mart management (Joyce, 2004). On September 24, 2003, a federal judge in California began considering a plaintiff's petition to include all 1.6 million women who have worked at Wal-Mart since late 1998 in a sex discrimination suit alleging Wal-Mart systematically denies women equal pay and opportunities for promotion. According to the plaintiffs, between 1975 and 1999, Wal-Mart had far fewer female managers in stores than its competitors, with only 34.5% vs. 56.5%, respectively (Freedman, 2003; Joyce, 2004). On June 22, 2004, U.S. District Judge Martin J. Jenkins ruled that this sex discrimination lawsuit could proceed to trial as a class action, in what could prove to be the largest private employer civil rights case in U.S. history (Joyce, 2004). Moreover, Wal-Mart is now facing an ongoing investigation by U.S. Immigration and Customs Enforcement (ICE) of its subcontracting of overnight cleaning services that employ illegal aliens. On October 23, 2003, ICE agents arrested 250 undocumented aliens at 61 Wal-Mart stores in 21 states (Schneider & El-Boghdady, 2003a). Federal officials announced at the time of the raid that wiretapped conversations suggested Wal-Mart executives knew the subcontractors were employing undocumented workers.

3. Community stakeholders: warm welcomes or chilly receptions?

The importance of local communities to Wal-Mart can be summarized by the following company statement:

Wal-Mart Stores Inc. believes each Wal-Mart store, Sam's Club, and distribution center has a responsibility to contribute to the well being of the local community. Our more than 3400 locations [in the U.S.] contributed more than $150 million to support communities and local nonprofit organizations. Customers raised an additional $75 million with the help of our stores and clubs. (Wal-Mart, 2004e)

Wal-Mart was ranked the number one Corporate Citizen in America in the 1999 and 2000 Cone/ Roper Report, an annual national survey regarding local philanthropy and corporate citizenship. According to the Foundation Center, Wal-Mart was ranked among the top five corporate foundations in giving in 1999 and 2000. More recently, in 2002, *Forbes* recognized Wal-Mart as being one of the most philanthropic companies in America; however, Wal-Mart's issues with local communities do not concern its philanthropic activities.

In the 1990s, Wal-Mart, along with such other "big-box" retailers as Target, Lowes, and Home Depot, became the focus of a national "antisprawl" movement, bringing together environmentalists, local business people, and residential homeowners in actively resisting what the National Trust for Historic Preservation (Washington, DC) defines as "poorly planned, low density, auto-oriented development that spreads out from the center of communities." The National Trust for Historic Preservation placed Vermont on its list of the 10 most endangered places in 2004, warning that the state's small-town charm is threatened by Wal- Mart. First placed on its annual list in 1993 because of Wal-Mart's plans to expand into it, Vermont, at the time, was the only state without a Wal-Mart. According to Al Norman, author of the 1999 book *Slam-Dunking Wal-Mart*, the environmental and land use issues that big-box retail stores bring to a community include (Norman, 1999):

- the impact of traffic on air quality standards
- the threat to water quality and aquifers
- the mismanagement of storm water and sewage
- the reduction of wildlife habitat
- the loss of open space and unique natural areas
- the homogenization of rural landscapes
- the expense of costly infrastructure
- the deterioration of historic commercial centers
- the overdependence on the automobile and Superhighways

While there have been occasional setbacks before city councils and land use and zoning boards, Wal-Mart rarely capitulates to community groups opposed to its building plans, but there is growing resistance to its Supercenter concept; not only in small-town America where environmental and small business survival concerns have dominated, but also in larger urban areas where economic issues are the primary drivers of local opposition. For example, in California, the Los Angeles City Council is poised to consider a proposal to forbid any store whose stock includes grocery items from exceeding 100,000 ft₂ in size (Wal-Mart Supercenters can range from 150,000 to 220,000 ft^2 in size). Los Angeles is following the lead established by the Alameda County Board of Supervisors and several other local governments in the San Francisco Bay area who, in 2003, passed similar land use ordinances.

Many city officials in California fear the arrival of the Wal-Mart Supercenters, believing they would place downward pressure on wages, as local businesses would need to reduce costs to compete, eliminate more jobs than create new ones, and leave more residents without health insurance. A study commissioned by the city of Los Angeles in 2003 concluded that the arrival of big-box stores would result in a net loss of jobs and force other businesses to lower wages and/or reduce benefits (Sanchez, 2004), and ultimately recommended approving restrictions on such megaretailers. However, in a Wal-Mart financed report issued in January 2004 by the Los Angeles County Economic Development Corporation, the study results offer a contrary economic impact scenario (Anderson, 2004). This study reported that the arrival of such megastores selling groceries could save households in Southern California an average of $524 per year once Wal-Mart reached a 20% market share, and that consumers spending those savings in other parts of the regional economy would help create far more jobs (17,300 in Los Angeles County alone) than would be lost from smaller businesses that could not compete with the major retailers. On the downside, it was noted that the presence of Wal-Mart Supercenters could be responsible for wage losses potentially as high as $258 million annually in Los Angeles County.

As a backdrop to its community-related problems in California, Wal-Mart's intended arrival with its Supercenters and groceries in the region is one of the issues involved in a 4-month strike by 75,000 employees represented by the United Food and Commercial Workers Union. Local grocery retail chains are now demanding wage and benefit concessions from employees, contending that, otherwise, union members risk losing their jobs to the Wal-Mart Supercenters. While no one knows precisely how much of an impact on retail wages Wal-Mart has had on the U.S. economy, the company's impact on wages in the South and Midwest has been significant since, after becoming the largest regional employer, it established wage rates for all retailers in the community.

In June 2003, Merrill Lynch released a study that found that Wal-Mart's Supercenters are not the supermarket chain "category killer," as popularly believed (Tatge, 2003). Wal-Mart has made few inroads into major urban areas, with 70% of its Supercenters located outside the top 100 metropolitan areas of the U.S., hardly the Republican-controlled and antiunion environment in which the company has flourished. While Wal-Mart is the top grocery retailer in America with a 15% market share and $50 billion in sales in 2002, less than 40% of its 7.8 billion increase in grocery sales for that year came from major metropolitan markets, where large supermarket chains Kroger, Safeway, Ahold, and Albertson's own over 70% of sales. In the top 26 markets with populations exceeding 2 million, Wal-Mart had a combined 2002 average market share of 3.65%. Merrill Lynch found that the real problem traditional supermarket chains face is weak demand and an inability to raise prices in a deflationary environment; not Wal-Mart pricing pressure. As they enter California and East Coast cities, Wal-Mart could face urban, Democrat-controlled, prounion shoppers who will boycott its Supercenters.

4. Supplier stakeholders: partnership at a cost

Wal-Mart management is dedicated to a "partnership" with its vendors to supply its stores with "low price" consumer merchandise. For Wal-Mart, price is the primary driver of its successful consumer business operations; consequently, reducing production costs is the mantra with which Wal-Mart's 21,000 suppliers are confronted: take-it-or-leave-it. In 2003, 7.5 cents of every nonautomotive dollar spent in a U.S. retail store went to Wal-Mart, making a contract with the retailer a necessity for even the largest consumer goods companies in America. Dial Corporation, a major consumer goods retailer, reportedly does 28% of its business with Wal-Mart. If Dial lost its Wal-Mart "partnership," it would need to double sales to its next nine customers in order to recoup the loss.

For basic commodity products, the price Wal-Mart will pay, and that is charged to consumers, must decline annually. However, Wal-Mart's emphasis on driving costs down can have negative consequences for suppliers offering quality merchandise. There is a trade-off; while unlike most general merchandise retailers, Wal-Mart does not charge "slotting fees" for manufacturer access to its shelves, it does establish strict delivery schedules and inventory levels, and heavily influences product specifications. There is little question that being a vendor to Wal-Mart can provide a supplier with significant increases in sales and market share; however, some manufacturers are forced to end their relationship with the company or risk losing their brand reputation with consumers. Or, if Wal-Mart executives do not agree to the pricing of a product, ostensibly because they do not believe it offers a good value to the customer, the product will no longer be carried by the retailer. Since the mid-1990s, Wal-Mart has

also challenged its suppliers by developing increasing numbers (over 1500) of "Great Value" private label products. Compared with the 15% profit margin offered by brand merchandise, private label goods generate profits as high as 30%. As Wal-Mart expands retail operations overseas where U.S. brands are less well known, private label brands promise potentially even higher profits.

The Wal-Mart organization is also well known for continuous operational improvements in the ability to handle, move, and monitor merchandise; consequently, it expects the same of its suppliers. Wal-Mart's discipline in its supply chain results in these businesses becoming more efficient, responsive, and focused. Leveraging its buying power, Wal-Mart forces suppliers to redesign all aspects of their operations from packaging to information systems, regardless of how problematic this might prove to be. In a recent study conducted by A.T. Kearney, it was found that Wal-Mart and other retailers stand to gain significant labor and inventory cost savings, 5% and 7.5%, respectively, from the adoption of electronic product codes and radio frequency identification tagging; efficiency savings that will come at the cost of manufacturers who must apply the tags to their goods (Ericson, 2003). While retailers will incur a onetime cost for installing readers and system integration at distribution centers and stores, manufacturers will face recurring costs of buying and applying tags to pallets and cases, per Wal-Mart requirement. Overall, however, A.T. Kearney found that Wal-Mart's buying power is "not a significant cost advantage" for the firm, and, in many cases, manufacturers actually make more money through Wal-Mart than through other retailers (The Economist, 2004).

What Wal-Mart wants, Wal-Mart gets from its suppliers; however, the company has a generally good reputation for integrity in its dealings with suppliers: it does not cheat, follows through on promises, and pays bills on a timely basis (Fishman, 2003). Most suppliers, however, are not located in the U.S. Wal-Mart launched a "Made in America" campaign in the mid-1980s, seeking out sources of domestic supply whenever possible. Today, the once heavily promoted mission has shifted to the backburner, and for a good reason: Wal-Mart now purchases the overwhelming majority of its merchandise from overseas. Not surprisingly, though, Wal-Mart critics point to the retailer's global pursuit of lower-cost goods as contributing to the accelerating loss of U.S. manufacturing jobs to China and other low-wage paying countries in Southeast Asia. In point of fact, the $12 billion worth of Chinese goods Wal-Mart acquired in 2002 represented 10% of all U.S. imports from the People's Republic of China. These purchases reached $15 billion, $7.5 billion purchased directly and $7.5 billion through its suppliers, for 2003. Of greater concern to Wal-Mart executives, however, are charges that these goods are manufactured in Third World sweatshops.

As the following statement illustrates, Wal-Mart strongly denies allegations of contracting with sweatshop manufacturers:

Wal-Mart strives to do business only with factories run legally and ethically. We continue to commit extensive resources to making the Wal-Mart system one of the very best. We require suppliers to ensure that every factory conforms to local workplace laws and there is no illegal child labor or forced labor. Wal-Mart also works with independent monitoring firms to randomly inspect these factories to help ensure compliance. In fact, we conduct more than 200 factory inspections each week to ensure these facilities are being run legally and ethically. (Wal-Mart, 2004f)

Wal-Mart states that it employs 100 auditors who annually inspect every one of its suppliers' factories operating in mainland China. In 2003, the retailer suspended dealings with about 400 suppliers, most for exceeding overtime limits, and another 72 factories were permanently blacklisted, nearly all for employing children under China's legal working age of 16. However, Wal-Mart does not conduct regular inspections of smaller factories that sell goods to the company through middlemen, nor does it inspect all its suppliers' subcontractors or the Chinese manufacturing operations of U.S. suppliers such as Mattel and Dell. Moreover, one labor organizer in China, Li, alleges that the supplier factories are notified before inspectors arrive: clean up their operations, create fake time sheets for the auditors, and brief workers on what they should tell the visitors (Goodman & Pan, 2004).

Wal-Mart pits one supplier against another, with the resulting competition for lower prices fueling longer employee working hours and lower wages. Li describes the following competitive environment:

> . . . these factories often require employees to work as many as 80 h per week during the busy season for $75 to $110 per month, violating Chinese labor laws. If Wal-Mart really wanted to monitor conditions among its suppliers, Li said, it could do so with surprise visits, longer inspections, and independent auditors. "But if they did that, prices would definitely go up." (Goodman & Pan, 2004)

Why does the Chinese Communist government continue this relationship? Wal-Mart, with retail operations throughout North America and Europe, offers the developing Chinese economy entrée into product markets that it could not acquire on its own. Furthermore, Wal-Mart's cost-reduction requirements offer the discipline which will improve production efficiency, thus making the Chinese factories more competitive and likely to acquire contracts from other major retailers. The question remains, however, whether this type of supplier arrangement, in the U.S. or overseas, will continue to remain attractive to Wal-Mart consumers in the long run.

5. Wal-Mart's nonmarket strategy

As witnessed by its financial standing in the business world, Wal-Mart has exhibited great success in the competitive market environment. Where the company has exhibited recent weaknesses is in its nonmarket environment, with legal and public relations issues involving employees, local communities, and suppliers receiving greater public scrutiny and tarnishing its corporate reputation; possibly affecting long-term profitability. According to Baron (1995a), the nonmarket environment consists of the social, political, and legal environment among companies and their public. To compete successfully, firms must embrace an integrated business strategy consisting of a market or competitive component and a nonmarket or public component (Baron, 1995b). Baron (1995a) believes that, to address nonmarket forces effectively, managers must formulate specific strategies to deal with them.

In 2002, Wal-Mart executives initiated a stakeholder survey of consumers, employees, local community leaders, investors, and suppliers. This corporate reputation survey, performed by corporate reputation consultant Fleishman—Hillard (Omnicom Group), was originally suggested by a Wal-Mart board member. The results of the stakeholder surveys indicate that:

- Consumers, while generally viewing Wal-Mart as an excellent retailer offering the lowest prices, reportedly mistrust Wal-Mart's labor practices and cite its negative impact on the surrounding community.
- Employees of Wal-Mart generally gave Wal-Mart high marks, but the company received little praise for its wages and benefits.
- Local community leaders, echoing Wal-Mart employees, negatively cited low-paying jobs.
- Investors (i.e., bankers) expressed similar problems that were cited by consumers, employees, and local community leaders, including low-paying jobs; however, these concerns appeared to have little or no impact on how they viewed Wal-Mart as a business investment.

The research found that many stakeholders view Wal-Mart as an employer of dead-end jobs, and that its performance as a corporate citizen is less than admirable. "They didn't see us as involved in the community as they might like," said Wal-Mart's chief spokesman, Jay Allen. "They didn't give us good marks on listening. Sometimes it was as basic as the parking lot was not clean, and that's not treating the community with respect" (Hays, 2003). As a result of the survey findings, Wal-Mart executives initiated a comprehensive, proactive nonmarket strategy to rejuvenate their tarnished corporate reputation.

6. Social strategy: accentuate the positive

Wal-Mart's corporate communications and marketing groups are developing external communications programs highlighting the retailer's employment and career opportunities, along with the company's local community "Good Works" philanthropy. According to Wal-Mart Annual Report, 2003, the company spent $676 million on advertising campaigns to attract consumers and improve its corporate reputation. The company, however, did not break out the amount spent on corporate reputation advertising campaigns. With 2003 even less of a banner media year for Wal-Mart, it would not be surprising to see increased expenditures for embellishing the company's reputation allocated for 2004. Furthermore, the company's operations group and the Wal-Mart Foundation are working together to make corporate local giving and involvement more visible and responsive to specific community needs. In early 2003, a series of television advertisements began to air, highlighting Wal-Mart's philanthropic contributions in the local communities where their retail and distribution facilities are located.

Around the same time, another series of television advertisements created by the Austin, Texas advertising firm GSD and M called "Good Jobs" began to air, emphasizing Wal-Mart's responsiveness to personal employee needs, without mention of low prices or selection of consumer products. The "Good Jobs" advertising campaign emphasizes female Wal-Mart managers and other employees providing testimonials regarding how they have benefited by working for the company. Bob Garfield, a columnist at *Advertising Age,* called the "Good Jobs" advertising series a smart strategy. "I'm embarrassed to say they work on me," he said, adding, ". . .in their ads, the employees seem like just plain folks who want to help me find the right brand of paper toweling . . .They're (Wal-Mart) well positioned for the moment" (Schneider, 2004).

To improve employee representation in the supervisory ranks, Wal-Mart announced in 2003 the formation of a Diversity Office, with the goal of recruiting and promoting from all segments of society and providing work environments allowing individuals to succeed on their own merits. Furthermore, for fiscal year 2004, a portion of management incentives will be tied directly to achieving diversity goals (Wal-Mart Annual Report, 2004).

7. Political strategy: working within the system

Wal-Mart's real estate group is considering how to give local government leaders more "ownership" in the design and location of Wal-Mart retail stores. Taking a different spin on this issue, Wal-Mart recently agreed to donate a 43,770-ft^2 building to the town of Bunkie, Louisiana. The building, which once housed a Wal-Mart store, was to be boarded up, and the municipal government requested the company to allow the town to subdivide the building and lease it to several small business tenants. The only restriction Wal-Mart required of the town was that the building should not be used for a discount store, warehouse club, or pharmacy. With some 300 so-called "dark" stores across the U.S., this seminal effort by Wal-Mart could be a positive community model to be followed in other locales.

Wal-Mart executives and spokespersons are becoming more engaged with the media, responding to critical news articles, editorials, and letters to the editor in print. Besides upper-level Wal-Mart managers, store employees have also taken it upon themselves to write letters to newspapers. Wal-Mart is aggressively using the ballot box to overturn local government ordinances restricting the opening of Supercenters. In 2002, voters in the California border town of Calexico overturned a government ordinance blocking Wal-Mart and other big-box retailers from doing business. In the Los Angeles suburb of Inglewood and in Contra Costa County near San Francisco, two localities where local government officials have sought to stop Wal-Mart Supercenters from opening, the company succeeded in getting measures on the ballot that, had they been approved by voters, would have cleared the way for its expansion plans. In Inglewood, the ballot measure was recently defeated by a vote of 61% to 39%, while in Contra Costa County, the Wal-Mart backed initiative was also defeated. "Not only are we more aggressive in our communications these days, but we are also becoming more savvy in using government affairs," said Wal-Mart spokeswoman Mona Williams. "Our critics make an awful lot of noise, and we need to ensure that our side of issues is heard as well" (Schneider, 2004). These political and media tactics will likely be necessary over the next few years, as Wal-Mart opens and expands scores of its 200,000 plus square-foot discount-supermarket stores in metropolitan areas where many communities are attempting to block such expansion.

An example of this proactive use of government affairs is highlighted in the recent publication of a study undertaken by Good Jobs First, a Washington, DC-based interest group that compiled the report with financing from the United Food and Commercial Workers International Union. It revealed that Wal-Mart has received well over $1 billion in state and local subsidies during its expansion from regional discount chain to world's largest retailer. According to Mona Williams, Wal-Mart spokeswoman, if the $1 billion figure is correct, Wal-Mart could make good use of the figure in its advertising. In the last 10 years, Williams said, Wal-Mart has collected more than $52 billion in sales taxes, paid $4 billion in local property taxes, and paid $192 million in income and unemployment taxes to local governments. "It looks like offering tax incentives to Wal-Mart is a jackpot for local governments" she said (Feder, 2004).

The retailer's increasingly diverse business interests have also prompted an expanded presence in Washington, DC. The company's Washington office, first opened in 1999, has grown to five staffers in the intervening 5 years; nevertheless, still a fraction of comparably sized firms such as General Electric. "The increased federal presence is driven by an increase in issues that affect our everyday operations," said Laurie Smalling, Wal-Mart's DC-based manager of corporate affairs (Vekshin, 2004). Furthermore, Wal-Mart has hired lobbyists, including the powerful Washington firm of Patton, Boggs, and Blow, to monitor legislation concerning consumer protection, ergonomics, port security, and prescription drug reform. According to Smalling, Wal-Mart's expanded Washington presence does not represent a shift in policy but rather was "an internal awareness" of the significance of federal policy.

This expansive federal policy involvement also extends to actively funding political candidates. As of November 2003, Wal-Mart's political donations were, according to the Center for Responsive Politics, $1.26 million, second only to the Goldman Sachs Group, with $1.6 million. At the same time, Wal-Mart is also the top political action committee (PAC) donor to federal candidates, contributing $1.028 million, with 84% gifted to Republican candidates. In the 2002 cycle of federal elections, Wal-Mart ranked 44th with $1.1 million among contributors nationwide; in 2000, the retailer ranked 128th with $457,050; and in 1998, the company ranked 356th with contributions of $135,750.

Congressman John Boozman (R-Arkansas), whose district includes the Bentonville headquarters of Wal-Mart, observes that Wal-Mart makes an effort to stay involved in Congress regarding the issues that affect the company and their customers. "They realize that the federal government is so intrusive and affects so much that they feel like its vital that their views are known when policies form," he said (Vekshin, 2004).

8. Legal strategy

Wal-Mart has acquired a reputation for aggressively litigating civil liability cases even when it would be less expensive to settle (Willing, 2001). Many legal analysts believe that Wal-Mart is sued more often than any other company in America; at any moment, Wal-Mart is confronted with about 8000 lawsuits, mostly personal injury suits involving employees. This Wal-Mart strategy has resulted in the pace of lawsuits stabilizing, as potential plaintiffs and their lawyers decide not to sue after weighing the costs of fighting the retailer. If it has to pay a settlement, Wal-Mart keeps the amount secret through confidentiality pacts. Even so, the company has recently adjusted its litigation policy, making a point of appearing reasonable, appealing fewer cases, and publicizing disputes it has resolved. This legal strategy reflects Wal-Mart's desire to not create further public relations problems through legal tactics; however, the retailer will aggressively use the legal system to implement its business expansion strategy. In January 2004, Wal-Mart filed suit against the Alameda, California County Board of Supervisors to overturn an ordinance banning the construction of Wal-Mart's Supercenters.

After the Fall, 2003 immigration-related raids, Wal-Mart retained Washington lawyer Martin Weinstein, a former federal prosecutor, to conduct an in-house investigation of its hiring and contracting practices. Weinstein concluded that Wal-Mart has cooperated with federal immigration authorities dating back to mid-2000 and had been assured it was not a target of the investigation. The results of this legal and public relations defense has, so far, been for naught, as Federal investigators are continuing with a grand jury investigation. Nevertheless, it shows that Wal-Mart is willing to investigate the legality of its own business practices and defend them in the public arena.

Forrester, a research company, predicted that "Wal-Mart will spend more legal energy than other retailers as it battles a barrage of lawsuits (including 33 putative class action suits alleging labor violations) and struggles to not get distracted by any more legal issues in 2004" (The Economist, 2004). To assist in this strategy, in January, 2004, the firm hired Tom Gean, a former U.S. attorney, to work with its operations compliance groups, which have been established to assist store managers in operating within laws and regulations (The Economist, 2004).

9. Conclusions

The results of their stakeholder surveys reveal that while Wal-Mart is viewed as a generally good corporate citizen and provides low-prices to the consumer, there are growing areas of concern found among all stakeholder groups; especially among consumers. Wal-Mart's corporate reputation, while still relatively intact, is showing signs of early deterioration. As Wal-Mart moves into urban metropolitan areas, they will face more demanding employees and consumers less amenable to tolerating unfair labor practices and willing to find other discount retailers who offer slightly less aggressive pricing in return for more acceptable labor, community, and supplier policies. According to Rosabeth Moss Kanter of the Harvard Business School, Wal-Mart brings out the tensions Americans feel regarding their dual roles as consumers and employees. For consumers, cheaper is better and it matters not where the products are manufactured. However, as employees and manufacturers, we are concerned, especially if inexpensive products mean our jobs could end up moving overseas. *Boston Globe* columnist Charles Stein believes that Kanter is on the right track but would go a step further, saying Wal-Mart has become a symbol of the anxiety Americans feel about capitalism as it is practiced in the 21st century; i.e., a global fastmoving contact sport (Stein, 2003).

Today's Wal-Mart is of high public profile and subject to media scrutiny commensurate with the world's most successful business enterprise. It is now responding to external threats with a concerted nonmarket strategy involving complementary social, political, and legal components. Wal-Mart's solid corporate reputation, as Wal-Mart executives know, is important to the continued expansion and financial success of the company. The evolving nature of this nonmarket strategy reveals potential for modest success. The company's social strategy, involving media campaigns focusing on female managers and community involvement, will help to educate many consumers on some of Wal-Mart's positive activities. Wal-Mart's political strategy of taking restrictive ordinances to the electorate has a "populist" appeal, and success at the ballot box will provide the firm with evidence of the popular appeal of its Supercenters, creating increased leverage in preordinance negotiations with local political officials. Political donations offer increased public policy visibility for Wal-Mart, with both political parties recognizing the company's active involvement in the electoral process; a necessity for a firm under such public scrutiny. In the civil litigation arena, a less confrontational approach emphasizing just settlements with litigants, especially consumers suffering physical injuries, will help enhance the company's reputation in the media.

Will Wal-Mart ever find itself the "darling" of the American union movement? Probably not, but neither will most of the American business community. Nonmanagerial retail jobs have never been the fast track for solid middle income wages and benefits. For full-time, nonmanagerial employees, Wal-Mart, like most other major retailers, will provide a modest paycheck that supplements the family's primary wage and benefits earner. Who is ultimately driving the quest for suppliers to provide lower-cost products and retailers to pay lower wages to employees? According to a 2002 study conducted by market research firm UBS Warburg, a Wal-Mart Supercenter offers an average price that is 14% below its competitors. The American consumer, 140 million strong, walks through the doors of Wal-Mart stores and Supercenters on a weekly basis. Those same consumers include countless union supermarket workers, many of whom would never work at Wal-Mart, but who would not hesitate to shop there (Schneider & ElBoghdady, 2003b). While showing discomfort with the Wal-Mart business model of low cost/prices and continuous expansion, the American consumer has yet to walk away from Sam Walton's stores. That day, however, may yet come.

References

Anderson, H. (2004, January 27). Analysis: Wal-Mart's effects not all bad. *Washington Times*, Retrieved February 9, 2004, from http://washingtontimes.com/upi-breaking/20040127- 073020-6356r.htm

Baron, D. P. (1995a). The nonmarket strategy system. Sloan Management Review, 37, 73–85.

Baron, D. P. (1995b). Integrated strategy: Market and nonmarket components. California Management Review, 37, 47–65.

Bianco, A., & Zellner, W. (2003). Is Wal-Mart too powerful? Business Week (6 October) pp. 100–104, 106, 108, 110.

Ericson, J. (2003, November 10). Wal-Mart will burden suppliers. *Line56: The E-Business Executive Daily*. Retrieved February 9, 2004, from http://www.line56.com/print/default.asp? ArticleID=5144

Feder, B. J. (2004, May 24). Wal-Mart's expansion aided by many taxpayer subsidies. *The New York Times*, Retrieved May 25,

2004, from http://www.nytimes.com/2004/05/24/business/24walmart.html?e=5040 and en=bbdf782af74

Fishman, C. (2003, December). The Wal-Mart you don't know. *Fast Company*, 77 (Retrieved February 5, 2004, from http://pf.fastcompany.com/magazine/77/walmart.html).

Fombrun, C. (1996). *Reputation: Realizing value from the corporate image*. Boston, MA: Harvard University Press.

Freedman, M. (2003, July 22). Wal-Mart's women trouble. *Forbes.com*. Retrieved February 9, 2004, from http://www.forbes.com/2003/07/22/cz_mf_0722wmt_print.html

Goodman, P. S., & Pan, P. P. (2004, February 8). Chinese workers pay for Wal-Mart's low prices. *Washington Post*, A1.

Hays, C. L. (2003, August 14). Wal-Mart opens wallet in effort to fix its image. *New York Times*, Retrieved February 1, 2004, from http://sfgate.com/cgi-bin/article.cgi?file=/ca/2003/08/14/ BU185832 DTL and type=printable.

Joyce, A. (2004, June 23). Wal-Mart bias case moves forward. *Washington Post*, A1–A8.

Norman, A. (1999). The case against sprawl. *Sprawl-Busters*. Retrieved February 9, 2004, from http://www.sprawlbusters.com/caseagainstsprawl.html

Resnick, J. T. (2002, May). Reputation matters: First industry rating of corporate reputation yields important insights. *Chain Store Age*, 41–42.

Roberts, P. W., & Dowling, G. R. (2002). Corporate reputation and sustained superior financial performance. *Strategic Management Journal*, 23, 1077–1093.

Sanchez, R. (2004, February 3). Los Angeles to Wal-Mart: Bigger's not always better. *Washington Post*, A3.

Schneider, G. (2004, January 24). Wal-Mart's damage control: Longtime price message takes a back seat to blitz designed to mend reputation. *Washington Post*, Retrieved February 6, 2004, from http://www.businessweek.com:/print/bwdailydnflash/jan2004/nf20040128_6990_db14.ht, E5.

Schneider, G., & ElBoghdady, D. (2003a, November 5). Wal-Mart confirms probe of hiring. *Washington Post*, Retrieved February 28, 2004, from http://www.arkansasnews.com/archive/ 2004/01/18/ WashingtonDCBureau/107320.html, E1.

Schneider, G., & ElBoghdady, D. (2003b, November 6). Stores follow Wal-Mart's lead in labor. *Washington Post*, Retrieved February 2, 2004, from http://www.walmartstores.com, A1.

Stein, C. (2003, November 30). Wal-Mart finds success, image breed contempt. *Boston.com*. Retrieved February 9, 2004, from http://www.boston.com/business/globe/articles/2003/11/30/wal_mart_finds_success_image

Tatge, M. (2003, June 30). As a grocer, Wal-Mart is no category killer. *Forbes.com*. Retrieved February 9, 2004, from http://www.forbes.com/2003/06/30/cz-mt-0630walmart-print.html

The Economist (2004, April 15). Wal-Mart: How big can it grow? Retrieved May 8, 2004, from http://www.economist.com/business/displayStory.cfm?story_id=2593089

Vekshin, A. (2004, January 18). Wal-Mart beefs up federal presence. *Arkansas News Bureau (A Stephens Media Group)*, Retrieved February 28, 2004, from http://www.arkansasnews.com/ archive/2004/01/18/WashingtonDCBureau/107320.html

Wal-Mart. (2004a). Recent awards and recognition. Retrieved February 2, 2004, from http://www.walmartstores.com

Wal-Mart. (2004b). Statements: Unions. Retrieved February 15, 2004, from http://www.walmartstores.com

Wal-Mart. (2004c). Why work for Wal-Mart? Retrieved February 7, 2004, from http://www.walmartstores.com

Wal-Mart. (2004d). Our commitment to people. Retrieved February 8, 2004, from http://www.walmartstores.com

Wal-Mart. (2004e). Our commitment to communities. Retrieved February 7, 2004, from http://www.walmartstores.com

Wal-Mart. (2004f). Statements:Sweatshop allegations. Retrieved February 15, 2004 from http://www.walmartstores.com

Wal-Mart. (2003, January). *Annual report.*

Wal-Mart. (2004, January). *Annual report.*

Willing, R. (2001, August 13). Lawsuits a volume business at

Wal-Mart. *USATODAY.com.* Retrieved February 2, 2004, from http://www.usatoday.com/news/nation/2001/08/14/walmart-usat.htm

World Economic Forum. (2004, January 22). Corporate brand reputation outranks financial performance as most important measure of success. Davos, Switzerland: Press Release.

*This manuscript was accepted under the editorship of Dennis W. Organ.
*Present address: Department of Strategic Management & Public Policy, The George Washington University, 2121 G. Street, NW, Munroe 203, Washington, DC 20052, USA.
E-mail address: tomhemphill@comcast. net

From *Business Horizons,* 2005, pp. 11-21. Copyright © 2005 by Elsevier Science Ltd . Reprinted by permission.

Managing for Organizational Integrity

By supporting ethically sound behavior, managers can strengthen the relationships and reputations their companies depend on.

Lynn Sharp Paine

Many managers think of ethics as a question of personal scruples, a confidential matter between individuals and their consciences. These executives are quick to describe any wrongdoing as an isolated incident, the work of a rogue employee. The thought that the company could bear any responsibility for an individual's misdeeds never enters their minds. Ethics, after all, has nothing to do with management.

In fact, ethics has *everything* to do with management. Rarely do the character flaws of a lone actor fully explain corporate misconduct. More typically, unethical business practice involves the tacit, if not explicit, cooperation of others and reflects the values, attitudes, beliefs, language, and behavioral patterns that define an organization's operating culture. Ethics, then, is as much an organizational as a personal issue. Managers who fail to provide proper leadership and to institute systems that facilitate ethical conduct share responsibility with those who conceive, execute, and knowingly benefit from corporate misdeeds.

Managers must acknowledge their role in shaping organizational ethics and seize this opportunity to create a climate that can strengthen the relationships and reputations on which their companies' success depends. Executives who ignore ethics run the risk of personal and corporate liability in today's increasingly tough legal environment. In addition, they deprive their organizations of the benefits available under new federal guidelines for sentencing organizations convicted of wrongdoing. These sentencing guidelines recognize for the first time the organizational and managerial roots of unlawful conduct and base fines partly on the extent to which companies have taken steps to prevent that misconduct.

Prompted by the prospect of leniency, many companies are rushing to implement compliance-based ethics programs. Designed by corporate counsel, the goal of these programs is to prevent, detect, and punish legal violations. But organizational ethics means more than avoiding illegal practice; and providing employees with a rule book will do little to address the problems underlying unlawful conduct. To foster a climate that encourages exemplary behavior, corporations need a comprehensive approach that goes beyond the often punitive legal compliance stance.

An integrity-based approach to ethics management combines a concern for the law with an emphasis on managerial responsibility for ethical behavior. Though integrity strategies may vary in design and scope, all strive to define companies' guiding values, aspirations, and patterns of thought and conduct. When integrated into the day-to-day operations of an organization, such strategies can help prevent damaging ethical lapses while tapping into powerful human impulses for moral thought and action. Then an ethical framework becomes no longer a burdensome constraint within which companies must operate, but the governing ethos of an organization.

How Organizations Shape Individuals' Behavior

The once familiar picture of ethics as individualistic, unchanging, and impervious to organizational influences has not stood up to scrutiny in recent years. Sears Auto Centers' and Beech-Nut Nutrition Corporation's experiences illustrate the role organizations play in shaping individuals' behavior—and how even sound moral fiber can fray when stretched too thin.

In 1992, Sears, Roebuck & Company was inundated with complaints about its automotive service business. Consumers and attorneys general in more than 40 states had accused the company of misleading customers and selling them unnecessary parts and services, from brake jobs to front-end alignments. It would be a mistake, however, to see this situation exclusively in terms of any one individual's moral failings. Nor did management set out to defraud Sears customers. Instead, a number of organizational factors contributed to the problematic sales practices.

In the face of declining revenues, shrinking market share, and an increasingly competitive market for undercar services, Sears management attempted to spur the performance of its auto centers by introducing new goals and incentives for employees. The company increased minimum work quotas and introduced productivity incentives for mechanics. The automotive service advisers were given product-specific sales quotas—sell so many springs, shock absorbers, alignments, or brake jobs per shift—and paid a commission based on sales. According to advisers, failure to meet quotas could lead to a transfer or a reduction in work hours. Some employees spoke of the "pressure, pressure, pressure" to bring in sales.

Under this new set of organizational pressures and incentives, with few options for meeting their sales goals legitimately, some employees' judgment understandably suffered. Management's failure to clarify the line between unnecessary service and legitimate preventive maintenance, coupled with consumer ignorance, left employees to chart their own courses through a vast gray area, subject to a wide range of interpretations. Without active management support for ethical practice and mechanisms to detect and check questionable sales methods and poor work, it is not surprising that some employees may have reacted to contextual forces by resorting to exaggeration, carelessness, or even misrepresentation.

Shortly after the allegations against Sears became public, CEO Edward Brennan acknowledged management's responsibility for putting in place compensation and goal-setting systems that "created an environment in which mistakes did occur." Although the company denied any intent to deceive consumers, senior executives eliminated commissions for service advisers and discontinued sales quotas for specific parts. They also instituted a system of unannounced shopping audits and made plans to expand the internal monitoring of service. In settling the pending lawsuits, Sears offered coupons to customers who had bought certain auto services between 1990 and 1992. The total cost of the settlement, including potential customer refunds, was an estimated $60 million.

Contextual forces can also influence the behavior of top management, as a former CEO of Beech-Nut Nutrition Corporation discovered. In the early 1980s, only two years after joining the company, the CEO found evidence suggesting that the apple juice concentrate, supplied by the company's vendors for use in Beech-Nut's "100% pure" apple juice, contained nothing more than sugar water and chemicals. The CEO could have destroyed the bogus inventory and withdrawn the juice from grocers' shelves, but

he was under extraordinary pressure to turn the ailing company around. Eliminating the inventory would have killed any hope of turning even the meager $700,000 profit promised to Beech-Nut's then parent, Nestlé.

A number of people in the corporation, it turned out, had doubted the purity of the juice for several years before the CEO arrived. But the 25% price advantage offered by the supplier of the bogus concentrate allowed the operations head to meet cost-control goals. Furthermore, the company lacked an effective quality control system, and a conclusive lab test for juice purity did not yet exist. When a member of the research department voiced concerns about the juice to operating management, he was accused of not being a team player and of acting like "Chicken Little." His judgment, his supervisor wrote in an annual performance review, was "colored by naïveté and impractical ideals." No one else seemed to have considered the company's obligations to its customers or to have thought about the potential harm of disclosure. No one considered the fact that the sale of adulterated or misbranded juice is a legal offense, putting the company and its top management at risk of criminal liability.

An FDA investigation taught Beech-Nut the hard way. In 1987, the company pleaded guilty to selling adulterated and misbranded juice. Two years and two criminal trials later, the CEO pleaded guilty to ten counts of mislabeling. The total cost to the company—including fines, legal expenses, and lost sales—was an estimated $25 million.

Acknowledging the importance of organizational context in ethics does not imply forgiving individual wrongdoers.

Such errors of judgment rarely reflect an organizational culture and management philosophy that sets out to harm or deceive. More often, they reveal a culture that is insensitive or indifferent to ethical considerations or one that lacks effective organizational systems. By the same token, exemplary conduct usually reflects an organizational culture and philosophy that is infused with a sense of responsibility.

For example, Johnson & Johnson's handling of the Tylenol crisis is sometimes attributed to the singular personality of then-CEO James Burke. However the decision to do a nationwide recall of Tylenol capsules in order to avoid further loss of life from product tampering was in reality not one decision but thousands of decisions made by individuals at all levels of the organization. The "Tylenol decision," then, is best understood not as an isolated incident, the achievement of a lone individual, but as the reflection of an organization's culture. Without a shared set of values and guiding principles deeply ingrained throughout the organi-

Corporate Fines Under the Federal Sentencing Guidelines

What size fine is a corporation likely to pay if convicted of a crime? It depends on a number of factors, some of which are beyond a CEO's control, such as the existence of a prior record of similar misconduct. But it also depends on more controllable factors. The most important of these are reporting and accepting responsibility for the crime, cooperating with authorities, and having an effective program in place to prevent and detect unlawful behavior.

The following example, based on a case studied by the United States Sentencing Commission, shows how the 1991 Federal Sentencing Guidelines have affected overall fine levels and how managers' actions influence organizational fines.

Acme Corporation was charged and convicted of mail fraud. The company systematically charged customers who damaged rented automobiles more than the actual cost of repairs. Acme also billed some customers for the cost of repairs to vehicles for which they were not responsible. Prior to the criminal adjudication, Acme paid $13.7 million in restitution to the customers who had been overcharged.

Deciding before the enactment of the sentencing guidelines, the judge in the criminal case imposed a fine of $6.85 million, roughly half the pecuniary loss suffered by Acme's customers. Under the sentencing guidelines, however, the results could have been dramatically different. Acme could have been fined anywhere from 5% to 200% the loss suffered by customers, depending on whether or not it had an effective program to prevent and detect violations of law and on whether or not it reported the crime, cooperated with authorities, and accepted responsibility for the unlawful conduct. If a high ranking official at Acme were found to have been involved, the maximum fine could have been as large as $54,800,000 or four times the loss to Acme customers. The following chart shows a possible range of fines for each situation:

What Fine Can Acme Expect?

	Maximum	Minimum
Program, reporting, cooperation, responsibility	$2,740,000	$685,000
Program only	10,960,000	5,480,000
No program, no reporting, no cooperation, no responsibility	27,400,000	13,700,000
No program, no reporting, no cooperation, no responsibility, involvement of high-level personnel	54,800,000	27,400,000

Based on Case No.: 88-266, United States Sentencing Commission, *Supplementary Report on Sentencing Guidelines for Organizations.*

zation, it is doubtful that Johnson & Johnson's response would have been as rapid, cohesive and ethically sound.

Many people resist acknowledging the influence of organizational factors on individual behavior—especially on misconduct—for fear of diluting people's sense of personal moral responsibility. But this fear is based on a false dichotomy between holding individual transgressors accountable and holding "the system" accountable. Acknowledging the importance of organizational context need not imply exculpating individual wrongdoers. To understand all is not to forgive all.

The Limits of a Legal Compliance Program

The consequences of an ethical lapse can be serious and far-reaching. Organizations can quickly become entangled in an all-consuming web of legal proceedings. The risk of litigation and liability has increased in the past decade as lawmakers have legislated new civil and criminal offenses, stepped up penalties, and improved support for law enforcement. Equally—if not more—important is the damage an ethical lapse can do to an organization's reputation and relationships. Both Sears and Beech-Nut, for instance, struggled to regain consumer trust and market share long after legal proceedings had ended.

As more managers have become alerted to the importance of organizational ethics, many have asked their lawyers to develop corporate ethics programs to detect and prevent violations of the law. The 1991 Federal Sentencing Guidelines offer a compelling rationale. Sanctions such as fines and probation for organizations convicted of wrongdoing can vary dramatically depending both on the degree of management cooperation in reporting and investigating corporate misdeeds and on whether or not the company has implemented a legal compliance program. (See the insert "Corporate Fines Under the Federal Sentencing Guidelines.")

Such programs tend to emphasize the prevention of unlawful conduct, primarily by increasing surveillance and control and by imposing penalties for wrongdoers. While plans vary, the basic framework is outlined in the sentencing guidelines. Managers must establish compliance standards and procedures; designate high-level personnel to oversee compliance; avoid delegating discretionary authority to those likely to act unlawfully; effectively communicate the company's standards and procedures through training or publications; take reasonable steps to achieve compliance through audits, monitoring processes, and a system for employees to report criminal misconduct without fear of retribution; consistently enforce standards through appropriate disciplinary measures; respond appropriately when offenses are detected; and, finally, take reasonable steps to prevent the occurrence of similar offenses in the future.

There is no question of the necessity of a sound, well-articulated strategy for legal compliance in an organization. After all, employees can be frustrated and frightened by the complexity of today's legal environment. And even managers who claim to use the law as a guide to ethical behavior often lack more than a rudimentary understanding of complex legal issues.

Managers would be mistaken, however, to regard legal compliance as an adequate means for addressing the full range of ethical issues that arise every day. "If it's legal, it's ethical," is a frequently heard slogan. But conduct that is lawful may be highly problematic from an ethical point of view. Consider the sale in some countries of hazardous products without appropriate warnings or the purchase of goods from suppliers who operate inhumane sweatshops in developing countries. Companies engaged in international business often discover that conduct that infringes on recognized standards of human rights and decency is legally permissible in some jurisdictions.

Legal clearance does not certify the absence of ethical problems in the United States either, as a 1991 case at Salomon Brothers illustrates. Four top-level executives failed to take appropriate action when learning of unlawful activities on the government trading desk. Company lawyers found no law obligating the executives to disclose the improprieties. Nevertheless, the executives' delay in disclosing and failure to reveal their prior knowledge prompted a serious crisis of confidence among employees, creditors, shareholders, and customers. The executives were forced to resign, having lost the moral authority to lead. Their ethical lapse compounded the trading desk's legal offenses, and the company ended up suffering losses—including legal costs, increased funding costs, and lost business—estimated at nearly $1 billion.

A compliance approach to ethics also overemphasizes the threat of detection and punishment in order to channel behavior in lawful directions. The underlying model for this approach is deterrence theory, which envisions people as rational maximizers of self-interest, responsive to the personal costs and benefits of their choices, yet indifferent to the moral legitimacy of those choices. But a recent study reported in *Why People Obey the Law* by Tom R. Tyler shows that obedience to the law is strongly influenced by a belief in its legitimacy and its moral correctness. People generally feel that they have a strong obligation to obey the law. Education about the legal standards and a supportive environment may be all that's required to insure compliance.

Discipline is, of course, a necessary part of any ethical system. Justified penalties for the infringement of legitimate norms are fair and appropriate. Some people do need the threat of sanctions. However, an overemphasis on potential sanctions can be superfluous and even counterproductive. Employees may rebel against programs that stress penalties, particularly if they are designed and imposed without employee involvement or if the standards are vague or unrealistic. Management may talk of mutual trust when unveiling a compliance plan, but employees often receive the message as a warning from on high. Indeed, the more skeptical among them may view compliance programs as nothing more than liability insurance for senior management. This is not an unreasonable conclusion, considering that compliance programs rarely address the root causes of misconduct.

Even in the best cases, legal compliance is unlikely to unleash much moral imagination or commitment. The law does not generally seek to inspire human excellence or dis-

tinction. It is no guide for exemplary behavior—or even good practice. Those managers who define ethics as legal compliance are implicitly endorsing a code of moral mediocrity for their organizations. As Richard Breeden, former chairman of the Securities and Exchange Commission, noted, "It is not an adequate ethical standard to aspire to get through the day without being indicted."

Integrity as a Governing Ethic

A strategy based on integrity holds organizations to a more robust standard. While compliance is rooted in avoiding legal sanctions, organizational integrity is based on the concept of self-governance in accordance with a set of guiding principles. From the perspective of integrity, the task of ethics management is to define and give life to an organization's guiding values, to create an environment that supports ethically sound behavior, and to instill a sense of shared accountability among employees. The need to obey the law is viewed as a positive aspect of organizational life, rather than an unwelcome constraint imposed by external authorities.

Management may talk of mutual trust when unveiling a compliance plan, but employees often see a warning from on high.

An integrity strategy is characterized by a conception of ethics as a driving force of an enterprise. Ethical values shape the search for opportunities, the design of organizational systems, and the decision-making process used by individuals and groups. They provide a common frame of reference and serve as a unifying force across different functions, lines of business, and employee groups. Organizational ethics helps define what a company is and what it stands for.

Many integrity initiatives have structural features common to compliance-based initiatives: a code of conduct, training in relevant areas of law, mechanisms for reporting and investigating potential misconduct, and audits and controls to insure that laws and company standards are being met. In addition, if suitably designed, an integrity-based initiative can establish a foundation for seeking the legal benefits that are available under the sentencing guidelines should criminal wrongdoing occur. (See the insert "The Hallmarks of an Effective Integrity Strategy.")

But an integrity strategy is broader, deeper, and more demanding than a legal compliance initiative. Broader in that it seeks to enable responsible conduct. Deeper in that it cuts to the ethos and operating systems of the organization and its members, their guiding values and patterns of thought and action. And more demanding in that it requires

The Hallmarks of an Effective Integrity Strategy

There is no one right integrity strategy. Factors such as management personality, company history, culture, lines of business, and industry regulations must be taken into account when shaping an appropriate set of values and designing an implementation program. Still, several features are common to efforts that have achieved some success:

• *The guiding values and commitments make sense and are clearly communicated.* They reflect important organizational obligations and widely shared aspirations that appeal to the organization's members. Employees at all levels take them seriously, feel comfortable discussing them, and have a concrete understanding of their practical importance. This does not signal the absence of ambiguity and conflict but a willingness to seek solutions compatible with the framework of values.

• *Company leaders are personally committed, credible, and willing to take action on the values they espouse.* They are not mere mouthpieces. They are willing to scrutinize their own decisions. Consistency on the part of leadership is key. Waffling on values will lead to employee cynicism and a rejection of the program. At the same time, managers must assume responsibility for making tough calls when ethical obligations conflict.

• *The espoused values are integrated into the normal channels of management decision making and are reflected in the organization's critical activities*: the development of plans, the setting of goals, the search for opportunities, the allocation of resources, the gathering and communication of information, the measurement of performance, and the promotion and advancement of personnel.

• *The company's systems and structures support and reinforce its values.* Information systems, for example, are designed to provide timely and accurate information. Reporting relationships are structured to build in checks and balances to promote objective judgment. Performance appraisal is sensitive to means as well as ends.

• *Managers throughout the company have the decision-making skills, knowledge, and competencies needed to make ethically sound decisions on a day-to-day basis.* Ethical thinking and awareness must be part of every managers' mental equipment. Ethics education is usually part of the process.

Success in creating a climate for responsible and ethically sound behavior requires continuing effort and a considerable investment of time and resources. A glossy code of conduct, a high-ranking ethics officer, a training program, an annual ethics audit—these trappings of an ethics program do not necessarily add up to a responsible, law-abiding organization whose espoused values match its actions. A formal ethics program can serve as a catalyst and a support system, but organizational integrity depends on the integration of the company's values into its driving systems.

---

an active effort to define the responsibilities and aspirations that constitute an organization's ethical compass. Above all, organizational ethics is seen as the work of management. Corporate counsel may play a role in the design and implementation of integrity strategies, but managers at all levels and across all functions are involved in the process. (See the chart, "Strategies for Ethics Management.")

During the past decade, a number of companies have undertaken integrity initiatives. They vary according to the ethical values focused on and the implementation approaches used. Some companies focus on the core values of integrity that reflect basic social obligations, such as respect for the rights of others, honesty, fair dealing, and obedience to the law. Other companies emphasize aspirations—values that are ethically desirable but not necessarily morally obligatory—such as good service to customers, a commitment to diversity, and involvement in the community.

When it comes to implementation, some companies begin with behavior. Following Aristotle's view that one becomes courageous by acting as a courageous person, such companies develop codes of conduct specifying appropriate behavior, along with a system of incentives, audits, and controls. Other companies focus less on specific actions and more on developing attitudes, decision-making processes, and ways of thinking that reflect their values. The assumption is that personal commitment and appropriate decision processes will lead to right action.

Martin Marietta, NovaCare, and Wetherill Associates have implemented and lived with quite different integrity strategies. In each case, management has found that the ini-

tiative has made important and often unexpected contributions to competitiveness, work environment, and key relationships on which the company depends.

Martin Marietta: Emphasizing Core Values

Martin Marietta Corporation, the U.S. aerospace and defense contractor, opted for an integrity-based ethics program in 1985. At the time, the defense industry was under attack for fraud and mismanagement, and Martin Marietta was under investigation for improper travel billings. Managers knew they needed a better form of self-governance but were skeptical that an ethics program could influence behavior. "Back then people asked, 'Do you really need an ethics program to be ethical?'" recalls current President Thomas Young. "Ethics was something personal. Either you had it, or you didn't."

The corporate general counsel played a pivotal role in promoting the program, and legal compliance was a critical objective. But it was conceived of and implemented from the start as a companywide management initiative aimed at creating and maintaining a "do-it-right" climate. In its original conception, the program emphasized core values, such as honesty and fair play. Over time, it expanded to encompass quality and environmental responsibility as well.

Today the initiative consists of a code of conduct, an ethics training program, and procedures for reporting and investigating ethical concerns within the company. It also includes a system for disclosing violations of federal pro-

Strategies for Ethics Management

Characteristics of Compliance Strategy

Ethos	conformity with externally imposed standards
Objective	prevent criminal misconduct
Leadership	lawyer driven
Methods	education, reduced discretion, auditing and controls, penalties
Behavioral Assumptions	autonomous beings guided by material self-interest

Characteristics of Integrity Strategy

Ethos	self-governance according to chosen standards
Objective	enable responsible conduct
Leadership	management driven with aid of lawyers, HR, others
Methods	education, leadership, accountability, organizational systems and decision processes, auditing and controls, penalties
Behavioral Assumptions	social beings guided by material self-interest, values, ideals, peers

Implementation of Compliance Strategy

Standards	criminal and regulatory law
Staffing	lawyers
Activities	develop compliance standards train and communicate handle reports of misconduct conduct investigations oversee compliance audits enforce standards
Education	compliance standards and system

Implementation of Integrity Strategy

Standards	company values and aspirations social obligations, including law
Staffing	executives and managers with lawyers, others
Activities	lead development of company values and standards train and communicate integrate into company systems provide guidance and consultation assess values performance identify and resolve problems oversee compliance activities
Education	decision making and values compliance standards and system

curement law to the government. A corporate ethics office manages the program, and ethics representatives are stationed at major facilities. An ethics steering committee, made up of Martin Marietta's president, senior executives, and two rotating members selected from field operations, oversees the ethics office. The audit and ethics committee of the board of directors oversees the steering committee.

The ethics office is responsible for responding to questions and concerns from the company's employees. Its network of representatives serves as a sounding board, a source of guidance, and a channel for raising a range of issues, from allegations of wrongdoing to complaints about poor management, unfair supervision, and company poli-

cies and practices. Martin Marietta's ethics network, which accepts anonymous complaints, logged over 9,000 calls in 1991, when the company had about 60,000 employees. In 1992, it investigated 684 cases. The ethics office also works closely with the human resources, legal, audit, communications, and security functions to respond to employee concerns.

Shortly after establishing the program, the company began its first round of ethics training for the entire workforce, starting with the CEO and senior executives. Now in its third round, training for senior executives focuses on decision making, the challenges of balancing multiple responsibilities, and compliance with laws and regulations critical to the company. The incentive compensation plan for executives makes responsibility for promoting ethical conduct an explicit requirement for reward eligibility and requires that business and personal goals be achieved in accordance with the company's policy on ethics. Ethical conduct and support for the ethics program are also criteria in regular performance reviews.

Today top-level managers say the ethics program has helped the company avoid serious problems and become more responsive to its more than 90,000 employees. The ethics network, which tracks the number and types of cases and complaints, has served as an early warning system for poor management, quality and safety defects, racial and gender discrimination, environmental concerns, inaccurate and false records, and personnel grievances regarding salaries, promotions, and layoffs. By providing an alternative channel for raising such concerns, Martin Marietta is able to take corrective action more quickly and with a lot less pain. In many cases, potentially embarrassing problems have been identified and dealt with before becoming a management crisis, a lawsuit, or a criminal investigation. Among employees who brought complaints in 1993, 75% were satisfied with the results.

Company executives are also convinced that the program has helped reduce the incidence of misconduct. When allegations of misconduct do surface, the company says it deals with them more openly. On several occasions, for instance, Martin Marietta has voluntarily disclosed and made restitution to the government for misconduct involving potential violations of federal procurement laws. In addition, when an employee alleged that the company had retaliated against him for voicing safety concerns about his plant on CBS news, top management commissioned an investigation by an outside law firm. Although failing to support the allegations, the investigation found that employees at the plant feared retaliation when raising health, safety, or environmental complaints. The company redoubled its efforts to identify and discipline those employees taking retaliatory action and stressed the desirability of an open work environment in its ethics training and company communications.

Although the ethics program helps Martin Marietta avoid certain types of litigation, it has occasionally led to other kinds of legal action. In a few cases, employees dismissed for violating the code of ethics sued Martin Marietta, arguing that the company had violated its own code by imposing unfair and excessive discipline.

Still, the company believes that its attention to ethics has been worth it. The ethics program has led to better relationships with the government, as well as to new business opportunities. Along with prices and technology, Martin Marietta's record of integrity, quality, and reliability of estimates plays a role in the awarding of defense contracts, which account for some 75% of the company's revenues. Executives believe that the reputation they've earned through their ethics program has helped them build trust with government auditors, as well. By opening up commu-

nications, the company has reduced the time spent on redundant audits.

The program has also helped change employees' perceptions and priorities. Some managers compare their new ways of thinking about ethics to the way they understand quality. They consider more carefully how situations will be perceived by others, the possible long-term consequences of short-term thinking, and the need for continuous improvement. CEO Norman Augustine notes, "Ten years ago, people would have said that there were no ethical issues in business. Today employees think their number-one objective is to be thought of as decent people doing quality work."

NovaCare: Building Shared Aspirations

NovaCare Inc., one of the largest providers of rehabilitation services to nursing homes and hospitals in the United States, has oriented its ethics effort toward building a common core of shared aspirations. But in 1988, when the company was called InSpeech, the only sentiment shared was mutual mistrust.

Senior executives built the company from a series of aggressive acquisitions over a brief period of time to take advantage of the expanding market for therapeutic services. However, in 1988, the viability of the company was in question. Turnover among its frontline employees—the clinicians and therapists who care for patients in nursing homes and hospitals—escalated to 57% per year. The company's inability to retain therapists caused customers to defect and the stock price to languish in an extended slump.

At NovaCare, executives defined organizational values and introduced structural changes to support those values.

After months of soul-searching, InSpeech executives realized that the turnover rate was a symptom of a more basic problem: the lack of a common set of values and aspirations. There was, as one executive put it, a "huge disconnect" between the values of the therapists and clinicians and those of the managers who ran the company. The therapists and clinicians evaluated the company's success in terms of its delivery of high-quality health care. InSpeech management, led by executives with financial services and venture capital backgrounds, measured the company's worth exclusively in terms of financial success. Management's single-minded emphasis on increasing hours of reimbursable care turned clinicians off. They took management's performance orientation for indifference to patient care and left the company in droves.

CEO John Foster recognized the need for a common frame of reference and a common language to unify the diverse groups. So he brought in consultants to conduct interviews and focus groups with the company's health care professionals, managers, and customers. Based on the results, an employee task force drafted a proposed vision statement for the company, and another 250 employees suggested revisions. Then Foster and several senior managers developed a succinct statement of the company's guiding purpose and fundamental beliefs that could be used as a framework for making decisions and setting goals, policies, and practices.

Unlike a code of conduct, which articulates specific behavioral standards, the statement of vision, purposes, and beliefs lays out in very simple terms the company's central purpose and core values. The purpose—meeting the rehabilitation needs of patients through clinical leadership—is supported by four key beliefs: respect for the individual, service to the customer, pursuit of excellence, and commitment to personal integrity. Each value is discussed with examples of how it is manifested in the day-to-day activities and policies of the company, such as how to measure the quality of care.

To support the newly defined values, the company changed its name to NovaCare and introduced a number of structural and operational changes. Field managers and clinicians were given greater decision-making authority; clinicians were provided with additional resources to assist in the delivery of effective therapy; and a new management structure integrated the various therapies offered by the company. The hiring of new corporate personnel with health care backgrounds reinforced the company's new clinical focus.

The introduction of the vision, purpose, and beliefs met with varied reactions from employees, ranging from cool skepticism to open enthusiasm. One employee remembered thinking the talk about values "much ado about nothing." Another recalled, "It was really wonderful. It gave us a goal that everyone aspired to, no matter what their place in the company." At first, some were baffled about how the vision, purpose, and beliefs were to be used. But, over time, managers became more adept at explaining and using them as a guide. When a customer tried to hire away a valued employee, for example, managers considered raiding the customer's company for employees. After reviewing the beliefs, the managers abandoned the idea.

NovaCare managers acknowledge and company surveys indicate that there is plenty of room for improvement. While the values are used as a firm reference point for decision making and evaluation in some areas of the company, they are still viewed with reservation in others. Some managers do not "walk the talk," employees complain. And recently acquired companies have yet to be fully integrated into the program. Nevertheless, many NovaCare employees say the values initiative played a critical role in the company's 1990 turnaround.

The values reorientation also helped the company deal with its most serious problem: turnover among health care providers. In 1990, the turnover rate stood at 32%, still above target but a significant improvement over the 1988 rate of 57%. By 1993, turnover had dropped to 27%. Moreover, recruiting new clinicians became easier. Barely able to hire 25 new clinicians each month in 1988, the company added 776 in 1990 and 2,546 in 1993. Indeed, one employee who left during the 1988 turmoil said that her decision to return in 1990 hinged on the company's adoption of the vision, purpose, and beliefs.

Wetherill Associates: Defining Right Action

Wetherill Associates, Inc.—a small, privately held supplier of electrical parts to the automotive market—has neither a conventional code of conduct nor a statement of values. Instead, WAI has a *Quality Assurance Manual*—a combination of philosophy text, conduct guide, technical manual, and company profile—that describes the company's commitment to honesty and its guiding principle of right action.

Creating an organization that encourages exemplary conduct may be the best way to prevent damaging misconduct.

WAI doesn't have a corporate ethics officer who reports to top management, because at WAI, the company's corporate ethics officer *is* top management. Marie Bothe, WAI's chief executive officer, sees her main function as keeping the 350-employee company on the path of right action and looking for opportunities to help the community. She delegates the "technical" aspects of the business—marketing, finance, personnel, operations—to other members of the organization.

Right action, the basis for all of WAI's decisions, is a well-developed approach that challenges most conventional management thinking. The company explicitly rejects the usual conceptual boundaries that separate morality and self-interest. Instead, they define right behavior as logically, expediently, and morally right. Managers teach employees to look at the needs of the customers, suppliers, and the community—in addition to those of the company and its employees—when making decisions.

WAI also has a unique approach to competition. One employee explains, "We are not 'in competition' with anybody. We just do what we have to do to serve the customer." Indeed, when occasionally unable to fill orders, WAI salespeople refer customers to competitors. Artificial incentives, such as sales contests, are never used to spur individual performance. Nor are sales results used in determining compensation. Instead, the focus is on teamwork and customer service. Managers tell all new recruits that absolute honesty, mutual courtesy, and respect are standard operating procedure.

Newcomers generally react positively to company philosophy, but not all are prepared for such a radical departure from the practices they have known elsewhere. Recalling her initial interview, one recruit described her response to being told that lying was not allowed, "What do you mean? No lying? I'm a buyer. I lie for a living!" Today she is persuaded that the policy makes sound business sense. WAI is known for informing suppliers of overshipments as well as undershipments and for scrupulous honesty in the sale of parts, even when deception cannot be readily detected.

Since its entry into the distribution business 13 years ago, WAI has seen its revenues climb steadily from just under $1 million to nearly $98 million in 1993, and this is an industry with little growth. Once seen as an upstart beset by naysayers and industry skeptics, WAI is now credited with entering and professionalizing an industry in which kickbacks, bribes, and "gratuities" were commonplace. Employees—equal numbers of men and women ranging in age from 17 to 92—praise the work environment as both productive and supportive.

WAI's approach could be difficult to introduce in a larger, more traditional organization. WAI is a small company founded by 34 people who shared a belief in right action; its ethical values were naturally built into the organization from the start. Those values are so deeply ingrained in the company's culture and operating systems that they have been largely self-sustaining. Still, the company has developed its own training program and takes special care to hire people willing to support right action. Ethics and job skills are considered equally important in determining an individual's competence and suitability for employment. For WAI, the challenge will be to sustain its vision as the company grows and taps into markets overseas.

At WAI, as at Martin Marietta and NovaCare, a management-led commitment to ethical values has contributed to competitiveness, positive workforce morale, as well as solid sustainable relationships with the company's key constituencies. In the end, creating a climate that encourages exemplary conduct may be the best way to discourage damaging misconduct. Only in such an environment do rogues really act alone.

Lynn Sharp Paine is associate professor at the Harvard Business School, specializing in management ethics. Her current research focuses on leadership and organizational integrity in a global environment.

Reprinted with permission from *Harvard Business Review*, March/April 1994, pp. 106–117. © 1994 by the President and Fellows of Harvard College. All rights reserved.

an ethical dilemma

HOW TO BUILD INTEGRITY INTO YOUR SALES ENVIRONMENT

Theodore B. Kinni

Contrary to the stereotypical view, sales-people are not predisposed to face any fewer, or any more, ethical dilemmas than anyone else. But that doesn't mean that sales organizations can't become ethical—and legal—nightmares. Just ask Lake Forest, Illinois-based TAP Pharmaceutical Products Inc.

According to a story in *Business Week*, (June 24, 2002—"A Whistle-Blower Rocks an Industry" by Charles Haddad), in 1995, when TAP hired Douglas Durand as vice president of sales, the company owned the best-selling prostate cancer drug, Lupron, which was generating $800 million in annual revenues. The only problem, as Durand quickly discovered, was that TAP was building and maintaining Lupron's market share illegally.

Durand found that TAP's sales force was busy sowing a minefield of explosive ethical and legal problems. With management's knowledge and approval, the company's salespeople were offering doctors a 2 percent kickback, in the guise of an administrative fee, to prescribe Lupron. They were also distributing undocumented samples of the drug and encouraging doctors to sell them—in addition to offering every one of the nation's urologists a game show's wealth of televisions, vacations and high-tech gadgets in return for treating their patients with Lupron.

The new sales exec tried to clean up the mess, but found himself ignored and shut out in TAP's numbers-driven business culture. Frustrated, Durand began documenting the abuses and, within a year, brought suit under the federal whistle-blower law. In October 2001, TAP paid an $875 mil-

lion fine to the government. Durand, who had left the company in early 1996, received $77 million for his evidence and testimony in the successful prosecution.

Admittedly, most sales organizations are not dealing with problems as extreme as TAP's—if you are, go straight to legal counsel. But every day, salespeople and their managers are faced with a variety of ethical dilemmas that have the potential to negatively impact their lives and their companies. The key question: How do you equip your sales force to deal with ethical dilemmas?

ethics flow downhill

A formal code of sales ethics is probably not the right place to start. "You can't just slap an ethics code on a sales force like a barnacle on the side of a whale," says Marjorie Kelly, publisher of *Business Ethics* and author of *The Divine Right of Capital: Dethroning the Corporate Aristocracy* (Berrett-Koehler Pub., 2001).

Instead, sales ethics should be an extension of the organization's ethics, which in turn are an extension of organizational values. At privately held Seventh Generation Inc., the nation's leading brand of non-toxic, environmentally safe household products, there is no code dedicated to sales ethics. "We don't look at sales ethics differently than we look at ethics in general," explains Jeffrey Hollender, president of the Burlington, Vermont-based company. "Sales ethics emanate from organizational values. And there is a lot of work that we do in developing organizational values that obviously then impacts everything we do. Quite honestly, we have never

found it necessary to define sales ethics any differently than we look at our general ethics."

San Francisco, California-based Charles Schwab & Company Inc., a company noted for having avoided the ethical melt-down among the stock brokerages, is another firm that has not found the need for a formal statement of sales ethics. "It's a values-driven company," says Parke Boney-steele, senior vice president of sales and service effectiveness. "So, our values are to be fair, empathetic and responsive in serving clients; to respect and reinforce fellow employees and respect the value of teamwork; to strive relentlessly to innovate in how we provide value; and then, to always earn and be worthy of our clients' trust. And that is what we are all about."

The fact that sales ethics do not require a dedicated code is not, however, to be construed as a free pass to ignore them. At both Schwab and Seventh Generation, sales ethics are always on the radar. Even when strong organizational values are in place, the application of broad-based ethics to the sales process remains a critical issue.

creating ethical specificity

"Salespeople need special training that says, 'Here are some boundaries,'" says Jeff Salters, programs director of Washington, D.C.-based Ethics Resource Center—"some things that you can and cannot do that will allow you to adhere to the code of ethics and still be an effective salesperson."

A PRIMER FOR HANDLING ETHICAL DILEMMAS

At one time or another, virtually every sales professional will face an ethical dilemma. SP asked ethics consultant and speaker Frank Bucaro how salespeople should deal with customers or employers who ask them to do something they consider unethical.

First, understand that unethical behavior is driven by emotions, such as greed, stress and fear. "You cannot deal with ethics on an emotional level," says Bucaro. "When emotions take control, ethics take a hit. So I encourage people when confronted with an unethical situation to take a break, step back."

Next, rationally analyze the situation. "There is a four-step process for considering an ethical decision. It takes some reflection," says Bucaro. "Number 1, you need to identify the action or behavior that is causing the problem. Number 2, what are the circumstances in which this is happening? By that I mean, what do we know about the situation; what you don't know can lead you to the wrong decision. Number 3, what are the criteria by which you are making this decision? Is it Sarbanes-Oxley? Is it the law? Is it the code of ethics? Is it because you think it is right or wrong? Identify the criteria. Number 4 is always, always, get communal wisdom. Find someone who is in your corner and bounce this off that person. We

sometimes get too close to a situation and don't always see what we need to see."

Finally, act. "Once you know what is acceptable and what is not acceptable, what is negotiable and what is not; then that is the line in the sand," says Bucaro of customer-initiated dilemmas. "You say, 'I really can't do that because it would jeopardize my credibility, our ethics, and the way this company is set up. I hope you can appreciate that, but this is why we can't do it.'"

And if your employer is the initiator? "Take the high road," says Bucaro. "That might mean saying, 'I am not quite sure I understand all of the reasons why you are asking me to do this, but let me share with you why I am concerned. And I would like your wisdom here in helping me understand why you are asking me to do this.'"

What if the boss says, just do it? "If they ask you to do that once and you do it, do you think they'll ask you to do it again? Sure," says Bucaro. "There is what I call the PTP Factor, that is the 'price to pay.' If the price is too high, you have to refuse. That's where the rubber hits the road. Either you believe in those values or you don't. Because if you make one exception, you will have to make many more."

> "Salespeople need special training that says, 'Here are some boundaries,' some things that you can and cannot do that will allow you to adhere to the code of ethics and still be...effective."

Salespeople need dedicated attention when it comes to ethics, not because they are less ethical than other employees, but because they face greater ethical exposures than most other employees. Patrick Murphy, professor at Notre Dame's Mendoza College of Business and director of the Institute for Ethical Business Worldwide, says, "One thing that makes selling ethics a bit different than other organizational ethics is that most salespeople are on the road. So, when they get hit with an ethical dilemma, often they have to deal with it on their own as opposed to in a meeting or checking with a boss down the hall. Organizations need to be sensitive to the fact that salespeople are often on their own and need to have a support structure."

The ethical support you create for your sales force should address two categories of ethical issues. There are issues that are generic to the sales discipline—that arise from the act of selling itself, such as overpromising—and those that are specific to your company and industry, such as the FDA's regulations for pharmaceuticals.

First and foremost, of course, are the legal issues, which Murphy identifies in the forthcoming textbook *Ethical Marketing* (Prentice Hall, August 2004), such as federal regula-

tions and applicable state and local regulations, including the Uniform Commercial Code, cooling-off laws, and Green River ordinances. Aside from notable exceptions such as the Lupron debacle, most salespeople don't stray into this territory and most companies are active about ensuring that they never do.

Less well covered, however, is ethics support that addresses what Murphy calls, "the gray areas of selling." These represent issues that, while not necessarily illegal, can cause great damage to sales careers and companies. They are:

1. The use of company assets, including abuses of equipment such as cars and computers, and expense reports;

2. Customer relationships, which includes such abuses as overstocking, overselling, overpromising, overtelling, and underinforming;

3. Competitor relationships, including disparagement, tampering and spying;

4. Relationships with peers and supervisors, including such abuses as territory poaching and false reporting;

5. Conflicts of interest, including improper disclosure;

6. Gifts and entertainment in excess of corporate and customer policies; and

7. Bribery and facilitation, specifically in countries in which they are accepted practices and not illegal.

"If companies have a formal policy regarding gray areas, then the salesperson can tell the customer that they are not allowed to offer tickets to more than one game once a season or once a month or things of that nature," says Murphy. "That

is where I think specificity, if you will, helps the salespeople when they get put in a tough spot."

translating ethics into reality

Ensuring the linkage between sales ethics and organizational values and creating policies that specify behavior is all well and good, but doesn't guarantee ethical compliance. After all, Enron had a value statement and a 65-page *Code of Ethics*, a copy of which now resides in the Smithsonian. So, how do you ensure that your sales force lives up to the highest ethical standards?

First, build ethics into your hiring process. "Alignment from a values perspective is about 50 percent of the equation on a new hire," says Hollender of Seventh Generation's employment process. "We would not want to hire someone who is 100 percent focused on the result and 0 percent focused on the process. What you have to find is people who are very committed to the result, but understand that the process through which they achieve that result is of equal importance. It's a very different mind-set."

"Forward-thinking companies are even going as far as doing initial testing to check for ethical values. They test salespeople prior to hire," says Anthony Zuanich, a veteran sales manager who worked at IBM and ADP before becoming senior vice president of sales at the HR Outsourcing division of Aon Consulting Worldwide, an arm of Chicago, Illinois-based AON Corp.

Second, provide new hires with written policies and ask them to sign them to indicate both comprehension and compliance. "Salespeople should get new-hire packets that document ethics issues and policies, including the ethical dilemmas that are unique to that company," explains Zuanich. "New salespeople should be educated and sign off that they agree to the policies, and will not harm the company's reputation as well as their own by not following these ethical guidelines."

Third, build ethics and values into the training curriculum. "Then its about reinforcement," says Schwab's Boneysteele. "We have it in our new-hire training, in our manager training, in our sales training, we always have conversations and discussions about values...we talk about it as vision and values as opposed to ethics."

Schwab's training is designed to help employees distinguish between appropriate and inappropriate behavior. "We have a segment where we ask people to come up with things that would be contra to the values and discuss them as part of our new-hire training," says Boneysteele.

The reinforcement of ethics extends into the training provided by sales managers. "As we ask for results, as every good sales manager should," explains Tony Zuanich, "we need to be aware of where there are areas where the salesperson could cross the line. You have to document those areas as a manager and point them out to the salespeople."

build ethics into the process

There are two adages that companies that are serious about creating a highly ethical sales forces would do well to keep in mind. "You get what you pay for" and "What gets measured, gets done."

"Sales ethics need to be designed into the process," says Marjorie Kelly. "This arises out of a recognition that incentive shapes behavior much more than codes. So companies need to look at how they have structured incentives and what kind of behavior that drives. Is your commission structure sending an opposite message from your ethics code?"

Seventh Generation, for instance, created an employee review system that uses 360-degree appraisals to evaluate behavior relative to the corporate values (community, growth, leadership, responsibility, service and trust) as well as performance. "Half of that evaluation is about their traditional business responsibilities, and half of it is about their behavior relative to the values of the

company," says Hollender. "Salespeople are evaluated not just on meeting sales objectives and managing expenses, but also in terms of the progress they make in growing from a personal perspective in ways that are in alignment with our values. And they cannot earn 100 percent of their bonus, even if they necessarily double the sales in their budget, if they aren't also making progress in this personal-development area, as well as some kind of community involvement and community service."

Ensuring the linkage between sales ethics and organizational values and creating policies that specify behavior is all well and good, but doesn't guarantee ethical compliance.

At Schwab, some of the gray areas of selling, such as conflicts of interest, have been effectively eliminated by the structure of the company and its compensation programs. "We've kept investment banking conflicts out of our business model," says Boneysteele. "Our customer-facing people are not compensated on whether or not a client picks a particular stock. We don't pay our front-line reps based on revenue that is generated by trading activity. So there are an awful lot of what might be industry gray zones that we just don't get into."

Here are a few more ideas for building sales ethics into the structure and process of sales:

1. Deliver ethics support to the field. "With technology, in particular cell phones and even instantaneous computer communication, your salespeople could literally step out of a meeting and call the office and get support and information," says Notre Dame's Murphy. "I think that companies need to use technology for their ethical benefit and encourage their salespeople to do the same.

2. Create a process for considering ethical issues. "Is there a hotline that I can call if I see something that is unethical or illegal happening?" asks ethics consultant Frank Bucaro. "Is there a number that I can call anonymously and report it?"

3. Use ethics violations as teaching tools. "In your weekly sales meeting," says Tony Zuanich, "take those dilemmas and use them to educate people. Explain what happened and discuss it."

4. Make ethics and values part of your sales presentation. "Even though it often takes time directly away from the sales

presentation," says Seventh Generation's Hollender, "we try to make the presentation of our values and operating principles part of what is presented to our customers, so that they understand our commitment, understand what to expect from us."

5. Make your policies public. Schwab maintains a "business practices disclosure" section on its public Website that explains exactly how representatives in 10 sales-related functions are compensated.

sales ethics compliance

Ultimately, the ethical level of a sales force is dependent on management's willingness to comply. If compliance and enforcement are ignored and/or applied inconsistently, salespeople will quickly learn that ethical behavior is not a priority.

The first issue in enforcement is consistency in compliance. "Very often organizations put policies and procedures into place that they'd like all of their employees to adhere to. However, many of them make exceptions when it comes to the sales force because the sales force is typically what helps to drive their profits," says Jeff Salters of the Ethics Resource Center. "The way we approach ethics here is, we like to talk about a consistency of message, a congruency of policies and procedures. So you can't state these principles and say, 'We want to adhere to the law, we want to adhere to our code,' and then make exceptions. Actual behavior trumps your stated policy."

Salters points to the pharmaceutical industry as an example: "Doctors might prescribe drugs that were approved for one purpose for other purposes. There are some firms that would discourage a doctor from doing that, even though it might limit the amount of sales they could make of that drug. There are regulations that say you should not sell a drug other than for its intended or approved purpose. When those lines become blurred, some firms try to adhere to a higher standard; some other firms wouldn't care."

The second issue is consistency in enforcement. "I think that in the selling function there is always that inclination or potential proclivity of the people in the higher sales management or up the marketing ladder to look the other way and not ask too many questions about how some salespeople get the sales they do," says Patrick Murphy. "And I think that in this day and age that really comes back to haunt people."

The only ethical answer is what Tony Zuanich calls a "no-excuse response." He says, "The severity of the ethics violation depends on what the issue was, but I think you always need to send a clear message with violators. That sends the message to the rest of the sales force that that kind of behavior will not be tolerated. And in the end, that kind of management will help the results of companies.

"I have and I will terminate employment," says Zuanich. "I will give you a very real one—a difficult case from a past employer. We had a person who was a top producer who gained a reputation for just having an incredible work ethic. We're talking about a salesperson who had a big ego. That person felt like a top gun—indispensable to the company—and the rules didn't necessarily apply. There was a policy about poaching in other salespeople's territories. The person was caught once and given a warning. It happened again and we sent a message. It's a tough thing to do for a results-oriented company, but we had to terminate our very top producer."

From *Selling Power,* October 2004, pp. 109-112. Copyright © 2004 by Selling Power. Reprinted by permission.

The Right Balance

The growing mature market is an attractive target for unscrupulous salespeople, who take advantage of seniors' supposed vulnerability in hopes of closing a deal.

But managers, beware: If your reps are selling unethically, the cost will, ultimately, far outweigh the benefit

Jennifer Gilbert

In December 2002, the Securities Division of the Office of Secretary of the Commonwealth of Massachusetts issued a cease-and-desist order against a company called Broker's Choice of America Inc. (BCA) and its founder, Tyrone M. Clark. The order prevented BCA and another firm founded by Clark, Senior Benefit Centers Network (SBCN), from committing any future violations of the state's Securities Act.

Clark's crime? Running "Senior Financial Survivor Workshops," allegedly designed to coerce seniors into selling their securities holdings and buying annuities, which are complex and controversial financial products, solely from his companies. Turns out Clark and the companies were not registered as investment advisers in Massachusetts. Yet according to an administrative complaint filed to the Securities Division on September 25, 2002—two months after *The Wall Street Journal* ran a story about Clark's so-called Annuity University, a two-day training school in which associates of his companies were taught how to sell annuities to senior citizens—associates of Clark's companies reportedly "used such specious titles as 'Certified Elder Planning Specialists' ('CEPS') to mislead the elderly and disguise the fact that the associates were insurance salesmen."

Meanwhile, Annuity University's teachings were unorthodox, to say the least. Among the lessons? That the optimal way to target seniors is to "assume you are selling to a 12-year-old who is blind yet smart," according to the complaint. "A major tenet in the training manual is that Respondents' associates must 'probe and disturb' the elderly client," the complaint further states. "Associates learn how to alarm seminar attendees by preying on their emotions."

A press release summarizing the December settlement stated that in consenting to the Securities Division's order, "Clark and the two companies neither admitted nor denied the findings of fact, conclusions of law, or allegations made in the complaint issued."

Although the Division of Securities, in Colorado, where BCA is based, does not license him, Clark does hold an insurance license with the Colorado Division of Insurance and is still operating BCA in that state, according to a Colorado Securities Division spokesperson. (Clark did not return phone calls to comment on the case.) But the case, while egregious, is not the only alleged incidence of such behavior. Seniors, with their increased life expectancy, are becoming a highly sought-after market. And with that allure has come a rash of companies and their salespeople tempted to target them with ethically questionable, condescending selling practices.

Older people have a significant amount of discretionary income. In fact, Americans age 50 and older hold a household net worth of $19 trillion, nearly twice the U.S. average, according to a survey from Senior Publishers Media Group (SPMG), a network of publications for seniors based in San Diego. Daryl Koehn, executive director of the Center for Business Ethics and the Cullen Chair of Business Ethics at the University of St. Thomas, in Houston, contends that individuals between ages 75 and 80 "are the wealthiest generation that the United States has ever seen." Most of them own their own homes and have paid off their mortgages, says Len Hansen, an author and expert on mature adults, based in Bellingham, Washington.

And their numbers are significant: Americans age 50 and older total 76.8 million, or one third of the entire U.S. population, according to the SPMG survey. And the size of the 65-plus group is growing: From 1990 to 2000, that segment grew 12 percent, from 31.2 million to 35 million, according to the U.S. Census Bureau. The American Association of Retired Persons (AARP) predicts that age group will grow at a rate of 1.8 percent through 2012. Further, the Census Bureau reports that the elderly population will increase dramatically in 2011, when the first baby boomers reach age 65. These facts come together to make them an attractive target for certain companies.

Some experts and salespeople argue that senior citizens are actually the most savvy consumers, having "learned by experience and from consumer news reporters to be more astute buyers," says Jacques Werth, president of High Probability Selling, a sales training firm based in Media, Pennsylvania.

But others believe mature individuals share common attributes that can make them particularly vulnerable to salespeople who choose, for the sake of closing a deal or earning a large commission, to take advantage of them. "They are easy to scam because they do have a lot of wealth and they have a number of traits that make them susceptible," Koehn says. "They get confused, and therefore become subject to unscrupulous salespeople who don't put in simple terms what the real products or features are."

In addition, many elderly no longer live near their children, and they may hunger for social interaction. "For many, going in and talking to a bank teller is the highlight of their day," Koehn says. They also have time to listen to pitches, making them particularly vulnerable to door-to-door salespeople, direct marketers, and telemarketers.

In many cases, the elderly also become too embarrassed to tell their children that they've been the victims of unethical selling practices. "They're not just easy targets," Koehn says. "They are easy to hit repeatedly because they don't talk to others about what's going on."

FRONT-PAGE NEWS

Besides the Clark case, other documented cases of similar targeting and ethically questionable selling practices abound. Last July, USA Today's **story, "AmSouth's Sales Tactics Draw Fire in Mississippi," recounted the first-ever joint investigation by state, federal, and industry regulators** of AmSouth Investment Services, based in Starkville, Mississippi, the brokerage division of AmSouth Bank. The investigation led to the subsequent departure of one of its top salespeople, Jim Benson Moorehead. Mississippi authorities accused Moorehead of encouraging elderly clients to invest in inappropriate products, such as variable annuities. In January 2003, Mississippi Secretary of State Eric Clark issued a notice of intent to revoke Moorehead's license to work as a securities broker in the state. According to a press release, "A routine examination by Clark's office in the summer of 2001 found that in a fifteen-month period, Moorehead generated approximately $1 million in commissions from selling variable annuities. This is an investment unsuitable for many investors, due to high risk and substantial charges for early withdrawal. Moorehead resigned from AmSouth in April 2001." The notice accused Moorehead of misrepresenting "variable annuity and mutual fund products during sales presentations by omitting important information about the investment or by making misleading, deceptive, and untrue statements to his customers."

A year later, in March 2004, Eric Clark and the Alabama Securities Commission assessed $225,000 in fines and penalties against AmSouth Investment Services for "failure to adequately protect investors in two states," according to a press release issued by the Mississippi Secretary of State's Office.

The case against Moorehead is currently in civil litigation, but AmSouth spokesperson Rick Swagler says: "We discovered [Moorehead's] wrongdoing and took prompt action to correct it in May 2001.... Over the past three years we've reviewed our processes and invested in technology and training to ensure we have the appropriate controls in place to ensure the securities we sell are suitable for the customer."

Moorehead, meanwhile, declined to comment on the case because of pending litigation.

Annuity sales to the senior investor have come under fire in recent years because many experts contend they are the wrong investment product for that market. "They pay extremely high commission to the broker, and the sale generally occurs because the client doesn't understand what the product is," says Edward A. H. Siedle, president of Benchmark Financial Services Inc., based in Ocean Ridge, Florida, a company that investigates money-management wrongdoing. "I had a seventy-six-year-old nanny taking care of my daughter," Siedle says. "She had purchased a variable annuity. Under the terms of the annuity, she couldn't take any money out for eight or ten years. I called her broker and said the woman will be dead before she can touch it."

Another case of alleged unethical selling practices involved The Kirby Company, part of a shrinking number of companies that still sell their products exclusively through independent distributors who go door-to-door. The Cleveland-based maker of high-end vacuums is a subsidiary of Scott Fetzer Company, which is a subsidiary of Warren Buffett's Berkshire Hathaway. Some of Kirby's independent distributors have been accused of unethical sales practices in the past, to the point that they were the target of a *Primetime Live* investigation in April 2002, after the ABC news show reported it found more than 1,000 complaints lodged against Kirby for questionable selling practices. According to consumer watchdog site ConsumerAffairs.com, in June, the Arizona Attorney General's office filed suit against two independent Kirby distributors who were accused of trying to gain access to consumers' homes by falsely telling prospects they were entered into a drawing to win $1,000 in groceries.

The salespeople were also accused of knowingly selling vacuums to elderly consumers who would not be able to use them because they were too large, and falsely telling people age 65 and older that they had three days to cancel the sale—when in fact, Kirby has a "Golden Age" policy whereby seniors can cancel within a year of purchase.

Separately, in October 2002, the Florida Agriculture and Consumer Services Commissioner said it had obtained refunds totaling $13,000 for 13 senior citizens who had filed consumer complaints with the office against S&T Distributors, who were accused of using high-pressure sales tactics to sell Kirby products. The seniors were refunded $1,000 each and were allowed to keep the vacuums; the salesperson was terminated.

Rob Shumay, Kirby's vice president of consumer and public relations, integrated marketing, and distribution, says, "the incidence of complaints involving Kirby's independent distributors is quite small compared to the number of in-home demonstrations they conduct. However, because our independent distributors are invited into a customer's home, any problems that may occur are magnified," he says.

To ensure that its distributors operate legally and ethically, Kirby management reviews distributors at least once a year and audits their business practices, Shumay says. "Kirby also reviews and verifies the sales of its independent distributors with customers, either in writing or by phone," he says. "Finally, Kirby takes disciplinary action against distributors," including withholding shipments and terminating agreements.

ON THE HORIZON

On many levels, steps are being taken to stamp out ethically questionable selling tactics when mature adults are the targets. For example, in the sale of annuities, "the law is changing," Siedle says. "It used to be that if you somewhere have it defined in fine print what you're doing, and you're not selling something that's outrageously inappropriate, that's okay. Now, investment companies are being held to a higher legal standard. What is evolving is a higher fiduciary standard that says that the product sold must be in the best interest of the investor," he says.

The Direct Marketing Association Inc. (DMA), a trade organization based in New York, has taken steps to prevent inappropriate tactics among its members. "We hear cases of violations of the guidelines every month," says Patricia Faley Kachura, vice president of ethics and consumer affairs at the DMA. "Often the complaint will be that a disclosure wasn't clear enough. If a disclosure doesn't meet [our standards], members can be found in violation, and they'll be asked by the ethics committee to change their practices."

In the end, the responsibility to curb unethical selling falls largely on managers' shoulders. Those who oversee staffs of reps selling to seniors must watch for signs of unethical behavior and take action to correct questionable activity. "Unfortunately…for people who happen to be less scrupulous already, the opportunity to earn commission gives them an opportunity to leverage unethical behavior into substantial income," says Michael Kitces, director of financial planning for Pinnacle Advisory Group Inc., a private wealth-management firm based in Columbia, Maryland. Kitces, who used to sell life insurance and annuities for a major life insurance company, says, "Those are the people managers need to be watching out for."

The documented cases of companies whose reps have used unethical tactics to sell often inappropriate products and services to the elderly are the most conspicuous examples. But tactics that fall into an ethically gray area might be more common than realized. "If a sales rep has a huge success rate, managers should probe a little bit as to how the success is being achieved," Koehn says.

What managers risk when turning a blind eye are potential tarnished corporate reputation, litigation, increased regulation, lost sales, and, perhaps, more. "We are living in an increasingly litigious society, where firms are sued by clients who feel they are not being treated in a fair and appropriate way," Koehn says. "And in many cases, they're losing."

And in the age of the Internet, stories of customers' bad experiences "no longer stay with that person, they go 'round the world. Companies shouldn't expect anymore that they can just sit on top of problems, because the problems will come out," Koehn says. And when problems come out, regulators take note. "They decide to look at other companies within the same industry who likely would have faced the same temptation."

Sales managers can be held legally accountable for their reps' unethical activities. "You could be sued for millions of dollars," says Patricia Gardner, CEO of Maximum Sales, a sales hiring firm based in Hunt Valley, Maryland. Particularly in the mortgage industry, "even vice presidents can lose their jobs" over what managers fail to do about ethical practices, she says.

Kitces says the solution is improved hiring and adequate oversight and training to teach appropriate, ethical sales tactics. Piece of Pie Marketing, a company that trains financial advisors to sell to the elderly market, holds a two-day course that teaches three main tenets, according to founder Mike Kaselnak: Engage in mutual respect; don't sell, tell, preach, or teach; and let them invite you in, that is, never force yourself on a client. It requires an upfront investment of time and money, but Kitces says it's worth it, because it avoids a buildup of unethical tactics that become tough to breakdown.

In the end, it behooves managers and their sales teams to monitor their practices when selling to seniors. Notwithstanding the legal and regulatory repercussions, it's just good business: If they manage properly and make sure salespeople are selling ethically, managers stand to gain a loyal, lucrative market.

Executive Editor **Jennifer Gilbert** *can be reached at jgilbert@salesandmarketing.com*

From *Sales And Marketing Management,* November 2004, pp. 25-28. Copyright © 2004 by VNU Business Media, Inc. Used with permission from Sales & Marketing Management.

Patagonia's Founder Seeks to Spread Environmental Gospel

Planet and profit aren't mutually exclusive, outdoor apparel maker Yvon Chouinard says.

Leslie Earnest
Times Staff Writer

Yvon Chouinard has climbed a glacier on the face of Mt. Kenya, survived an avalanche on Minya Konka in Tibet and kayaked down the Yellowstone River through a treacherous rock wall canyon. He has also helped preserve millions of acres of wild lands in the U.S. and South America—all this on top of building an outdoor apparel business with $240 million in sales.

But the founder and chairman of Ventura-based Patagonia Inc. is now facing what could be his biggest challenge: convincing corporate America that environmental awareness can be a profitable business model.

Chouinard has a new book, "Let My People Go Surfing: The Education of a Reluctant Businessman," which describes the pitfalls of growing a business too fast and the perils of polluting. In a nutshell, he wants people to think first about the planet.

It is, he admits, "a hard sell."

The 66-year-old Chouinard—who backed into a career when he began making climbing tools almost 50 years ago—isn't brimming with optimism. "I'm very pessimistic about the future," he said during a recent interview at his Ventura office. "I don't feel like we've had much impact yet."

Even his own company has a long way to go, he observed ruefully. He noted that he recently paid $2 million to install solar panels over a parking lot—which is filled with employees' gas-guzzling SUVs.

He hopes the book, which will be released nationwide Monday, will make a difference.

In it, Chouinard describes how, after working through successes and failures, he began seeing Patagonia as a potential model for other businesses.

Environmental groups and some business leaders say it has done just that.

"Patagonia made a difference because they stood out as a leader in the apparel industry," said Todd Larsen, managing director of the environmental activist group Co-op America. "They're a true success story."

Patagonia's decision to switch to organic cotton in 1996, for example, prompted other companies to think harder about the materials they used to make clothing.

Chouinard also co-founded 1% for the Planet, an alliance of 175 small businesses that have agreed to give at least that amount of sales to environmental groups.

But business consultant Michael Kami, whom Chouinard sought out for advice more than a decade ago, holds out little hope that others are likely to follow his lead. Although corporate givers are plentiful, few businesses incorporate doing good into their business plan, Kami said. Usually, charitably inclined executives make a killing and then start handing out money.

"He's very rare," Kami said.

Observers note that a major reason Chouinard can implement his vision at Patagonia is that the company is, and always has been, privately held. With shareholders watching from the wings, it's much harder for a publicly held business to follow such a vision.

Chouinard has kept his focus on the environment "at the expense, I'm sure, of major commercial success in growing his company," said Dick Baker, chief executive of Irvine-based Ocean Pacific Apparel Corp. "He's a very different animal than virtually all public companies."

Chouinard is known for his blunt, often downbeat, assessments of the state of the planet and the shortsightedness of corporations. He describes American businesses as "lemmings" and says free trade and globalism are "absolutely killing us." As for the stock market, it's "evil," partly because shareholders get only a sliver of a company's tangible worth, he says.

So uncompromising is the 5-foot-4-inch-tall Chouinard about his principles that pal Tom Brokaw calls him the "tiny terror."

The former NBC anchor has known Chouinard for 20 years; the two have climbed Mt. Rainier and the Grand Tetons together. As Brokaw sees it, Chouinard and the outdoors are inextricably linked. "It's his whole world," Brokaw said.

Said Baker, "He is an eco-warrior in its purest sense.

"Does he piss people off? Absolutely. But he's been doing that for 30 years."

From the outset, Yvon Chouinard didn't seem destined for business success.

Born in Maine, he got his Gallic name from his father, a French Canadian from Quebec. As a child, Chouinard was bored by school, developed an "attitude" and hung out with "fellow misfits," his book says. As a young outdoorsman, he considered politicians and businessmen "greaseballs" and viewed corporations "as the source of all evil."

But he became an entrepreneur in spite of himself, to make better climbing tools.

Chouinard's father helped him build his first shop in 1957 out of an old chicken coop in the backyard of their home in Burbank, according to the book. In 1966, he moved to Ventura to be closer to the surf, setting up shop in a tin boiler room of an abandoned slaughterhouse.

In the late 1960s, Chouinard Equipment Co. added clothing to its product mix, a line that eventually was dubbed Patagonia and became a separate apparel company.

Chouinard took an environmental stand early, providing a little money and work space for Friends of the Ventura River and, in 1985, pledging 10% of pretax profit to environmental groups. (In 1992, that was changed to 1% of total sales or 10% of pretax profit, whichever is greater.)

The first major crisis occurred in the late 1980s, when Chouinard Equipment was hit with several lawsuits claiming that the company provided improper safety warnings with its gear. The lawsuits were settled out of court, and the company's insurance premiums shot up 2,000% in a year, prompting Chouinard Equipment to file for Chapter 11 bankruptcy protection in 1989, Chouinard said.

Employees bought the assets and moved the restructured company, Black Diamond Equipment Ltd., to Salt Lake City in 1991.

Meanwhile, soul-searching was underway at Patagonia as the company began to see its rapid growth as "unsustainable" and in conflict with its principles.

"Had we kept growing at that rate, we would have been a $1-billion company in no time at all," Chouinard said. The company would have had to sell to department stores and ultimately to discounters, he said, driving down prices and quality. "That would have negated everything we were in business for."

That year, as the nation entered a recession, Patagonia—struggling with distribution and other problems—hit a wall. Dealers canceled orders, and the bank cut Patagonia's credit line. On July 31—the "darkest day in the company's history," according to the book—the company laid off 120 workers, about 20% of the workforce.

After a trip to Argentina, during which Patagonia's managers took a hard look at the direction of the business, they adopted a values statement. It said the Earth was in peril and vowed that Patagonia would "re-order" its values, making all future decisions "in the context of the environmental crisis," the book says.

The company took a fresh look at the way it made clothes, and it became the first to make fleece jackets using recycled bottles instead of polyester. It also reined in growth. It currently sells to 700 retailers, many of them small specialty stores. It also sells through its own chain, which comprises about 40 stores in the U.S., Europe, Asia and Chile.

"I could call Nordstrom, maybe tomorrow, and sell I don't know how many millions of dollars' worth of stuff," Chouinard said. "You just have to say no. And that's what we're doing here."

The company banned paper cups and plastic trash-can liners from its offices and built an extension to its headquarters using 95% recycled materials. Children at the company's day-care center help wheel the cafeteria's kitchen scraps to the corporate compost heap. Diaper-changing tables are blanketed with used computer paper.

Not that Patagonia claims purity. Chouinard says he's still a polluter who makes many products using nonrenewable resources. So he's doing "penance"—Patagonia has contributed more than $22 million to environmental groups since 1985, Chouinard said, and he and his wife, Malinda, co-owner of the company, also give 30% of their salaries. Royalties from his book also will be donated, he said.

Businesses such as Patagonia are part of a larger movement that was born in the 1970s and have been gathering steam over the last decade, said Jason Mark, California director for the Union of Concerned Scientists, a nonprofit advocacy group that conducts research related to energy and climate changes.

Today, rising energy costs are driving a "new wave of consciousness among the bean counters in corporate America," he said. "The question is, what's the estimated return on their investment?"

Environmental groups and business owners say Patagonia is making a difference by proving that a company can incorporate sound environmental practices into its business model and still be successful.

"When [Chouinard] says, 'I've never made an environmental decision that hasn't turned out to be profitable,' I think it raises eyebrows and causes people to say maybe we should be looking at that as well," said Matt McClain, spokesman for the Surfrider Foundation, a San Clemente-based environmental organization that works to protect oceans and beaches.

Patagonia does not disclose earnings, so its claim of profitable altruism is hard to quantify, although the company says it has always been in the black. Patagonia's sales have been uneven in recent years but are expected to rise 4% to $242 million in 2005 over last year. That would be 19% above 2000's revenue.

Outdoor equipment retailers say Patagonia's commitment to the environment is a selling point.

"That environmental message resonates with a lot of customers," said Nicole Fallat, spokeswoman for Recreational Equipment Inc., which sells the Patagonia brand in its 80 REI stores across the nation. "They're one of our biggest brands in action sportswear."

In fact, Patagonia's stand regarding organic cotton, which is grown without using pesticides, even caused REI to be more conscious of the materials it uses in its private-label apparel, Fallat said. Patagonia has proved that it's "OK to be green," she said. "You're not going to lose your customers just because it costs a dollar more."

After attending an "organic exchange" meeting at Patagonia last year, outdoor and fitness apparel maker Prana of Vista, Calif., increased its use of organic materials in its clothing, general manager Demian Kloer said.

"We've been steadily increasing them every season since," he said, even though the effort eats into profit. "There's a cost associated with going organic, but the long-term benefits far outweigh the short-term cost."

But many consumers simply don't care whether a product is organic or not, according to research conducted by Hartman Group in Bellevue, Wash.

Some consumers may indeed desire a "soul connection" with the product they buy, but that loyalty weakens as the price starts to rise, said Jenny Zenner, client service manager for the market research firm. "There is price resistance," she said, "even if they buy it for their children."

Chouinard would be the first to admit that there are easier ways to make a buck, especially now that the outdoor apparel industry has fierce competition even from the likes of Ralph Lauren and Tommy Hilfiger.

Unlike other wealthy businessmen, Chouinard said, he doesn't keep pushing because he likes "the game."

"I don't have that much interest in the game," he said. "But I'm very pessimistic about the fate of the world, and I wouldn't be able to sleep at night if I didn't feel like I was doing what I could about it."

And it's not as if he's having a bad time. In fact, Chouinard is out of the office for much of the year on outdoor adventures. Even then, he insists, he is helping the business—trying out its fishing waders in Canada or tropical gear in Tahiti.

"Somebody has to test it somewhere," he said with a smile.

From *Los Angeles Times*, October 9, 2005, pp. 25-28. Copyright © 2005 by Tribune Media Services. All rights reserved. Used with permission.

UNIT 5

Developing the Future Ethos and Social Responsibility of Business

Unit Selections

Key Points to Consider

- In what areas should organizations become more ethically sensitive and socially responsible in the next five years? Be specific, and explain your choices.

- Obtain codes of ethics or conduct from several different professional associations (for example, doctors, lawyers, CPAs, etc.). What are the similarities and differences between them?

- How useful do you feel codes of ethics are to organizations? Defend your answer.

Student Website

www.mhcls.com/online

Internet References

Further information regarding these websites may be found in this book's preface or online.

International Business Ethics Institute (IBEI)
http://www.business-ethics.org/index.asp

UNU/IAS Project on Global Ethos
http://www.ias.unu.edu/research/globalethos.cfm

Business ethics should not be viewed as a short-term, "knee-jerk reaction" to recently revealed scandals and corruption. Instead, it should be viewed as a thread woven through the fabric of the entire business culture—one that ought to be integral to its design. Businesses are built on the foundation of trust in our free-enterprise system. When there are violations of this trust between competitors, between employer and employees, or between businesses and consumers, the system ceases to run smoothly.

From a pragmatic viewpoint, the alternative to self-regulated and voluntary ethical behavior and social responsibility on the part of business may be governmental and legislative intervention. From a moral viewpoint, ethical behavior should not exist because of economic pragmatism, governmental edict, or contemporary fashionability—it should exist because it is morally appropriate and right.

This last unit is composed of articles that provide some ideas, guidelines, and principles for developing the future ethos and social responsibility of business. The first article, "Ethics for a Post-Enron America," discloses how trust, integrity, and fairness are crucial to organizations fulfilling their basic fiduciary duties to serve the interests of shareholders and the public. "Hiring Character" presents a look at business leader Warren Buffett's practice of hiring people based on their integrity. The next article reflects why managers and leaders must take a more active role in addressing ethical issues with the organization.

Ethics for a Post-Enron America

John R. Boatright

The high-profile scandals at Enron, WorldCom, Global Crossing, and Tyco, among others, combined with the spectacular dissolution of the accounting firm Arthur Andersen, are more than business failures. Numerous and voluminous news reports have revealed egregious failures by top executives and their advisers—including accountants, investment bankers, and lawyers—to fulfill their basic fiduciary duties to serve the interests of shareholders and the public.

A fiduciary duty is a duty of a person in a position of trust to serve the interests of others. Accordingly executives are fiduciaries who are pledged to serve the interests of shareholders. Yet, some have manipulated earnings, hidden debts, and falsified accounting records, all in order to exercise their lavish stock options at their shareholders' expense. Accountants who perform audits for the benefit of the investing public have permitted many instances of so-called "aggressive accounting" and approved financial statements that subsequently proved false. Investment bankers have helped executives to develop complex financial transactions that generated phantom earnings or removed unwanted debts from the balance sheet.

All the while, the banks' analysts, who are supposed to be objective, were giving favorable evaluations of the securities of companies with which the banks were doing deals, and the banks' brokers were filling their customers' portfolios with these same securities, even as they sometimes denigrated them in internal communications. And the lawyers who blessed many of these accounting and financial shenanigans were acting as though their clients were the executives who hired them and not the shareholders, who were ultimately paying for their services.

In each of these cases, the moral wrong is simple: a failure to fulfill a fiduciary duty, generally because of a serious conflict of interest. That this kind of behavior is immoral, and often illegal, is clear, but what challenge does it pose beyond recognizing that it is wrong and attempting to prevent it? Some argue that existing laws and the force of the marketplace are sufficient, so that nothing more needs to be done. Indeed, many of the wrongs in the recent scandals are slowly being rectified. Congress has mandated new rules to ensure that directors and auditors are "independent," which is another way of saying "free of conflicting interests." Among the many provisions of the Sarbanes-Oxley bill, for example, are the requirements that audit committees be composed entirely of independent directors with no ties to management and that accounting firms doing audits refrain from performing certain nonaudit services that could bias an audit. Similarly, Eliot Spitzer, the New York State attorney general, has forced some major investment banks to increase the independence of analysts to reduce the risk that their ratings of stocks will be influenced by the banks' deal-makers.

Although these efforts to reinforce fiduciary duties by removing conflicts of interest and restoring objectivity may produce some improvements, they do not address the most important challenge posed by the recent scandals. The effectiveness of fiduciary duties as a regulator of business conduct has been seriously undermined in the past two decades by several developments in the American business system. In particular, executive compensation tied to performance, the combining of auditing and consulting by accounting firms, and consolidation in the financial-services industry have produced powerful new incentives that have been major factors in the recent scandals. Restoring the traditional fiduciary duties in the face of these developments will be a difficult, if not impossible, task.

There are alternatives, however. Imposing fiduciary duties is one form of regulation that relies heavily on moral force, but market-based regulation that seeks to alter the incentives is another form. The challenges in this post-Enron era, then, is to determine which form of regulation, or what combination of these forms, can best secure the kind of ethical business environment in which future Enrons will not occur.

WHAT WENT WRONG?

We cannot propose reforms to prevent another Enron, much less understand the post-Enron world, without a firm grasp of why the recent scandals occurred. The stories are complex, and each one is different, but they all share some common features. Each case involves a business strategy gone awry, executives determined to boost short-term stock price by any means, directors who failed to detect warning signs, accountants who acquiesced in aggressive accounting, investment bankers who structured questionable financial deals, and lawyers who showed how to achieve the desired results with a plausible legal veneer.

A major factor in the scandals of 2001 is an increased focus on share price. This greater attention to stock price began in the early 1980s during a period of hostile takeovers, when a high share price was the best defense against a takeover. The impetus for high executive compensation tied to performance came originally from companies taken over that needed to raise share price quickly. Institutional investors encouraged this trend because it seemed to promote good corporate governance by aligning executives' interests more closely with those of shareholders. Finance theorists, most notably Michael Jensen, further supported this idea with arguments drawn from agency theory, which studies the problems of a principal (in this case the shareholders) controlling an agent (the CEO). Reducing the loss from an inadequately controlled CEO would more than offset the high executive compensation—or so the theory goes. Executives also became enamored of rising stock prices, not only because of their option-rich pay packages, but also because a high stock price opened up a growth strategy of making acquisitions.

A second important factor is the deregulation that occurred in the past two decades. Market deregulation, especially in energy and telecommunications, began a scramble to develop business models for a future that no one could accurately predict. It is significant that the biggest bankruptcies occurred at Enron (an energy-trading company) and at WorldCom and Global Crossing (in telecommunications). The novelty of these companies required new accounting methods that tested generally accepted accounting principles (GAAP). How should Enron price long-term contracts for delivery of energy, for example? Or how should WorldCom and Global Crossing classify unused telephone lines and optic-fiber cable? (WorldCom counted lease payments for idle capacity as capital investments, which is garden-variety accounting fraud.) At the same time, investment banks were developing sophisticated financial instruments that permitted, to cite just one example, loans that could be booked as trades. In this deregulated financial environment, Enron became more like a hedge fund than an energy company.

In addition to market deregulation, in the 1990s the legal liability of accounting firms and investment banks was reduced. It is difficult for a company to commit massive fraud without the complicity of its accountants, bankers, and lawyers. However, a 1994 court decision held that accounting firms and investment advisers could not be held liable for "aiding and abetting" fraud in securities transactions, and the 1995 Private Securities Litigation Reform Act protected investment banks from class-action suits for alleged securities fraud. Although this liability deregulation was introduced to make business more efficient, it had the unintended consequence of weakening a powerful constraint on accounting firms and investment banks.

The third factor, and perhaps the most significant, is simultaneous changes in the compensation structures for executives, accountants, and investment bankers. The rapidly escalating pay for CEOs has become heavily weighted with stock options that must be exercised within a narrow period. This time limit, combined with the importance of meeting analysts' expectations, produced great pressure to achieve short-term results. To

achieve the needed results, earnings management, which has long been used to iron out small wrinkles in financial statements, was now used to fashion figures out of whole cloth.

Further, accounting firms had discovered that it was far more lucrative to sell consulting services to their audit clients, thus tempting the firms to go easy on audits lest they lose the consulting business. And investment banks found that they could make more money doing deals with large companies than by servicing individual brokerage clients. As a result, analysts touted the stock of companies with which the deal-makers were doing business and encouraged the firm's brokerage customers to stuff their portfolios with these stocks. Individual investors were further shunted aside as investment banks made their most lucrative opportunities, such as shares in hot initial-public offerings (IPOs), available to their CEO-clients. These CEOs received thinly disguised kickbacks for bringing their company's business to the investment bank.

> **The American business system is schizophrenic in that it combines a market system built on the pursuit of self-interest with a system of fiduciary duties, in which one party is pledged to serve the interests of another. This system has worked because of the compartmentalized professional roles of those with fiduciary duties.**

The effect of these changes is that what had previously been a system of healthy checks and balances became a united front, at the expense of investors. Instead of having opposed interests that served to protect investors, these entities now had an unhealthy common interest. The fiduciary duty that executives owed to shareholders took a back seat to the pursuit of a short-term increase in stock price. Accountants, who had formerly policed financial reports to protect the public, now had a strong incentive to help executives to do whatever was necessary to boost share price so as to keep them as consulting clients. And investment bankers no longer served as trusted advisers to their customers, scouting out the best securities. They found it more advantageous to work with executives and accountants to finance deals that raised stock prices, even if this meant selling out their customers.

This broad-brush indictment also overlooks many factors, but it does paint a picture of a systematic failure with multiple causes. It is like a major industrial accident that happens when a number of small mishaps, inconsequential by themselves, occur together with catastrophic results. Although the individual failures are predictable, their occurrence together is highly improbable and hence not easily foreseen. Lacking an understanding of the convergence of factors that led to the Enron collapse and to other bankruptcies, the people involved could not easily appreciate the risks they were taking. For the most part, they were playing the game with which they were familiar, unaware of how treacherous the playing field had become.

WHAT IS TO BE DONE?

The American business system is schizophrenic in that it combines a market system built on the pursuit of self-interest with a system of fiduciary duties, in which one party is pledged to serve the interests of another. This system has worked because of the compartmentalized professional roles of those with fiduciary duties. Public accountants, stock brokers, and lawyers have operated as professionals who serve clients—or, in the case of public accountants, the public. Even CEOs and other top executives have generally viewed themselves as quasi-professionals and have taken their fiduciary duties seriously.

However, the compartmentalization of those with professional roles has been seriously eroded in recent years by several factors. One is the enormous compensation packages that have become common in recent years. These are designed to align executives' interests with those of shareholders so as to solve the agency problem of how to induce executives to serve the shareholders' interests. Whatever the merits of this strategy, one effect is to replace a moral and legal mechanism with a purely market mechanism. Fiduciary duties are now less important as a means for restraining executive behavior because the market is now being employed to achieve the same end.

Another factor is the consolidation of multiple services in accounting firms and investment banks. Accounting firms now provide many internal accounting and financial-information systems, advise on tax strategies, and offer appraisals and fairness opinions. In a similar manner, investment banks that mainly served large corporate clients merged with those that offered brokerage services mostly to small individual clients. As a result, brokers and analysts, who have always operated with both fiduciary duties and market mechanisms, now find themselves with even greater conflicts.

A third factor is the devaluation of some professional services. Auditing is a cost to companies that must be borne because the service is mandated by law. The cost is passed along to the intended beneficiaries, the investing public, but investors have little control over the price or the quality of audits. Similarly, securities analysis is a cost for brokerage firms that is also passed on to investors. Thus, corporations have an incentive to skimp on audit costs, and investment banks on the costs of analysis. In the recent bull market, investors had less interest in both

the quality of audits and the quality of research because they found that everything they bought unfailingly increased in price. As a result, accounting firms and investment banks have tended to treat auditing and analysis, respectively, as loss leaders to attract more lucrative business. These professional services have thus become peripheral to the more basic business services of consulting and investment banking.

> **This erosion of professional roles and decline of fiduciary duties is the reality of the post-Enron era. Although efforts can be made to reverse this development, doing so might require changing executive compensation and breaking up accounting firms and investment banks.**

This erosion of professional roles and decline of fiduciary duties is the reality of the post-Enron era. Although efforts can be made to reverse this development, doing so might require changing executive compensation and breaking up accounting firms and investment banks. Congress has grappled unsuccessfully with the issue of executive compensation, and the proposal by Arthur Levitt, the former chairman of the SEC, to separate auditing and consulting services was soundly rejected. And the consolidation of the banking industry has so collapsed the distinctions between investment banks that serve large clients and those engaged in retail brokerage that any return to the past would be very difficult.

Would we really be better off if we could put on the brakes and return to the pre-Enron period? After all, high executive compensation tied to performance might actually provide greater protection for shareholders than would a sense of fiduciary duty. The problem in the recent scandals is not that the pay packages were too large, but that they did not create the right incentives. Arguably, corporations and shareholders are better served by multipurpose accounting firms that can attract the best people and provide economies of both scale and scope. And financial supermarkets that offer a multitude of services also might serve everyone better. In any event, the market is telling us that these kinds of consolidation are more efficient and that they can be undone only at a price.

What is the alternative? Despite their importance, fiduciary duties are a second-best means of regulation. They are generally employed in relations in which one party agrees to serve the interests of another. If the obligations in question can be fully specified and embodied in contacts, then there is no need for fiduciary duties. Fiduciary duties, which are general, open-ended obligations to act for the benefit of another, are employed, then, when precise rules are not possible. For example, the main reason for imposing a fiduciary duty on executives to serve the shareholders' interests is that shareholders cannot specify in detail what executives should do to serve their interests because the situations that might arise are unpredictable. However, tying executive compensation to performance gets around this problem without the need for fiduciary duties+. A market mechanism that appeals to self-interest, rather than an ethical and legal duty, is used instead.

> ## An alternative to more rules is the European approach of employing accounting principles instead of rules. A principle-based accounting system, which prescribes general goals instead of specific means, allows accountants to choose, and auditors to approve, the accounting methods that provide the truest picture of a firm's financial situation. However, the European system requires a greater reliance on the integrity of the persons doing accounting and auditing.

Although accounting is a highly rule-bound activity, the rules still leave considerable discretion that accountants can use to benefit one party over another. The fiduciary duty of public accountants to serve the public is one way of ensuring that the public is served. However, the new Public Company Accounting Oversight Board, which was created by the Sarbanes-Oxley bill, is charged with creating even more rules and with conducting reviews of audits. The result of such efforts may further constrain the accounting profession and reduce the need for fiduciary duties. In addition, more accounting information is now available from corporations, and it may be possible in the near future for investors to have real-time access to company books. Such a development would reduce the need for audits and provide an external check on their quality.

Some people argue that there are already too many rules in accounting and that their number merely encourages the search for creative ways of getting around them. An alternative to more rules is the European approach of employing accounting principles instead of rules. A principle-based accounting system, which prescribes general goals instead of specific means, allows accountants to choose, and auditors to approve, the accounting methods that provide the truest picture of a firm's financial situation. However, the European system requires a greater reliance on the integrity of the persons doing accounting and auditing. American accountants already have the authority to depart from GAAP if doing so provides a truer picture, but few take advantage of this opportunity because it imposes a burden of proof that can be avoided by merely following the rules. In addition, the pursuit of principles should lead to the best methods of accounting, which can then be codified in rules. In return, these rules prevent unnecessary disagreements over the best methods. It is probably better to have precise rules wherever they are possible and to leave principles for difficult cases that are less amenable to rules.

The problem of biased analysis by investment banks has a very easy solution. Instead of guarding the independence of analysts or requiring analysts to disclose any conflicts, which are among the current proposals, encourage the development of a larger market for analysis. If analysis has value, then it will be purchased by investors, and analysis from a provider with a reputation for objectivity will bring a higher price. Part of the problem with analysis at investment banks is that top-notch analysts receive more in salary than brokerage customers are willing to pay for, and so the money for their high pay can be generated only by adding value to the bank's deal-makers, which creates a conflict of interest. The best solution, then, may be to invest only as much in analysis as buyers will pay for in the marketplace.

CONCLUSIONS

Both fiduciary duties and market-based regulation aim at a common goal, which is to reduce risk. In particular, investors run the risk that executives will enrich themselves at the shareholders' expense, that a company's financial statements will not be accurate, and that a broker's advice will not be sound. In each case, the solution has been to impose fiduciary duties that reduce the risk with a promise, in effect, not to take advantage of investors. Executives, accountants, and brokers each promise to act in the investors' interests. Rules on conflict of interest further reduce the risk to investors by prohibiting situations in which the parties might be tempted to break this promise.

However, the goal of reducing risk can be achieved in a number of ways. A market-based system of regulation would shift the risk away from investors and back to the parties that now have fiduciary duties. For example, if accounting firms cannot be held liable for "aiding and abetting" clients in fraud, then they bear little risk in facilitating "aggressive accounting." Removing this protection would require accounting firms to engage in more extensive risk management so that they would, in effect, be regulating themselves more closely. In short, if accounting firms and investment banks bore more of the risk of the activities for which they now have a fiduciary duty, then investors would have less need to rely on this kind of obligation to serve their interests.

There are drawbacks to such a regulatory approach. An increased risk burden would lead to less risky behavior, which might not be in investors' interest given that greater risk leads to higher returns. This burden involves a cost that would most likely be passed along to investors because accounting firms, for example, might spend more money on audits or buy more insurance. However, fiduciary duties also have a cost, and so in the end the choice of regulatory approaches may depend on a trade-off between effective protection and the cost of that protection.

However this issue is ultimately decided, it is clear that in this post-Enron era the fiduciary duties of the various players in the American business system have become less-effective protections for investors and the public. This erosion of a traditional means of regulation has resulted from many changes that have taken place in recent years, some of them highly beneficial. The challenge we face, then, is deciding whether to strengthen these fiduciary duties, in part by effectively reducing conflicts of interest, or to find other means of protecting against the kinds of scandal that Enron represents.

John R. Boatright is the Raymond C. Baumhart, S.J., Professor of Business Ethics in the Graduate School of Business at Loyola University Chicago. He currently serves as the executive director of the Society for Business Ethics, and is a past president of the Society. He is the author of the books *Ethics and the Conduct of Business* and *Ethics in Finance*. His current research focuses on ethics in finance and corporate governance. He received his PhD in philosophy from the University of Chicago.

Reprinted from *Phi Kappa Phi Forum*, Vol. 83, No. 2 (Spring 2003) pp. 10-15. Copyright © 2003 by John R. Boatright. Reprinted by permission of the publisher.

Hiring Character

In their new book, *Integrity Works,* authors Dana Telford and Adrian Gostick outline the strategies necessary for becoming a respected and admired leader. In the edited excerpt that follows, the authors present a look at business leader Warren Buffett's practice of hiring people based on their integrity. **For sales and marketing executives, it's a practice worth considering, especially when your company's reputation with customers— built through your salespeople—is so critical**

Dana Telford and Adrian Gostick

This chapter was the hardest for us to write. The problem was, we couldn't agree on whom to write about. We had a number of great options we were mulling over. Herb Brooks of the Miracle on Ice 1980 U.S. hockey team certainly put together a collection of players whose character outshined their talent. And the results were extraordinary. We decided to leave him out because we had enough sports figures in the book already. No, we wanted a business leader. So we asked, "Who hires integrity over ability?"

The person suggested to us over and over as we bandied this idea among our colleagues was Warren Buffett, chairman of Berkshire Hathaway Inc.

Sure enough, as we began our research we found we had not even begun to tell Buffett's story. But we were reluctant to repeat his story. Buffett had played an important part in our first book. And yet, his name kept coming up. So often, in fact, that we finally decided to not ignore the obvious.

Perhaps more than anyone in business today, Warren Buffett hires people based on their integrity. Buffett commented, "Berkshire's collection of managers is unusual in several ways. As one example, a very high percentage of these men and women are independently wealthy, having made fortunes in the businesses that they run. They work neither because they need the money nor because they are contractually obligated to—we have no contracts at Berkshire. Rather, they work long and hard because they love their businesses."

The unusual thing about Warren Buffett is that he and his longtime partner, Charlie Munger, hire people they trust—and then treat them as they would wish to be treated if their positions were reversed. Buffett says the one reason he has kept working so long is that he loves the opportunity to interact with people he likes and, most importantly, trusts.

Buffett loves the opportunity to interact daily with people he likes and, most importantly, trusts.

Consider the following remarkable story from a few years ago at Berkshire Hathaway. It's about R.C. Willey, the dominant home furnishings business in Utah. Berkshire purchased the company from Bill Child and his family in 1995. Child and most of his managers are members of the Church of Jesus Christ of Latter-day Saints, also called Mormons, and for this reason R.C. Willey's stores have never been open on Sunday.

Now, anyone who has worked in retail realizes the seeming folly of this notion: Sunday is the favorite shopping day for many customers—even in Utah. Over the years, though, Child had stuck to his principle—and wasn't ready to rejigger the formula just because Warren Buffett came along. And the formula was working. R.C.'s sales were $250,000 in 1954 when Child took over. By 1999, they had grown to $342 million. Child's determination to stick to his convictions was what attracted Buffett to him and his management team. This was a group with values and a successful brand.

Arnie Ferrin, longtime friend of Child, said, "I believe that [Child] is a man of extreme integrity, and I believe that Warren Buffett was looking to buy his business because he likes to do business with people like that, that don't have any shadows in their lives, and they're straightforward and deal above-board."

This isn't to say Child and Buffett have always agreed on the direction of the furniture store.

"I was highly skeptical about taking a no-Sunday policy into a new territory, where we would be up against entrenched rivals open seven days a week," Buffett said. "Nevertheless, this was Bill's business to run. So, despite my reservations, I told him to follow both his business judgment and his religious convictions"

Proving once again that he believed in his convictions, Child insisted on a truly extraordinary proposition: He would personally buy the land and build the store in Boise, Idaho—for about $11 million as it turned out—and would sell it to Berkshire at his cost if—and only if—the store proved to be successful. On the other hand, if sales fell short of his expectations, Berkshire could exit the business without paying Child a cent. This, of course, would leave him with a huge investment in an empty building.

You're probably guessing there's a happy ending to the story. And there is. The store opened in August of 1998 and immediately became a huge success, making Berkshire a considerable margin. Today, the store is the largest home furnishings store in Idaho.

Child, good to his word, turned the property over to Berkshire—including some extra land that had appreciated significantly. And he wanted nothing more than the original cost of his investment. In response, Buffett said, "And get this: Bill refused to take a dime of interest on the capital he had tied up over the two years."

And there's more. Shortly after the Boise opening, Child went back to Buffett, suggesting they try Las Vegas next. This time, Buffett was even more skeptical. How could they do business in a metropolis of that size and remain closed on Sundays, a day that all of their competitors would be exploiting?

But Buffett trusts his managers because he knows their character. So he gave it a shot. The store was built in Henderson, a mushrooming city adjacent to Las Vegas. The result? This store outsells all others in the R.C. Willey chain, doing a volume of business that far exceeds any competitor in the area. The revenue is twice what Buffett had anticipated.

As this book went to print, R.C. Willey was preparing to open its third store in the Las Vegas area, as well as stores in Reno, Nevada, and Sacramento, California. Sales have grown to more than $600 million, and the target is $1 billion in coming years. "You can understand why the opportunity to partner with people like Bill Child causes me to tap dance to work every morning," Buffett said.

Here's another example of Buffett's adeptness at hiring character. He agreed to purchase Ben Bridge Jeweler over the phone, prior to any face-to-face meeting with the management.

Ed Bridge manages this 65-store West Coast retailer with his cousin, Jon. Both are fourth-generation owner-

managers of a business started 89 years ago in Seattle. And over the years, the business and the family have enjoyed extraordinary character reputations.

Buffett knows that he must give complete autonomy to his managers. "I told Ed and Jon that they would be in charge, and they knew I could be believed: After all, it's obvious that [I] would be a disaster at actually running a store or selling jewelry, though there are members of [my] family who have earned black brits as purchasers."

Talk about hiring integrity! Without any provocation from Buffett, the Bridges allocated a substantial portion of the proceeds from their sale to the hundreds of coworkers who had helped the company achieve its success.

Overall, Berkshire has made many such acquisitions—hiring for character first, and talent second—and then asking these CEOs to manage for maximum long-term value, rather than for next quarter's earnings. While they certainly don't ignore the current profitability of their business, Buffett never wants profits to be achieved at the expense of developing ever-greater competitive strengths, including integrity.

It's an approach he learned early in his career.

Warren Edward Buffett was born on August 30, 1930. His father, Howard, was a stockbroker-turned-congressman. The only boy, Warren was the second of three children. He displayed an amazing aptitude for both money and business at a very early age. Acquaintances recount his uncanny ability to calculate columns of numbers off the top of his head—a feat Buffett still amazes business colleagues with today.

At only six years old, Buffer purchased six-packs of Coca-Cola from his grandfather's grocery store for twenty-five cents and resold each of the bottles for a nickel—making a nice five-cent profit. While other children his age were playing hopscotch and jacks, Buffett was already generating cash flow.

Buffett stayed just two years in the undergraduate program at Wharton Business School at the University of Pennsylvania. He left disappointed, complaining that he knew more than his professors. Eventually, he transferred to the University of Nebraska–Lincoln. He managed to graduate in only three years despite working full time.

Then he finally applied to Harvard Business School. In what was undoubtedly one of the worst admission decisions in history, the school rejected him as "too young." Slighted, Buffett applied to Columbia where famed investment professor Ben Graham taught.

Professor Graham shaped young Buffett's opinions on investing. And the student influenced his mentor as well. Graham bestowed on Buffett the only A+ he ever awarded in decades of teaching.

While Buffett tried working for Graham for a while, he finally struck out on his own with a revolutionary philosophy: He would research the internal workings of extraordinary companies. He could discover what really made them tick and why they held a competitive edge in their markets. And then he would invest in great companies that were trading at substantially less than their market values.

Ten years after its founding, the Buffett Partnership assets were up more than 1,156 percent [compared to the Dow's 122.9 percent], and Buffett was firmly on his way to becoming an investing legend.

In 2004, Warren Buffett was listed by Forbes as the world's second-richest person (right behind Bill Gates), with $42.9 billion in personal wealth. Despite starting with just $300,000 in holdings, Berkshire's holdings now exceed $116 billion. And Buffett and his employees can confidently say they have made thousands of people wealthy.

We often ask business leaders one simple question: Which is more dangerous to your firm—the incompetent new hire or the dishonest new hire? It's the part of our presentation where attendees sit up straight and start thinking.

We always follow the question with an exercise on identifying and hiring integrity. Though it becomes obvious that many of the executives and managers haven't given employee integrity much thought, most of the CEOs in the audiences are increasingly concerned about hiring employees with character.

So, how do you hire workers with integrity? It's possible, but not easy. It is important to spend more time choosing a new employee than you do picking out a new coffee machine. Here are a few simple areas to focus on:

First, ensure educational credentials match the resume. Education is the most misrepresented area on a resume. Notre Dame football coach George O'Leary was fired because the master's degree he said he had earned did not exist the CEO of software giant Lotus exaggerated his education and military service and the CEO of Bausch & Lomb forfeited a bonus of more than $1 million because he claimed a fictional MBA.

It is important to spend more time choosing a new employee than you do picking out a new coffee machine.

Job candidates also often claim credit for responsibilities that they never had. Here's a typical scenario:

Job candidate: "I led that project. Saved the company $10 million." Through diligent fact checking, you find an employee at a previous employer who can give you information about the candidate:

Coworker: "Hmm. Actually, Steve was a member of the team, but not the lead. And while it was a great project, we still haven't taken a tally of the cost savings. But $10 million seems really high."

How do you find those things out? Confer with companies where the applicant has worked—especially those firms the person isn't listing as a reference. Talk to people inside the organization, going at least two levels deep (which means you ask each reference for a couple more references). Talk to the nonprofit organizations where the person volunteers. Tap into alumni networks and professional associations. Get on the phone with others in the industry to learn about the person's reputation. Check public records for bankruptcy, civil, and criminal litigation (with the candidate's knowledge). In other words, check candidates' backgrounds carefully (but legally, of course).

We find that most hiring managers spend 90 percent of their time on capability-related questions, and next to no time on character-based questions. In your rush to get someone in the chair, don't forget to check backgrounds and be rigorous in your interviewing for character. Hiring the wrong person can destroy two careers: your employee's—and your own.

Ask ethics-based questions to get to the character issue. We asked a group of executives at a storage company to brainstorm a list of questions they might ask candidates to learn more about their character. Their list included the following questions:

- Who has had the greatest influence on you and why?
- Who is the best CEO you've worked for and why?
- Tell me about your worst boss.
- Who are your role models and why?
- How do you feel about your last manager?
- Tell me about a time you had to explain bad news to your manager.
- What would you do if your best friend did something illegal?
- What would your past manager say about you?
- What does integrity mean to you?
- If you were the CEO of your previous company, what would you changer?
- What values did your parents teach you?
- Tell me a few of your faults.
- Why should I trust you?
- How have you dealt with adversity in the past?
- What are your three core values?
- Tell me about a time when you let someone down.
- What is your greatest accomplishment, personal or professional?
- What are your goals and why?
- Tell me about a mistake you made in business and what you learned from it.
- Tell me about a time when you were asked to compromise your integrity.

It's relatively easy to teach a candidate your business. The harder task is trying to instill integrity in someone who doesn't already have it.

Of course, we don't want to imply that it's impossible. Sometimes people will adapt to a positive environment and shine. Men's Wearhouse has certainly had tremendous success hiring former prison inmates, demonstrating everyone should have a second chance.

But integrity is a journey that is very personal, very individual. An outside force, such as an employer, typically can't prescribe it. It's certainly not something that happens overnight. That's one reason many of the CEOs we have talked with prefer promoting people from inside their organizations when possible.

Don Graham, chairman and CEO of the Washington Post Company, said, "There's a very good reason for concentrating your hires and promotions on people who already work in your organization. The best way to predict what someone's going to do in the future is to know what they've done in the past—watch how people address difficult business issues, how they deal with the people who work for them, how they deal with the people for whom they work. You may be able to put on a certain face for a day or even a week, but you're not going to be able to hide the person you are for five or ten years."

Graham tells a story about Frank Batten, who for years ran Landmark Communications and founded The Weather Channel. "Frank is a person of total integrity," Graham says. "Frank once said, 'When you go outside for hire you always get a surprise. Sometimes it's a good surprise. But you never hire quite the person you thought you were hiring.'"

What do you look for in a job applicant? Years of experience? College degree? Specific skill sets? Or do you look for character? If so, you're in good company.

Years ago, Warren Buffett was asked to help choose the next CEO for Salomon Brothers. "What do you think [Warren] was looking for?" Graham asks. "Character and integrity—more than even a particular background. When the reputation of the firm is on the line every day, character counts."

Don't like surprises? Then hire people who have integrity. Want to ensure a good fit with the people you hire? Then hire people who have integrity. Want to ensure your reputation with customers? Then hire people who have integrity.

Are we saying that nothing else matters? No. But we are saying that nothing matters more.

From Integrity Works: Strategies for Becoming a Trusted, Respected and Admired Leader by ***Dana Telford*** *and **Adrian Gostick**. Copyright 2005 by Dana Telford and Adrian Gostick. Reprinted with permission of Gibbs Smith, Publisher.*

From INTEGITY WORKS, June 2005, pp. 39–42. Copyright © 2005 by Dana Telford and Adrian Gostick. Reprinted by permission.

Why corporations can't control chicanery

Saul W. Gellerman
Management Consultant, Denver, Colorado

> Sadly, as this issue went to press, we learned that Dr. Gellerman had passed away from post-surgical complications. We hope that this article stands in tribute to his wit, insight, and professional dedication. And we extend our condolences to his family.

Business ethics is taught , to one extent or another, one guise or another, in most business schools. But many complain that the schools are not teaching enough of it, or not teaching it well, given the many recent instances of mischief in high places in corporate America. Such a position is naive; personal ethics are "made" well before people reach the point of attending a business school. There are ways, however, to think realistically about the causes of corporate malfeasance and to guard against them.

Recent corporate scandals prove that the lessons of previous scandals have not yet been learned. Management still blames rogue employees, and pundits still blame business schools. Most companies would rather not touch the real cause: pressures that push management to test the boundaries of the permissible. As a result, some executives are inevitably confronted with more temptation to do the wrong thing, and more opportunity to do it, than they can resist. Policies that assume everyone will nobly rise above that combination are unrealistic. The best defense lies in painful structural changes that minimize both the temptation and the opportunity to loot the company and defraud investors.

It happens, on average, about every 12 years: Someone who works for a big company gets caught cooking the books. In a smaller company, the same offense might not be newsworthy. But if the company is well-known, the media—whose job, after all, is to sniff out headlines—react swiftly. Swarms of reporters descend on the company, with prosecutors and politicians not far behind. In a matter of hours, another of corporate America's household names is all over Page One, mired in a messy, potentially damaging scandal.

Management usually defines its predicament as being primarily a problem in public relations, and calls in the damage-control experts. And right there—in diagnosing the problem as a mere crisis in reputation, rather than the inevitable result of the way they do business—the seeds of yet another corporate disaster, due to sprout in about another 12 years, are sown. It will probably strike a different company, but that makes it all the more dangerous, because the next corporate victim will be blind to the lesson not learned by the first one. The next big scandal, in other words, could strike any big company.

Short-term effects

Next, top executives, taking their cue from the wily police chief played by Claude Raines in Casablanca, proclaim themselves to be "shocked, shocked!" at the unauthorized misconduct of a few rogue employees—who promptly become ex-employees. Public relations consultants then prescribe massive doses of good works, such as well-publicized sponsorships of socially beneficial programs (prenatal health care? adult literacy?), to associate the company's name in the public's mind with doing the right thing—conspicuously. Thanks to the public's notoriously short memory, the whole unpleasant episode is soon forgotten. Today's horrendous scandal inevitably becomes tomorrow's stale news—unless, that is, the prosecutors or the regulators strike pay dirt during the discovery phase of their investigation, and if the company's attorneys can't head them off. That could cause the company to implode, which is what happened to financial giants E.F. Hutton and Drexel Burnham about a dozen years ago. Their current counterparts include the once-mighty Arthur Andersen and WorldCom.

He was expressing the essence of the dilemma in which executives find themselves: to go as far as they dare in a lucrative but dangerous direction without ever quite going too far.

Convictions are, of course, the ultimate PR disaster. Firms do not want to do business with a demonstrably crooked company, if only because their own stockholders would surely question their sanity for even thinking of it.

Avoiding corporate destruction is the best reason for companies to rein in the chicanery of their own employees. But as that continuing 12-year cycle indicates, their track record is not very good. There are three reasons for that. First, management is ambivalent about really clamping down on the kinds of mischief that can get a company into serious trouble. Second, when they do try to get a handle on it, they are likely to use ineffective methods. Third, they are likely to shrink from the kinds of drastic structural changes that could halt these abuses altogether.

Managerial ambivalence

A corporation's executives are caught between avoiding the sanctions of the authorities and the displeasure of the stock market. They are forever in the gray zone between maximizing profits and risking the incursions of inquisitive reporters and ambitious prosecutors. (Rudy Giuliani, be it remembered, made his reputation by sending Michael Milken to jail.)

Executives are also in competition with those of other companies, whose profit performance becomes the standard by which their own is judged. They are thus constantly pushed toward the fuzzy, indistinct line that separates barely acceptable practices from those that are intolerable. It should not be surprising, then, that they send mixed messages to the middle managers who make the company's day-to-day, tactical decisions.

I once attended a management meeting of a company that had to walk a fine line between competitiveness and a looming antitrust injunction. A top executive, addressing an audience of middle managers, pounded the lectern for emphasis as he shouted at the top of his lungs, "We want our competitors to survive!" To which he added, in a clearly audible stage whisper, "barely."

He was, I think, expressing the essence of the dilemma in which executives find themselves: to go as far as they dare in a lucrative but dangerous direction without ever quite going too far. You can bet that when the Enron scandal hit the headlines, many a corporation ordered an immediate review of its own accounting practices and put any questionable tactics on hold. How much document-shredding went on in companies that were not (at least not then) the targets of investigation is a fascinating but unanswerable question.

This much is certain: When executives send mixed messages, their subordinates are left to decipher their real meaning. The usual translation is: "If the rewards are not enough to motivate you, we don't need you. Just do whatever you have to do to make your numbers. And remember, anyone stupid enough to get caught will be hung out to dry."

Of course, hardly anyone is foolish enough to say such things for the record. But all that executives really have to do is hint to their subordinates that the race will be won by the most audacious among them, rather than by the most deliberate, and then leave them to draw the necessary inferences. So it should not be surprising when subordinates decide that lifting debts from the balance sheet and stashing them somewhere else, or masking ordinary expenses as long-term investments, is what their bosses really had in mind. Most executives are likely to welcome the results such tactics bring, and do not condemn them until someone outside the company finds out, or until an insider blows the whistle.

For all these reasons, executives tend to approach internal reforms with mixed feelings. For many of them—perhaps most—the bottom line is their highest priority, especially if their own compensation is tied to it. That makes them reluctant to give up a tactic that has already worked to their advantage. But from a longer-range perspective, any given quarter's bottom line is a secondary goal. The primary goal, always, is corporate survival. In the long run, you can make a lot more money from a steadily profitable company that is still in business than from a spectacularly profitable company that lost the confidence of its customers and is now deservedly defunct.

Ineffective methods I: Preaching ethics

When executives undertake to prevent future scandals, they usually seek to prevent "misunderstandings" of their policy guidance. The most common way of doing this is to provide employees with a written "Code of Ethics," most of which states boldly, but imprecisely, that the highest standards of decency, honesty, and fairness are demanded of everyone at all times, and that deviations from those standards will not be tolerated. The main problem with these codes is that they are seldom referred to after the hoopla with which they are introduced has died down. For all practical purposes, they are forgotten after a few months simply for lack of emphasis.

Recognizing the inadequacy of trying to control behavior by merely distributing documents, many companies have gone one step further by bringing in consultants to provide ethics training. Usually these are academics with credentials in philosophy who have "majored," so to speak, in the study of ethics. Their objective is to arm employees with analytical methods that enable them to discern where a line can be drawn between right and wrong.

These consultants illustrate their message with case examples of how easily one can be tempted, or deceived, into taking the wrong turn when making what appears on the surface to be an ordinary business decision. But these courses usually amount to little more than highly sophisticated Sunday School lessons.

There is no question but that an intelligent student will come out of them with an intellectual grasp of ethical principles and how they apply to on-the-job decision making. That such an understanding will beget ethical behavior on the job—especially when the actual challenge occurs long after the course has ended, under heavy pressure for results, in the presence of dangled temptation, and in a culture that stresses winning at all costs—is at best dubious.

Giving the right answer to an ethical problem in a classroom, and applying that same answer in the heat of battle, are two very different things. Unless a way can be found to make what are usually near-instantaneous, gut-level decisions in an atmosphere of classroom-like serenity, under the benign guidance of a professor who has your best interests at heart (as distinct from a demanding boss who will not take "no" for an answer), providing employees with formal training in ethics will be an exercise in futility.

Training does not get at the root of the problem, which is not a lack of ethical intent or ethical wisdom, but rather the circumstances in which most critical managerial decisions are made. Thus, a student may in fact be conversant with such advanced ethical concepts as the Categorical Imperative of Immanuel Kant, or the Utilitarianism of Jeremy Bentham, but will either completely forget them at the moment of decision or discard them as irrelevant when that decision must be made under fire. Knowing full well that what you contemplate doing is wrong is not, alas, an effective deterrent when the rewards of wrongdoing are extravagant, the risks of being found out seem remote, and the consequences of not doing what your superiors seem to want can be devastating to your career.

Ineffective methods II: Excluding unethical employees

Another popular but equally ineffective method used by companies that want to avoid potentially dangerous scandals is to try to prevent unscrupulous people from getting into positions in which they could harm the company. Psychologists are brought in to try to weed out executive candidates who seem overly predisposed to cutting corners or bending rules. The psychologists attempt to peer, as it were, into the innermost psyches of candidates for high-level positions, usually by administering various tests, studying their life histories, and/or interviewing people who have known them well at various stages of their lives.

Giving the right answer to an ethical problem in a classroom, and applying that same answer in the heat of battle, are two very different things.

To authorize such screening requires a great deal more faith in the predictive powers of psychological methods than their record would justify. Many executives are aware of that but reason that in the event of another failure they can always say they did all they could to prevent it.

Psychologists operate on the (correct) assumption that some people are more likely than others to simply brush rules aside and let the consequences be damned. If individuals carrying that trait can be screened out before they acquire the power to make fateful decisions, the company will be spared the disastrous consequences of their rashness. (The flip side of that screening is that you also eliminate people of uncommon initiative.) The psychologists survey candidates for jobs in which critical decisions can be made, hoping to ensure that only men and women of probity, wisdom, and self-restraint get to make the really big ones.

The sad truth seems to be that when it pays to do the wrong thing, someone will. Singling out that "someone" in advance is at best impractical and at worst improbable.

In practice, there are two severe problems with this approach, either of which is enough to invalidate it. The first concerns its feasibility: Can executive crooks actually be weeded out before they do irreparable harm? The second concerns the realism of its underlying premise: Is corporate misconduct actually the work of just a few "bad apples"—that is, a handful of incorrigibly unscrupulous executives? When you dig down into the details, the feasibility question turns out to be tougher than it may appear at first. There are not just one but two types of potential offenders whom the psychologists have to detect.

First, there are those for whom self-serving, irresponsible acts are a way of life. Clinically, these people are usually diagnosed as psychopaths. Fortunately for society, they are relatively rare. Fortunately for employers, most of them quickly acquire the kinds of records that human resource departments routinely screen out. But their very scarcity makes hunting for them among the employees of a big company rather like hunting for a few needles in an enormous haystack. There may not be any of them there in the first place; and if there are, their disdain for rules is likely to be blatantly obvious without tests.

The second target for the psychologists are people whose morals are not especially rigid and who might not be above doing the wrong thing if they encountered sufficiently permissive conditions. This group is likely to be quite large. The practical problem they present is that excluding them from positions of power would probably make a majority of employees, virtually all of whom are innocent, the targets of discrimination. Many a capable, promising, and heretofore honorable employee would be ruled ineligible for higher-level posts if the absence of a stern, steely character were considered a disqualification.

Among the remaining few—those whose characters were deemed "impervious" to temptation (the quotation marks are unavoidable)—it might be difficult to find those who were also sufficiently imaginative and decisive to handle executive responsibilities. The practical result is that management has little choice but to take its chances on executive candidates who might, under the wrong circumstances, present risks of wrongdoing.

Then there is the question of whether psychologists can actually make all those distinctions accurately and reliably. The long answer requires at least a semester in a good psychology program, because of the inherent difficulty in trying to demonstrate such things incontrovertibly. The short answer is: Probably not.

The origins of unethical conduct

The sad truth seems to be that when it pays to do the wrong thing, someone will. Singling out that "someone" in advance is, for the reasons just discussed, at best impractical and at worst improbable. Many employees—possibly even most—will resist the temptation, but in a large enough group, someone will give in. And it only takes one aggressive risk-taker, or a few, to ease a company onto the initially lucrative but inevitably slippery slope that leads, all too readily, to its own destruction.

Why do they do it? What motivates people who usually have a lot to lose (in most cases, a career that was off to an excellent start) to risk everything on a fast buck? Every corporate scoundrel probably had his own set of motives. But the one common denominator that influenced all of them is that they did it because they could. The opportunity was there, and they seized it. Had there been no opportunity, they would still be what they were before the fatal temptation presented itself: highly regarded, promising employees with a great future and perfectly clean records.

In other words, whether one's behavior is going to be ethical or unethical is, to a large extent, situational. It is not the result of an inadequate understanding of ethics, or of fault lines within one's character, but of being in the wrong place at the wrong time.

A wise sociologist once observed, "The main reason there aren't more affairs is that there aren't more opportunities." The same can be said of resorting to creative accounting, of bribing employees to put their own interests above those of clients, even of defrauding widows and orphans. Opportunity, not ignorance or inherent evil, is the culprit. If that thought strikes you as too cynical, answer this question for yourself: Suppose you are out of town, alone, in a city where you know no one and no one knows you. You enter a taxi cab, and as it rushes off toward your destination you notice beside you, on the back seat, the wallet of a previous passenger. It is stuffed with hundred-dollar bills. What will you do?

Obviously, there will be some kind of identification in that wallet, so what you should do is contact its owner and arrange to return the wallet and its contents to him. But the question I am asking is not what you should do, but what you *would* do. If you returned the wallet, many would applaud your honesty. Yet many others would call you a fool. (After all, they might note, those would be tax-free dollars.)

The only way to get a definitive answer to the question would be to put you in a taxi in a strange city, with no one but yourself in a position to see what actually happened. Absent that ultimate test, all of us have a right to be at least somewhat skeptical about what each of the rest of us would do. And if that is the case, it should not be surprising if circumstances that management deliberately creates, or knowingly tolerates, can lead people with previously unblemished records to reach for those fast bucks.

Exalted ideas about human nature have no place in a realistic plan to control employee misconduct. To achieve that goal, you have to start with the following assumptions: that everyone (with no exceptions) is at least potentially dishonest; that temptation and opportunity are the two main contributors to potential dishonesty; and that the best way to keep everyone honest is to eliminate, or at least severely restrict, both of them.

Bad apples or bad barrels?

An old saying has it that a few bad apples, if not removed, can spoil all the other apples in the barrel. That is the principle underlying the attempt to screen out unreliable managers before they rise too high in the hierarchy. But the attempt itself is probably futile. To pursue the analogy, the problem is not with the apples (that is, the individual executives themselves) but rather with the barrel (the system of constraints and licenses in which they operate).

John C. Coffee, Jr., a professor at the Columbia Law School, dealt with exactly that problem in analyzing the reasons why auditors at Enron and elsewhere acquiesced in their clients' attempts at "earnings management." During the 1990s, he noted, the costs to auditors of doing that went down, while the benefits went up:

> The costs declined because in several decisions the Supreme Court made it harder to sue accountants, while Congress passed legislation that, among other things, reduced their maximum liability.... In any profession, but especially for custodians of the public trust, advocacy and objectivity cannot be safely combined. (Coffee 2002)

In other words, the government, not just greedy executives, had a hand in this. Constraints designed to dissuade accountants from colluding with clients to misrepresent their earnings, or at least to present them in an extremely optimistic light, had eroded because of decisions taken by both the judicial and legislative branches. Risks that had been thought foolish under prior rules now seemed worth thinking about. Inevitably, someone experimented with tactics that had previously been discouraged, just to see what would happen. And when nothing happened, others followed suit. Soon, methods that might once have been considered unthinkable became, instead, the norm.

The need for structural change

Bigger fines and stricter enforcement of existing rules are not the answer. That is because so many minds are virtually programmed to seek ways around restrictions on personal freedom—especially when it pays to evade them. Ingenuity always wins out over regulation. Instead, the way to keep all those perfectly clean records as clean as ever lies in structural changes that remove either the incentive to misbehave or the opportunity to do so, or (preferably) both. Of course, such changes come with a price tag attached.

The solutions suggested here are hardly panaceas. They cannot make any of these problems disappear altogether, and they certainly are not painless. But the present sorry situation of American business demands challenges to the kinds of established thinking that got us into this mess. Four areas seem especially ripe for structural change: boards of directors, organization structure, executive pay, and the auditor-client relationship.

Boards of directors

In theory, boards are the shareholder's (and the public's) last line of defense against managerial chicanery. In practice, they have been overly acquiescent and (in too many cases) insufficiently inquisitive about what is really going on in the companies they allegedly govern. For both reasons, boards have come under fire from critics who see them as too chummy with, and therefore too easily conned by, management.

Much has been written about the role of inside directors, whose service on the board of a company they also manage would appear to involve an inherent conflict of interest—not unlike that of a fox guarding a hen house. It is true that inside directors bring with them a detailed, expert knowledge of company operations to which outside directors often need access. On the other hand, there is no good reason why outside directors could not question any manager who had information they needed without having to give him a vote on the board's policy decisions.

Inevitably, someone experimented with tactics that had previously been discouraged, just to see what would happen. And when nothing happened, others followed suit. Soon, methods that might once have been considered unthinkable became, instead, the norm.

But another issue regarding board performance, though at least as important as the "inside vs. outside" question, has received less attention: the board's competence to carry out its duties. Some boards appear to have been asleep at the switch while great harm was being done to their companies. Enron's board, for example, got into an unseemly finger-pointing contest with management once the extent of the firm's accounting shenanigans began to emerge.

Do boards consist chiefly of semi-informed, easily satisfied figureheads capable of presiding over a company but not actively steering it? I doubt that. But to the extent that there may be any truth at all in that stereotype, it is probably because directors are simply playing the role they have been given to play. Keeping their hands off, leaving the heavy lifting to management, and being satisfied with only a general overview of how the company is achieving its reported results is what is commonly expected of them. Nevertheless, we must ask whether it is indeed possible for anyone to bear the ultimate responsibility for a company's fortunes with such a loose grip on its reins.

Another issue that has not received enough attention is the fact that board members (with the frequent exception of the chairman) serve on only a part-time basis. Outside directors, of whom so much more is now expected than before, usually have full-time jobs elsewhere and necessarily treat their directorships as secondary responsibilities.

If boards are to do what they are supposed to do—control their firms, rather than merely preside over them—they will have to become the antithesis of what they have been. And if we are to have active, hands-on, fully informed boards of directors, a majority of them will have to serve full-time. They will also have to be given the authority of a military inspector-general: the right to go anywhere, ask any question of anyone, and apply appropriate sanctions to whoever attempts to conceal information from them.

Will management like this? Of course not. Will relationships between such a board and its management become tense and adversarial? Possibly. But are these prices worth paying to put the representatives of the owners actually in charge of their company? That is a question on which reasonable people may differ. For myself, I suggest that fewer scandals, and fewer bear markets prolonged and worsened by shareholder disgust, would make all that discomfort well worth it in the end.

Organization structure

Organizations with built-in conflicts of interest have tried to enjoy the best of both worlds by erecting so-called "Chinese Walls" (prohibited contacts or discussions) in order to separate employees who could collaborate too easily in ways that could compromise the firm's integrity.

The most striking recent example of an unsuccessful attempt to prevent corruption by merely forbidding it was Merrill Lynch.

Investment bankers realized that having securities analysts under the same roof with them could be a huge competitive advantage when seeking corporate underwriting accounts. So the "wall" was breeched by giving analysts a financial stake in obtaining underwriting business, simply by inducing them to add some undeserved luster to their evaluations of the prospective client's company.

Trying to repair the wall by punishing those who have breeched it or by increasing the penalties for those who try it in the future are probably futile, simply because the incentive is still there. The problem at Merrill Lynch was not the villainy of a few investment bankers, or the willing collaboration of a few financial analysts, but rather the common corporate roof over both of them. Their ready access to each other made the deception of the company's brokerage clients possible, and perhaps even inevitable.

The only way to eliminate both the incentive and the opportunity for this kind of gambit is to spin off one of the two units into a separately owned and managed company. Of course, that would also eliminate opportunities for perfectly legitimate synergy.

Like the executive who wanted his competitors to survive (barely), brokerages that are also investment bankers have to walk a fine line between maximizing their profits and risking the loss of their reputation. It would be a hard choice, because in all probability the sum of the profits generated by two totally separated units would be less than those produced by those same units under a single but perpetually endangered corporate ownership.

Executive pay

Some CEOs and other high-level executives have been grossly overpaid, at the ultimate expense of the companies' shareholders. During the stock market boom of the late 1990s, this attracted little comment because everyone else was prospering too. But when stock prices fell early in the new century, questions arose about whether the earnings of the 1990s that had pumped up those prices were real—and complacency over executive pay quickly changed to outrage.

How much are top executives worth? In the real world, they are worth whatever a board of directors, conscious of its fiduciary responsibility to shareholders, sees fit to pay them. The real issue is not the pay package itself but the basis on which it is calculated, usually a fiscal year. But as we have learned to our sorrow, earnings often have to be recalculated long after they were first officially announced, and fiscal "skeletons" sometimes don't emerge from wherever they were buried until years afterward.

In other words, the problem is not so much in the size of the pay package as in the payment schedule. The only way for the directors of a big company to be reasonably certain that the performance on which an executive's pay is based has been accurately measured is to let enough time pass between its initial calculation and the actual transfer of funds. That means sequestering the incentive component of an executive's pay for several years, and then paying it out gradually over a period of several more years. Boards might even consider attaching strings to those payouts, in the form of mandatory reimbursement, in the event subsequent discoveries make those initial reports questionable. Until those initially reported earnings are no longer uncertain, these executives can live on their salaries (an arrangement that most non-executives would consider neither cruel nor unusual).

Will CEOs and other beneficiaries of lucrative pay packages like this? Of course not. But it will give them an incentive to see to it that there are no hidden accounting tricks, errors, or omissions in the reports they pass on to their boards. And if a board has to stiffen its spine to face down a CEO who finds these restrictions too onerous, that is exactly what their shareholders have a right to expect of them.

Auditors and the audited

The incentive for external auditors to collaborate with a client's attempts to present its financial reports in the most favorable light is to keep the client's auditing business. In the past, there was often an even bigger incentive: to keep the client's consulting business. But even if—as now seems likely—auditing firms have to get out of the consulting business, the temptation for auditors to please the people they are paid to police will still be there. The problem is not that corporate accountants (or their boss, the chief financial officer) are inherently

dishonest. Instead, the problem lies in the structure of their relationship with their auditors. The auditors are hirelings whom the company can dispense with as it pleases and simply replace with other auditors. The effect is that the company is expected to police itself, which places both the temptation and the opportunity to coerce the auditors squarely in the hands of the client's financial staff. It should not be surprising that some people on that staff, realizing how much power they have, decide to exercise it.

The solution is term limits for auditors. They should contract with their clients to prowl through their books for a fixed number of years, with no options for renewal. Since there is no point in trying to hold on to a client you are going to lose anyway, auditors would have no incentive to bend over backwards to please the client. They could then return to the at least quasi-adversarial relationship that their respective roles require of them.

All of the changes prescribed here are strong medicine. They won't taste good, and they probably won't go down easily. But boards and management must recognize that the likely alternative is yet another round of scandals, possibly even worse than this one, perhaps a dozen or so years down the road. Sooner or later, the public and its elected representatives will declare that enough is enough and force changes like these (or even tougher ones) down the throats of both guilty and innocent companies. It would be much better for all concerned if companies undertook the necessary reforms by themselves, now, without waiting for that.

References and selected bibliography

Coffee, John C., Jr. 2002. Guarding the gatekeepers. *New York Times* (13 May): A17.

From *Business Horizons,* May/June 2003, pp. 17-24. Copyright © 2003 by Elsevier Science, Ltd. Reprinted by permission.

Index

Index

Test Your Knowledge Form

We encourage you to photocopy and use this page as a tool to assess how the articles in *Annual Editions* expand on the information in your textbook. By reflecting on the articles you will gain enhanced text information. You can also access this useful form on a product's book support Web site at *http://www.mhcls.com/online/*.

NAME:

DATE:

TITLE AND NUMBER OF ARTICLE:

BRIEFLY STATE THE MAIN IDEA OF THIS ARTICLE:

LIST THREE IMPORTANT FACTS THAT THE AUTHOR USES TO SUPPORT THE MAIN IDEA:

WHAT INFORMATION OR IDEAS DISCUSSED IN THIS ARTICLE ARE ALSO DISCUSSED IN YOUR TEXTBOOK OR OTHER READINGS THAT YOU HAVE DONE? LIST THE TEXTBOOK CHAPTERS AND PAGE NUMBERS:

LIST ANY EXAMPLES OF BIAS OR FAULTY REASONING THAT YOU FOUND IN THE ARTICLE:

LIST ANY NEW TERMS/CONCEPTS THAT WERE DISCUSSED IN THE ARTICLE, AND WRITE A SHORT DEFINITION:

We Want Your Advice

ANNUAL EDITIONS revisions depend on two major opinion sources: one is our Advisory Board, listed in the front of this volume, which works with us in scanning the thousands of articles published in the public press each year; the other is you—the person actually using the book. Please help us and the users of the next edition by completing the prepaid article rating form on this page and returning it to us. Thank you for your help!

ANNUAL EDITIONS: Business Ethics 06/07

ARTICLE RATING FORM

Here is an opportunity for you to have direct input into the next revision of this volume.
We would like you to rate each of the articles listed below, using the following scale:

1. **Excellent: should definitely be retained**
2. **Above average: should probably be retained**
3. **Below average: should probably be deleted**
4. **Poor: should definitely be deleted**

Your ratings will play a vital part in the next revision.
Please mail this prepaid form to us as soon as possible.
Thanks for your help!

RATING	ARTICLE	RATING	ARTICLE
	1. Thinking Ethically: A Framework for Moral Decision Making		34. Truth in Advertising: Rx Drug Ads Come of Age
	2. Business Ethics: Back to Basics		35. Rejuvenating Wal-Mart's Reputation
	3. Advice from Aristotle on Business Ethics		36. Managing for Organizational Integrity
	4. Truth or Consequences: The Organizational Importance of Honesty		37. An Ethical Delimma: How to Build Integrity into Your Sales Environment
	5. Why Good Leaders Do Bad Things		38. The Right Balance
	6. Best Resources for Corporate Social Responsibility		39. Patagonia's Founder Seeks to Spread Environmental Gospel
	7. Flip-Flop Over Faculty Fingerprints		40. Ethics for a Post-Enron America
	8. Corruption: Causes and Cures		41. Hiring Character
	9. Where the Dangers Are		42. Why Corporations Can't Control Chicanery
	10. Sexual Harassment and Retaliation: A Double-Edged Sword		
	11. The Under-Reported Impact of Age Discrimination and Its Threat to Business Vitality		
	12. Where Are the Women?		
	13. How Corporate America is Betraying Women		
	14. 50 and Fired		
	15. Into Thin Air		
	16. Hall Monitors in the Workplace: Encouraging Employee Whistleblowers		
	17. On Witnessing a Fraud		
	18. Birth of the Ethics Industry		
	19. Academic Values and the Lure of Profit		
	20. Like the Smoke of a Blazing Room		
	21. The Parable of the Sadhu		
	22. Does It Pay to Be Good?		
	23. Trust in the Marketplace		
	24. How Women Are Changing Corporate America		
	25. Old. Smart. Productive.		
	26. The Truth About Drug Companies		
	27. Eminent Domain: Is It Only Hope for Inner Cities?		
	28. Debate Flares Anew Over Violence in Video Games		
	29. Values in Tension: Ethics Away From Home		
	30. Managing Ethically with Global Stakeholders: A Present and Future Challenge		
	31. Fakes!		
	32. The Perils of Doing the Right Thing		
	33. Is Marketing Ethics an Oxymoron?		

(Continued on next page)

BUSINESS REPLY MAIL
FIRST CLASS MAIL PERMIT NO. 551 DUBUQUE IA

POSTAGE WILL BE PAID BY ADDRESEE

McGraw-Hill Contemporary Learning Series
2460 KERPER BLVD
DUBUQUE, IA 52001-9902

NO POSTAGE
NECESSARY
IF MAILED
IN THE
UNITED STATES

ABOUT YOU

Name   Date

Are you a teacher? ☐   A student? ☐
Your school's name

Department

Address   City   State   Zip

School telephone #

YOUR COMMENTS ARE IMPORTANT TO US!

Please fill in the following information:
For which course did you use this book?

Did you use a text with this ANNUAL EDITION?   ☐   yes ☐   no
What was the title of the text?

What are your general reactions to the *Annual Editions* concept?

Have you read any pertinent articles recently that you think should be included in the next edition? Explain.

Are there any articles that you feel should be replaced in the next edition? Why?

Are there any World Wide Web sites that you feel should be included in the next edition? Please annotate.

May we contact you for editorial input?   ☐   yes ☐   no
May we quote your comments?   ☐   yes ☐   no